On the Street

ISBN 978-1-912122-53-0

 A catalogue record for this book is available from the British Library.

Designed by Sylvia Ugga
Edited by Miranda Harrison
Proofread by Kirsty Watling
Printed in the UK by Gomer Press
Typeface: Financier, Cardone

MIX
Paper from responsible sources
FSC® C114687

Edwin Heathcote

On the Street

In-Between Architecture

HENI Publishing, London

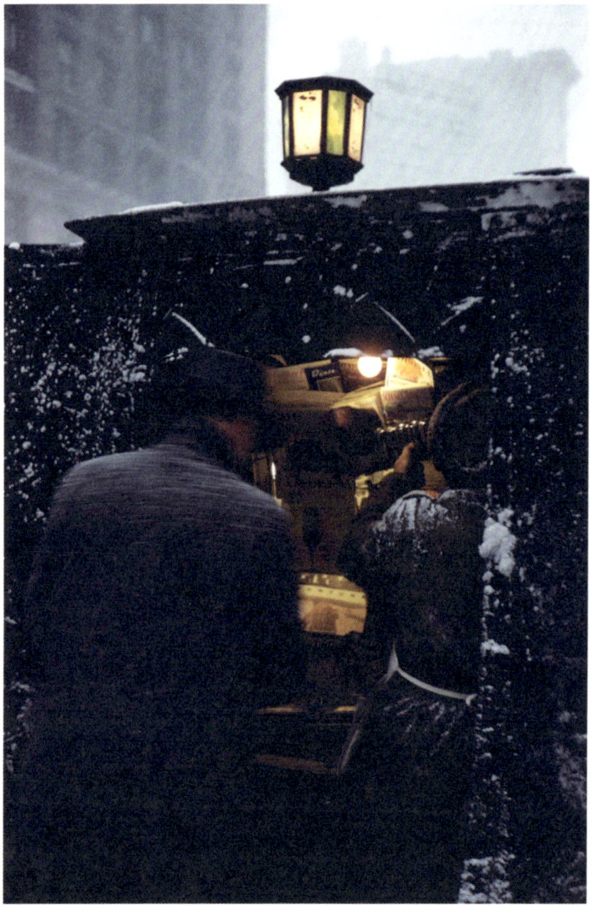

Newspaper Kiosk, 1955
Saul Leiter

Contents

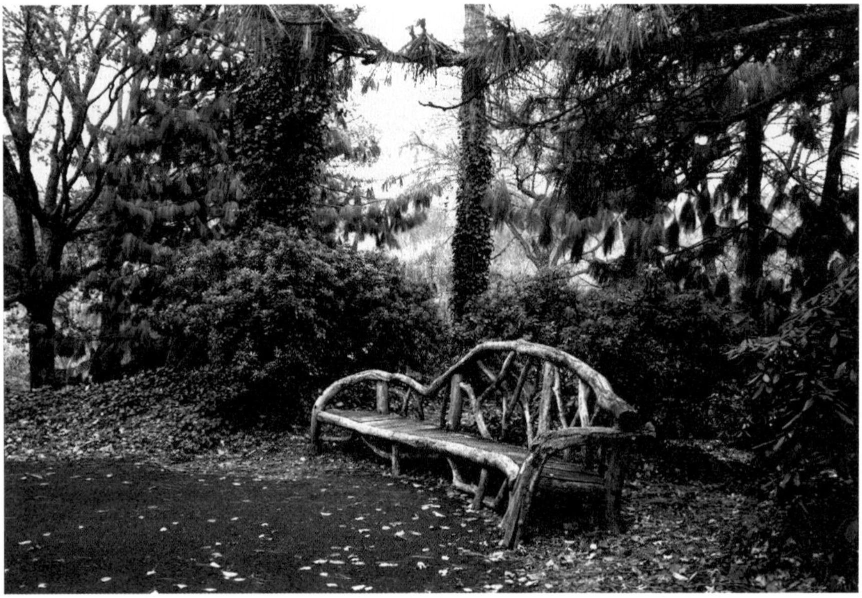

New York, US (Olmsted; Vaux), 2000
Mark Pimlott

Acknowledgements

The main thanks here should go to the engineers, the stallholders, the parks workers, the labourers, the municipal, communications and sanitary departments whose work goes almost entirely uncelebrated and yet without whom there would be no life on the streets. I should also acknowledge the designers and makers of the almost endless variety of street furniture who remain mostly anonymous, this book is a kind of thank-you note. I'd also like to thank my family, my wife Krisztina, my daughters Lili and Ella for their patience as I stop, once again, to take a snap of a drain cover, a lamppost or a phone box. I would also like to thank my friends and family for never telling me this was a stupid idea.

I'd also like to thank the dozens of others who have helped with advice, conversation, with encouragement or with their wonderful work. These include Tom Emerson, Christian Küsters, Mark Pimlott, Sue Barr, Will Scott, Arthur Tress, Christopher Howse, Sir Kenneth Grange, Richard Wentworth, the Ironbridge Gorge Museum Trust and many others.

I'd like to pay tribute and give posthumous thanks to others who helped me along but who are no longer here, notably Charles Jencks, Michael Sorkin, whose wisdom, words and company I miss all the time, and also Michael Wolf.

The idea for this book emerged from a short series I wrote for The Financial Times *and I'd like to thank Helen Barrett, the then commissioning editor, for having the nerve to publish those essays on what others might have thought a mundane subject for the pages of a national newspaper. I'd also like to thank Jan Dalley, for many years my editor at the newspaper, for her support and confidence, and my other editors and former colleagues, notably Peter Aspden.*

I'd like to thank Joe Hage and his colleagues at HENI for making these ideas into a book which had existed in my head for years but which I am delighted, and slightly surprised, to see in print. Finally, I'd like to thank my father, Graham Heathcote, some of whose photos are included here. He was the biggest bibliophile I have ever known, a journalist, a lover of print, a reader and an immeasurable influence. I dedicate the book to him, even though he is no longer here to see it.

Preface

This is a book about public space. About the street. And, perhaps, about the last great unexplored arena of public architecture. Or rather, the layer of urban artefacts that represents an in-between architecture. Street furniture - that category of things which punctuates our journeys through cities and accompanies us in the streetscape but to which we have become inured and almost blind - is, in its way, more essentially urban and enduring than the buildings which frame those public spaces. Its proportions relate directly to the human form, mediating between building and body: kiosks and booths for vendors and telephones, drinking fountains, bollards, benches, signposts, streetlights positioned so that they illuminate just the right field for human vision. On the pavements and kerbs we feel it directly through our feet, in the handrails of steps we grip or stroke it with our fingers as we so rarely touch any other part of the city. Street furniture relates every bit as much to the human body as does the furniture in our homes, even if much of it exists to repel rather than attract or accommodate us. The endless barrage of things which inhabit our streets are our inanimate companions on a walk, appearing and disappearing on each journey but always there.

It is also, however, a layer of stuff that is considered as ephemeral. Street furniture fulfils a function, and once that function is defunct it is often treated with a ruthlessness which betrays its years of service, its mass, its wear and familiarity. We have allowed so many of these things to disappear, from delicate gaslights and modernist dustbins to public toilets and drinking fountains, yet they were and, at least in their physical presence, still are, pivotal elements of the streetscape and the civilised city. I will not make the arguments that these things are all special. In fact, their delight quite often stems from their apparent banality. Beauty is a much-abused notion in architecture and design, a charged word which brings with it entire worlds of politics, prejudice and nuance. There are, without doubt, beautiful items of street furniture, but the real charisma of these objects lies in the territory between the quotidian and the sublime, the constant tug of war between utility, amenity, cost and affection, history and modernity, between the public and the private, between architecture and landscape.

This is not anything like a conventional history of street furniture. That would be something entirely different. It might also be a little depressing, a sad story of decline, neglect and loss. Neither is it comprehensive, because there are some categories of things which I find boring and have nothing to say about and others about which there is so much to say (public sculpture, for instance) that they would demand an entire book on their own. It is not a taxonomy and neither does it try to cover too much of the world. Instead it pivots around my home city London, with occasional excursions to cities I am at least a little familiar with, to Paris and New York in particular. And above all it is personal. Recollections and images from my own mind mingle with snaps I've taken on my phone, encounters both personal and physical. Ultimately I hope it might be something slightly uplifting, a plea to find delight and surprise in the most seemingly ordinary of moments. It is also, I hope, a book that can be flipped through. Not to be read in order, not in one sitting, but dipped into. I would be quite happy if readers enjoyed only the photos and regarded the texts as extended captions.

Dorothea Lange memorably said that 'the camera is an instrument that teaches people to see without a camera'. As I am suggesting here that we don't necessarily always see street furniture, I have turned to photography to better illustrate the often surprisingly prominent presence it has in framing our public lives and defining the city at a human scale. These mass-manufactured, often massive and often over-familiar objects are so ubiquitous that we can afford to ignore them but, in the world of street photography, the street fittings reclaim their presence in the civic sphere. It seemed to me that photography is the medium, more than any other, which will allow us to see these things again and to begin to understand their status as parallel inhabitants of the city.

As I have been writing this over the past few years, entire new typologies of street furniture have emerged: hand sanitiser dispensers, tape stuck to benches to enforce social distancing, electric vehicle charging points in garish plastic, gum receptacles, new public bins with underground containers, 5G masts and CCTV camera poles. This book was mostly written during the strange period of the Covid-19 epidemic and, through lockdowns and the officially sanctioned walks, I tried to look again at this layer of stuff. It gave me something to do on otherwise interminably repetitive exercise strolls. But it also allowed me the time and space to see and to find things that were, in their own ways, wonderful.

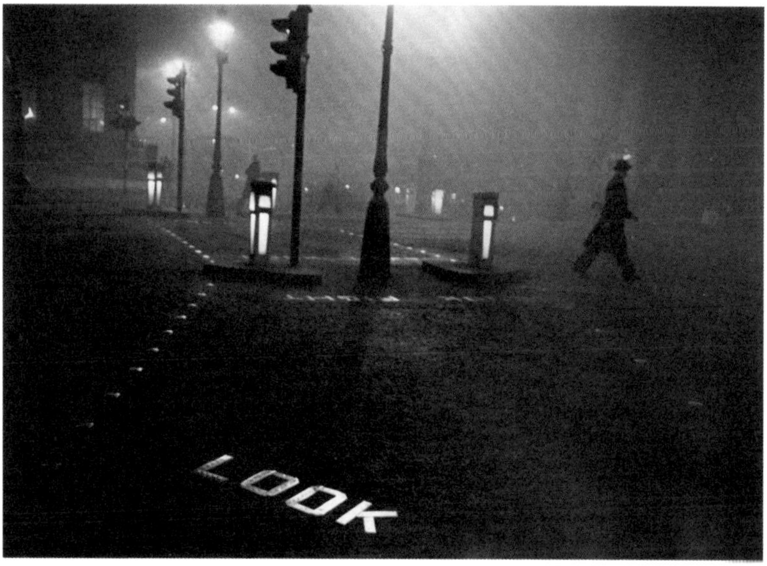

London, 1952
Robert Frank

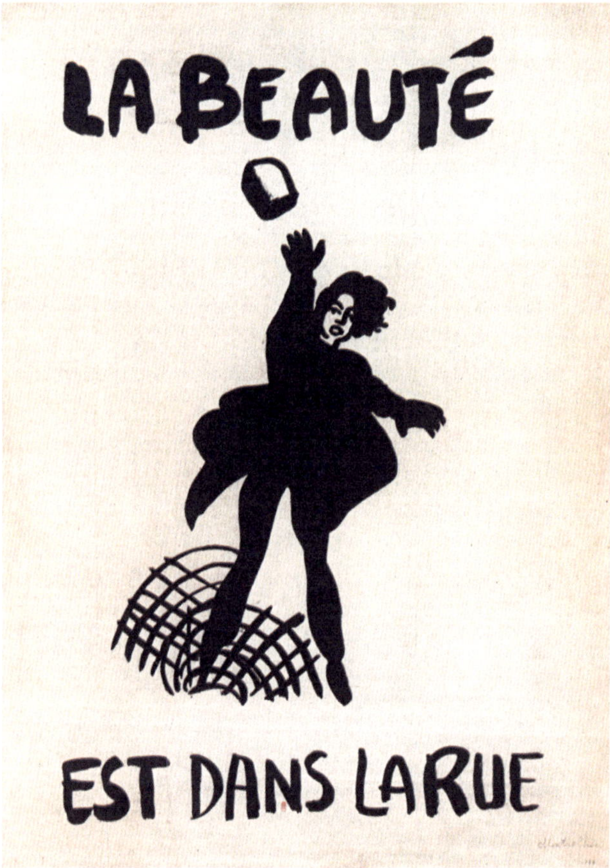

Beauty is in the Street, Paris, May 1968
Poster by Atelier Populaire

Introduction

'*Sous les pavés, la plage*!' Beneath the paving stones, the beach. These words were graffitied across Paris in 1968. They became the rallying call of the protesting students who ripped up the Paris cobbles to pile them into barricades and hurl them at the police, and found that the granite setts were bedded in sand. The beach. It was the perfect metaphor. The Situationists attempted to reimagine the city as a playground, to transform streets built for military marching and capitalist consumption into a labyrinth of puzzles, reconfiguring and subverting the metropolis as a place of idle wandering and free association.

I always thought, though, that the Situationists missed a trick. There is an idea of a submerged city, a fantasy city, a Calvino-esque inverted city or urban playground yet to be discovered that offers something new - but have we really exhausted the possibilities of the visible city, the city above? The 1968 protests found in the surface of the paving a way of tearing the fabric of the city apart in the most visceral way, flaying it of its stone skin, and reconfiguring that material membrane as ammunition, throwing the stones at the police, weaponising the substance of the city itself.

In that idea of the street as surface, as a taut membrane, a skin covering a body, and in the graffiti scrawled directly above it on the white stone walls of the bourgeois buildings like urban tattoos, they missed the things on the surface.

There is a layer of the city which we seem to rarely see, the skein of structures and fittings which populate the pavement and which modulate our movement through and experience of the city while remaining oddly invisible. It is a realm almost untouched by architects and architecture, left to traffic engineers, utility companies, manufacturers, anonymous designers and back street workshops. Although it might be largely invisible to us it has proved very visible to photographers, they have somehow managed to understand this layer of stuff more perceptively. Perhaps this most functional area paradoxically appears more manifest as image than as reality.

The very idea of 'street furniture' is odd. Furniture is the object-language of the interior, the street is its opposite. The French contrast *meubles* (furniture) with *immobilier* (real estate), the mobile and the immobile, and the odd bastardisation of *mobilier urbain* exists in a paradoxical in-between world. The phrase 'street furniture' at first conjures images of abandoned soggy sofas on the pavement, or stray, broken chairs. The real, strange, ad hoc world of street furniture is however, in its way, the indicator of modernity, the excrescence of the technologies which make the city such an amenable place to live. It is the architectural expression of the infrastructure of the urban commons. There are the streetlights and the stink pipes, the telecoms, phone and postboxes, each announcing the arrival of a radical new technology or medium. There are the steam vents and the hotdog stands, the food carts and the newspaper kiosks. There are market stalls and trestle tables, fire hydrants and benches, anti-homeless spikes and pissoirs, piss-protectors and mud scrapers. And each new layer of technology adds its presence to the streetscape, the 5G masts, electric vehicle chargers and solar-powered parking meters. Each new skein of things can provoke almost insane hostility; parking meters were vandalised when they were introduced in the mid-20th century, resented for impinging on the freedom that was the essence of automobility. As I was writing this, 5G masts were being burnt and vandalised by those who believed it was a malignant force, a spreader of digital disease or a government conspiracy. Yet that realm of things, the layer of fittings which can so affect our streets remains mostly unregulated, unregarded and unexamined.

Ubiquity breeds invisibility. Street furniture is part of the realm that Georges Perec described as the *infraordinaire*, the infraordinary, the opposite of the exotic - the endotic. Yet you only need to get a glimpse into a telephone exchange box with its incomprehensible viscera of coloured cables, or the tangle of pipes excavated beneath the pavement, to see that even the everyday is a front for a complex system which is the result of incredibly refined technologies and highly developed networks.

What might seem banal may contain almost unimaginable material history and echoes of other forms. You might find bollards made from cast-iron cannon, or milestones indicating the many miles of distance to a city that you are already now clearly in, evidence of how the metropolis has metastasised to consume its surroundings. There are surprising stories: London's famous phoneboxes were designed by the architect of Battersea Power Station and based on a tomb designed by the 18th-century architect Sir John Soane for his wife. You might find cast-iron streetlights decorated with dragons, sea serpents and gods, and advertising columns which once concealed urinals or entrances to underground tunnels. Street furniture can be used to express state or municipal power and presence, or it can be employed to empower citizens. It is both deeply political and a reminder of complex webs of regulation and urban identity, as well as being paradoxically radically invisible. Even the great theorists of the city - Walter Benjamin, Georg Simmel, Henri Lefebvre, Siegfried Kracauer and others - only skirt gently round the subject, despite almost endless texts about the use of the streets, their meaning, subversion and re-enchantment. If streetlights are mentioned it is only the abstract light they cast that is dwelt on, not the physical presence of the object.

It is precisely this layer of unseen architecture, the city in between street and building, that this series of short essays is dedicated to. It is not about taste and it does not seek to denigrate or rank the interventions through aesthetics. It is not a gazetteer or a guide, rather it is an attempt to focus a little attention on a neglected realm which arguably shapes our experience of the city almost as much as the most expensive buildings. It is about how this layer of stuff can inhibit our journeys through the city or our interaction with it, but at other times it can enrich and transform the streets, making them more complex, more interesting and more human.

It is also an intensely and unapologetically personal look at this world of partially seen things. It is based on and in the city I know best, London, but it touches on others. Much of it is reminiscence, and perhaps much of that is misremembered or subtly changed in my own retelling. These objects have inserted themselves into the collective imagination but mostly only as background, and in attempting to bring them into clearer view perhaps you change their nature, in the way that observation can alter the status and position of a sub-atomic particle.

Obviously a city is defined by its buildings, its macro-scale, its architecture and its most prominent landmarks - but it might equally, and perhaps surprisingly, be instantly familiar from that background layer of things, its street furniture often so distinctive and particular. Most major historic cities have evolved a language of objects almost entirely their own. If a set designer wants to evoke an English street, a red phonebox and postbox might be enough to do the trick. For New York it might be a steam vent or fire hydrant and a hotdog cart, for Paris an Art Nouveau ironwork Metro exit. Street furniture and the kind of in-between architecture which populates the pavements defines the experience of walking through the city. We live in our homes but we engage with a city through its streets; we inhabit the metropolis against a background of fittings and, when we travel, we notice the small differences acutely. The same is true of the street surfaces. It is a very different experience to tramp the pavements of a Georgian London Square, the sandy surface of Birdcage Walk, the cobbles of Montmartre, the wavy black and white stones of Rio's beaches or the pock-marked and pot-holed streets of Downtown New York. Surfaces matter - the way they wear, the way the rain runs off them, the way they puddle in particular places or reflect the neons above. Children play the game of avoiding cracks in the paving stones, the pavement insinuates itself into their world as a hopscotch grid or a framework for superstitions. It appears differently if you're on a skateboard, on roller-skates, in a wheelchair, pushing a buggy or delivering from a trolley; tiny differences in texture radically alter the feel of the city.

I was prompted to think about the subject by one small but particular encounter. I was in New York for a brief trip, staying at a hotel a few blocks from Central Park. This bit of the Upper East Side is hardly known for its buzzing street life; rather it is a neighbourhood of upscale condos and corporate behemoths with a few restaurants catering to the business lunch market, the usual smattering of chain coffee shops and the occasional dazzlingly-lit drug store. Coming from London I don't even try to fight the jet lag any more, I just accept that I'll wake around 3am and prop myself up in bed writing emails and waiting for someone who sells coffee to open up. On this occasion, assuming I was facing a long, uncaffeinated slog until 7am at the earliest, I opened up my curtains and noticed a coffee cart being set up in the street below. The stainless steel wagon was unhitched from a car and powered up; its bright light fizzled on and its warmly wrapped inhabitant started laying out his things in the clear-fronted compartments. I pulled on my coat and shoes and bought, for less than three dollars, a coffee and a pastry from the vendor. The cart was a fiercely bright spot of light amidst the still-dark commercial towers and empty stores, a little glimpse of hope for a weary soul. The city, which had looked like a dead zone of darkness and inhospitable steel and glass, suddenly felt populated and alive, illuminated by the bright glare of the vendor's lamps. Here, in the middle of perhaps the richest neighbourhood in the richest city on earth, it was left to a recently newly arrived Syrian immigrant to animate the streets, to bring the city to life single-handed. Of course on the way back I noticed homeless bodies wrapped up against the early Spring cold, cleaving to doorways and near subway vents which warmed them a little, with one lucky enough to have found a park bench, elevated from the cold seeping from the ground. You are never alone in the streets of a big city, but the temporary metal cart with its generator buzz, its bagels and doughnuts stacked high and its improvised architecture knocked-up in a workshop somewhere on the edge of an outer borough transformed the street. Bringing it alive.

When I was young and used to stay out late - in bars, at gigs, playing snooker at dodgy, subterranean all-night clubs or drinking in dark, sticky, stuffy basements (all that was left after the pubs closed at 11pm) - one of the thrills of a Saturday night was to get tomorrow's papers from the news kiosk near Tottenham Court Road Underground Station, sometimes still warm from the presses. I'd read the Sunday papers on the bus home in a fug of cigarette smoke, drunken conversation and condensation, the windows misted up from a deck full of passengers' rain-sodden coats and steamy, drunken breath.

Newspapers had a different importance then, almost exalted; their arrival was anticipated. Getting hold of them on the day before the publication date was like living a little in the future, getting ahead of time. If the point of living in the city is its speed, its heart rate, then tomorrow's newspapers were an accelerant, a shot of urban adrenaline. Most of those kiosks have disappeared now, victims of changing patterns of consumption and the triumph of the digital over the physical. And the street is noticeably poorer for it. They functioned as connectors with the world, bonding the local to the international, and they would function as a means of reading the world without leaving the local; you could browse the headlines on the front pages on the street.

The coffee cart, the news kiosk and the park bench are a part of this world which exists at street level, a world as rich in architecture, design, social interaction and stories as any architecture which might seem more substantial, more massive, more expensive. These items have, perhaps inevitably, formed the backdrop to street photography and film since the beginnings of both. Although architects and designers might have often failed to notice this interstitial landscape of things (or perhaps to care about them), those who have looked at cities through a lens have not. For photographers and for those documenting the life that flows through the city, street furniture became the props in the production design of urban life, the hardware which enabled the city's software to run, its citizens, to navigate the city and mark their place. It became a parallel population of things, a foil and a familiar language of urbanity. The poles, lampposts, signs and bins become visible as a kind of armature for everyday life in the public sphere.

Whether in a Brassaï photograph of an empty bench or an image of a New York fire hydrant spewing water on to street urchins as a welcome relief from a summer heatwave, street furniture has a presence in visual culture which does not seem to have translated into design culture. That's why I've attempted to view the subject, in part, through the lens, mediated by a history of photography which has relied heavily on street furniture since its very beginnings. This is also a book about pictures, about how these objects have formed an indispensable foil to some of the most familiar images of our era. Street photographers but also photojournalists, fashion photographers and amateur snappers taking family photos have leant on street furniture as a layer of visual props and a code for urbanity, a supporting cast of objects in dialogue with models and subjects. It is as if these things become more visible when filtered through the gaze of an observer. These most tangible of things are brought suddenly to life through being captured in two dimensions.

Outside of the privileged medium of the photograph, however, this remains a realm of the unloved, the utilitarian and the unsentimental. For many years the phonebox or booth seemed an indispensable architecture of the urban realm, a connective device and a conduit from the street to the wider world. Now those that remain look forlorn and without purpose, an unemployed architecture. The newsstands are fast disappearing while new forms of furniture appear - the endless array of bleak, clunky boxes for telecommunications or the ugly, plasticky pillars for electric vehicle charging, barely considered yet permanently present.

Despite an ongoing decline in so many areas, this is also paradoxically a boom-time for street furniture. A new securitisation of the streetscape is emerging, sprouting new forms of furniture in an effort to resist everything from skateboarding and sleeping rough to truck-bombing. The City of London's 'Ring of Steel' security measures introduced a new language of fear into the street, a system of control which turns the last bastion of publicness into an airport security gate. Huge, hideous poles with spiked collars supporting CCTV cameras have shot up from our pavements. Stone blocks which look like benches turn out to be protecting privately owned public plazas from car bombs, while their edges are protected by anti-skateboard studs. Bollards and planters are designed to resist weaponised vehicles and their roots now reach deep into the earth. The new language of street furniture is concerned less with public utility than with the imposition of control. The once decorative and elegant language system of phoneboxes, postboxes, streetlights and fountains, each an invention to improve everyday life in the streets, has given way to the architecture of security and surveillance in which every citizen is understood as a potential threat.

This radical reversal of the nature of the public realm shows how intimately street furniture reflects the changing nature of civic space, how it denotes the demarcation between public and private, how it conveys meaning and responds and adapts to perceived threat and change. On the other hand, street furniture can also embrace the powerless, the street hawkers and food vendors, the homeless sleeping on a park bench, but is almost always in the first instance an expression of power, a built manifestation of systems of control.

The question is, what kind of meaning does our contemporary streetscape communicate? Throughout the history of public space, urban markers have been used to convey a sense of place, of centre, connection and of context, national and urban identity, as well as to overlay a geometry, a way of marking and mapping space. A milestone expresses distance but is itself also a marker of that particular location, the longer it survives the more the thing itself becomes the object of interest and affection. These things are simultaneously both sign and signified. So pivotal were milestones to the Roman Empire and its obsession with measuring and mapping that to move or molest a milestone was punishable by death. A market cross places the centre of a settlement, its symbolic place of exchange; the pump or fountain becomes a meeting place, a place to wash, drink or water animals. A clock becomes somewhere to meet at a certain time. A postbox is a connection to a wider network, a society. It is a node but it is one which also carries the monogram of the king or queen, an expression of state power and also a sacrosanct object. Tampering with the post is a strangely serious crime as, like moving a milestone, it represents a rejection of order. And where is society without order?

Street furniture presents a constantly changing matrix in between buildings and people, an intermediate field of objects like the condiments on a dining table, an indispensable part of the scene which is nevertheless itself a moveable feast. The manner in which it has been portrayed, documented and reflected is often as interesting, if not more so, than the way it is used and the way it has changed. Through photography, art and film it continues to inhabit our visual imagination as much as it does our streetscape and it has populated popular culture just as vividly as our cities. Street furniture inhabits the city as a surrogate for our vertical, and occasionally horizontal, bodies. It casts nets of shadow across our walls and pavements, its forms are adapted to patterns of urban life and in its presence it suggests habitation.

In these short essays I've tried to examine just a few aspects of the history, meaning and representation of street furniture, its changing status and the ways in which it has been mediated. These objects can tell us stories about material culture, manufacture, fashion, technology, power, surveillance, revolt, protest, how to behave and how not to. It can tell us about the ways we use and inhabit the city. But also, I have attempted to outline my own encounters with these things, the role they might have played in my recollections. Through surprising finds, family photos, fading memories and memorable moments, this is a particularly personal book about a subject which is understood as municipal and anonymous.

Street furniture works hard for us. It lights our way and helps us to see, to sit, to eat and to walk. The least we can do then, is to acknowledge this oddly under-explored yet most public of architectures. The beach may still be beneath the pavement, but remember also that other slogan of 1968: '*La Beauté est dans la rue*' (Beauty is in the Street).

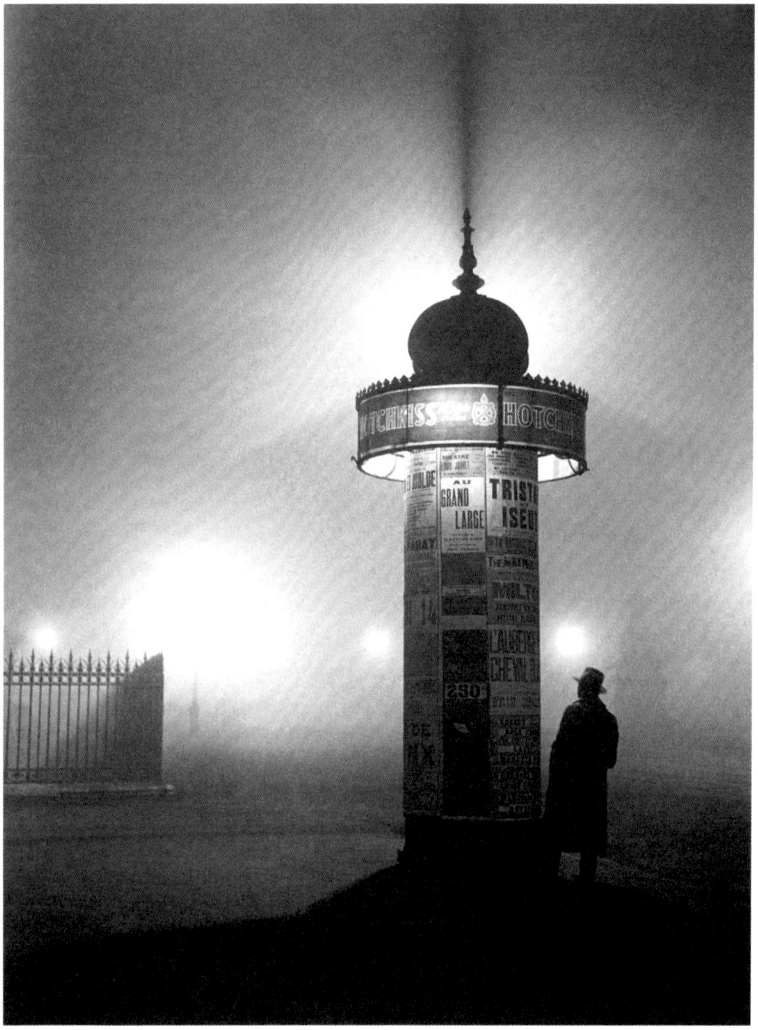

Colonne Morris, 1933
Brassaï

Advertising

Hungarian-born, Paris-based photographer Brassaï took the haunting and well-known photograph shown opposite. A silhouette of a man looks at a *colonne Morris* (Morris column) - the familiar, cylindrical Parisian advertising column. It is a foggy night. The column appears as a beacon, a refuge from the darkness. This is a picture of a city defined by its street furniture in which text gives solace, the company of words and intimations of pleasures to come. We instantly know which city we are in. The architecture has disappeared, receded into the mist and all that is left is the advertising column, the glow of the streetlights, a sculpture in the distance and the sharp profile of a railing on the left. And, of course, the figure. It is, in its way, a photograph of urban existentialism: a man, with words, on his own in the city.

Other cities have defining items of street furniture - think of London's red pillarbox or New York's fire hydrants - but the Morris column is one of the most evocative. It is a gazetteer, a shelter, a public resource and an illuminated urban marker. Perhaps surprisingly, it is not at all Parisian in origin. In 1854, in Germany, Ernst Litfass was outraged by the haphazard bill-posting which plastered and, as he saw it, visually polluted the city walls, and proposed the column as a way of centralising notices and posters in one urban node. Litfass's original design was ascetic and proto-modernist, a simple metal cylinder. His idea caught on and the Litfass column quickly became a ubiquitous presence on the streets of German cities, with over 50,000 erected by the end of the 19th century. Paris followed in 1868, when Gabriel Morris, a printer of playbills and theatrical posters, introduced a more elaborate French version, capped with an exotic onion dome and a frilly frieze. It formed a part of the huge programme of works the city was undertaking and quickly became, along with the streetlights, newsstands and fountains, an indispensable element of the cityscape. A second generation of columns was designed by architect Gabriel Davioud, who was responsible for so many of the street furniture patterns rolled out in the Haussmannisation of the city: the benches, lamps and fountains.

This more elaborate Parisian version owed its form not only to Litfass's design but also to another fundamental piece of Parisian street furniture - the pissoir. This too was a cylindrical or spiral-plan column of green-painted cast iron, often capped with an exotic cupola, and often plastered with handbills and posters. Within a couple of decades most of Europe, from Barcelona to Berlin, was employing some form of advertising column. Their appearance coincided, not incidentally, with a golden age of graphic design, a period in which artists of the calibre and fame of Henri de Toulouse-Lautrec and Pierre Bonnard were commissioned to design posters for theatres and cabarets. But it also arrived in parallel with new ways of reading the city - literally. In his novel *À La Recherche du Temps Perdu* (*In Search of Lost Time*), Marcel Proust wrote:

> Every morning I would hasten to the Morris column to see what new plays it announced. Nothing could be more disinterested or happier than the day-dreams with which these announcements filled my imagination, day-dreams which were conditioned by the associations of the words forming the titles of the plays, and also by the colour of the bills, still damp and wrinkled with paste, on which those words stood out.

In Brassaï's photo, a lone figure stands reading the posters on the Morris column, while the rest of the city fades into the fog. These columns were a way of translating the city into text, something legible, a way of understanding their nightlife. With their striking lithographs and expressive fonts, they became a kind of street art, expressing the culture of the city and turning the street into a spectacle, a place to linger. The original German cover of Erich Kästner's best-selling *Emil and the Detectives* shows the eponymous group of boys hiding behind a Litfass column, spying on their target. In countless spy films, agents tailing suspects pretend to be reading notices on columns if their mark turns round. Here the column becomes a fragment of a city in which anything might be a clue, can be read as Sherlock Holmes before he had turned London into a series of maps and diagrams to be understood and interpreted for the solving of crimes.

For Proust though, the columns became a vehicle of escape, into a fantasy world of smokey, lime-lit nightclubs and theatres. The advertising column also became a more visceral means of escape - for Harry Lime, for instance, in Carol Reed's stunning *The Third Man*, who uses a Viennese Litfass column as an escape route to the city's sewers, its literal underworld. It was an image drawn on again in *Men In Black II* when Agent Black runs into a Manhattan Morris column to escape raging aliens. In fact, all kinds of myths arose about the contents of the Paris columns, most famously that they contained spiral stairs which led down to the catacombs under the city. If they actually contained anything at all, it was usually street cleaning equipment - brooms and snow shovels and, perhaps, the buckets of paste and brushes used to put up the posters.

Eugène Atget, chronicler of the objects, corners and shopfronts which haunted Paris as the last traces of its medieval past were erased, seemed to make a speciality of Morris columns. They pop up frequently in his work, portrayed almost as surrogate figures in the city. He seems to have enjoyed the cornucopia of text, the sheer density of words but, unlike most other photographers, Atget sought out those with hybrid functions; they often also housed flower sellers, ticket booths, transport inspectors and other traders. These things that seem so blind as objects did, after all, sometimes turn out to have rich interior lives.

The columns were commercial, a franchise as well as a public service, so they tended to be sited in the busiest, most prestigious neighbourhoods as well as, of course, near the theatre and entertainment districts. Haussmann's grand new boulevards with their wide pavements proved perfect for this emerging archetype. In photography the *colonnes Morris*, sited so prominently in the best quartiers, became one of the great clichés of Parisian imagery. From Robert Doisneau to Ilse Bing, photographers used them as surrogate figures in the cityscape or as characters in a kind of conversation with the figures reading them. In a neat turn of meta-advertising, companies would occasionally have a Paris scene captured and then enhance their ads on the columns in the end product, turning them into postcards which they would distribute - mechanically reproduced words inserted into the city and given physical presence, then recorded, enhanced and reprinted and recirculated; the city as image of itself. It is an odd quirk that Paris, so proud of its street furniture and so distinctive in its landscape of objects, should have its two most characteristic designs bearing oddly British-sounding names: the Morris column and the Wallace Fountain.

Paris still has its Morris columns, but the old models were all replaced in the 1980s with retro-repro versions by advertising giant J.C. Decaux (they have been changed again since then). Where once they displayed playbills or information about events and culture (both high and low) or about particular places and the city, now they have become a tool supplied by the global advertising industry, displaying ads for big brands such as cosmetics, and high-profile campaigns for movies. They have stayed the same, but become something else. There is nothing to read now, just the memory of a form that was once a part of something much bigger.

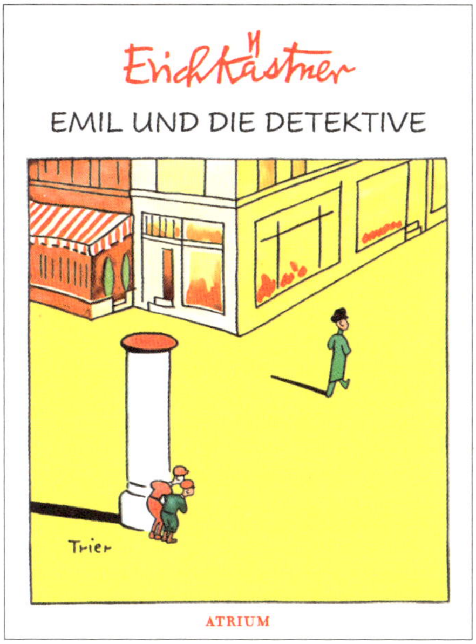

German cover of Emil and the Detectives*, 2018 edition*
Cover by Walter Trier

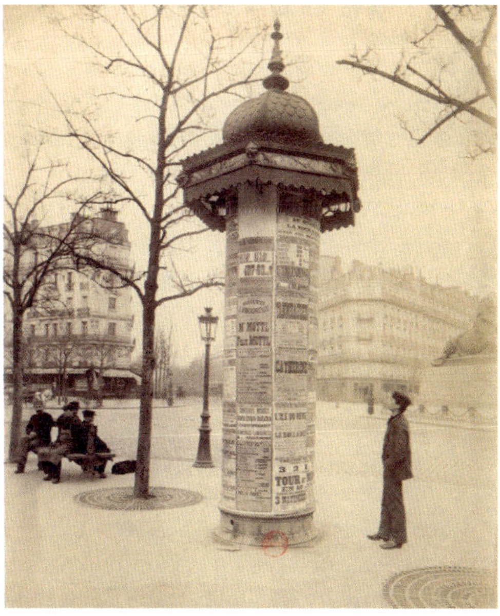

*Colonne Morris, Place Denfert Rochereau, Paris, c.*1898
Eugène Atget

Anti-pissing

One of the most familiar odours of the big city is the sour, strident smell of piss. Puddles of urine coalesce in dark alleys and unlit corners, in doorways and gutters, as dogs and men (and it is usually men) do what needs to be done and what there is often little other provision for. Piss has been a perennial problem for the city. The appearance of pissoirs, urinals and public lavatories in the 19th century marked a heroic effort to counter the problem, catalysed by new ideas about morality, decency and hygiene, but it is an effort that has shamefully been allowed to fade. As municipal budgets are ruthlessly cut and facilities monetised, and as moral outrages attached themselves to the alternative uses that were found for lavatories, pools of piss have reappeared in the city's darker corners.

The scene of a drunken yuppie pissing against the walls of the luckless family in Bong Joon Ho's *Parasite* becomes the perfect metaphor for the way in which life's misfortunes puddle against their dingy basement apartment, and it foreshadows the flood which comes later, both physical and psychic. The dream of piss appears here as a symbol and an omen. Studies of London in the 19th century frequently detailed the shock of their authors at encountering cellars and basements crowded with the poor, deluged by human waste, living amid the effluent of the city above. The most extreme versions of these may now have disappeared (in the world's wealthier cities, at least), but the problems of piss persist.

Building owners have been struggling for centuries to make corners and walls unattractive to potential pissers, and the range of devices and deterrents they have come up with is impressive and inventive. There are spiked railings and domed bollards, steel panels and iron flanges. None, of course, can actually stop people urinating. But what they can do is to deflect the stream back, on to shoes and trousers. They are, in a curious way, the opposite of urinals.

Clifford's Inn Passage, just off Fleet Street, for instance, features a ribbed iron flange on one wall, at just the right angle to direct the run-off on to shoes. Another can be seen at the north-east corner of the Bank of England, this one an iron quarter-circle above a curving infill. A corner of St Paul's Cathedral also has a fierce-looking piss-protector, this one a spiky wrought-iron construction to stop potential passers getting anywhere near, and there's another, not in a corner but very spiky, on the side of Mansion House.

Norwich too, for some reason, seems to have had a lot of problems with corners which it has tried to resolve in creative ways. It is useful to wander down the steps that take you from Rosebery Avenue to Warner Street, down beneath the iron viaduct. Each landing has a lumpy piss-protector in its corner. They do not seem to be doing their job spectacularly well, but they do at least present opportunities for creative alcoholic littering. The opera in Paris has some good, spiky examples, a little like half a bear trap suspended in the corners. Cities from Amsterdam to Barcelona have attempted to address the problem with bespoke solutions to particular problem corners.

Many of these devices were built in an era when apartments had no toilets, but even in our age of burgeoning domestic bathrooms it's not an issue that has gone away. The piss still flows through the city but, as a typology, urine deflectors seem now to be only a historic memory and an occasional eccentric discovery in its dingiest, darkest corners.

Archiving

The city can be ruthless towards memory. Places long and fondly remembered disappear overnight. Bars and cafés, once vessels of warmth, memories and conviviality are shuttered and ripped out, empty shells replacing once well-worn and complex surfaces which revealed the traces of decades of use. To live in a city is to feel time and change, to succumb to the impression that you are ageing as the points of reference for your youth are flattened and disappear one by one. A certain alienation appears almost inevitable. Yet, despite this merciless role of transformation and disappearances, the city can be an archive of itself, a meta-narrative of texts and attractions, media and ghosts.

To be down in the Tube when posters are being stripped back, layer by layer, to reveal fragments of half-remembered images and events can induce a breath-stopping moment of recognition and the collapsing of time. To see a bland acrylic fascia shop sign being removed from a business that was always going to fail, revealing an old, far more durable, hand-lettered sign beneath, can bring a bit of the city back to life, giving a glimpse of an alternate universe in which that café or bar had survived. I was recently in a small street off Leicester Square, London's nexus of churn, and a small strip of green and gold mosaic signage had emerged from beneath a newer fascia. Like the sign, my memory has faded, is intermittent. I think it read 'Café Monaco', but I may be wrong. It was weirdly arresting, a little fragment of swinging sixties pleasure exposed to the light again. I went back to photograph it but it had gone, along with the building it had been attached to.

The ephemera of the city arrives in waves. At one time most of the words were painted directly on to buildings, the city an incredibly dense palimpsest of layers of text, advertising for board and lodging, meals, brands, barbers, real estate, solicitors, tonics - everything. To peer at a photo of Victorian London or fin-de-siècle Paris is to be overwhelmed by the sheer amount of text. Every surface - the shop windows with arcs of words, the engraved brass ledges and spandrels beneath their displays, the awnings, the walls, the signs, the hoardings, the railings, the walls of stations, town halls, theatres and factories - is plastered with copy. The city is an endlessly updating essay about itself, a hypertext in which everything refers to something else in the city, constantly connecting.

More ephemeral notes come and go. At one time London's phoneboxes were wallpapered with cards for local sex-workers, an entire visual language made possible by cheap computers, mobile phones and digital printers. It was the first time, perhaps, that porn imagery appeared in the streets themselves, away from the heavily policed sex shops or the top shelves of newsagents. At other times it was ads for gigs, new albums or club nights plastered over empty shopfronts, along with festivals and shabby Russian circuses. The doorways of the music shops of Denmark Street were papered with notices for musicians wanted (usually drummers) or PA systems for hire. Then there were tear-off strips on bus stops and missing cat or teenager notices on lampposts. And, of course, the now ubiquitous memorials for stabbed teens or crushed cyclists. The city once ran on the fuel of newspapers, printed in proximity beneath the streets, delivered multiple times a day in different editions through complex networks to be sold at stands and kiosks with big-print lurid headlines of the scandals and catastrophes of the day for the front of their box-stands. All of this was wrapped up with the endless torrent of news itself at the end of each day and pulped. But the headlines survive in photography. What better way to capture a cataclysmic event than in a picture of a drowsy newsstand vendor, with the latest assassination, declaration of war and peace or resignation right there beside her?

Beyond text there is the technology which allows the city to operate, layers of new systems which become critical to the smooth functioning of everyday life and yet which can entirely disappear, leaving only remnants of what was once ubiquitous. The coal that once heated and powered the greatest city the earth had ever known, Victorian London, is now only evident in the lost urban medallions of coal-hole covers and a few fragments of industrial archaeology. The names of the telegrams and tram companies powered by cables are still inscribed into cast manhole covers, as are long defunct manufacturers, the foundries of a once industrialised London. Obsolete layers of technology are tangled up together and threaded through the city - the upright and bright blue police call boxes which were once available to use for free, and the phone kiosks now repurposed as defibrillators or ATMs. This archaeology of infrastructure exists between history and future, not yet abandoned but adapted, bodged and appropriated. Manholes for one technology are reused for something else; telegraphs for broadband, gas for TV. The traces are everywhere. The city, as Walter Benjamin suggested, is like a detective novel in which nothing truly disappears and every action leaves its mark.

And then there is the city itself, constantly churned, the demolition and rubble, rubbish and refuse. The wallpaper revealed when an adjacent house is demolished, the sooty, convoluted tracks of chimneys snaking up gable walls, the doll's house glimpse of an interior once the walls which defined it have gone. It is all still there, in some dump or other, not too far away, beneath an artificial hill made of the city itself. If you live in it long enough, everything in a city changes. But perhaps nothing is ever completely lost.

Ascending

Stairs and steps can be part of the street, and they can be apart from it. They can be the street itself and they can be the border. In a stoop they become the in-between zone which is private and yet part of the street, constructed of the same stone or draped in the same asphalt as the pavement yet placed behind the property line. An iron fire escape is resolutely not a part of the street, stopping short, dangling just out of reach and yet utterly indispensable in forming the character of that street. A back alley with a web of fire escapes and the deep, complex net of shadows they cast is an utterly distinctive urban moment in which the possibility of private catastrophe looms over the public realm.

When a city meets a hill, the street becomes a stair. From Montmartre to Bunker Hill, Lisbon to Medellin, moments of ascent impart a very specific character, pulling the street towards the sky. Photographers love stairs because they give the illusion of depth inside the picture itself, increasing engagement, pulling the viewer into the frame. Geoff Dyer writes eloquently about this in his book on understanding photography, *The Ongoing Moment*: 'Stairs serve as hills', he writes, 'metaphors, that is, for the further exhaustive endeavours that lie ahead: climb them and there will be other, possibly better views, other photographs.'

Most photographers shoot from the bottom to give that sense of ascent and depth, and to induce in the viewer, perhaps, a little sympathy for a figure slowly climbing into the distance. Henri Cartier-Bresson loved city stairs, but he liked to look the other way. The composition in his photo of Scanno in Abruzzo (p.24) exploits the curve of the stair and the slender uprights of the railings, but it is the black-clad women, one with a tray of pastries on her head, which draw the eye. The pastries echo the cobbles on the street surface and the stair winds down out of view, beyond the piazza, intimating another layer beyond. In a shot of Sifnos, Greece, from a decade later, a girl running up the stairs catches the eye but, as in Scanno, the steps, the street and the architecture are indistinguishable, a single, continuous membrane of surface undulating almost like waves on water while the walls begin to pick up the crow-step pattern of the stairs; one becomes the other. Cartier-Bresson's photo of Hyères (p.24) looks down a set of stairs in the Provençal town. Here, his decisive moment is the cyclist passing by below. There's a little filmic expressionism in the swirling stair and handrail, halfway between *The Cabinet of Dr Caligari* and *Vertigo*, but there are other hints too. Squint and you can almost detect the shape of a human eye, distorted but present with its pupil at the centre where the handrail curls around with the arc of the curve as an eyelid. Or you might discern an echo of the spoke of the bicycle, absent from the wheels themselves as the shutter speed captures only the tyres, blurring the rest. The spiralling stairs become static versions of the spinning wheels.

In Cartier-Bresson's photo of the Kamondo stairs at Galata in Istanbul (p.24), the steps become a stage, an urban theatre with figures distributed artfully, actors of urban life. Unusually for him, the camera is looking up the stairs. We are positioned more as an audience than an omnipresent hovering eye. These stairs, dating from the late 19th century, blend a Baroque sensibility (all sumptuous curves and swelling forms) with an almost proto-Art Nouveau approach, all with a hint of Michelangelo's lava-flow steps at the Laurentian Library in Florence. There's a postbox

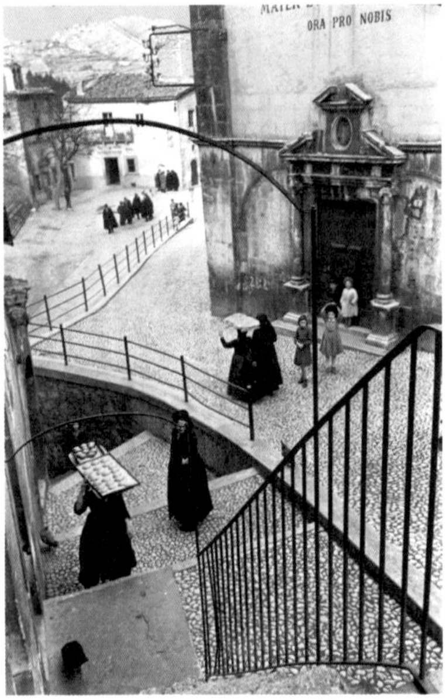

Scanno, Abruzzo, 1951
Henri Cartier-Bresson

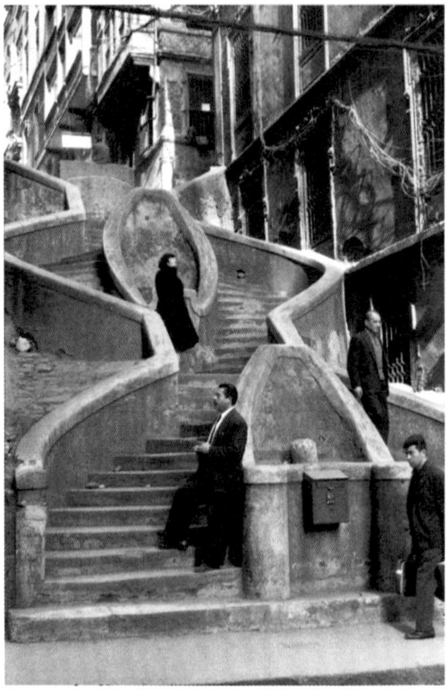

Galata, Istanbul, 1964
Henri Cartier-Bresson

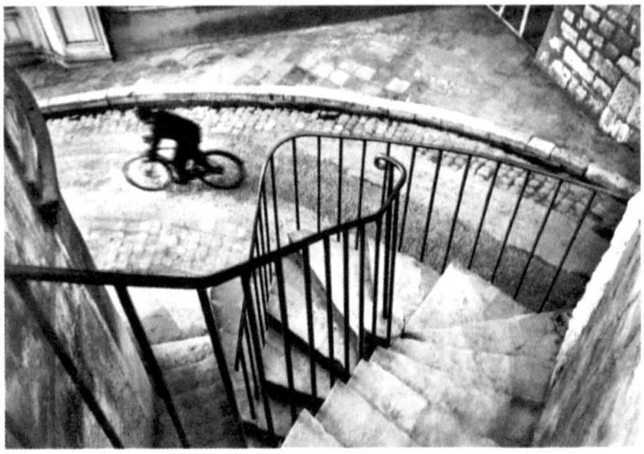

Hyères, The Var Department, 1932
Henri Cartier-Bresson

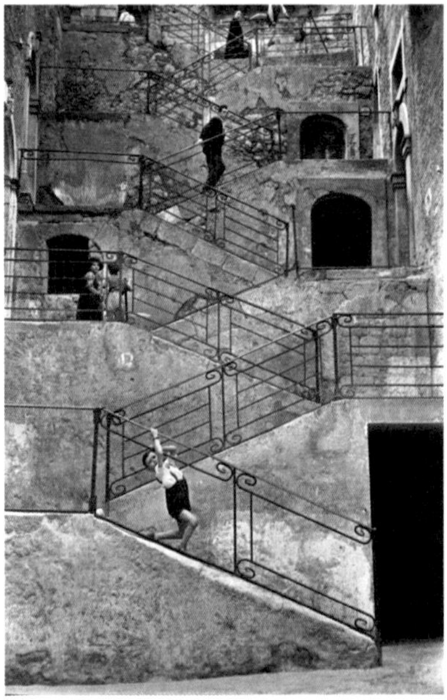

Leonforte, Sicily, 1956
René Burri

stuck slightly incongruously to the bottom of the steps, where you might expect a fountain or some more symbolic gesture. More recently the municipality has attempted to address this incongruity by placing a few potted trees at the bottom, though it looks not much less odd.

René Burri in his 1956 shot in Leonforte takes a similar view - straight on, looking slightly up at the seemingly endless stairs, figures placed perfectly to tell a story about the layered complexity of an old city. A couple of women chat, a young man ascends, looking back at the photographer, but it is the little boy hanging off the handrail who truly inhabits the space and the photo. The subtly wrought iron is spindly and delicate, with a simple spiral detail which picks up the back and forth of an ascent up the stair. It is the way in which they recede that makes the photo so mesmeric; your eye can't help but ascend from the dark opening at the bottom right corner.

For André Kertész, photographing a fire escape in New York in 1949, the figures also appear as actors, or perhaps backstage hands working on the gantry which forms the armature for urban life. The deep shadows cast on the brick wall and the complex angles and black lines cast off in all directions recall, as does Cartier-Bresson's work, the fragmented geometries of Expressionism. There's something here of the divide between front and back of stage: at the front are the buildings, the skyscrapers and towers, the Art Deco city; backstage are the fire escapes and vast flank walls, the workers and the shadows. The ironwork is a separate layer of infrastructure, like so much of the iron in the city, from the lampposts to the manhole covers. It looks like it could almost be teased out, unthreaded from the fabric of the city, but then the whole thing might just fall apart.

The same illusion of depth and the metaphors of ascent into the light into descent into the depths have made street stairs a favourite of filmmakers too. A staple of horror, film noir and the psychological thriller, the internal stairs feature vividly in nightmares induced by everything from *Nosferatu* and *The Shining* to *Psycho* and *Double Indemnity*. But the city stair, though perhaps a little less familiar, makes appearances in countless scenes of epic and operatic tragedy as well as the most slapstick of comedies. Sergei Eisenstein's endlessly referenced and much-parodied Odessa steps scene in *Battleship Potemkin* (1925) uses descent as a metaphor for the catastrophe of the massacre, as soldiers pursue the crowd downwards and a solitary pram runs out of control down the steps. But it is preceded by a brief scene of a woman picking up her dead child and reversing the action, moving briefly up the stairs, against the flow, as if to suggest the boy's ascent towards the heavens. Alexander Rodchenko's striking 1929 photo *The Stairs* similarly shows a woman cradling a child up the steps, but here it is the geometry, the diagonal hatching of the shadows, which makes the image.

Three years later Laurel and Hardy's *The Music Box* uses a street stair equally brilliantly in its story of two bumbling removal men trying to transport a pianola up a steep set of stone stairs. The Sisyphean effort is magnificently filmed, with all its pratfalls and disasters, and the punchline is that they could have just taken it up the hill around the side on their cart. Remarkably, those steps are still there, in Silver Lake, just off Sunset Boulevard.

Between them, these two scenes expose the urban stair as a site of endless struggle, and both are, in their own very different ways, stories of class (the maltreated sailors of Odessa and the oppressed deliverymen of California). Urban stairs might also stand in for an inner descent into madness, exquisitely exemplified in Joaquin Phoenix's unsettling dance scene in Todd Phillips's *Joker* (filmed in the Bronx). The steps are still the street, but with extra depth and metaphor they become even more irresistible.

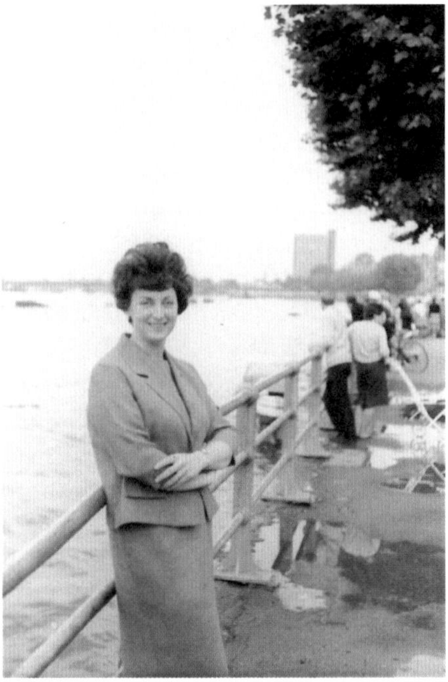

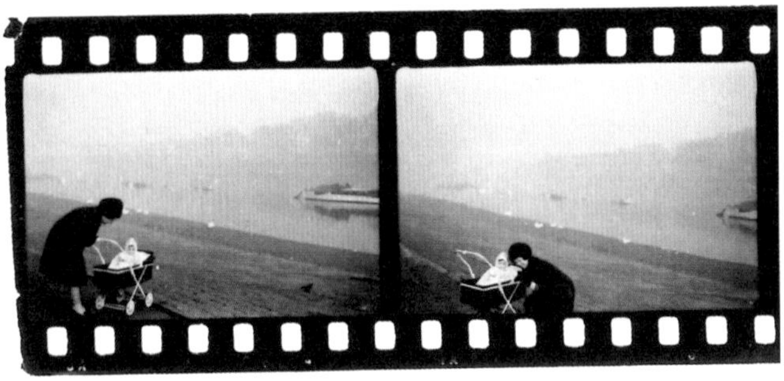

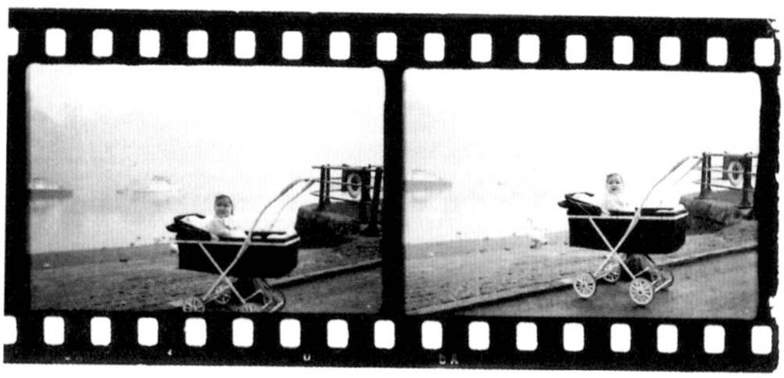

Top: *The author's mother at Thames Embankment, Putney*, 1964
Bottom: *The author as a baby at Thames Embankment, Putney*, late 1960s
Photographs by Graham Heathcote

Balustrading

There are fences which exclude and railings which attract. Along an embankment or a seaside promenade, railings are designed to be leant on. It is easy to rest a foot on a lower horizontal rail, to peer out aimlessly at the water or the landscape. They may be barriers between street and water, but they attract us right to the edge and allow us to enjoy that moment in between. Railings and balustrades assume we are slapstick clowns unable to not fall over any available edge (yet think of Venice, where almost every street is bounded by water which you can fall into at any point, free of railings). They are also in themselves a framework for being in public. Stand around in a public place and you might gather questioning looks; lean on a railing and you are clearly legitimately indulging in the view, being in the street, using the city, in contemplation or conversation. They can facilitate idling.

Bert Hardy's famous 1951 shot of two young women sitting on a railing on the Blackpool seafront is a piece of pure theatre. Apparently Hardy managed to take it the exact moment a gust of wind came and, in a moment to prefigure Marilyn, lifted Pat Stewart's skirt. Stewart, it turned out, was a dancer and Tiller Girl, not unused to showing her legs, but the photo hadn't been posed. The two women had appropriated the railings as seats, yet must surely have been aware of their prominence - after all, they are looking back towards the street, not out to sea.

Two years after Hardy's shot, John Christie was arrested while apparently leaning on the railings on the Thames Embankment in Putney, just about outside the flat I'd live in 40 years later. At least that is how it was portrayed in the film *10 Rillington Place*, where Richard Attenborough leans on the railings looking at the river when a passing policeman recognises and arrests him. The river has not washed away his sins. His is the opposite of theatre. A dull-looking man attempting to avoid being noticed, he is facing away from the street.

Those same railings appear in a photo of my mother, dated 1964 in pen on the back. They become the foil for the figure and a device which shoots a diagonal up across the picture plane, leading the eye to a vanishing point virtually exactly level with my mother's gaze. Leaning against them, her weight is countered with that diagonal, giving the picture a kind of kinetic balance. The railings appear again in contact strips I recently found, of a small fellow sitting in a pram. I must have been aged about one and, though this is probably some kind of memory caused by the photo rather than vice versa, this is, I have always thought, my earliest memory. My dad was about to take the photo but then, I think, had gone to look at something else, perhaps with my mum, and I felt some kind of anxiety that I'd been abandoned. It is a memory of a feeling rather than an event. In the background you can just make out a lifebelt and, behind that, on the other side, Bishop's Park partly obscured by a painterly and picturesque mist. This was the 1960s and London still had its foggy reputation to live up to. Now replaced with wooden-topped, clunkier versions, the railings act as crowd barriers for the Boat Race, perches for seagulls, and something to lean on for summer pub drinkers.

A good railing, with cast-iron uprights, does not separate realms, it brings them closer together. To lean and relax and look into the distance on a railing is to be able to appreciate whatever it is you are being protected from - the water, the drop, the sea. Close enough.

Barring

We often read about breaking down barriers. It is one of the great clichés of contemporary culture and a huge, clunking metaphor. But, together, all the different barriers make a kind of concrete poetry. I find it all a little depressing, so to save me from writing about them, here is an incomplete inventory of urban barriers:

* Railway level crossing
* Crowd control barrier
* Highway traffic barrier
* Traffic cone
* Bridge barrier
* Concrete and steel anti-truck barrier
* Longitudinal Channelising Devices
* Jet blast barrier
* Barrier gates
* Steel swing gates
* Parking access control gates
* Tyre killer
* Motorbike inhibitor
* Speed bump
* Planter barrier
* Velvet rope and polished brass posts
* U chicane
* Crash barrier
* Anti-cycling barrier
* K-frame barrier
* Mobile vehicle barrier
* Hydraulic anti-ram barrier
* Water-filled barrier
* Riot-control barrier
* Mobile police cordon
* Protective bike stand
* Noise barrier
* Wedge-plate barrier
* Manual lifting arm
* Guardrail safety barrier
* Police tape
* Hazard tape
* Protective planter
* Bollard
* Wooden trestle
* Rising boom arm barrier
* Steel arch
* X-ray gates
* Height restriction barrier
* Chain post
* Turnstile
* Utility barrier
* Traffic cone barrier
* Mesh barrier
* Steel hoop barrier
* Expanding high-visibility safety barrier
* Hydraulic bollard
* Road blocker
* Hydraulic high-security rising road blocker
* Parklet
* Random boulder
* Spherical bollard

Booking

The Bouquinistes of Paris, who can claim a history of over half a millennium of *plein-air* bookselling, have, perhaps, refined street furniture to its most seductively minimal means. Their simple stalls attached to stone walls along the Seine open like writing desks, their tops flipping up so that a blind, dumb box becomes an entire shopfront lined with words and pictures, creating its own roof, illuminated in the dark, early evenings of winter and radiating reading and warmth. Posters, prints, pamphlets and postcards supplement the books to create a suspended landscape of printed matter set against the scenery of the city, an outdoor gallery. It can seem as if all photographers have had a go at capturing this spectacle of the street books and their browsers. From Robert Doisneau's strong, almost choreographed scene of pairs of figures in long overcoats and stark, black trees on a sweeping curve along the river (1947) to Inge Morath's 1954 view of elegant women in cinch-waisted cocktail dresses browsing the prints (p.30), the row of riverside booksellers has come to be one of the great visual clichés of intellectual Paris, a city in which words are inscribed on the *quais* and the second-hand booksellers are protected by statute.

One anonymous image, dated apparently from 1929, seems to embody this image of Paris. A sign reading 'English Book Stall' pokes out of one of the boxes, while the eye is led via the perspective line of a repaired section of asphalt to a Morris column with its exotic dome (another embodied display of text in the city). The right of the picture features a cropped streetlamp with a tapering ladder resting against it. The books and the advertising column between them indicate a city of words and spectacle, of literature converted into drama by everyday life; the lamp represents Paris as the City of Light and also the electric invention which allows nights of reading. The relationship of these simple boxes to the books they contain is clear - they open up like books themselves, an *architecture parlante*, books covers transformed into street furniture, while the padlocks that secure them overnight recall the locks on *incunabula* in old libraries before printing made books accessible. Another familiar image, Brassaï's *Professor Louis Dimier* (early 1930s), shows an almost caricatured image of the old intellectual bending over the books to get closer to the titles. With his cane held behind him and his bowler and beard, he is the archetype of the book browser, oblivious to the street.

Over the channel in London a few years later, in *c.*1936, Wolfgang Suschitzky captured a group browsing the shelves outside a Charing Cross Road bookshop (p.30). Like Professor Dimier they are hunched over the titles, but are so densely packed that the books themselves are completely obscured. It is almost as if they are praying. In a famous and striking wartime photo taken by an anonymous Associated Press photographer three years later, a boy is shown sitting on what appears to be a rolled-up shopfront shutter, reading a book amid the ruins of a bookshop. I suppose this too is Charing Cross Road. Windows have been smashed by the bombing of the Blitz and books strewn all over the place, beautifully illustrating the fragility of the border between bookshop and street (a line blurred so successfully by the boxes of books). Here it is the shelves in the shop's doorway which create the zone of public, outdoor books rather than boxes outside, a model still occasionally seen, though increasingly rarely.

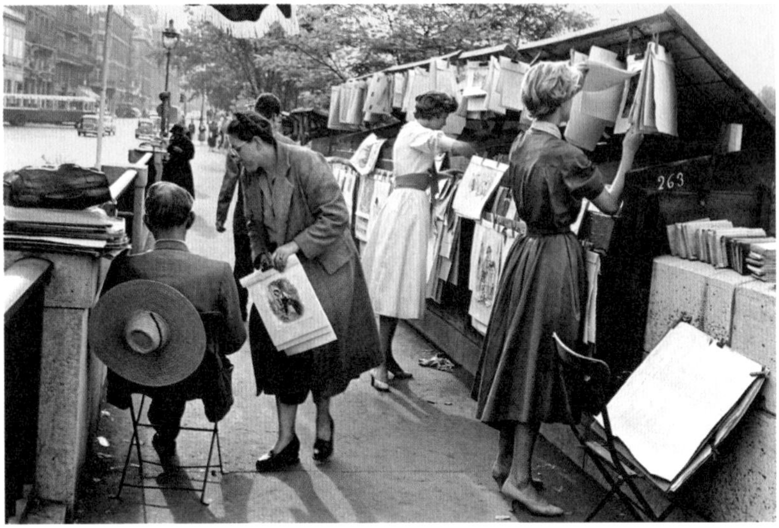

Booksellers along the Seine, 1954
Inge Morath

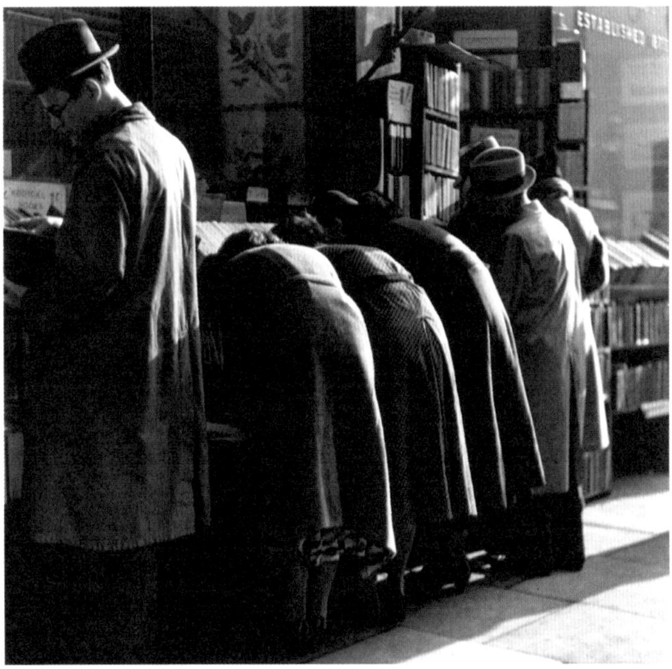

Charing Cross Road, London (book shop), c.1936
Wolfgang Suschitzky

Charing Cross Road today is a sad sight for a bibliophile; barely a couple of second-hand bookshops survive in what was once an entire street of them. At least it has fared better than the streets around St Paul's, the one-time centre of the industry and now completely bereft of anything to do with books or publishing. There are still book carts outside one bookshop however, and someone is always browsing. At Strand Books, on New York's Broadway, you are more likely to encounter actual crowds rifling through the slightly soiled titles on carts outside the store. From the homeless and the retired with time on their hands to students and tourists, the books (here displayed on cobbled together but charming wheeled shelves) always seem to attract attention, they have a kind of magnetism. Anyone who truly likes reading finds it difficult to pass such a display without at least a sideways glance.

Most cities seem to have evolved some form of indigenous book stall or cart, albeit not as institutionalised (or protected) as those of Paris. In London it is the trestle tables and storage boxes beneath draughty Waterloo Bridge. Boston has its wonderful shelves with their slender pitched roofs lining West Street. The huge College Street in Kolkata houses its book stalls in a kind of ad hoc informal architecture, echoing the corrugated metal and blue tarpaulin-roofed dwellings in the city's informal neighbourhoods. Here the massive piles of books become such a mass that they become walls and labyrinths, with paperbacks as bricks, books as architecture. Istanbul has the densely packed and stepped old book market of Sahaflar Carsisi with a delicate and beautiful canopy of trees and ivy supplementing the overhanging eaves of the stalls. The Welsh town of Hay-on-Wye built itself an architecture from books, its ramshackle book stalls lining the streets and now its main attraction. And in Tokyo the side alleys of Kanda Jimbocho are lined with membranes of books like paper siding, the curtains and canopies of tarpaulin rain protection ruched out of the way to give them a slightly theatrical effect.

As books become less a part of the public culture, and as everything continues to migrate online, and libraries, so long fought for and so hard won, wither under political apathy, there has been a small revival in the adoption of books to foster a new sense of public property and street furniture as public good. Little carts of red books have popped up, or shelves outside front gardens. Free lending libraries have cropped up in unlikely places, often public structures; bus shelters, on walls, outside houses and on old shelves in the city. And phoneboxes around the world have been converted into refuges for freely available used books by communities - the cheering sight of one mode of communication being replaced by a much older one.

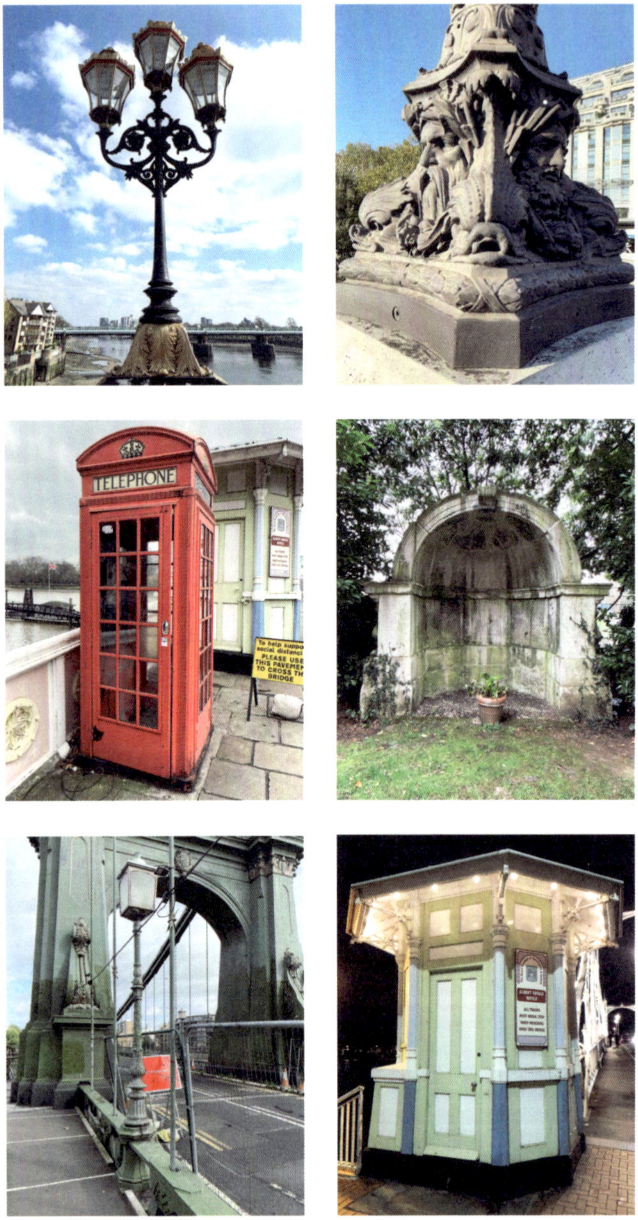

Top row, left: *Putney Bridge, London*; right: *Pont Neuf, Paris*
Middle row, left: *Albert Bridge, London*; right: *stone apse from London Bridge*
Bottom row: *Hammersmith Bridge, London*; right: *Albert Bridge, London*

Bridging

Bridges are in-between structures, contested between one side of the river and the other. They create a crossing in which the pedestrian in particular feels a certain momentary sense of freedom. The release from the walls of the city, the tight streets and the canyons of towers and the sudden breath of air that comes from a river, the cool breeze blowing along its length, can trigger a moment of urban clarity in which the city itself suddenly becomes visible and comprehensible, and the mind is cleared, prepared for the other side.

Bridges are those rare mechanisms through which a municipality gets a chance to express itself through grand design. Situated between architecture, engineering and infrastructure, they are by necessity profoundly functional, but through civic pride and vanity often also ambitious, slightly pretentious and extremely ornate. I don't entirely suggest that bridges themselves be understood as street furniture (although you might argue that something like London's Tower Bridge is exactly that, a perfect symbolic embodiment of Victorian municipal functional infrastructure), but because they are inevitably representative of a certain kind of metropolitan expression and self-image they become the places where the actual street furniture attached to them is allowed to be its most extravagant. And because they are so intimately tied up with a city's idea of itself they often retain fittings like lamps, seats and railings far more effectively than the streets to either side, which tend to succumb to successive waves of obsolescence, function and fashion. Bridges are familiar and beloved, they soon become listed and protected and, as such, tend to be preserved in their entirety, including all the fixtures and fittings that might otherwise disappear if they were less valued.

For two decades I lived in a flat overlooking Putney Bridge on the Thames in London. An elegant but perhaps not outstanding stone structure from the 1880s, it resembles the 1830's version of London Bridge which was subsequently sold to the US and now stands in Lake Havasu City in Arizona (a town now famous chiefly for having London Bridge). My former bridge, Putney Bridge, designed by the engineer famous for the London Embankment and its sewer system, Joseph Bazalgette, is made magical by its lights. The triple in-line lanterns with their solid cast-iron base and curlicued shafts are things of wonder, things that would nevertheless surely have long disappeared if they weren't a part of a protected structure. They were designed for gas but survived electrification and even the widening of the bridge. The surrounding streets have gone through a panoply of lights, from gas to electric, from iron to concrete and back again to fake heritage, all the way to utilitarian poles. But these ridiculously ornate lights survive.

In their form they aren't a million miles from those on the Pont Alexandre III in Paris. Closely spaced and elaborate, with etched glass scallops, iron bulrushes and lions' feet, these French fancies are a mongrel mix of Belle Epoque excess and metropolitan pomposity. Hammersmith Bridge (the next bridge upstream from Putney) similarly maintains its ornate lights as part of the iron structure that really might be thought of as street furniture in its entirety.

On London's Albert Bridge (1873) the four toll booths survive, two on either end. At twilight, with lightbulbs twinkling under their overhanging eaves, they look like kiosks at some ghostly funfair, promising something seductive and yet all locked up. They're compelling structures, octagonal in plan with an almost Chinese roof and cast-iron columns with elaborate brackets. They certainly wouldn't have survived if the bridge wasn't listed and the same is true of the single red phonebox on the south side. Together with the old gas lamps on the bridge and a cabmen's shelter a few yards away, they make quite a street furniture ensemble.

The opposite is true of another series of odd survivals. When Old London Bridge was demolished in 1832, the stone alcoves, in the form of apses (which dated from a 1762 restoration), were saved and a few are now scattered throughout the capital. There is one in the grounds of Guy's Hospital, another in Victoria Park in Hackney and yet another, weirdly, in the grounds of a 1930s block of flats in East Sheen, a leftover from when these were the grounds of a grand house. It has no seat, just a vaulted stone canopy with a couple of flower pots beside it.

Perhaps the city in which bridges come closest to crossing over into street furniture's domain is Venice. This is a city where the bridges are inseparable from the streets and alleys, a connective tissue criss-crossing the canals. With steps, handrails, balustrades, bollards and sculpted stone, they force you to engage with the nature of this city built on water. When seen, almost inevitably with the mooring posts, the hanging lights and the gentle hum of boats passing under, they become part stoop, part street, their steps as seats and their surfaces as public places, suspended piazzas now repurposed as selfie stations.

Occasionally, due to their scale or eccentricity, a bridge might even *become* the city. Sydney Harbour Bridge, Brooklyn Bridge, Tower Bridge, the Golden Gate in San Francisco, the Chain Bridge in Budapest, the Charles Bridge in Prague - each is, in its way, a piece of utilitarian design which comes to define the city it connects. That zone over the river seems to be protected by sentiment as well as legislation, a sliver of perpetuity allowing the bridge and its components to survive as a microcosm of a street from another age. The bridge is literally an in-between zone, and it preserves within and upon it a streetscape of things from another age.

Calling

The phonebox is an enigmatic piece of architecture. A kind of glass coffin for communication, it is simultaneously a very personal and a very public place - a refuge and a fish bowl. It is also, now, almost perfectly obsolete. Yet because they are protected, because they offer opportunities for advertising or because they might, in some rare circumstances, still be needed, they frequently survive, these odd, glass sarcophagi for a defunct technology.

The first public phonebox was installed in Berlin's Potsdamer Platz as early as 1881, almost as soon as the first phones became available. But perhaps the most perfect manifestation of this miniature building type is the classic and quirky red British K2 phonebox. The design dates from an architectural competition in 1924 which was won by Giles Gilbert Scott, designer of Liverpool Cathedral and both Battersea and Bankside power stations (the latter now Tate Modern). Scott based his design for the phone kiosk on the rather unlikely model of Sir John Soane's 1815 mausoleum for his wife, Eliza, in Old St Pancras churchyard. One of the architect's original prototypes (modelled in timber rather than the more familiar cast iron) can still be seen beneath the arch of the Royal Academy on Piccadilly.

You might argue that, with the mausoleum inscribed in its design, the phonebox has a kind of morbidity embedded in its form. It is its own memorial. I can't help thinking of a film that had a profound impact on me as a child, Antonio Mercero's *La Cabina* (*The Telephone Box*, 1972). This Spanish TV short silently tells the story of a man who enters a glass phonebox to make a call, finds the phone isn't working but is then unable to exit. The door stays resolutely shut and concerned passers-by are unable to help. Engineers enter the scene and they too are unable to free the captive caller. Finally a phone company flat-bed truck arrives and the whole phonebox is lifted on to the back and hauled away, to both the crowd and the occupant's relief. At one point, stuck in traffic on the truck like a caged animal, the phonebox prisoner sees another identical phonebox with another man trapped inside. For a moment they just look at each other from inside their respective phoneboxes, until the lights change and they pass. It is a moment of subtle and absolute horror, a recognition of the end in the way that a doppelgänger is always supposed to indicate, though the double here is of course the kiosk. The journey ends in a vast subterranean warehouse packed with phoneboxes full of live and dead occupants. But the final scene is the most chilling - the engineers back at the square install a new phonebox and leave its door just slightly ajar.

This phonebox is more akin, perhaps, to Snow White's glass coffin, another intimation of death. But it is also a typically Spanish, subversive and surreal take on the city (this was still the Franco era and it can be taken as a Kafka-esque metaphor for becoming trapped in bureaucracy or a state that leaves you unable to speak out, ironically to communicate). It reveals something of the psychic awkwardness of being isolated and cocooned yet in full view while talking (or failing to be able to get through) to someone somewhere else entirely. Phone booths pop up in movies of every different hue from *Goodfellas* to *The Blues Brothers*. The brilliantly offbeat and shocking *Oldboy*, for instance, sees the protagonist snatched from a phone booth and imprisoned, the isolation of the glass box somehow anticipating his subsequent years

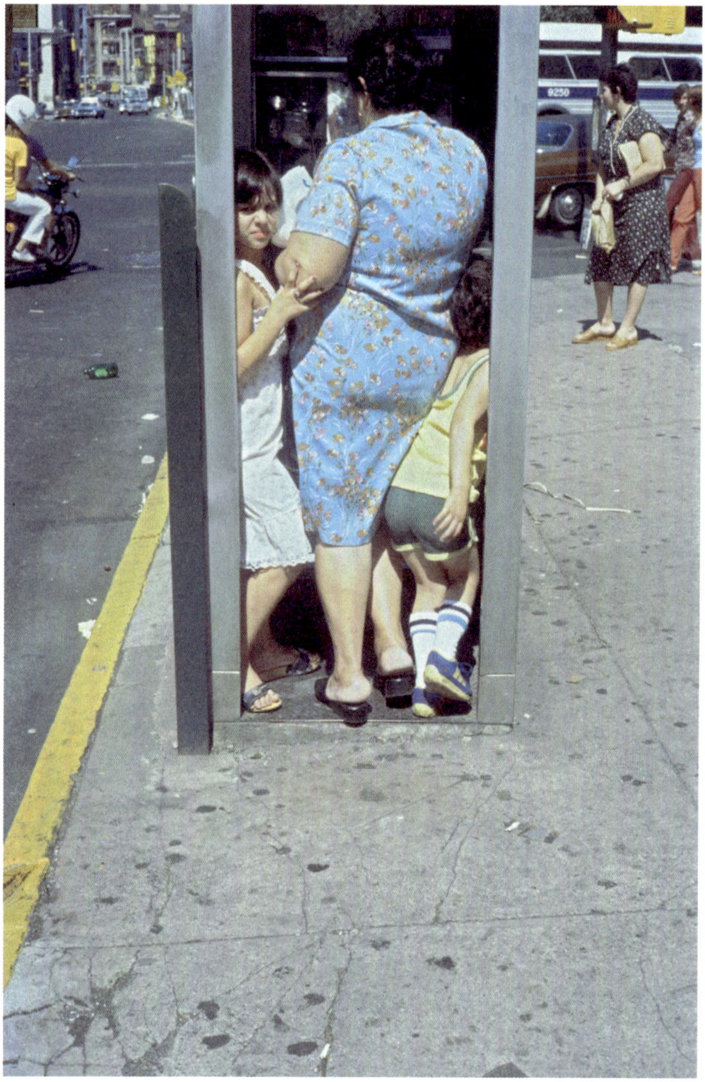

NY, 1988
Helen Levitt

of solitary confinement in surveilled captivity. For Tippi Hedren's character in Hitchcock's *The Birds* it becomes a cage - with the birds on the outside. In his *Dial M for Murder* it becomes a voyeuristic soundbox to witness failed murder over the line.

The phone booth might represent an experience of disembodiment, alienation, intensified angst and horror but also of transformation - and transportation. Cartoon strips of Clark Kent rushing to his nearest phone booth to change into his Superman costume led to endless parodies and homages of this same idea. From *Doctor Who* to *Bill & Ted's Excellent Adventure*, the phone booth became a place of transition, from one state to another or even one dimension and another. It is curious how enduring this trope has been. In *The Matrix*, one of the first movies to imagine a techno-dystopia (or utopia, depending on how you see it) enabled by the digital, the phone booth becomes the portal between the real and the simulated worlds. Really, a phone kiosk? It abides as an archetype precisely because of that status as a portal. Where once cities had gates, barriers to entry and exit, they then had phoneboxes, places highlighting precisely the connection to other places. That they resembled sentry boxes was a welcome absurdity. They were sentinels and switchboards, presences in the city emphasising both connection and disconnection. There was the phone line but there was also the isolation in full view.

Perhaps in the response to that clear design for a single, vertical body, booths are at their oddest when they accommodate more than a single body. Helen Levitt's famous 1988 photo of a phone booth with a mother squeezed in between her two children recalls a weird postwar craze for 'phone booth stuffing'. College kids began trying to see how many of them could squeeze into a booth and they would be snapped, limbs akimbo and bodies compressed behind glass. For a moment in which sex was absented from the public discourse, it seems a curiously intimate activity, all that proximity and touching - perhaps that was its attraction. It spread across the world, to the UK too, though not to quite the same extent, but the end of the 1950s had seemed to die a merciful death.

British popular culture was particularly pickled in the mythology of the phonebox. Perhaps the British version is more robust, more architectural and certainly more visible (except in Hull, where examples are, curiously, beige rather than red) than its global counterparts, which are often little more than plastic bubbles like 1960s salon hairdryers. From the cover of David Bowie's *Ziggy Stardust* to *The Ladykillers*, the phonebox keeps popping up in. But even in Hollywood (*The Blues Brothers* again, *Phone Booth*, *Blow Out*, *Dirty Harry* or its pale imitation *Die Hard 3*) phone booths remain a persistent presence.

The British booth, with its red livery, pierced crown decoration and vertical form, positions it somewhere between sentry box and postbox, symbols of the status quo, the state, the queen, and the General Post Office which then still owned the network. Thus they became ubiquitous in the iconography of tourist tat: phonebox keyrings, fridge magnets, money boxes, biscuit tins. That status is fading now, a quarter of a century after they became defunct but it has not disappeared. The whiff of nostalgia lingers like the sour smell of the booths.

Perhaps it is partly to do with an appearance of shelter and warmth. Phoneboxes always appeared as nighttime beacons, lanterns in the streetscape which indicated escape from the cold and rain, and provided communication and the warmth of conversation. They were the smallest of civic buildings - open, undiscriminating and genuinely public. But they are over-sentimentalised. The phoneboxes I remember from real life (and I used them a lot) were something very different. It is difficult to compute today, with our instant access to communication, that we once needed phoneboxes. To enter one was to cocoon yourself in an instantly recognisable funk of human odour. Their concrete floors were stained and streaked with bodily fluids and carpeted with fag-ends and the residues of suspiciously sticky substances. To enter was to be enveloped in a warm, moist mist of stale cigarette smoke and the smell of recently departed humanity, wet woollen coats and sweat. If you found a phone that was unvandalised, you then had to keep popping coins in a conversation flecked with beeps and clicks as your money began to run out and you fumbled for more. The phonebooks suspended on hinged brackets were invariably shredded or soaked, graffiti was scratched into the surfaces, and the ash trays were full to overflowing. In their latter days, the interiors of British phoneboxes became a rich and colourful collage of ads for sex-workers, with 'discipline services', 'real models' and 'genuine photos' of pre-op transexuals blue-tacked on to the panes of glass. These cards were themselves about transformation, bodies changing into something they had not been, insanely sexualised images of women you might have assumed looked not entirely like their representations.

On the other hand, the level of amenity designed into the interior of the K2 was impressive. There was the phonebook on its hinged fitting but there was also a shelf (for a hat or a handbag), that ash tray and, in the original models, a hook for an umbrella. That level of bespoke domesticity and consideration for the accoutrements of everyday life surely went some way to endearing it to its public, at least in theory. These kiosks were also, and this is largely now forgotten, often the only sources of electricity in rural areas. There are stories of people removing the lightbulbs to plug in their electric shavers or even kettles and toasters. It is a reminder of rural precariousness and one we would do well to remember. Many areas remain almost stubbornly resistant to mobile signals and the phoneboxes are all that there is in an emergency. At the time of writing, the UK is disposing of three quarters of its phone booths, which will not, I suspect, end well.

The few surviving K2 phoneboxes represent a particularly contemporary piece of heritage, an architecture devoted to technology, manufactured in cast iron in imitation of classical plaster and timber mouldings, and referring in its form to a Regency tomb and a Roman pendentive vault. It somehow embodies a cartload of particularly British concerns, an attempt to conceal technology in the cloak of history, a blend of heavy industry and manufacture and historical reference, of modernity and tradition, high-tech and nostalgia. The subsequent designs for phoneboxes, which were more resolutely modern and easier to manufacture and maintain, never attained the same status as the K2. That sentry-box design had somehow become engrained in the culture.

In the 1960s the GPO began to experiment with more modern designs. Neville Conder's 1962 version, for instance, was a very slick, minimal modern design with chamfered edges but it was Bruce Martin's K8 design, introduced in 1968, which won out. With rounded corners to the single large windows on each side it was a simpler kiosk, still elegant, still red, stripped of the inessential detail. A few dozen still survive. Class, as ever, entered the equation in British design. During the 1970s and '80s some neighbourhoods got new kiosks (few looked any good), while the poorest estates got a canopy on a stick in the freezing cold.

Other countries, especially ones with warmer climates, developed very different architectures. There were the hairdryer-style plastic hoods which covered your head only, and there were minimalist glass boxes, moulded plastic pods and mini-pagodas. On the streets of Brazil and beyond in Latin America, and as far as Africa, there was and still is the 'big ear' - a rare instance of a female designer making a major impact with a much-loved piece of street furniture. The wonderful *orelhão* was designed in 1971 by Shanghai-born Brazilian architect Chu Ming Silveira, then working at the Companhia Telefônica Brasileira. It was a response to vandalism inflicted on more traditional kiosks and the unbearably hot temperatures endured inside a glass box. These outsize eggshells, usually in yellow, present a slightly surreal moment in the street, their tilted domes often inhabited by legs and torsos with unseen heads. Cartoonish and fun, they also perform well, the dome providing acoustic isolation and protection from the rain and at least a little privacy.

In Malta and Gibraltar, there were British colonial boxes left unglazed to allow the breeze to filter through. The Netherlands had the ultimate modern phone booth. Designed by Leendert Cornelis van der Vlugt and Johannes Brinkman (architects of the astonishing Van Nelle Factory in Rotterdam) in 1932, it is a piece of pure industrial design in galvanised steel and glass, a mini-modernist house. Completely glazed and with slender steel sections, it is still a remarkably modern-looking design. Even the stripped graphic ('Telefoon') on a blue background is more memorably vivid than any recent designs. This is not a Superman changing box. In the best functionalist manner, there is nowhere to hide, an X-ray architecture in which the use is completely exposed, the user still a part of the street. There are a few still studded around Holland, mostly outside (or inside) museums, but the one I remembered outside the Boijmans van Beuningen in Rotterdam seems to have gone, a casualty of upgrading.

The phonebox is, of course, now almost totally obsolete. The ubiquity of the mobile phone has made them virtually pointless. Ed Ruscha's painting *Site of a Former Telephone Booth* (2005), featuring an expanse of sky framed by a streetlight pole and a section of slender tree trunk, is full of pathos, the end of an era, the booth not even present. But it is unsentimental. Things change. Street furniture, no matter how close it might appear to architecture, is ephemeral and expendable.

Yet is there still a purpose the phonebox might serve? Many of Britain's K2 boxes have survived because they are in conservation areas. The architecture of technology has become heritage, like the technology itself. It suggests that street furniture can still be beautiful, even if its function has been superseded. Phoneboxes have become so much a part of the physical and psychic landscape that they have become indispensable. Today you are probably more likely to find old phoneboxes in bars, stores, clubs or converted to shower units in self-consciously quirky interiors. Some have been converted into micro-libraries in an effort to maintain their status as tokens of that disappearing idea of a public building. Others have been made into greenhouses, art installations, pub furniture or espresso bars, and there is now even a market for crude reproductions. Some new phoneboxes have appeared, unhappy, distorted versions (one is a funereal reimagining of the K2 in black but open, like a bus shelter), clearly designed for billboards rather than calling, the unused phone an excuse for sticking a huge ad in the middle of the pavement. Others pretend to be Wi-Fi hotspots or charging stations; again the ad is both the real medium and its message.

It is difficult to believe that today such an exquisite piece of architecture could be commissioned and developed from one of Britain's leading architects. The day of the phonebox is gone. We all now exist in our own bubbles of communication, without shelter or warmth and only the little light from the screens of our phones, the digitally deracinated. The phonebox is relegated to heritage, as redundant now as horse troughs and public drinking fountains, a fragment of a memory of a public architecture of privacy inscribed on the city streets in the most public way possible. That some surviving examples have now been fitted with defibrillators is a pleasing reflection on a typology which had been inspired by a mausoleum. Perhaps, like those in *The Matrix*, they can become portals to another chance rather than memorials to a defunct technology and an age of publicly owned architecture.

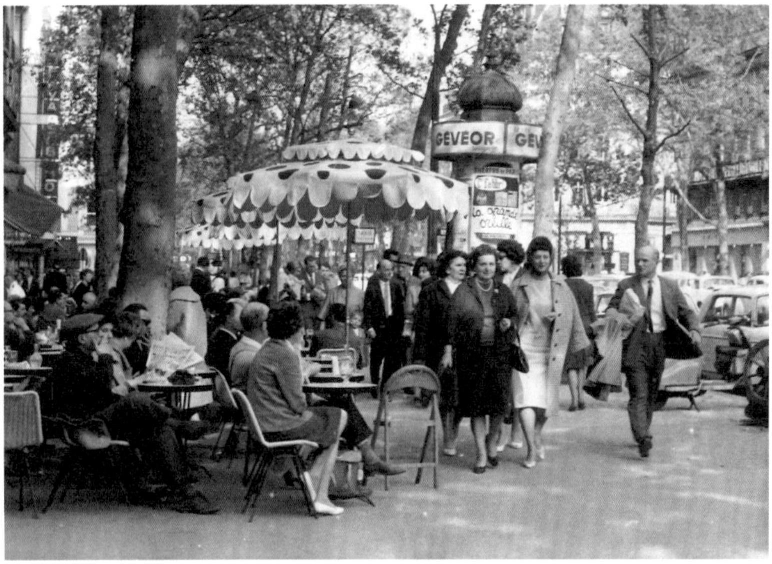

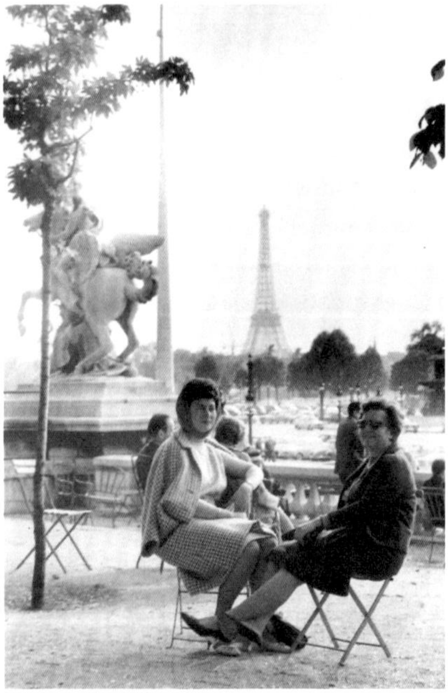

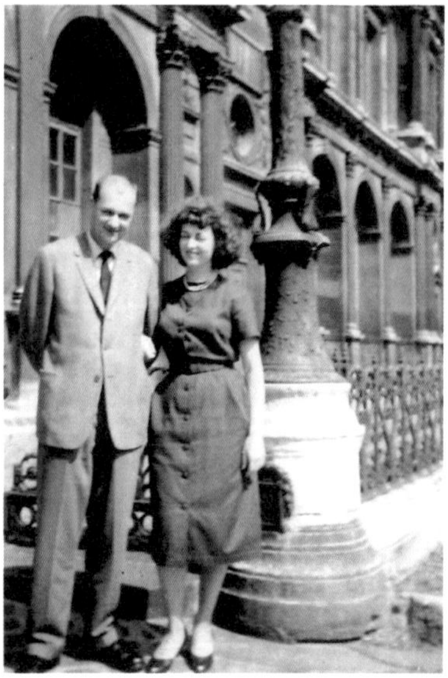

Top and bottom left: *The author's mother and grandmother in Paris,* 1963
Bottom right: *The author's mother and father in Paris,* late 1950s

Capturing

As I was writing this book, I was also clearing out the house in which I grew up. The sadness-and-nostalgia tinged sorting through seemingly endless piles of papers, the books, the boxes, the stuff. Days lived in dust and the dry, papery smell of things untouched for decades. I thought I'd taken all the family photos back home but, towards the bottom of another pile, I found a shoebox and inside, hundreds of photos, mostly of people I don't know. But among them were a few taken by my father. He was not a great photographer but he did manage a few atmospheric and evocative snaps, evocative at least for me – they picture an era from before I was born which seems impossibly distant now, yet they also have a kind of directness which makes them, at least for me, compelling.

The place and date were written on a few photos in my mother's hand: Paris, 1963. They're nothing more than the usual tourist snaps, my mother and her mother sitting and walking in Paris, posed, unposed, but always somehow self-conscious. One photo, of the pair walking down an unnamed boulevard, features a Morris column directly above them, pointing almost like an arrow. The name of a drinks firm around its rim is prominent: Geveor, a wine brand. (In Robert Doisneau's classic colour shot it is Suze, a bitters drink.) The street is cluttered with the polka dot umbrellas of the cafés, the café chairs themselves, each a different design, each looking out towards the streets, oriented not for conversation but for watching the city itself, the flow of people. A street sweeper's cart stands upside down to the far right and, perhaps surprisingly, the streetlight is a breezily modern design, a slender pole splitting into two brackets with twin lamps pointing down at the pavement and road. Now that same city is full of what look like much older fittings, imitation Belle Epoque lights with gas-style lanterns. The image of cities changes as they try to become more like a particular idea of themselves.

Then I came across another photo of the same trip, probably the same day – the outfits are the same, the coat draped over my mother's shoulders, the headscarf. Here too the panoply of street furniture and fittings comes into view as you look. I had just returned from Paris the day before, reflecting on these pictures. I'd been to the Jardins de Tuileries to look at the chairs, prompted by looking at photographers' studies of the groupings. The cluster of chairs from the 1960s is ad hoc, each one a little different to the others, an accumulation of designs from bent metals to timber slats, folding and non-folding versions. The chairs have character.

There are plenty of vertical accents here. The Eiffel Tower, of course – these are tourist photos after all. But also the spindly tree, the tapering flagpole behind the equestrian statue, and in the Place de la Concorde, which was then a huge car park, a grid of elaborate iron streetlamps. There is the balustrade with its fat balusters, a low wall, railings and folded chairs stacked against another tree. It is an entire ecosystem of things, each addressing an aspect of comfort or containment, accessibility or art, things which, together, constitute the city but which also embody bodies. Each item refers to our verticality or our seated postures in the city, accommodating our forms as they did the forms of our forebears. I wonder how long those two chairs stayed like that after my mother and granny posed for the picture. Were they taken and subtly shifted immediately afterwards? What happened to them? The chairs that have replaced them are uniform, elegant, but with less character. Probably more comfortable. And the one on the left looks like it is laughing.

The discovery of these photos embodied and pre-empted everything I was writing about. And then, just as I was wrapping up the writing, I found another image, this one from an earlier trip. My parents didn't have a lot of money, they didn't take holidays abroad until much later in their lives, so a trip to Paris was a big deal. This one, taken of my mother and father two years after they were married, has a different feel, stiffer, more conventional, which might just be a reflection of the times - the 1950s versus the 1960s. My father seems exactly as I remember him, even though this was taken a decade before I was born. His fashion sense never changed, the same sports jackets (rarely a suit), a knitted tie. There appear to be three figures in the shot - my mother, my father and a lamppost. The building in the background is, I think, the Louvre, in the days before buildings were cleaned. Still soot-stained and dark, the architecture is the same tone as the cast-iron shaft of the light which itself is the same tone as the subdued dress my mother is wearing. This is still a city in black and white.

It interests me that they chose this spot in which to pose. Like so many of the models photographed in Paris and London at around the same time, the street furniture is being used as a foil for the figure. The cast-iron shaft anchors the two bodies in space and in place, in Paris (because where else has such elaborate lampposts, where else than the City of Light?). As Charles Marville found when he captured these monumental works of public utility and beauty in his photos of 19th-century Paris, street furniture is not just background but often a character in its own right. Just as the umbrellas, the Morris column and the Eiffel Tower situate my mother and grandmother in the larger scheme of the city and in scale, so the lamppost mediates between the insane grandeur and scale of the Louvre - palace as presentation of power - and the human figures. These pieces of street furniture create a landscape of objects between the body and the city in which we can more easily find ourselves, which is why they have themselves been such perennially popular subjects for photographers, filmmakers and artists, and why they pop up so frequently in the most personal of artefacts.

These snaps are nothing more than snatched images of people in a city, though of course to me they mean more. But they show the peculiar status of street furniture as an in-between architecture, a matrix of public goods which gives us comfort in the immensity of the city and, over time, in the gap between reality and memory, portrayal and real life. Between the living and the dead.

Cashing

A curious bank transaction took place on 27 June 1967, when TV comic actor Reg Varney took out a tenner from the world's first ATM (Automated Teller Machine) at a Barclays Bank in Enfield. There is more than one strange thing about this story. The first is that the US wouldn't get an ATM until 1969. The second is that Reg Varney was not particularly famous (*On the Buses,* which became huge, was two years later). The third is that the first ATM *in the world* was in Enfield.

One of the most mysterious pieces of street furniture to a traveller from the past would be an ATM. I remember my daughter, when very small, being disappointed to discover that the money given to you by the machine was your own. Although quite literally a hole in the wall, a controlled leak, ATMs create a connection between the street and the securest of buildings - the bank. It is debatable, I suppose, whether they are street furniture or more closely related to shopfronts. But it seems to me that they derive from a lineage of open-all-hours vending machines, which once dispensed everything from stamps and bubblegum to condoms and chips and then went out of fashion (in most, but not all, countries). Which is exactly what is happening to the ATM now.

The rapid decline of cash is leading to a corresponding decline in the use of ATMs around the world. Banks are reducing their networks of machines, often leaving smaller towns with no access to cash at all. But it was a thrilling story while it lasted. To be able to access ready money outside bank hours (which were always infuriatingly short and often bizarrely random) made the world available. The capacity even today to be able to take cash out of an ATM in another country (especially those where cash is more respected and used) seems a kind of miracle if you remember the days when you needed to exchange your money into that currency before you left.

There were stories about stolen pin numbers, about people being marched to machines at knife- or gun-point and forced to withdraw cash. There were CCTV videos of villains in mechanical diggers ripping ATMs out of walls and others of hackers slotting in mocked-up cards for cash. There were incidents of scammers fitting dummy fronts to record keystrokes and others of cameras aimed at pin pads to capture pin numbers. The odd thing about these machines is that, unless you are one of these characters, you are withdrawing your own cash, so a transaction is like transporting a case of notes around with you, unlocking it and taking a few out.

Architecturally, ATMs were also a curious hybrid. Often built into the walls of Victorian buildings, with their dependable, classical, rather boring and safe architecture, these machines breached the walls with lurid colours, lights, screens and splashed, illuminated logos. In the days before most people were used to living their lives through keystrokes, the ritual of stiffly poking in a pin was almost nerve-racking, a transaction directly with a machine which, at any point, might decide to swallow your card. ATMs changed the landscape, bringing the dream of constant consumption and 24-hour availability a little closer. Now they are being displaced by the cards designed to be inserted in them and by the phones we now carry and rely on for services that were once provided by myriad pieces of street furniture: clocks, newsstands, photo booths, phonebooks and the rest. They are one more almost obsolete piece of street furniture. My bank, where I was a customer for 40 years, recently shut down. Its ATM removed, it has become a literal hole in the wall - a bleak but now very visual gag about banks and security.

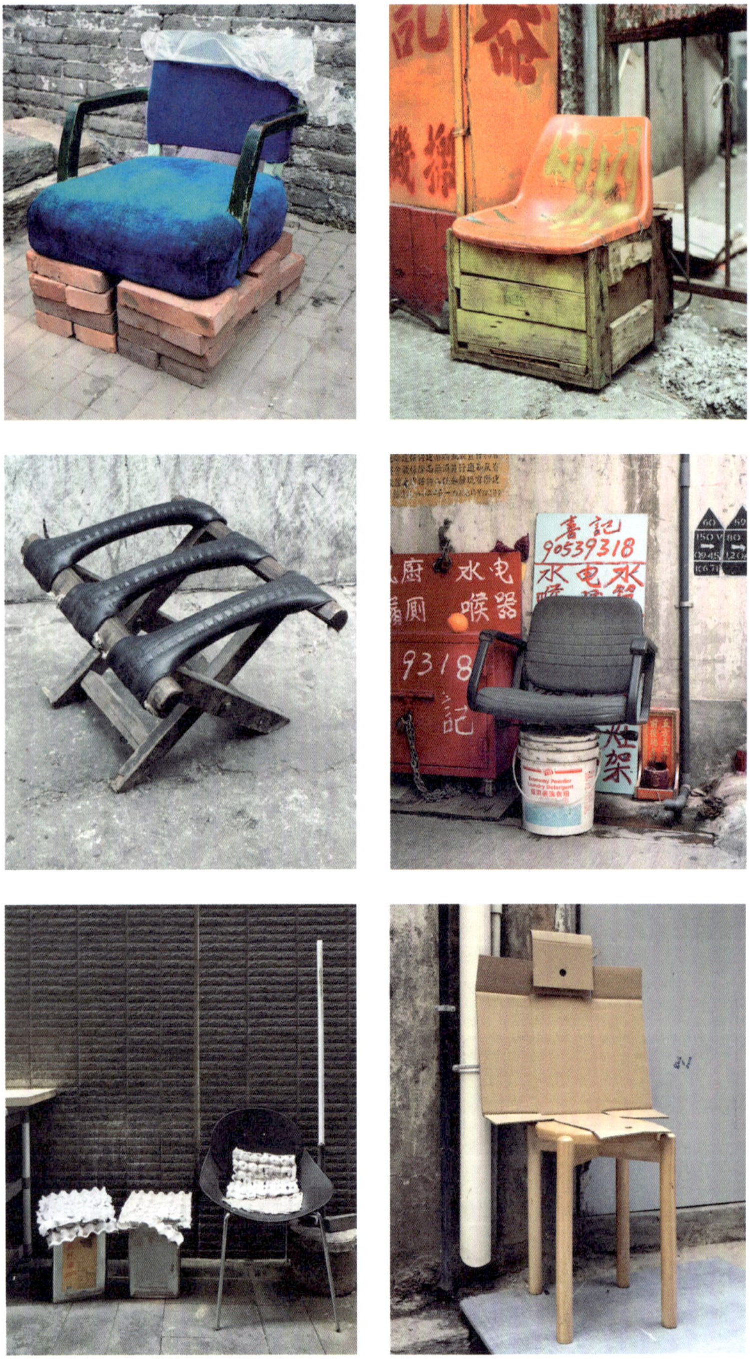

Photographs from the series Bastard Chairs, 1995–2017
Michael Wolf

Chairing

There is a category of furniture that is not street furniture, yet which is simultaneously also, arguably, the most successful street furniture of all. The chair. Not the classy café chair, nor those pieces of park furniture fixed to the ground and facing each other at an oblique angle, but the millions of cheap, mass-produced, almost universal chairs - appropriated, adapted, reused, rescued and repaired - all across the world which are put into service as street seats, private but in the public realm.

Michael Wolf's documentation of these seats in his series *Bastard Chairs* is an endless wonder of ingenuity and survival. He presents us with portraits of DIY masterpieces of bodging, of using the materials at hand to create site-specific seats adapted to the needs of place and person, site and body. Drawn mostly from Hong Kong, where he lived, and mainland China, he portrayed Frankenstein-seats made from hybrid parts, often using cannibalised bits of existing or broken mass-manufactured seating supplemented with anything from bricks and boxes to tyres and buckets. Occasionally they are quite brilliant pieces of work - ad hoc, almost Dadaist, responses to the smooth perfection of modern, mass-manufactured design.

Occasionally they involve only small adjustments to existing products. I am always very taken with the plastic garden chairs with two legs on one side sawn down to adapt them to be being used, sideways, on a set of steps. There are car seats stripped from long-gone chassis and placed on piles of bricks and there are injection-moulded school chairs boosted up on crates creating strangely beautiful hybrids. They are a response to particular conditions in the street - a lack of outdoor space, a lack of indoor space, the desire to sit outside and watch the world - and they are tailored to the particular demands of that location. These chairs are rarely objects into which much work or expense will have gone. Being in the public realm they are vulnerable, they need to be robust enough to be left outside and function over a long period of time, but with too little value or too specific a set of qualities to be worth stealing. As the marketplace becomes increasingly crowded with designs and commodities that are so complex they defy hacking or adaptation (from cars to phones), cheap chairs remain remarkably open to re-styling. That they can be re-purposed or made more comfortable or more appropriate with only the most basic of materials, with no use of tools at all, gives them a quality of incredible endurance and usefulness.

These adapted chairs are something different to the off-the-shelf plastic chairs you see all over the world, from Lagos to Naples, Mexico City to Bali, but they exist in the same world. They are gestures of minor appropriations of public space where there is no provision for conviviality, or where that provision is inadequate or tailored poorly to local conditions and customs. The placing of a pair of plastic chairs outside a front door while their occupant chats or pods peas is a way of inhabiting the city and blurring the lines between the public and private through the most accessible of means. It is a way of *being* in the city. It is street furniture because it is in the street but it is, unlike most street furniture, bottom up. Even these seemingly disposable chairs are taped up and adapted, kept in service after they should be gone. Because they are in the street, the less value they have, the better.

Chairs are, of course, not only used for sitting. They are used frequently (as so wonderfully documented by Richard Wentworth in his photographic series *Making Do and Getting By*) for propping open sash windows, for reserving parking spaces and as tables and ledges. They have tape draped over them to indicate space-in-between, and brooms balanced on them to save a spot in the road for a skip or a van.

Because they are so associated with the body and with sitting, chairs have come to act as a cipher for people and for presence. To plant a chair means that someone human has been here and will be here again. They populate a city without the presence of people. And, as such, they probably deserve more rights and better treatment than we give them.

Charging

As if cars didn't take up enough of the public realm already, an entire new layer of infrastructure and street furniture is currently being introduced to enable them to charge off the electricity grid. Umbilically wired in to the system, drivers have managed to monopolise a little more public space.

The widespread introduction of EV charging points while, of course, good for the environment, coincides with a moment of extreme inadequacy in their design and an apparent total lack of regulation or oversight. As was historically the case with so much street furniture, the early stages of the roll-out of a new typology are a trial and error experiment driven by the private sector and with a typical fragmentation of designs and approaches. At the moment the model seems to be a garishly coloured plastic post with some kind of coloured illumination to indicate whether it is charging or not. Rather than being conceived as public utilities, they seem to be individual exercises in branding and visibility. It is difficult to think of a more inadequately designed type of street furniture (with the possible exception of the UK's wildly hideous water bottle refilling stations). Rather than adding interest or pleasure to the public landscape, they introduce new hazards, clutter and visual incoherence. And why should pedestrians be made to suffer the consequences, having further space taken away from them? Some are already incorporated into lampposts where trailing cables make perfect trip hazards. Perhaps they could eventually be buried and installed in the roadway itself.

When cities reinvented themselves for new technologies, whether by introducing streetlighting, accommodating telephone boxes or electric grids, the effects were widely distributed and often created with amenities as a by-product. Even humble coal holes were treated as decorative medallions in the pavement, embellishing rather than diminishing the pedestrian path. Each new technology brings with it disruption and puzzlement as to how it might be absorbed into the landscape. Can there be some extra benefit for EV chargers? Can they bring to the public realm something else besides continuing justification for the dominance of the landscape by private vehicles? It doesn't look good so far, but perhaps if legislators demand some extra amenity it might become a possibility. What might that amenity be? Could we flash charge our phones perhaps? Might they be installed in public seating? Or could they be buried, manifesting themselves as exquisite objects flush with the pavement? I have no idea, but they have, surely, got to improve.

Classicising

Much of this book is, effectively, about a layer of the quotidian which remains largely unseen. It is, largely, about the municipal and the mundane, albeit occasionally picked up by photographers and brilliantly framed as a kind of urban sculpture. There is, however, another type, that is not quite spectacular but is certainly striking. And no-one did it better than Jože Plečnik. The Slovene architect redefined the centre of his hometown, Ljubljana, through public buildings, bridges and spaces but, arguably even more critically, through street furniture.

This is something very different from the standard, penny-pinching, picked-from-a-catalogue commodities which have defined most of the history of modern street furniture. What Plečnik did was to use street furniture as a way of asserting an identity for a small, then still provincial, capital to create an infrastructure of aesthetics which built on history, antiquity, invention and modernity. There is nothing quite like it.

The streets of Ljubljana are dotted with items of incredible invention, and once you have noticed a few, you will find more. There are Ionic columns reimagined as streetlamps with bulbs hanging like ripe fruit from their volutes. There are rustic park benches in stone and columns surmounted by globes or candle lights, and there are kiosks built like Roman temples nested within larger temples. Most striking of all is the triple bridge - a piece of infrastructure transformed into a public space with pedestrian paths forking away from the traffic in the centre and lamps like balusters. Everywhere you go in Ljubljana, from the parks and squares to the cemetery and the churchyards, you can't help but almost trip over a bollard, an obelisk, a shelter or a fountain in a form you've never seen before, inevitably designed by Plečnik.

The architect had worked in the atelier of Otto Wagner in Vienna, the birthplace of modernism, and then moved to Prague in 1911 - the city where Cubism was briefly (and weirdly) torn from the canvas and transplanted into the city, becoming a sculptural, expressionistic style which presaged Art Deco in its extravagant angularity. In Vienna he was an adherent of the Secessionist style, which attempted to apply fine design across every level of the city from hospitals to tableware; in Prague he worked on the Castle, making a series of brilliant interventions into the solid fabric - new entrances, stairs, elaborate courtyards, gardens and promenades - making it an urban space. When he came home to Ljulbljana in the early 1920s he was apparently shocked by its lack of columns. Putting this right, the result was a series of fantastical Ionic columns, on buildings, in promenades, market halls and as streetlights and monuments, as architecture and street furniture. Plečnik believed the Ionic column was the Etruscan order and that the Slovenes were the successors of the Etruscans. He went about creating a national language (spurious as it may have been) from almost nothing.

While working in Prague, Plečnik would have seen Emil Králíček's Cubist lamppost (1913) near Prague's Wenceslas Square, an eccentric hybrid of column, lantern and seat with a Brâncuși-like shaft and star-section lantern. It became a minor sensation, but stayed a one-off. Plečnik, whose budget for urban improvements was modest, scrimped on stone paving (often laying concrete or gravel surfaces instead) and saved the money instead for moments of dignity, creating street furniture as theatrical events in the cityscape and through them a coherent language of public space. This was no modernist effort at harmonisation and homogenisation of fittings, rather each was treated as a variation on a theme, each with its own sense of surreal delight and even absurdity. Neither were these new languages intended to become catalogue items, each were designed for a specific site.

These elements, then, came not only to define the streetscape but to contain it, so that public piazzas and pavements became interiors in their own right, as architectural spaces. You might also argue that, along with that invention and sense of playfulness in form, it was an attempt to create a national identity through the most quotidian elements - and this came with its own problematic dose of nationalism. Parallels with Rome and the Etruscans were made consciously, an attempt to graft a grandeur on to the history of a small nation that had always been on the fringe, washed over by the empires of Italy and the Austro-Hungarians. They were part of a project of deliberate separation from Austria-Hungary, a Slavification and a Slovenisation through streetlights. It worked. It remains brilliantly original and eye-catching. But it has never been copied.

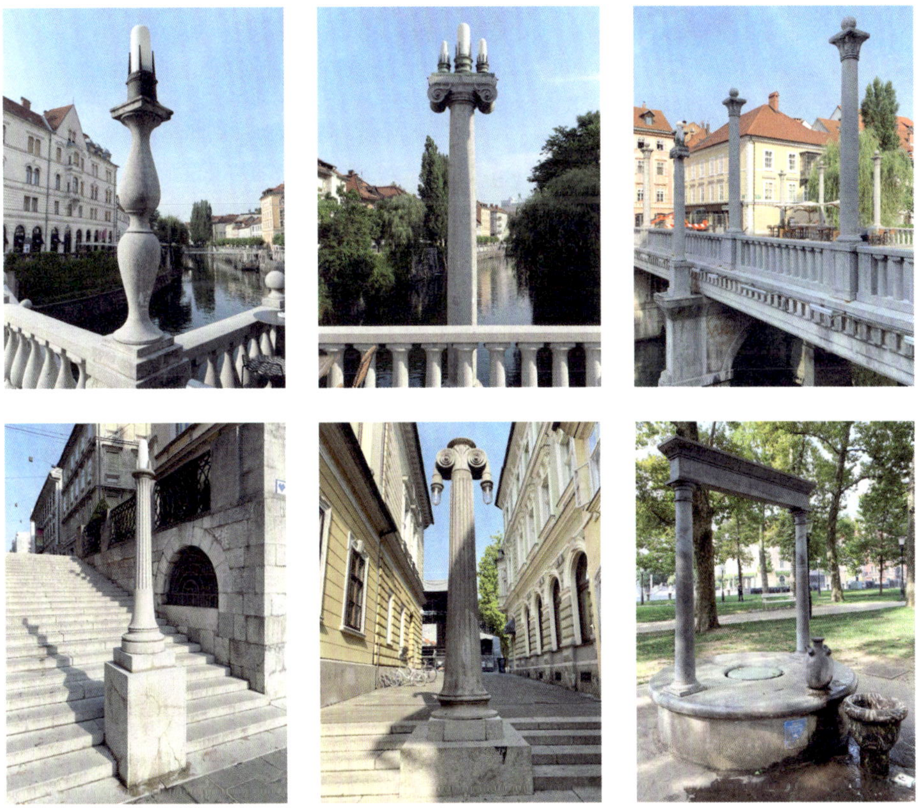

Ljubljana street furniture by Jože Plečnik

Clustering

Street furniture, it seems, can get lonely. To alleviate this tendency, items often seem to be clustered together. In this way, single objects suddenly acquire a kind of urban presence, the impression of a Morandi-like still-life, inanimate things accruing gravitas from proximity, from their composition - though, arguably, this is almost always a result of expediency rather than conscious design. The massing of these very different or, occasionally, very similar items can create little moments of city serendipity. It can look convivial or urbane, or it can look ridiculous.

I've been recording some of these clusters for a while now. Sometimes they create a kind of mini-metropolis with its own curious skyline. These congregations of readymades can resemble a landscape of toys assembled by a child - a toy soldier, perhaps, beside a much smaller scale Matchbox car. An accidental cluster might look like a kind of catalogue, a dispersed display of the available options for acceptable, heritage-inflected street stuff. It can look deliberate: the barrages of anti-truck defences currently popping up all over London and New York, perhaps, or the concrete bench/barrage/bollard combinations in front of a row of old phoneboxes by London's Law Courts. Occasionally the clusters can have a Dadaist quality to them (it is all in the juxtaposition), or they might embody a moment of slapstick or sly comedy, a magical merging of sign and symbol (a 'Men at Work' sign in front of a concerned-looking fountain). And sometimes these little ensembles are bathed in pathos: two bollards, victims of bad driving, leaning away from each other as if they couldn't bear to be together, or two lampposts, one old but yet to be decommissioned, humiliatingly forced to stand beside its usurper. More often they are just banal, an expression of the piecemeal accumulation of objects placed by people who don't really care and by bodies which don't communicate with each other because everything is fragmented and privatised, and the pavements are disregarded in a way that highways never would be.

The main road outside my old house, for instance, is becoming crowded with items for new uses, suffocating the actual pedestrian route (see p.52, right). The latest are a 5G pole, two signs announcing the beginning of a Low Emission Zone, and one clunky pole supporting a CCTV traffic camera - all against the background of a burgeoning and rapidly reproducing bank of steel communication cabinets. One forlorn postbox, the paint peeling from its curved top, is all that's left from an era when it was thought that perhaps street furniture might be given a little dignity. Ironically, in an age of ubiquitous marketing and branding, the only item which revels and excels in its identity is Victorian, from an age when the Post Office was a cipher for the state and the empire, rather than a privatised entity burdened by debt in a ruse to avoid paying tax on its profits.

These often odd, usually accidental and occasionally wonderful juxtapositions are a pleasing distraction. The grouping in itself becomes a game in which actions are seemingly uncoordinated and the map is used in abstract to place the things that will become the background to our lives. They are the result of a streetscape conceived as a utility rather than an amenity (if it is thought about at all). But that does not mean we should not enjoy their adjacencies.

Communicating

Early in April 2020, as the Covid-19 pandemic was sweeping across the UK and the first lockdown had, officially at least, confined people to their homes, there was a spate of fires as crowds started to gather and attempt to burn down 5G communication masts.

There was something almost pagan about it - a mad, superstitious rumour spread via social media platforms marinaded in conspiracy theories that 5G was somehow connected with the Coronavirus, leading to mobs turning up and torching communication equipment. It was something like a belief in witchcraft and its attendant burnings at the stake. Street furniture, normally seen as so benign, or at least inert, suddenly became the locus of mass hysteria.

The connection with Covid was non-existent but perhaps the rage at this particular, seemingly innocuous, target could be justified. 5G is the harbinger of that great marketing black hole, the *Internet of Things* and its dumb twin brother, the *Smart City*. All this tech might allow us to download a movie on to our phones in four seconds, but it also represents the final phase of what Shoshana Zuboff has catchily christened 'Surveillance Capitalism'. It will see the street, that public realm, fully incorporated into the horizon of blanket surveillance, the last vestiges of urban invisibility disappeared. Already there are lampposts which incorporate CCTV cameras and 5G network gear. They remind us, perhaps, that the arrival of streetlighting in the city had its moralising dimension in its illumination of the shadier corners in which denizens often enjoyed the anonymity and invisibility brought by darkness. Artificial lighting was often seen as an imposition, an expansion of the surveillance state and a kind of attempt at gentrification of the night, making streets safe for the respectable bourgeoise at the expense of the working classes and working women whose work benefitted from not being too visible.

London famously already has the most extensive network of CCTV cameras outside China. The implications of such 360-degree mass surveillance are critical in undermining any sense of individual freedom in the city, even if we take into account the radical shifts in digital monitoring we impose on ourselves through our mobile phones, credit cards and oysters. Somewhere between the terrorism of the IRA in the late 20th century and Islamicist extremists more recently, and in the idea that the answer to personal security in cities for women and oppressed groups is an infinitely expanding network of cameras, we have reached this state. Yet, astonishingly, there is almost no research to show that cameras deter violent crime. It is true that footage has been useful in tracking down terrorists after the event, but the tragedies themselves continue. At the time of writing, incidentally, the UK has something approaching six million CCTV cameras.

The aim is not only to survey but to influence behaviour through the knowledge that you are always on camera, the constant nagging nervousness that you are being watched. The incorporation of tech into streetlights and telephone poles makes street furniture complicit in this conspiracy; it subverts the seemingly dumb structures through making them digitally sentient and radically reshapes our relationship with this architecture of communication.

The explosive proliferation of communications technology has also necessitated a burgeoning and ill-considered landscape of boxes and cabinets, often clustered together as various network providers install their equipment on to pavements. Odd cityscapes of metal boxes begin to pop up, alternative miniature switchboard skylines of communication impinging on narrow pavements and already limited public space.

The rhetoric of connection is of an invisible, benevolent blanket wrapping us in connectivity so that we can consume at any moment through our phones. The reality is that not only are we the product, with our data being harvested by every network mast we pass, but that this network is reliant on a very tangible series of manifestations. We don't generally see the server farms and data centres, the latter are usually deliberately obfuscated in bland buildings. But we are increasingly aware (or if not necessarily always aware then increasingly hemmed in by) this burgeoning infrastructure of data. Yet while historic forms of street furniture, from coal plates to phone kiosks, were treated with a kind of reverence so that their forms would communicate their purpose and their presence as decorative, elegant objects, this new layer of communication manifestation is being kept deliberately obscure and dumbly blank. The opprobrium heaped on 5G by those pandemic protestors, that almost occult sense of something being amiss and of these objects harbouring technology that could be turned against us, has hardened this determination to keep these objects under cover, present but inconspicuous. The result is an emerging language of non-communication - dumb, blind boxes which are reluctant to reveal their purpose and chunky, clumsy steel poles which elevate their gear to increase the spread of the signal but also seem to be lifting their tech out of reach, fearful of repercussions.

There is an irony that the emerging architecture of communication should be so reluctant to communicate anything of itself, to develop a visual or symbolic language which might help us better understand and embrace it, or to provide some extra amenity. But it is perhaps precisely that reluctance to express anything at all through its form that communicates a generalised unease, an unsettling sense that this is something that the networks would like to pretend is somehow ethereal and virtual with no real-world effects. It is, in fact, a huge burden on data centres and a massive capture of information being built to enmesh us further in a culture of consumption, in which we are being unwittingly consumed, packaged, sold-on and surveilled in our every move, turn and swipe.

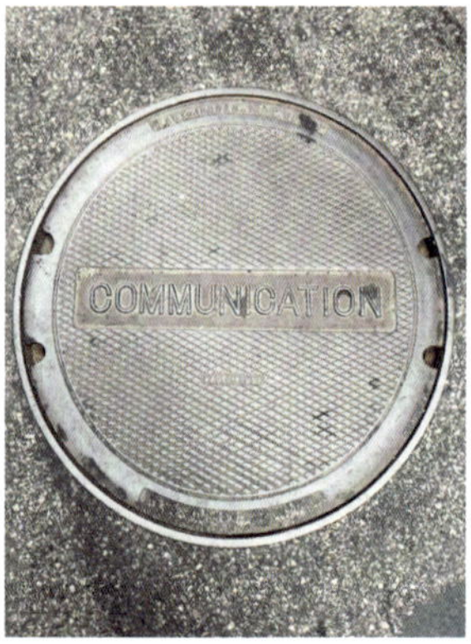

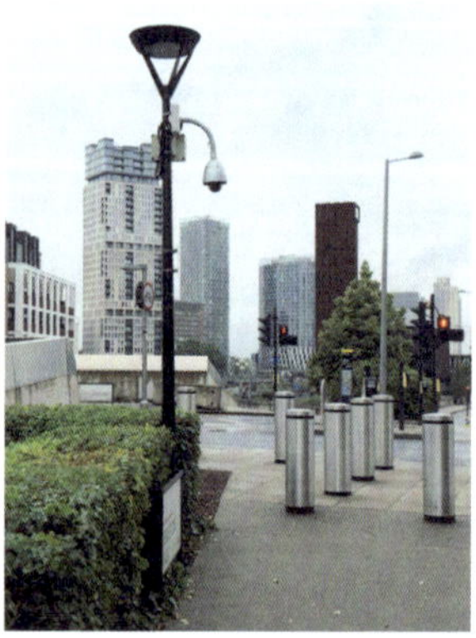
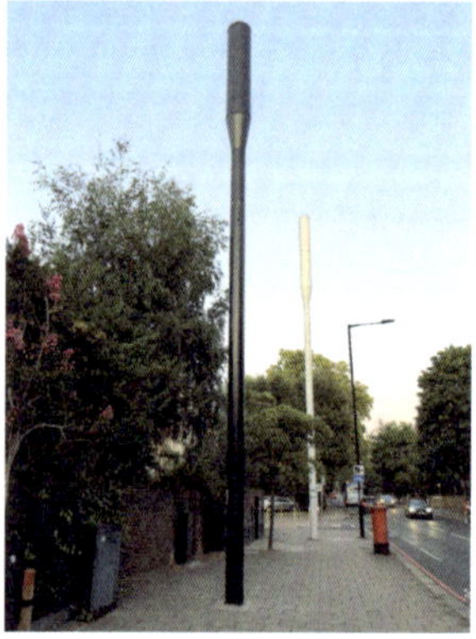

Left: *New York*; middle: *Stratford, London*; right: *Putney, London*

Commuting

A lot of street furniture is not only a thing in itself but an intimation of a world underground - the manhole covers, steam vents, water hydrants and coal holes - and even the streetlights suggest a subterranea of cables and viscera, gas and steam pipes and so on. But the most conspicuous underground conduits are the ones that carry people; the way they manifest themselves at street level is perhaps the chunkiest and most substantial category of street furniture. Metro systems are the most comprehensive of urban branding systems, and they say a lot about how the city sees itself. We read larger cities often as much through their subway maps as through our knowledge of their streets, relating real locations to their positions on the map and understanding where we are often in a more coherent way than our own inevitably piecemeal understanding of the city.

Nowhere could this be clearer than in the Art Nouveau excrescences of Paris Metro stops. When applied to architecture there was often something fake about Art Nouveau, a retrospective exercise in window dressing, an appliqué architecture. But here, applied to a new typology which was all about suggestion rather than substance, it proved perfect. Iron - mined from the earth, manufactured in an inferno, poured when white hot and molten, pliable and superheated - seemed suited to this new public underworld. Situated perfectly on the cusp of the fin-de-siècle and built mostly around 1900 (when the World Exposition was being held in the city), these alien-looking, cast-iron constructions formed a very visible gateway to another realm. They suggest a strange blend of the organic and the industrial, the commuters, the citizens and the technology of the trains, all tainted by the darkness of the underground.

Hector Guimard's designs evoked the Metro as an experience straight out of Jules Verne, a gateway to an adventure. The Metro entrances were perfect pieces of street furniture. They comprised the sign in its distinctive lettering (*Metropolitain*), the shelter (some with glass canopies), the descent (via the stairs) and in some instances a light, a red lava lamp glowing like something from the centre of the earth and hanging like a forbidden fruit from the twisted iron. They became so familiar that Art Nouveau, already a French construction, became known as *'Le Style Metro'*.

The rest of the world's cities settled for something more prosaic, with functional exits and entrances contained within a cage of iron leaving the signage to do the heavy lifting and the urban branding. New York's versions feature integral streetlights with glass globe lamps, unambitious, functional, a little industrial; they echo the raw, undressed engineering of the stations just below the street with their riveted columns and beams and basement barrel vaults. Like the stripped, industrial, riveted, elevated subway lines, this was a language of unadorned construction, never easily confused with anything more refined. Some of the earlier designs, all now disappeared, resembled a kind of kiosk architecture, almost like something from a park with domed roofs, greenhouse glass and that Parisian street furniture paint. There is a recreation of one at Astor Place, and the original can be seen in a 1937 photo by Berenice Abbot. Martin Lewis's depiction of these subway hoods in *Late Traveller* (1949), showing a woman descending the stairs, is a perfect illustration of their presence and their offer of another world below.

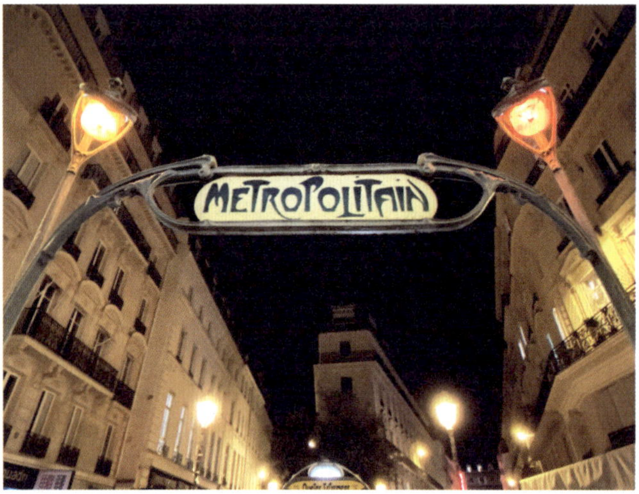

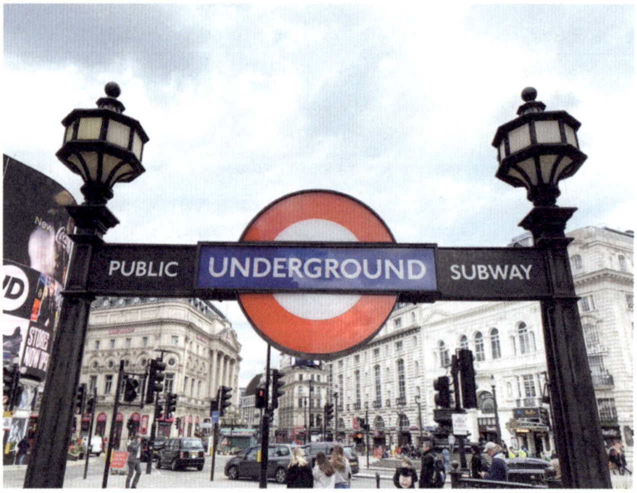

Above: *Paris Metro entrance*
Below: *London Underground entrance*

These kiosks were modelled on the system in Budapest, which boasted the world's second subway system after London (dating from 1896). Those originals have also disappeared, but they seem to have been remarkable. Vaulted, richly ornamented structures, they resembled something between a tomb, a reliquary and a toilet.

London's Underground entrances, the first in the world to this newly mined transport realm, were mostly integrated into the architecture of the city with ox-blood red entrances or unassuming portals, but in a few cases where they come up in the middle of the street, at Piccadilly Circus or Bank for instance, they manifest themselves as furniture, with pairs of elegant lanterns atop elaborate stems and the Underground roundel as a central element, the badge of identity. The hybridisation of lights and logos acts not only as a sign but, perhaps, to suggest that all is illuminated underground, nothing to be afraid of down there. The underground, as the Underground had proved, was the space of modernity. Just as services, the gas pipes and telegraph cables, electricity and even subterranean postal railways were running below the pavements, the arrival of trains, first steam and then electric, confirmed the urban subterranean as a layer of technology; the tube was just another kind of conduit.

London Underground's roundel was designed in 1908 (originally looking more like the Martini logo) and refined by Edward Johnston in 1919. One of the best and most recognisable pieces of urban corporate identity anywhere on the planet, it became a piece of street furniture in its own right. Its graphic modernity (in a city then dominated by historicising architecture) indicated the technological nature of the underground. The repetition of that branding below and above the surface linked what could have seemed a detached, dark space to the streets above. That it acted as a light, illuminating the way, was both brilliant branding and urban ingenuity, making it seem like a symmetrical reflection of the city - just as the blue band bisects the red circle, as above, so below; modern, light and familiar.

Concretising

The fetish for concrete hit street furniture hard. Sometime soon after the Second World War concrete developed a kind of aura, benefiting from an assumption among architects, designers and civil engineers that there was nothing it could not do. It was also around this time that highway engineers began to take on the responsibilities for planning the appearance of public space in most of the Anglo-Saxon cultures. Previously street furniture had been left to a diverse and dispersed non-system of municipal councils, parishes, businesses, utilities and institutions, but from the 1930s, and with the increasing perception of the future as one inevitably based around the car, power became concentrated (and congealed) in the hands of the highway engineers - and their priority was almost always vehicular rather than pedestrian traffic.

As they were planning and constructing their new networks of motorways, bridges, bypasses, underpasses and everything else in concrete, it seemed only logical that the fittings they specified to punctuate them should be formed in the same material. It started with streetlights and a truly strange array of concrete designs which somehow managed to be neither truly modern nor historical, neither elegant nor definitively ugly. Lamps hung like odd plums from question-mark-shaped uprights and 'swan-necked' pillars, and catalogues showed weird configurations of hydra-headed lamps, late Art-Deco inflected designs and even, bizarrely, some more reminiscent of Art Nouveau, a movement which had never taken off in the UK in the first place. Plan forms varied similarly from tapered hexagons and chamfered squares to slender footprints which flared out and then back in again like the handle of a table knife or an anorexic coffin.

Some looked a little like hokey sci-fi ray guns, others like fish bones. Occasionally, just occasionally, there appeared austere, elegant and attenuated designs that succeeded in bringing a touch of sleek modernity to suburbia. There was an interesting sympathy between the acres of pebble-dashed semis which had been built along the UK's burgeoning network of A-roads in the 1920s and '30s and the knobbly, gravelly sandy-grey posts of the new concrete streetlights. Gateposts, garages and driveways were all made of the same material. It made a kind of sense, a gradual carpeting of concrete. Architects and self-appointed arbiters of taste were aghast at their poor designs, but the concrete lampposts just kept coming. They were, it turned out, just the beginning. The knobbly beige aggregate-rich lampposts were supplemented later by entire ranges of street furniture of every description.

As Brutalism (after the French *béton brut*, 'raw concrete') began to take hold in architectural culture from the end of the 1950s, street furniture too became brutalised. What had been spindly designs in delicately cast iron, painted wooden slats or steel mesh were reconceptualised as miniature expressions of mass in the urban landscape, little shots of pedestrian Brutalism. Most common were the chunky bollards which appeared everywhere. Designs ranged from tapering, dome-topped cones, blunt-ended bullets, thick cylinders, fat phalluses, rounded lumps and chunky cigars to ribbed rods and massive balls. They acted as little punctuation marks of modernism speckling every corner of the country with a little self-contained dose of pre-cast avant-garde.

In shopping centres and pedestrianised precincts there were massive concrete dustbins, benches and planters with chunky aggregate stuck in cream-coloured cement. On bleak bypasses people stood shivering, standing on concrete paving stones under concrete bus shelters with even the bus-stop sign itself a mini-skyscraper of concrete, a lumpy central section designed to display the bus timetable. There were concrete tower blocks and streets in the sky, stairs, ramps and lamps - by the early 1970s people could easily find themselves entirely enveloped in concrete, a total environment, a *Gesamtkunstwerk* in which any sudden movement scraped the knuckles and rain stained every surface like urban tears. This was the city moulded by modernity, conceived in concrete.

But that structural wonder-material proved oddly unstable, a peanut brittle of cement and aggregate. Massive concrete bollards were counter-intuitively fragile, a little knock would make them crumble while rusting rebars acted like tumours cancerously consuming their insides. It became common to see bollards seemingly suspended mid-air on spindly, rusty steel innards. Rebars began appearing throughout the surfaces of concrete benches and concrete lampposts, X-raying themselves like fracture-clinic snapshots. Massive benches on a scale that suggested eternity began to crack and crumble, often after only a decade or so. Concrete's moment was surprisingly short, perhaps only the quarter century between 1950 and 1975. It was replaced in many cases by the oddest of things, the material it had not so long ago usurped - brick.

By the late 1970s (the fever dream of late modernism), the concrete fetish began to fade in favour of a softer Scandi-modernism, the organicism of Alvar Aalto. The dream was still of the moulded, total environment, but this was to be one tempered by a material more obviously of the earth, more clearly fired, containing fragments of landscape and green, less certain of its status as a harbinger of utopia and rather attempting a new contextuality. Low brick walls swept up to become seating, whole benches of brick were made in what was seen as a less alienating material. The Barbican's low brick table-shaped seats are a good example of how, even here in a concrete utopia, brick had begun to win territory back.

Concrete returned, however, in the wake of the terrorist bombings, first with the aftermath of Oklahoma City and then again in a bigger way after 9/11. But this time it was not in the dignified, sculptural sense of carefully tailored and meticulously designed objects that complemented the best Brutalist architecture, but rather in the form of ungainly chunks of pre-cast blocks craned into place in a hurry. Concrete found itself revived as protection from truck bombs and blast barriers, improvised blocks of dumb mass. Supposedly temporary, they have somehow never quite been replaced. Concrete, now understood not only as a wonder-material but as an environmentally damaging crisis for construction, is here to stay, and often in all of the worst kinds of ways.

Containing

On the 26 September 1864, a massive crowd gathered in Brussels to witness the flight of a photographer in a huge balloon which he had christened 'The Giant'. Gaspard-Félix Tournachon, otherwise known as Nadar, pioneered aerial photography from the covered wickerwork gondola of his great inflatable in which he had a fully equipped laboratory for developing, as well as a café and, rather unexpectedly, a billiards table. He had launched his balloon, then the biggest in the world, the year before in Paris, inspiring his friend Jules Verne to write *From the Earth to the Moon*. In Paris, the balloon's launch had attracted a crowd estimated at half a million (a third of the population of the city) and, fearing a repeat of these scenes, the mayor of Brussels, Jules Anspach, ordered a ring of barriers to be set up around in the botanical gardens around the launch site.

Anspach had transformed Brussels, rebuilding the city as a major capital, and has been compared in his influence to Baron Haussmann in Paris. Yet the name given to those barriers by posterity was not Anspach's but Nadar's. In Belgium and in Holland, crowd control barriers are, apparently, still often referred to as Nadar gates. The supreme irony is that the barriers made for this first known large-scale deployment of the type are named after an eccentric bohemian aviator, caricaturist, novelist and radical photographer, rather than an order-loving technocrat. During the Commune of 1870, in fact, Nadar used his balloons to relay messages and letters from the barricades - in the process also inventing airmail.

There does not seem to be much to indicate the precise design of those barriers, but if you look at a photograph from the time (the photographer of the photographer, ironically, remains anonymous), there appears to be a mix of saw-horse type barriers (the type used by the NYPD and which have only just been retired) and X-braced, almost Roman-looking timber gates. The saw-horses make sense. Even in New York similar barriers are still occasionally brought out, painted blue and used for community events, for sedate street markets and festivals. New York now has, like most of the rest of the world, the galvanised steel modular products which they refer to as 'French Barriers', which sounds like a kind of contraceptive.

The slightly obscure origins point to the ephemerality of barriers, things with little historic value ascribed to them. Though if I wanted to make the slightly strange case for the intimate, perhaps even inseparable, relationship between street furniture and photography which I hint at throughout this book, it might be hard to find a more concrete example than this bizarre link.

This simple piece of street furniture, if that is what it is, has become universal and ubiquitous. Much of the range of street furniture, from bollards and streetlighting to CCTV cameras, is about control, but few other items are as intimately tied in to policing the city as these banal barriers. Before protests and celebrations alike, before big sporting events and demonstrations, the arrival of the barriers stacked and nested on a flat-bed truck is a harbinger of police presence - the barriers are the vanguard. They are there to delineate access, to confine and compress and to control the crowds. That they might be reminiscent of prison bars is not, perhaps, entirely accidental. The barriers create a cage for the crowd. The old American versions, surely based on the then ubiquitous carpenters' saw-horses (timber then being the cheapest and most available material in the US), were daubed in stencilled lettering 'Police Line Do Not Cross'.

If one definition of street furniture is that it creates some amenity to the public, then barriers are the opposite, limiting public space and access, temporarily creating police property, fences for creating new offences.

They are joined in their presence by that similarly ubiquitous and sad sight of yellow police tape. The fluttering ribbons remaining after a crime scene investigation are surely as mournful a trace of litter as there is in the city. Police tape has a history stretching back only to the 1960s, where it originated in the US, but it has become an enduring icon of contemporary life in a way few other such media have. Now draped all over houses and student halls at Halloween and a staple of TV shows and the movies, crime scene tape is a remarkably efficient way of marking a territory with minimal means. Before it there were cops, using their bodies to block the way. Now there is tape, crime scenes and police lines can be stretched to vastly greater areas, colonising huge chunks of a neighbourhood and excluding neighbours. An almost omnipresent barrier in the movies and in crime shows, it effectively expresses the limits and impermanence of freedom in what otherwise appears to be public space, highlighting the fragility of the access we are allowed.

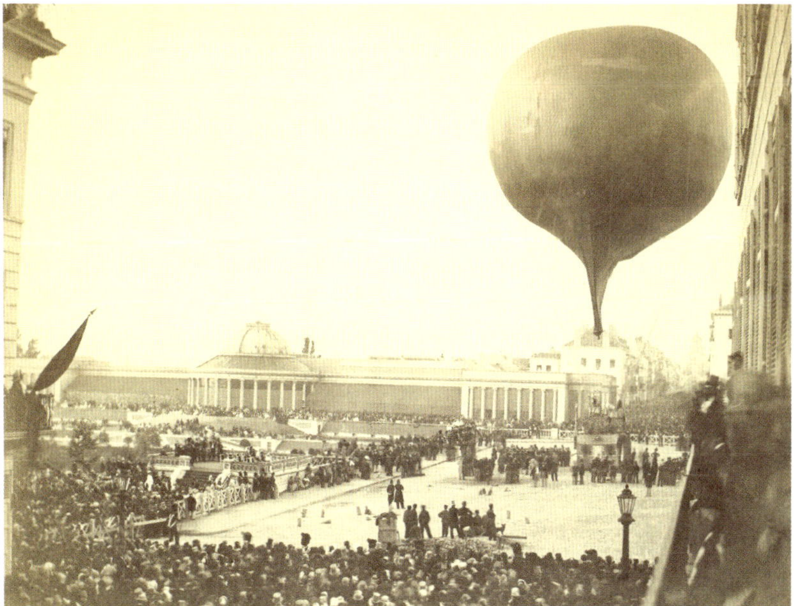

Third ascension of 'The Giant' in Brussels,
26 September 1864
Ghémar Frères

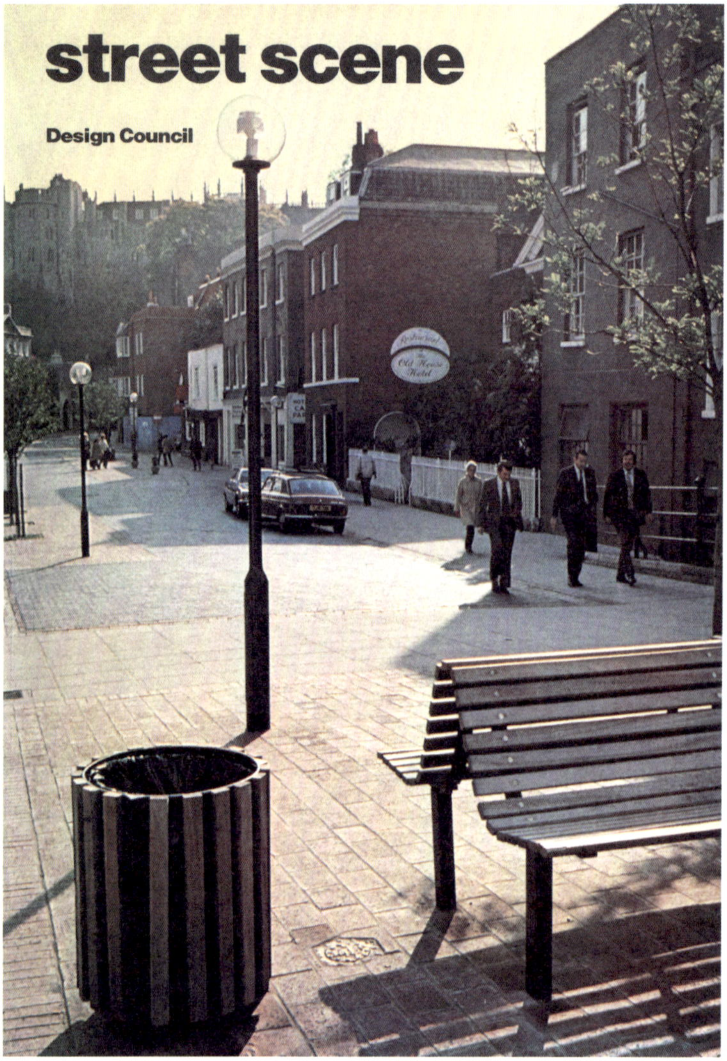

Cover of Street Scene*, published by the Design Council*, 1976
Photographer unknown

Co-ordinating

My slightly faded 1976 edition of *Street Scene* (it still reeks of cigarette smoke) is evidence of an era when street furniture was being conceived as a suite of objects. It was the era of late modernism in which heritage had been recognised but the impetus was still with a state-sanctioned, benevolent modernist notion of taste. And that taste was for a range of products which could be specified by architects, highway engineers and landscape designers to create a harmonious urban environment in which the street furniture would play a part in visually tying together a fast-changing cityscape. The pedestrianisation of town centres was being rolled out across the UK, new estates were being built - both council and private - and new municipal architecture with generous public spaces and amenities was still being designed by councils and government bodies. This was the era before the Thatcher revolution, which assumed only the private sector could be trusted with construction.

The cover of my brochure depicts a pedestrianised street with a pair of back-to-back slatted benches and a slatted litter bin in the foreground. A row of simple, glass-globe-topped streetlamps recedes into the distance - a little provincial and anonymous, but very simple and very modern. It is an ensemble, in its materials (black-painted metal and timber) and its aesthetics (stripped-down, unfussy municipal modernism). Inside, a drawing (p.62) illustrates in eight frames what had happened to the British townscape, from a scene of two men chatting on a bench in a bucolic landscape to a crowded nightmare of visual clutter and ill thought-out street furniture in which the buildings have been blotted out by fittings and any semblance of public space destroyed by the sheer amount of stuff. It is a drawing very much in the vein of Gordon Cullen's illustrations for the 'Outrage' issue of *Architectural Review*. Interestingly, though, it doesn't feature any cars which were, arguably, the real cause of change in the townscape, the de facto privatisation of huge swathes of public space. The text alongside advocates for specification from a single, well-designed range: 'A properly co-ordinated system of street furniture is immeasurably more flexible than a haphazardly chosen array of individual products.'

There is much in *Street Scene* about eliminating unnecessary posts - how, for instance, to suspend a traffic sign from a streetlight to save space and more on why, for some reason, streetlamps with angled heads are inferior to glass globes. There is an illustration of a small public space with the right kind of clustering of things (p.63): benches, vitrines, phoneboxes and trees. 'A complex and pleasant group of items of furniture', the caption reads, 'in an open space creates interest and provides a focus of attention.'

Seating is well considered everywhere, and bus stops too seem to have been given much thought. This is, in its way, the last phase of the paternalist era in which the Design Council knew better and advocated for its version of a gentle and practical modernism, still inspired by the ideas of the movement's early forebears - the industrialised, mass-produced, minimal designs which would inevitably lead to a more harmonious environment and a coherent public realm. Traffic engineering meets social engineering.

In fact, until around this time the public realm in Britain had been an accumulated landscape of ad hoc additions with new technologies arriving and being added before a formal language

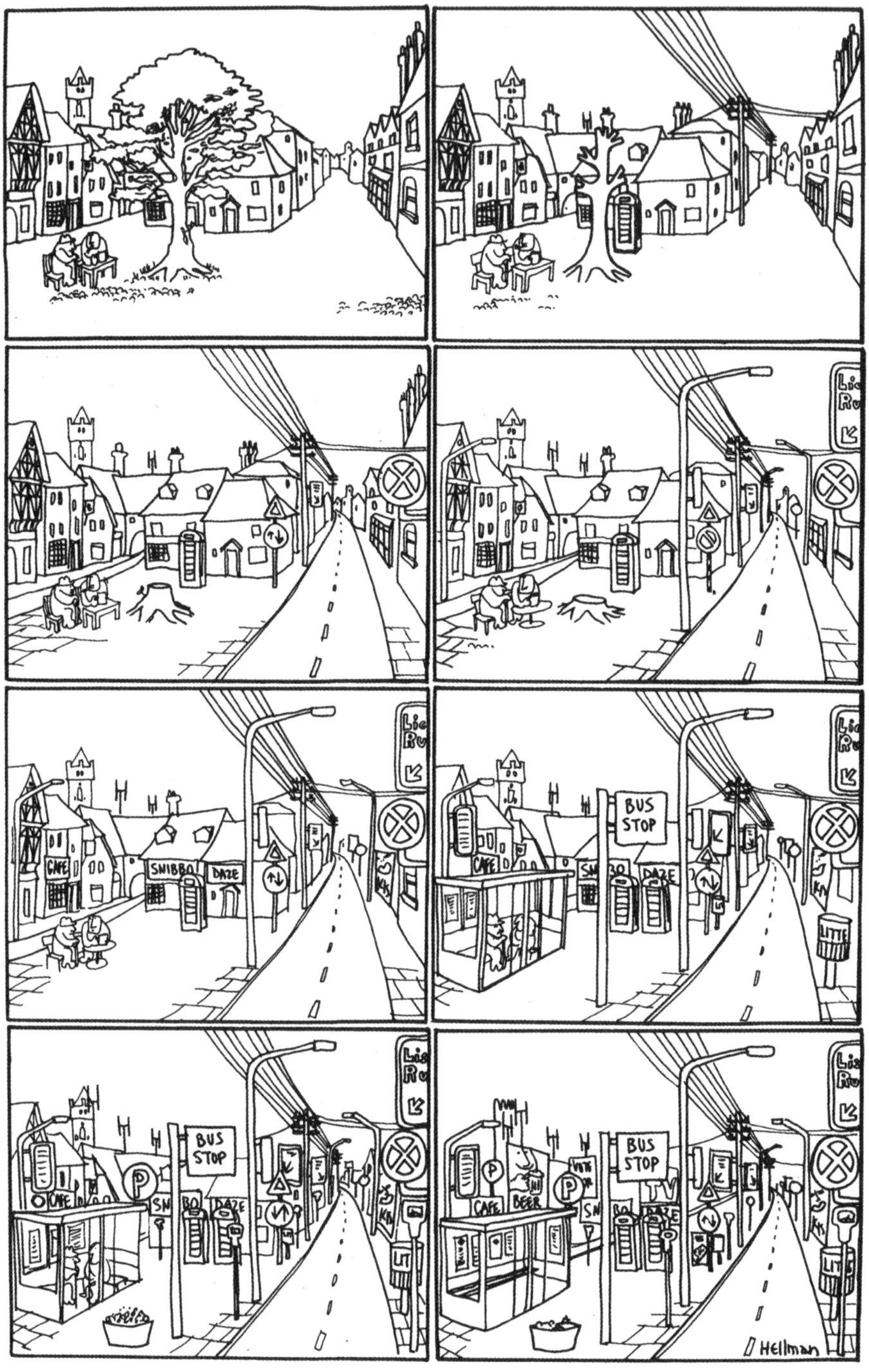

Page 10 of Street Scene, 1976
Illustration by Louis Hellman

had necessarily been finalised. That 'incoherence' of the historic streetscape now clearly bothered architects and planners. It was an era when planning as a profession became obsessed with a notion of design being 'in keeping' with its surroundings, conservation areas burgeoned, and new buildings and fitting might be expected to 'enhance' the nature of an area. The modern fittings, however, discriminated between an architectural environment and one of the street, in which the former was expected to be mixed and the latter co-ordinated, the former historic, the latter modernist. It didn't last. By the early 1980s, history was back and the catalogues were again dominated by reproduction items (faux gas lamps and Victorian-type benches).

Incredibly, despite being published well into my own lifetime, I'd suggest that virtually nothing from this prolific era in which a blanket uniformity was attempted across the landscape of street furniture, actually still survives today. Lights have been replaced as technology developed, benches have rotted away or been replaced by more prestigious or 'authentic' historic types to appeal to residents' sense of identity, bins are long gone and replaced by chunky plastic versions, and bus stops have gone through innumerable manifestations since those rather elegant versions. The public landscape today is fragmented and incoherent, except on the private estates and privately owned public spaces where it has become a part of the developer's branding and is understood as enhancing financial and rental value. Everything changes so that everything can remain the same.

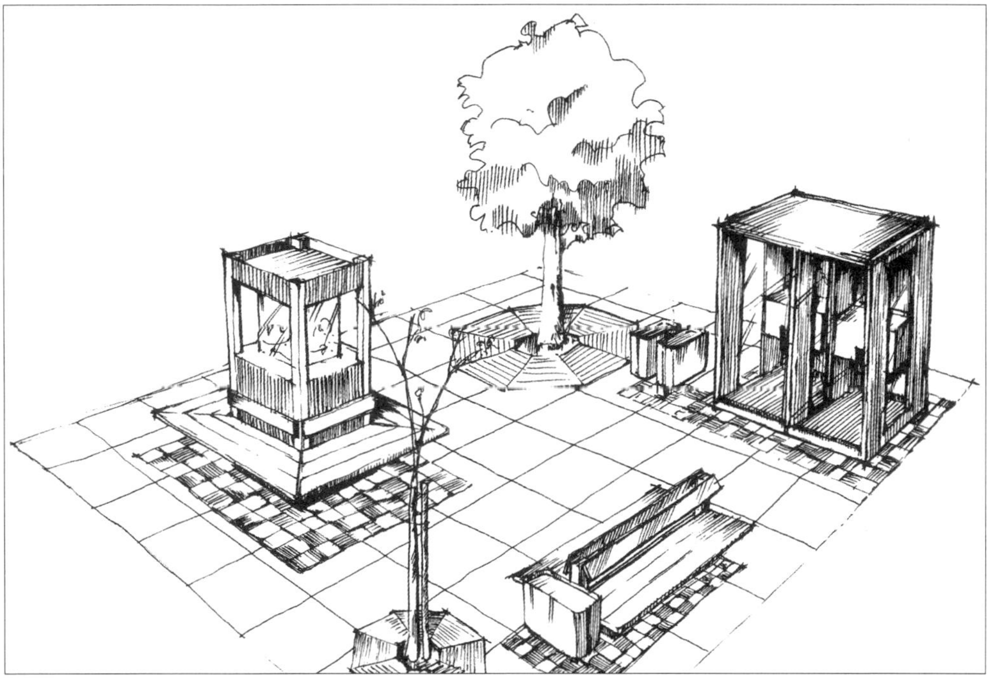

Page 17 of Street Scene, 1976
Artist unknown

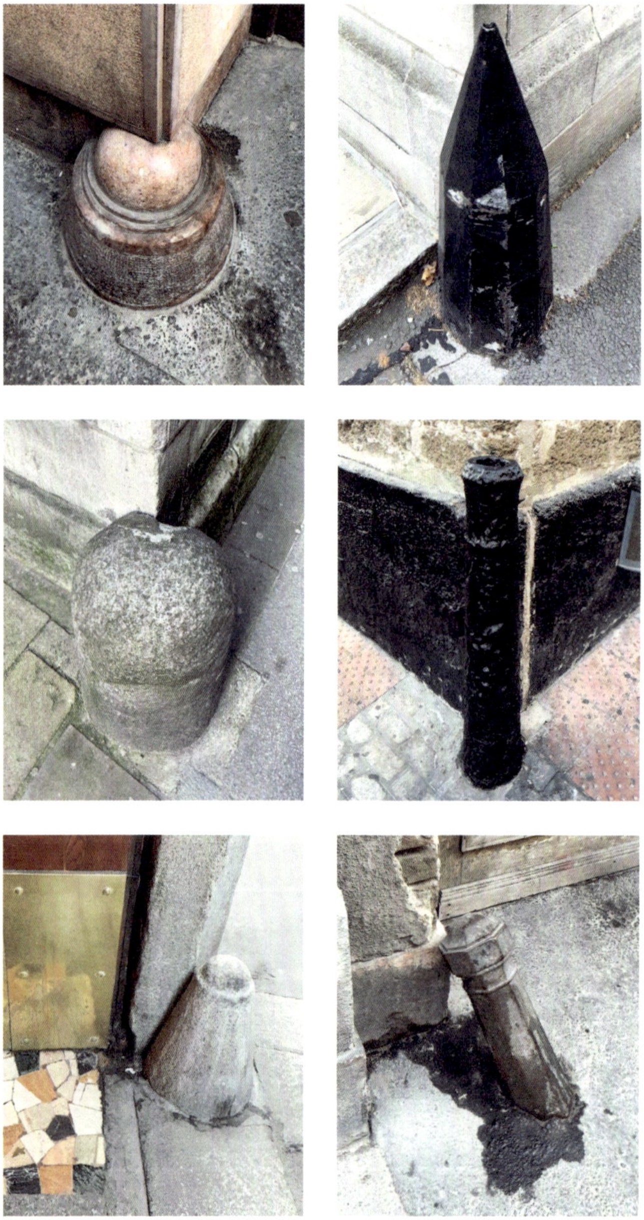

Continental corners

Cornering

They are there to protect the corners of private buildings but they are placed in the public realm. Corner protectors, spur stones or guard-stones are among the oldest and most enduring pieces of street furniture. Effectively shin-pads for architecture, they were designed to protect stone, brick and plaster corners from cart-wheels and carriages. They can be beautiful things, situated somewhere between architecture, ornament, street furniture and utility.

In Italy most are carved from stone, usually simple and lumpy - a portion of a sphere, a bollard, a bracket - but occasionally more ornate, carved into curious forms, often worn away by weather and friction. They may, in some cases, be *spoglia*, the remains of former stone architectures (often Roman) appropriated to protect the newer structures which have succeeded them. They may even, like bollards, be reused cannon, pressed deep into the ground.

London, with its less dense fabric, fewer stone structures and courtyards necessitating carriages manoeuvring through tight entrances, has fewer corner protectors, though there are still examples scattered through the city. In Paris they tend to be made of cast iron. Resembling London's boot scrapers a little, they are often extremely elaborate, with lions' heads or Rococo forms, occasionally resembling cannonballs or bollards bent over into quarter circles by some Herculean blacksmith.

In Ireland they are blessed with the wonderfully evocative name of 'jostle stones', which suggests they act to soak up the busyness of the street, as architecture's shock absorbers.

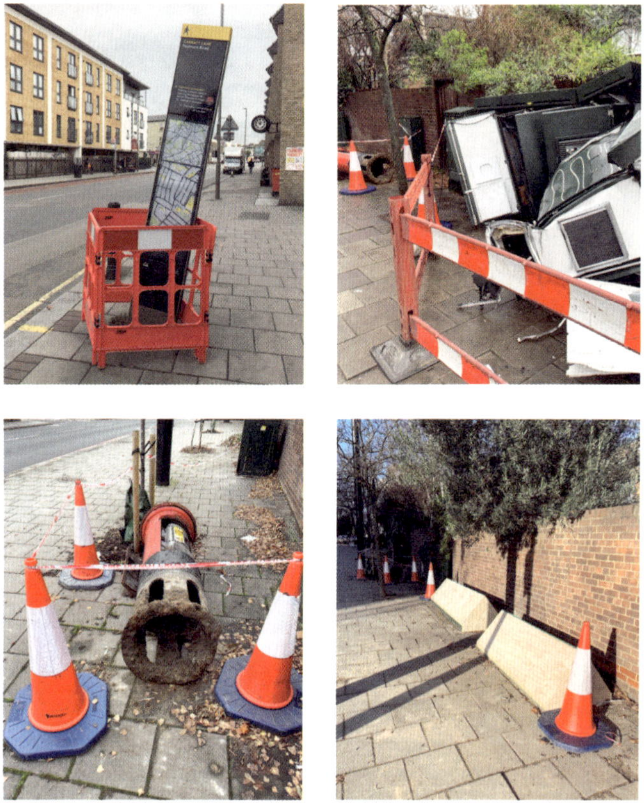

Crash scene victims, London

Crashing

If we think of items of street furniture as figures inhabiting the landscape, in their verticality and presence much like us, then we must also consider their mortality. To look at a photo of a city from a century ago is to see a very different scene: long-lost technologies like trams, telegraphs and telephones, the plethora of facilities from drinking fountains and horse troughs to public toilets which have long since been abandoned, dried up or sold off. We barely even notice their slow deaths or even their removal once they become defunct. And yet their cumulative disappearance has undoubtedly led to an impoverishment of the street and the public realm. Those ornate streetlights which illuminated every downtown in the US, for instance, eventually went because they caused problems for parking cars, scratching and denting their bodywork.

Alongside this cumulative disappearance, however, is a more dramatic strain of damage - the brutal collisions of fast-moving cars and fixed fittings, resulting in crumpled steel barriers and leaning lampposts, fallen trees and the paving stones they take with them as root systems pull up into the air. The brutality of these events was recently brought to my attention when something crashed into the expanding ensemble of poles and communication boxes at the end of my London street. Something had clearly got out of control and ploughed into the boxes, taking with it an old cast-iron postbox. The scene was a kind of carnage, the impact of the collision inscribed in the twisted metal, the viscera of the cables hanging out like guts and veins. The orange of the hastily erected barriers and emergency tape made it look somehow worse, yet more of a crisis, like the aftermath of a fatal accident (which I hope this was not).

Worst of all, though, was the postbox. Postboxes have a very particular manifestation and little thought is probably given to the way in which they meet the earth. Here, the postbox was lying on its side, placed a little way from the spot to which it had presumably been rooted for over a century. Its muddy base was now exposed, a solid root which flared out into a hoop of earth-encrusted iron perhaps a third as tall as the red-painted postbox itself. The curved door of the pillarbox had been pulled from its hinges by the impact and was lying beneath it like a broken limb. I have no idea what happened to the driver of whatever caused this catastrophic mess, but the postbox appeared to have been killed. The hole where it once stood was filled in with tarmac, the iron pillarbox itself removed. What was left of the comms boxes and their mess of wiring was also removed, and the holes covered by a pair of enigmatic structures. Appearing in the form of a pair of beautifully made pyramidal plywood coffins, they looked like some primitive *tumuli*, ancient coffins for a contemporary communications technology. Flanked by a pair of traffic cones, as if to suggest that cars had something to do with this, this formalised intimation of the presence of traffic looked like a classical arrangement.

There was something apt in the very handmade, archetypal funereal forms tailored for these remains of digital technology, a clash as aesthetically and formally striking as the impact itself. All these technologies - post, cables, power, fibre-optic - had gone in a single moment of lost control. Yet not much changed. I now walk to a postbox sightly further away, but how often do I post anything? The broadband is seemingly no different. I think my landline still works, but then I never use it. What, exactly, did all those cables do anyway?

Deterring

Much of the landscape of objects on our streets is to do with the delineation of territory and the protection of property - bollards, chains, steel barriers, cameras, corner protectors and so on. In recent years, though, there has been a hyperinflation of the products of deterrence and surveillance which has, arguably, transformed the physical streetscape in a more profound way than any single layer of street furniture ever has before. An entire new language of defensive designs has emerged: huge lumps of steel and concrete, chunky bollards and planters designed to defend against truck bombs and weaponised cars, CCTV cameras, barriers, spikes and bars. The improvised nature of these objects, their incongruity and alienness, might suggest that a new class of objects has had to be created, one without precedent or historic form. It all seems oddly ad hoc, retro-fitted, ill-fitting and brutally ugly.

The irony inherent in the changes wrought to defend against these new threats is that defensive architecture is the oldest architecture of all, with city walls, gates, spikes, moats, the portcullis and ditches. There is little that is novel in the challenges our cities face, except perhaps the technologies. Bridges were defended, their entrances guarded by sentries and constricted by toll booths. Public buildings and palaces were also made robust enough to resist attack, their defence embodied in the thickness of their walls. During the world wars whole new layers of defence were added, from pill-boxes for machine gunners to bunkers and air-raid shelters. Each era is forced to address the inadequacies of its defences but ours, perhaps grown accustomed to peaceful conditions and the idea of an open city, appears to be doing it badly.

The language of contemporary street furniture can sound like an architecture of paranoia: 'hostile vehicle mitigation solutions', 'counter-terrorism barriers'. The threat is real, but does its visual expression exacerbate the situation? There are many examples of integrating defensive measures with more civic typologies, such as concrete planters that double up as barriers, deceptively solid benches, bike stands that act as bollards, bollards which emerge from underground and so on. But in opening cities to traffic we have opened them to car bombs and to the weaponisation of vehicles as battering rams and people killers. Perhaps only now are we seeing the madness of having allowed vehicles to entirely dominate our streets.

The nature of threat has changed. So also has the tolerance for particular behaviours. Benches were once hospitable to the homeless or the lost, the penniless, the paralytic. Modern benches use a barrage of techniques to preclude their use for lying down, from armrests dividing the seats to various configurations making them more like chairs than benches. Comfortable-looking ledges in the centres of cities have been covered in 'anti-homeless spikes', a strange studded look which recalls a punk biker jacket worn by a paragon of corporate culture. Metal studs punctuate the edges of stone benches and ledges to stop skaters grinding along them. All these devices effectively undermine the publicness of the public realm.

There are occasional upsides. Fear of truck bombs has led to the pedestrianisation of many spaces, and a few scattered ugly objects might occasionally be a price worth paying. But public space belongs to everybody and everybody should be made comfortable and welcome. Otherwise, it is not public any more.

Disappearing

As a small child, I used to go with my mother to a greengrocer on the High Street. I'd often wait outside as the shop was tiny and next door was a coffee roaster's. Through the vent in the window flowed a fog of the most incredible aroma, a steaming cloud of pure coffee which I'm convinced is responsible for my addiction to espresso. Smell leaves intense memories. But only a couple of feet away the smell would shift to the sour, acrid scent of urine, disinfectant and toilet cake. In the middle of the road was a gent's lavatory, underground, surrounded by iron railings and topped with an illuminated sign. Beside that was a tall, elegant streetlamp of, I think, a Victorian variety and the whole little traffic island was surrounded by a set of heavy iron bollards. On the pavement was a news kiosk, a slightly ramshackle structure crowded with titles, fags and mags, two evening papers and boards behind mesh with roughly written headlines about ropey exclusives. A bare bulb illuminated the inside so that it looked, to me as a small child, a little like a puppet show, a Punch and Judy booth.

Everything in that ensemble is gone now. Some of it may never have even been there, except in my head. Street furniture, like memory, is fragile. Structures which seem embedded in the city, like the subterranean toilets and the massive iron bollards, can disappear overnight - filled in, taken out, replaced, disappeared. The architecture of the historic city is increasingly protected, the structure of the streets becoming a heritage theme park, but the parts we actually engage with, the shopfronts, the streetlights, the phoneboxes and toilets still seem inordinately vulnerable. Even in conservation areas they are conceived as utilities, somehow separate from the broader field of architecture which is so protected. Nothing lasts forever and this is not a plea to keep everything as it was. Rather it is an observation that everything changes but these layers live on, in the mind if not the street, piling on top of each other.

Rudolf Steiner thought that mankind's memory was inherently spatial and geographic, that in order to truly remember things we would have to return to where those memories were made. Perhaps, he suggested, our ancient landscapes were studded with sticks as markers of events and places where food or resources were once found. We tend to think of a memory palace as an interior architecture, a house with rooms representing facts or rhetorical flourishes. But could it be, instead, a landscape? A streetscape even, in which these markers appear as street furniture, as lamps and lavatories, smells and shop displays and signs, steps and stalls and kiosks? And what then happens when these markers disappear? Do our memories go with them, or do they just distort, fading into hazier recollections around half-remembered frameworks of things which might, or might not have been there?

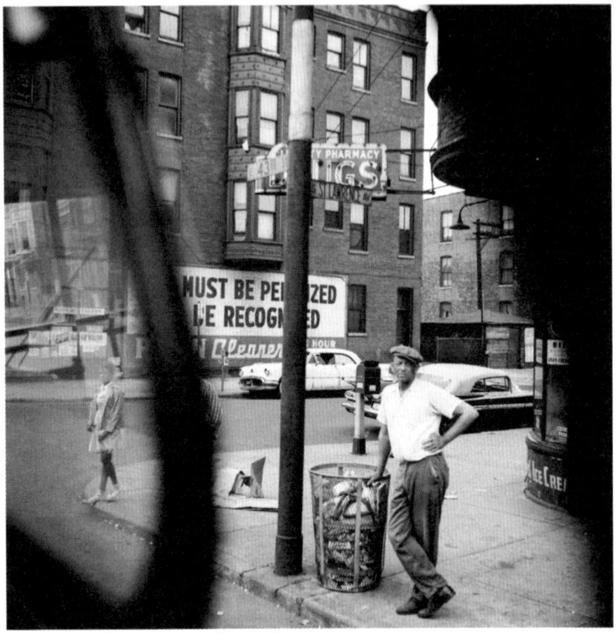

Chicago, IL, June 19, 1961
Vivian Maier

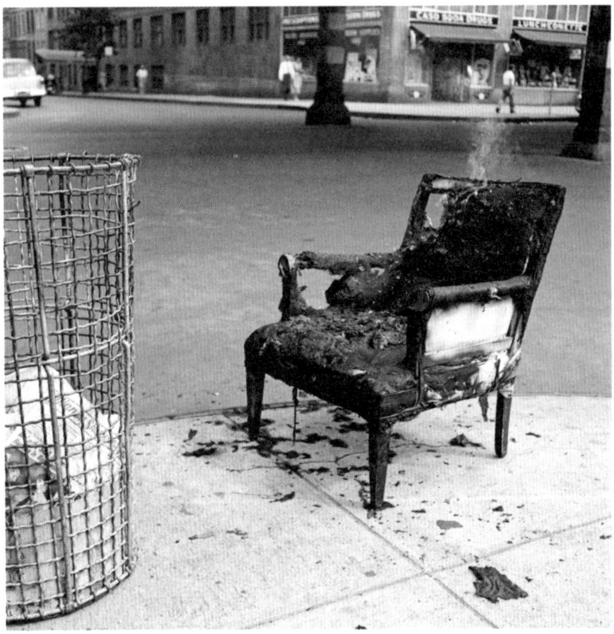

New York, NY, July 23, 1954
Vivian Maier

Discarding

There's an inevitability to litter bins in street photography. They are just there. But in Vivian Maier's photos they seem to take on an accidental starring role. It is a strange thing that these ubiquitous, normally almost invisible receptacles should take centre stage in the urban theatre she records, yet there they always seem to be.

A shot taken from a passing bus captures a pose so perfect it is almost classical. A man in a flat cap stands hand on hip, the other hand resting on a trash can. It is a blend of the Apollo Belvedere and the Resting Satyr. But with a bin. Dead centre of the shot is not the dustbin but the street sign, which perfectly bisects the shot. The bin is a prop and yet, despite its lightweight mesh construction, it anchors everything, earthing the figure to the ground like the tree stump in classical compositions which served to shore up figures' legs and support the weight of the sculpture.

Or you might look at Maier's photo of the dialogue between a bin and a burnt-out chair. Still smouldering, the blackened seat looks like it might have accommodated a victim of spontaneous combustion, wisps of smoke rising like a ghostly emanation. The bin, however, is just a bin. It gives the scene a kind of absurdity, these two pieces of furniture in conversation on the street. Or take a look at the photo of a man, a father, I suppose, taking something off the sole of his son's shoe (it must, surely, be his son). He is perfectly centred but the composition is made by the hydrant, the garbage can and a traffic light pole, which seems to be supporting his head as if he was impaled. The bin is passive, empty, a mesh containing nothing, but its presence completes the holy trinity of New York street furniture.

We might then move to Chicago, and to perhaps one of the most arresting and now familiar images Maier made. The visual interest here is in the three figures in vivid lemon yellow, the perfect trio, but again it is the bin, perfectly framed by the two gents in matching yellow shorts and socks, which draws the eye into the centre. It is a strange scene; all the figures look to our left, making us wonder what, exactly, is happening there. It seems paintings are being sold on the pavement, as there's more art on the other side of the road. But despite everything that's going on here - the skyscrapers in the background, the skybridge spanning the street behind, the long, old-school American cars and the statue cropped at the neck - the bin is still the unmoving centre. You might suggest a metaphor for the fleeting nature of urban life, the transience of the image, the decisive moment and its passing into history.

The bin is nothing and it is everything. Rubbish is an archive, the traces of the preoccupations of the city, its food, its wrapping, its news, its remains. It is what is left of the city's contents and consumption after a long day. Watching a homeless figure rooting through the rubbish always makes me wince, not because of the hygiene but because it stands for a kind of desperation and a terrible failure. Can we not, even in our fantastically rich societies, provide for the poor? But you might also look at it as a kind of urban harvesting, a form of research. Perhaps these lonely figures are engaging with the essence of the city right there, in the bin.

Maier was herself apparently deeply attracted to the contents of dustbins. Not rooting around in them but in recording their contents, particularly when they featured some kind of toy. Maier was employed as a nanny in New York and took her camera everywhere. The children in her care all relate stories of having to hang around while she took a photo of some apparently obscure subject. Dolls, clowns or teddies in the bin unsettle. They exude a sense of the uncanny, the intimate in the public, the throwing away of childhood. They work too easily as metaphors. Surely Maier's day job, the position of a nanny who was intimately involved in the upbringing of children one day and possibly dismissed and homeless the next, had some bearing on these images. They express the fickleness and the impermanence not just of childhood but of the condition of life itself.

Things out of context in a bin have passed, already, from one world into the next, from the world of the working everyday to the taboo realm of rubbish. They create their own speculations and short stories: the new bouquet of flowers stuffed in the bin? The broken umbrella, the half-full bottle perched on top, a book? What is the story behind these things? The bin is a portal, a transitional space, a black hole which disrupts the normal patterns. These photos show that a bin creates its own gravity, a strange attractor.

Unlike most street furniture the bin is unstable, changeable. Its function is to contain detritus for just a few hours; it needs to be emptied, occasionally moved. The wire waste baskets of New York as photographed by Maier were an intriguingly domestic solution; lightweight, see-through, robust, easy to move, the office-desk out-trays of the city. With time most city bins became increasingly heavy, bulkier and more fixed. They became smooth-sided in an attempt to deter rats, rodents and racoons.

Then came the terror. In London, with the regular appearance of IRA bombs, flimsy transparent plastic bags began to replace solid bins, see-through things in case there was a device, flapping condoms of civic insecurity. Before that, certainly in my childhood, there had been a fashion for bin burning. Setting fire to the contents inside the metal container so that the hard plastic cover would melt. It created surreal moments, Dalí-esque blobs of plastic spilling out over the pavement like lava. The heat of the city. It was bad. But also good, an irresistible metaphor for something or other.

There was a time, late modernism you might call it, probably the 1960s and '70s, when bins were taken seriously, solid pieces of hardware conceived as part of an urban infrastructure. That era is gone. There was an incredible array of bins from aggregate-studded concrete barrels to one particular type with splayed vertical timber slats and sitting on a metal tube leg bolted to the ground - which I remember particularly vividly as one of the ubiquitous objects of the 1970s and yet which has entirely disappeared. Rarely now will you find an enigmatic trash can or a bin with charm or charisma. But they're still there, in the background, doing their job. It is just that, perhaps, we have very few Vivian Maiers capable of transforming them into art.

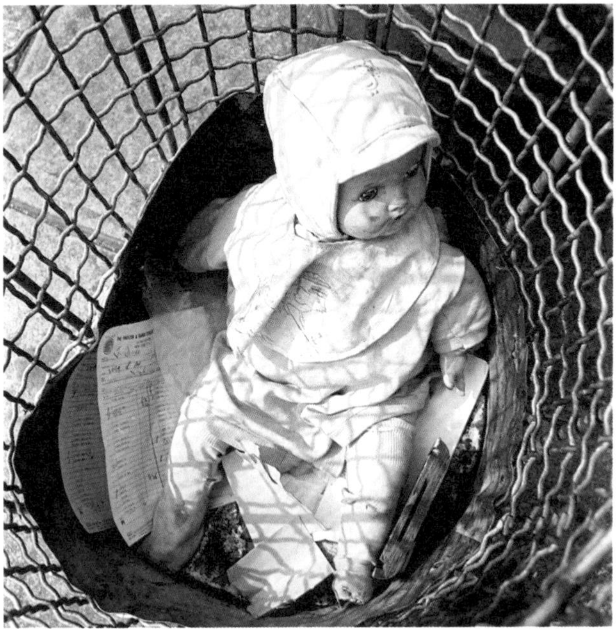

New York, NY, June 1953
Vivian Maier

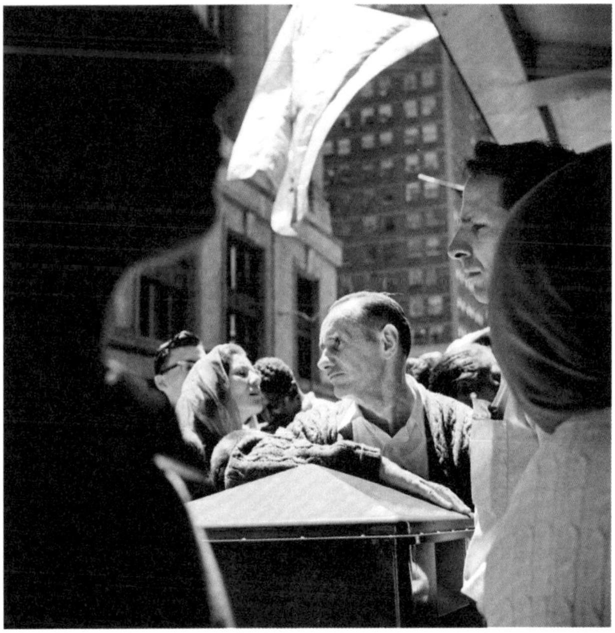

Chicago, IL, no date
Vivian Maier

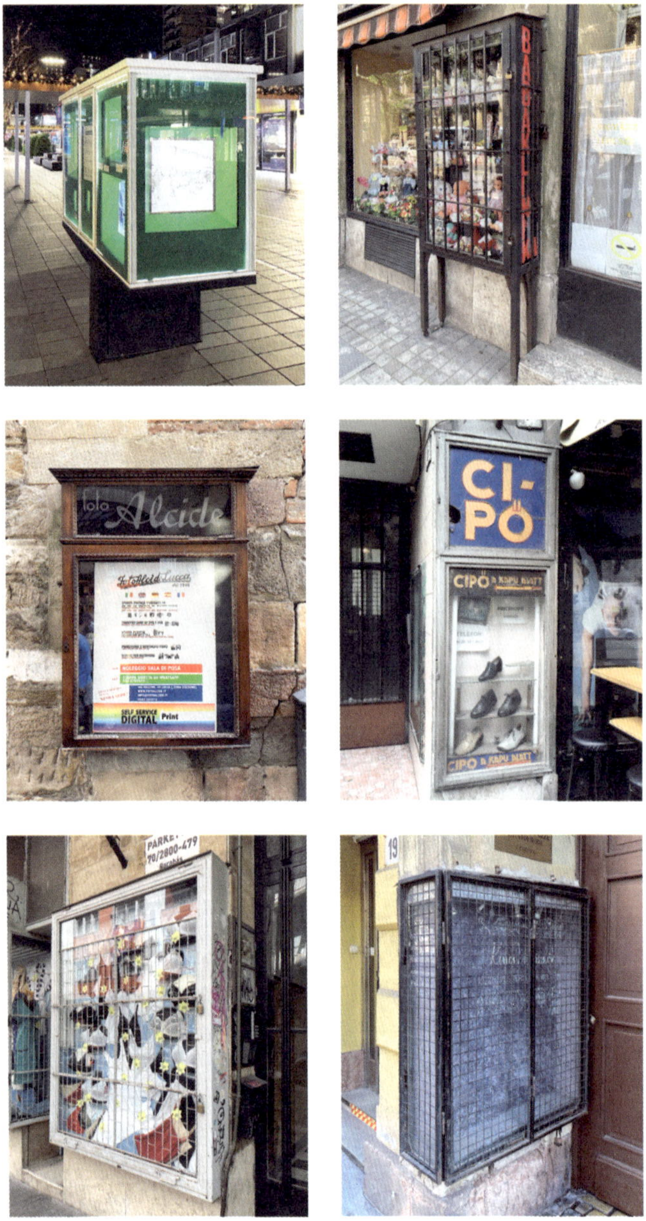

Top row, left: *Rotterdam*; right: *Budapest*
Middle row, left: *Lucca, Italy*; right: *Budapest*
Bottom row: *Budapest*

Displaying

The vitrine seems an unlikely item of street furniture. This fragile glass case for precious objects is more domestic than civic, or perhaps more redolent of a museum than a shopping street. For most of us the vitrine might evoke a corner in our granny's house, a cabinet full of porcelain pin-trays, flowers, and perhaps a couple of family photos. Yet vitrines also had their moment in the modernist city as illuminated reliquaries of commodified product, microcosms of the department stores and shopfronts, spotlighting an individual item or range as if it were ineffably precious.

For me the vitrine seems more a product of communist-era Central Europe than the capitalist West. You'd come across them in Berlin or Budapest, always more Prague than Paris. They were, in their way, a product of the modernist dream of *Lichtarchitektur*, the concept of an architecture capable of metamorphosing into something different after dark - into an inversion of itself where solids become light, dark windows and doors become bright. Architects in the 1920s sought to create a cinematic city, transforming the night into a theatrical journey, by using neon strips running horizontally across buildings and up specially designed towers, or attenuated banded windows giving the impression of car headlights caught in a long-exposure photo. Critical to this were the shopfronts, strips of light and glimpses into stores which blurred the boundaries between street and shop, inside and out, public and private. It created an enhanced sense of depth along the pavement and made the street a channel of light and desire. You still get the idea in the remarkable windows of the former Simpson's of Piccadilly (now Waterstones) or Heal's in Tottenham Court Road, where the windows recede and curve into the depth of the shop, stripping reflections away and seemingly creating an open space. You feel you can reach in and touch.

Street vitrines were an extension of this deliberate blurring of the borders between interior and exterior, enclosing a little fragment of the storefront into a glass case on the street itself. Europe's first pedestrian precinct, Rotterdam's Lijnbaan (designed by Jo van den Broek and Jacob Bakema in 1953), was speckled with vitrines in the middle of the roads where cars might otherwise have been. The effect was a kind of museum of consumption, a low-key exhibition, commerce as culture - an effect amplified by the occasional piece of public art interspersed with the showcases. There are still a few vitrines in the Lijnbaan, with one, I think, an original. They no longer have consumables inside but rather are used to display the history of the Lijnbaan itself, the metanarrative of vitrines displaying vitrines. The modern vitrines look quite slick, the old one rather heavy. Perhaps they needed to be more firmly rooted; this was a neighbourhood completely flattened by bombing. The lightness of the modern architecture was critical but it couldn't be seen to be too ephemeral, it needed, also, to be grounded in the new reality.

These pedestrian shopping streets with their central vitrines as treasure chests of consumption spread across Europe as city architects came on pilgrimages to Rotterdam. Warsaw and Prague in the East delivered their versions, so did Hamburg in its similarly brutalised centre. But so also did Stevenage in the UK, which kept the planters and even the exact same desk-lamp-type streetlights - but not the vitrines.

I don't remember the heyday of the European vitrine. Instead I remember an era when, all over Central Europe, the vitrines seemed peculiar survivals in cities which had somehow endured communism and emerged into a new era of capitalism. With lights blinking in the glare, the vitrines found themselves redundant. No-one seemed to know quite what to do with them. Weirdly, it seemed to me, communism had been responsible for the survival of these sidewalk symbols of commodity fetish. Perhaps in a system where choice was limited and new purchases were a luxury to be looked forward to, products retained more of an aura.

There were different kinds of vitrine, all of which, in some way, served to extend the shop window into unexpected spaces. In Budapest, when I lived there in the early 1990s, there were glass cabinets wrapped around courtyard entrances, luring strollers in through often dark, dingy, dank-smelling doorways which would otherwise have remained unknown. That illuminated shallow box, barely more than a glazed noticeboard, enriched and enlivened the streetscape. The products displayed were frequently bizarre. The corporate chains had yet to arrive in big numbers so store owners were left to curate their own displays. There were hand-painted mugs besides military, fake SS daggers and real Soviet fur hats and watches looming over porcelain peasant figures. In others, leatherworkers or watch repairers advertised their shops with broken clocks or tatty belts. There were fox-fur collars advertising furriers who worked nearby in tiny basements, and basic toiletries pointing to new 'pile-em-high' stores.

Free-standing vitrines, standing on the pavement itself, could only work in cities with wide boulevards, which explains why London only ever had a few scattered examples. Those that survived are disappearing, even from cities where they were once a common sight. The parade of vitrines on Berlin's Kurfürstendamm, currently decked out in high-fashion funereal black and stamped with the global language of luxury of the big brand names, gives some idea of what they might once have been. In socialist days they were employed for occasional flashes of colour in an often-drab retail landscape, suggesting a mythical wealth of goods. I remember one in Budapest which housed a single shoe, long slipped from its pedestal, faded by the sun with insects buzzing around the lights inside. It was quite an installation.

Walk through most provincial Mediterranean cities and there will be some remnants of this typology. There is something in these vitrines suggesting a family resemblance to the glass-fronted reliquaries you sometimes find in Catholic churches containing a skull, a bone or some item of clothing associated with a saint.

Vitrines weren't entirely absent from the streets of Britain, but they were thin on the ground. They tended not be stuffed with commodities but with exhibits for public education. I came across photos of an austere grouping of sculptural vitrines marking the pedestrianisation of Thetford's town centre sometime in the 1970s. It wasn't clear what they were displaying but it appeared to be an exhibit about the pedestrianisation itself. It might have been a last fling for planners celebrating their own much-maligned profession in public.

Today the few remaining vitrines are scattered in airports and stations, malls and plazas, remnants of an attempt to grab a little more of the street for retail relegated to the spaces of privatised interchange. Mid-market business hotels in Germany, Austria and Switzerland seem one of the last holdouts. Sometimes even the automatic revolving doors feature a display of products in a glazed central section, slowly spinning forever.

In a way, the vitrines made the street into an exhibition space. Resolutely commercial yet also somehow always a little anachronistic, they made products surreal by stripping them of their contexts. They suggested the precious in the context of the mundane while straining themselves to be almost invisible, even banal.

Documenting

Charles Marville was the official portraitist of street furniture. Employed as the photographer of the city of Paris in 1862, he produced a remarkable and beautiful record of the streetlamps, kiosks, advertising columns and pissoirs of a city being radically rebuilt. And he depicted them as figures in the city streets, urban artefacts with dignity. His task was to document the old city of slums and narrow medieval alleys and to record the new city emerging to the grandiose plans of his boss, Baron Georges-Eugène Haussmann. Marville worked closely with Gabriel Davioud, the chief architect of the Service des Promenades et Plantations which was responsible for the huge programme of *le mobilier urbain*. This was defined as 'the ensemble of objects or devices or apparatuses, public or private, installed in public space and tied to a function or a service offered to the collectivity' - which is probably the finest description of street furniture ever given.

Marville's photography of street furniture and, in particular, of streetlights, was itself part of a propaganda programme to promote the city's achievements in modernisation and to justify its status as the City of Light. The photos were exhibited in expos and fairs around the world, portraits of the cast-iron static citizens of the new streets. These were the harbingers of modernity and it is, perhaps, difficult today to understand quite how radical these interventions really were. Streetlights opened up the city in the hours of darkness, expanding the experience of its public spaces deep into the night. Haussmann's urban 'improvements' - new pavements and wider streets, the destruction of the city's slums and the ejection of their criminal underclass - was a bourgeois triumph. Neighbourhoods which had previously been too dangerous after dark could be opened up, the city made safe for its wealthier citizens. New urinoirs or pissoirs concentrated the yellow liquid within little shielded, roofless structures. The city's nighttime attractions were advertised on *colonnes Morris*, cast-iron cylinders with exotic French Empire hats which became the city's scrapbooks and glowed through the night; newspapers could be sold from specially designed kiosks. The full panoply of street furniture as the emblem of the modern metropolis began to emerge in a co-ordinated programme of improvement and amenity.

Marville shot these objects with the same reverence with which he photographed the statuary on the façades of Gothic cathedrals and the fountains of old Paris. He shot them as portraits, affectionate depictions of street furniture as dignified embodiments of the spirit of the place - even if they were, by their very nature, mass-produced.

If you look at Marville's early photos of the old streets of Paris, pre-Haussmanisation, they are mostly empty. There is the occasional horse or curious worker, but the generally low vantage point of the camera gives prominence to the ranks of bollards and wall and corner protectors which punctuated the pavements at the junction of the walls which defined the streets. Where he photographs the busy market of Les Halles, the crowds of porters and traders dissolve into a mist with the long duration of the exposure. The workers disappear, they evaporate. The stone bollards must stand in for them. In the same way, the later layer of lamps and kiosks becomes a cipher for the hard-working citizens populating the new streets.

Haussmann was concerned that the new designs should be beautiful but also modest, that the streetlights, for instance, should not be elevated on stone pedestals but should stand directly

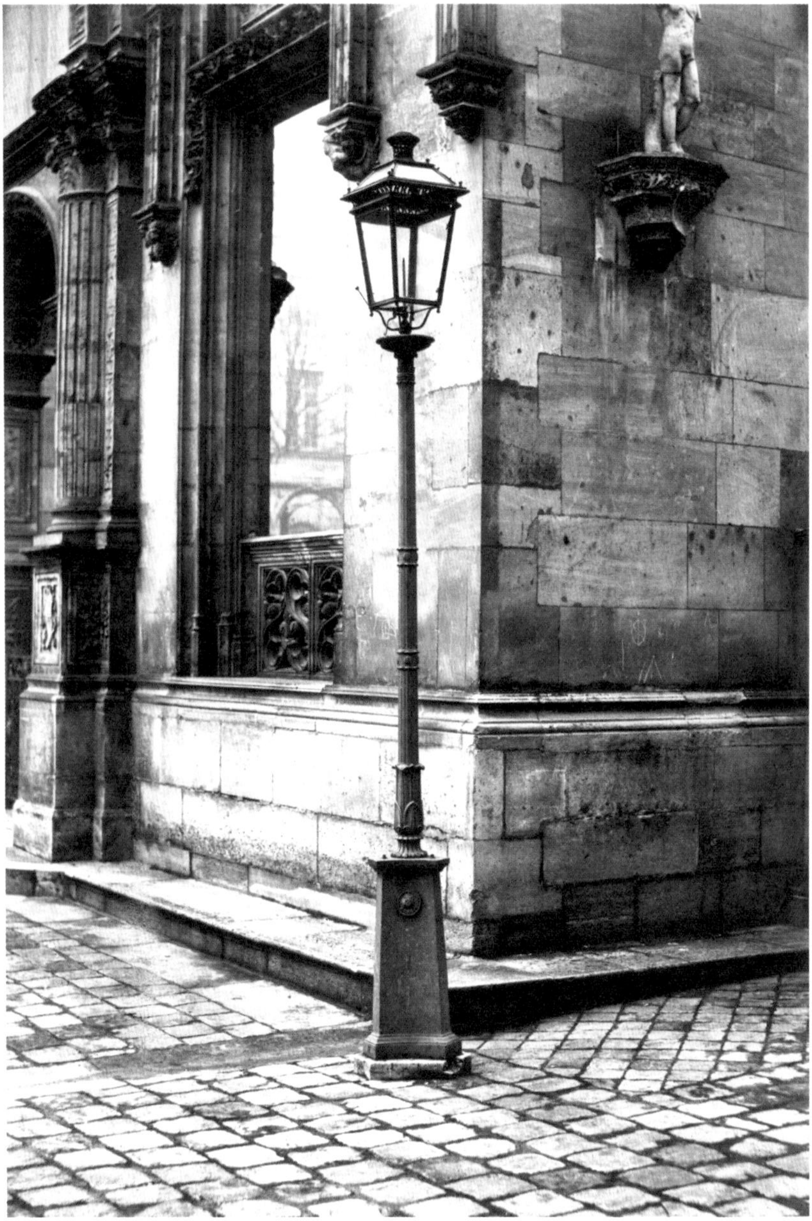

Entrance to the École des Beaux-Arts, 1878
Charles Marville

from the pavement to create a direct connection with pedestrians and with the street itself. They were to be elegantly, but not opulently, decorated, restrained bourgeoisie but not effete dandies. The way Marville captured them emphasises the coincidence between the body and the product. Always placed in the centre of the frame and viewed from approximately eye level, we encounter each item as we might a passerby on the street. They are rooted to the road and there is always just enough of the setting shown to understand the context - a street corner of elegant boutiques, an arch through to a palatial hotel, a grand avenue in a park where the streetlight's verticality chimes with the stone sculptures. These are not presented as products but as inhabitants in their own right, a parallel citizenry cast in iron.

In the 1860s photographic technology was unable to capture night, to work in the dark, so at the heart of Marville's marvellous photos there is an absence - light itself. The thing the streetlamps were designed for is invisible - the capacity to illuminate. This might have rendered the photos representations of dumb objects, but instead they are portrayed as friendly, humane additions to the streetscape, a civilising presence. They have not been emasculated by the daylight, rather they while away the hours alongside the citizens on the streets. Waiting to perform.

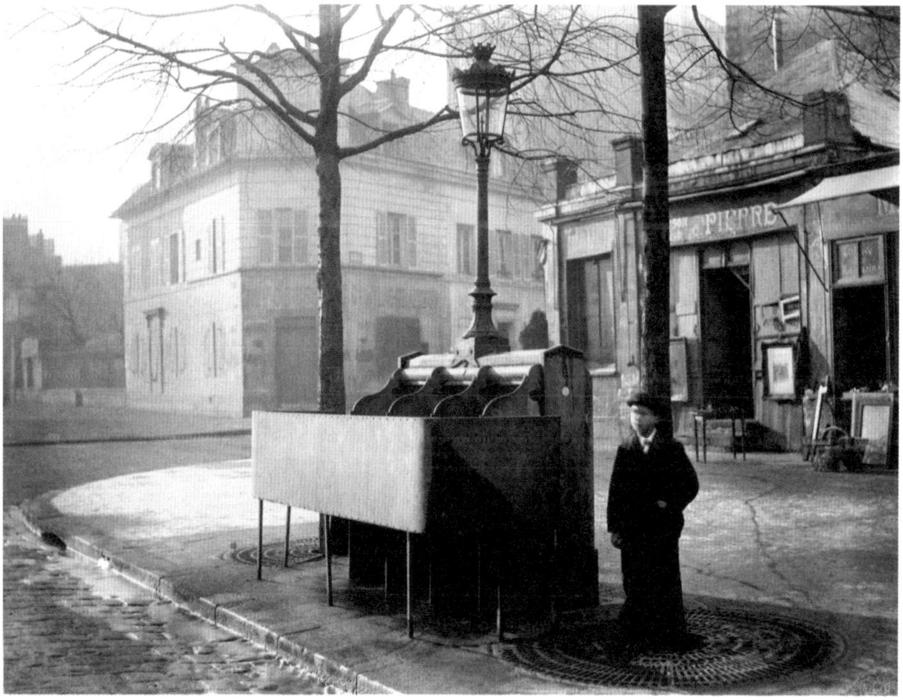

Urinal with Three Stalls, Chaussée du Maine, 1862/68
Charles Marville

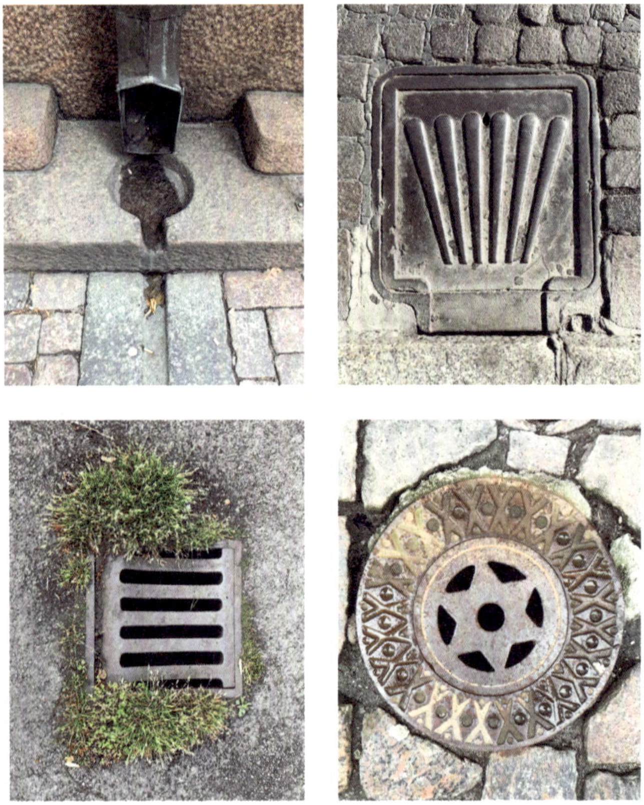

Top row, left: *Helsinki*; right: *Mantua, Italy*
Bottom row, left: *London*; right: *Copenhagen*

Draining

Against the wall under the portico of the church of Santa Maria in Cosmedin in Rome is a strange object, looking a little like a pancake with a face or one of those camembert man-in-the-moon images George Méliès used to conjure for early cinema. Christened the *Bocca di Verita* (the mouth of truth), the disk is thought to be a Roman drain cover, possibly from the Temple of Venus. It might have drained rainwater from the open oculus in the ceiling or even, perhaps, the blood of ritually slaughtered bulls. The legend is that if a liar puts their hand in the mouth it will close shut permanently, hand and all. Its most famous outing was in the film *Roman Holiday* in which Gregory Peck's photographer joshes with Audrey Hepburn's naive princess by pretending his hand has been trapped. There is a famous image of Hitchcock solemnly sticking his hand in, and another of Brigitte Bardot doing it a little less seriously.

In the film of Stephen King's *It*, the sinister clown Pennywise appears behind the grate of a storm drain (inspired, apparently, by a drain in King's hometown, Bangor in Maine). Things, including paper boats and arms, disappear down the drain. There is, it seems, something innately terrifying about drains. As street furniture goes they are without doubt the most banal items, but perhaps it is the mystery of what goes on below the streets that gives them this aura of other-worldliness. Whatever it is, they are also probably the longest-lived and least changed items of streetware. In Rome today, amid the ruins but even, on occasion, in the working streets, you can come across paving stones with pierced patterns, sometimes simple slots, sometimes a grid of circular holes. They are Ancient Roman drain grates. More elaborate and impressive versions can be seen in museums, such as that from Bothwellhaugh Fort in Lanarkshire (now in Glasgow's Hunterian Museum) with a six-petalled flower carved into its centre and a chevron rope ring carved around it.

Few pieces of street furniture, excepting perhaps bollards, survive so well and with their design and purpose so unchanged. The main difference is material. Stone gave way to cast iron during the industrial revolution. Slots and grids remain the language of the grate. Thanks to their smartphone-sized openings, slots now seem to be giving way to grids with smaller, square holes, but otherwise designs have remained the same. When the architect Adolf Loos designed his now-revered Michaelerhaus on Vienna's Michaelerplatz (1909–11), a contemporary cartoonist parodied the building's unadorned grid of windows by depicting the architect peering into a drain with an iron-grid grate, getting his inspiration from the sewers. The drain cover is the great survivor, suggesting a place where you might always be able to lose something.

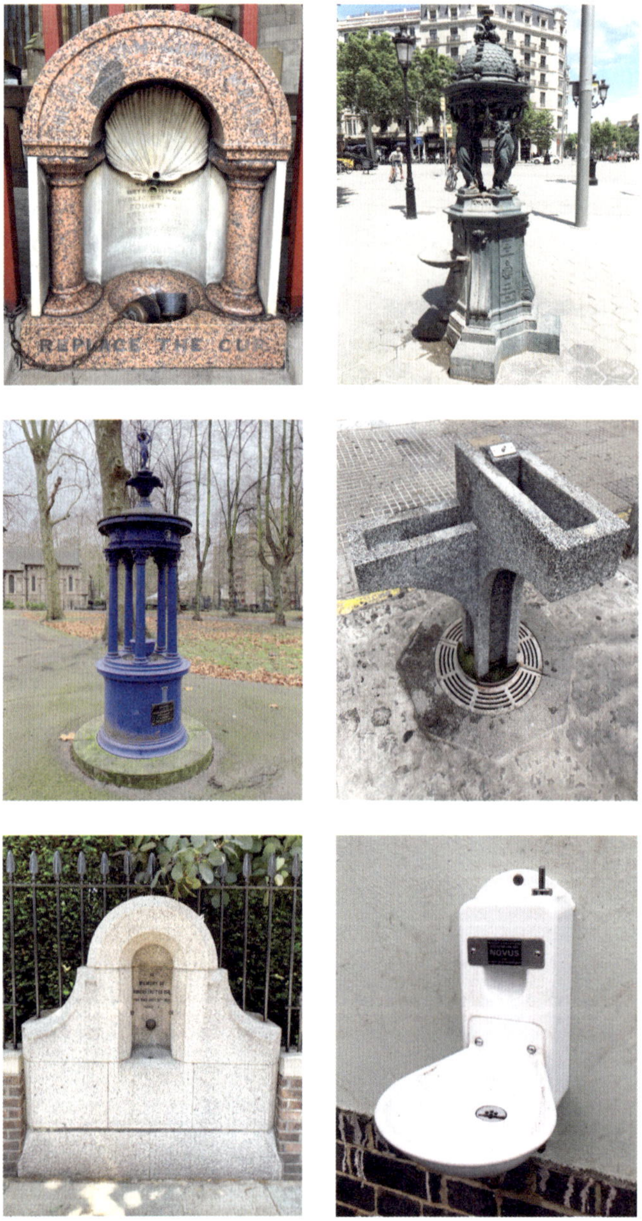

Top row, left: *Holborn Viaduct, London*; right: *Wallace drinking fountain, Paris*
Middle row, left: *St Pancras, London*; right: *Cadiz, Spain*
Bottom row, left: *South Kensington, London*; right: *Barnes, London*

Drinking

One million plastic bottles of water are bought globally every minute. For the UK, at the time of writing, the figure is 35 million each day. We know the destination of many of these - back in a symbiotic relationship with water, floating around in the sea. The solution is simple: public fountains. In the 19th century, cities managed to provide drinking water in the streets, yet today that simple public gesture has been abandoned in favour of this insane cycle of consumption and waste involved in bottling, transporting and discarding those billions of bottles.

The drinking fountain is, in its way, a symbol of the civilised city, a generous public gesture which makes the metropolis liveable. And it is nothing new. The public drinking fountain is an amalgam of two other urban archetypes: the decorative fountain and the water pump. The former was a monumental installation, probably sculpted with figures, rocks and scallops, to honour some wealthy patron; the latter was a utilitarian vertical stand with a handle. The Romans (of course) had public drinking fountains and some, almost unbelievably, still function. They might be in the form of a lion's head or a sun-face spouting water from the mouth, usually with a sarcophagus or bath-shaped trough below from which animals could drink. In later centuries, in the UK, water from pumps was recognised as a potential source of infection. As piping became more extensive, fountains dedicated to clean drinking water were introduced. Five years after John Snow traced a cholera infection to a single pump on Soho's Broadwick Street in 1854, the first public drinking fountain in Britain was erected. Funded by the newly minted Metropolitan Drinking Fountain Association, the fountain is still there, by Holborn Viaduct. The basin sits in a niche with a scallop-shell above it, framed by red granite columns and an inscription reading 'Replace the cup'. Two metal mugs are attached by chains as was the case with all subsequent public drinking fountains. Naturally, this being London, it doesn't work.

The water might have been clean, the mugs maybe not so much. If you return to Cornhill, near the surviving pump, you'll see an even more elaborate fountain from a little later, with four basins, the rings that would have fastened the cups and exquisitely carved columns, all crowned with a gas lantern - truly multi functional furniture. Sadly the water-carrier figure from the centre is missing. Set into the side of the Theatre Royal, Drury Lane, meanwhile, there is a hideously monumental drinking fountain complete with rusticated base and bust of actor/theatre manager Augustus Harris. In Grasmere, up in the Lake District, there is a fountain by a dry-stone wall dedicated to William Wordsworth. Built in 1889, it is perhaps the most complete item of English street furniture, combining a trough (with a little lower-level extension for dogs), a Romanesque niche for the fountain and a stone bench on the other side. Kindness to animals, a drink, fake medieval nostalgia and a nice sit-down - the perfect English day out embodied in one piece of street furniture.

By 1879 there were almost 800 public drinking fountains in London, and by this time other big cities had got going with their own programmes. In Paris, drinking fountains were introduced by an Englishman, a philanthropist named Richard Wallace. (There is one in London, standing outside his former home, just off Oxford Street, which now houses the eponymous Wallace Collection.) Wallace came into money, very big money, inherited from his father. While Paris was under siege in the Franco-Prussian War, he distributed bundles of cash to the poor and, once the war was over, turned his attention to fresh water which was lacking in many neighbourhoods. He donated the money to design, manufacture and install 50 fountains (which quickly became known as 'Wallaces'). The fountains, cast in iron and painted green like the rest of the street furniture, were once as much a part of the cityscape as that other English-sounding creation, the Morris advertising column. With their four finely sculpted female figures representing Kindness, Simplicity, Charity and Sobriety (sculpted by Charles-Auguste Lebourg) supporting a domed canopy (Ionic capitals sprouting from the tops of their heads), the fountains became urban markers, clearly visible, democratic and elegant. They featured sculpted sea creatures to inscribe the symbolism of water in their fabric; the caryatids were placed close enough together so that horses would not be able to drink from them and high enough that dogs would not be able to access them either. A small metal cup was placed in the trickle of water at the centre and chained to the iron.

That fourth caryatid, Sobriety, reveals much about the ulterior motives for the provision of public drinking water. Of course these were works of generosity, but they were also part of an effort to reduce alcohol consumption among the working classes by encouraging them to drink water. They were genuinely democratic; the homeless and the itinerant were welcome here. In Britain and the US their installation was supported by the powerful Temperance movement. On one side of the Tompkins Square fountain in New York (*c.*1888), for example, the word 'Temperance' is inscribed. In London, many fountains were positioned deliberately outside pubs. There always was an agenda. And there is again today. Now it is plastic. The urgent need to reduce those millions of bottles has revivified the discussion of fountains, but it begins with another familiar issue - hygiene. Public water fountains suffer from an image problem, exemplified in that dirty cup on a chain at Holborn Viaduct. Despite John Snow's discoveries, the concept of germs was still poorly understood in the 19th century, but by the early 20th century the cups began to disappear. But how were thirsty citizens supposed to drink?

An immediate and shocking image is Elliott Erwitt's blurry, unsettling snap of segregated water fountains in 1950. On the left is a streamlined Art Deco piece of kit ('White'); on the right is a basic basin ('Colored'). This unconscionable practice of segregation ended in 1965.

There have always been fears over 'sharing', whether with 'the other' or whether just with each other. Designers have found ways around it. If you look at the 'whites' fountain you'll see

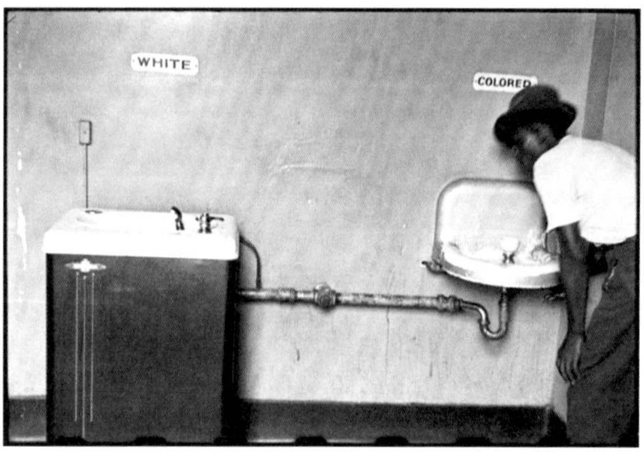

Wilmington, North Carolina, 1950
Elliott Erwitt

a familiar-looking cowl - something I recall vividly from fountains at my schools in London. In white enamelled metal with a toggle for a tap, those fountains somehow provoke a super-harp pang of nostalgia and angst, years of playgrounds, sports fields, parks and changing rooms, the slightly metallic tang of the water, the dribble down the chin. They felt like an inevitable presence of institutional life. A combination of Covid, germaphobia and municipal budget-cutting has led to their seemingly permanent demise.

One rather lovely solution to the bacteria issue can be seen in the fountains in Rome known as *nasone* (big noses), installed from the 1870s onwards. Looking like a fat, cast-iron bollard they have a bent spout sticking out, the water permanently flowing. Cupping your hand over the spout makes the water squirt out of a hole punched in the top of the pipe, shooting straight into your mouth. Most versions that I've seen in airports, gyms and public buildings now have two fittings, a geyser and a slim, tubular tap for refilling bottles, which might not be robust enough for use in the street.

Italy remains a cornucopia of fountains. From baroque clamshells and stone posts to cast-iron fittings and Rococo niches set into the walls of palazzi, the variations appear endless; water has been used effectively as a locus of public activity and lifted through ornamentation. It seems barely believable that some are survivals from Ancient Rome, still fed by their system of aqueducts, bringing pure spring water into the city. Yet they are. Interestingly, they often feature *grotteschi* - fantastical monsters, flat-faced gods and water creatures (the word 'grotto' emerges from the same source and these too often featured fountains). There is an incredible sense of enjoyment in these civic amenities, moments of light relief, beautifully sculpted. They were, at least in part, an expression of the power and munificence of the Roman state, conveyed in stone and symbols. They also hinted at the origins of the water, its mystery. Just as on maps with mythical creatures in the margins, so water conjures up images of nymphs and sprites, of Neptune and mermaids.

London has been careless with its fountains. Most are dried up, filled with leaves and litter. It is a shocking waste of a technology and an existing infrastructure. The city had something like the Wallace fountains, a series of Neoclassical structures scattered throughout the streets. There is one still present in St Pancras Old Church Gardens, painted a vivid blue and only a few steps from the tomb Sir John Soane designed for his wife Eliza which inspired Sir Giles Gilbert Scott's design for the telephone box. The fountain found momentary fame when it was used as the setting for a Beatles photoshoot, the band members spitting water while recording *The White Album* in summer 1968. It appears to have been painted in a more French-looking green at the time.

Which brings us to contemporary drinking fountains. On an unseasonably warm spring day, in 2016, I went to Borough Market where some of the first of a new range of London fountains had been installed. There weren't queues but there was a constant stream of people, refilling their plastic bottles (it takes a long time to fill a 1.5l bottle). So they work and there is, clearly, demand. How, then, do these new fountains live up to the legacy of aesthetic embodiment of the public good? The answer seems to be they don't even bother. They are shockingly ugly, big lumps of welded tube painted municipal green. There is no pleasure here, just utility. Other versions are executed in lurid blue plastic with stupid logos in moulded plastic intended to act as markers.

Every few years or so there are efforts to create something a little more pleasing. Michael Anastassiades's extremely elegant 'fleet' design is a faceted column with a slightly concave top and a central split through which water is delivered in an elegant arc. An object of rare beauty, it seems to have taken seriously its relationship to other classic British street furniture designs. A few examples were installed by the specially formed London Fountain Company, but they have yet to appear in greater numbers. Once a staple of the civilised city, drinking fountains have been allowed to decline. There are signs of revivals across the world, but they remain painfully slow.

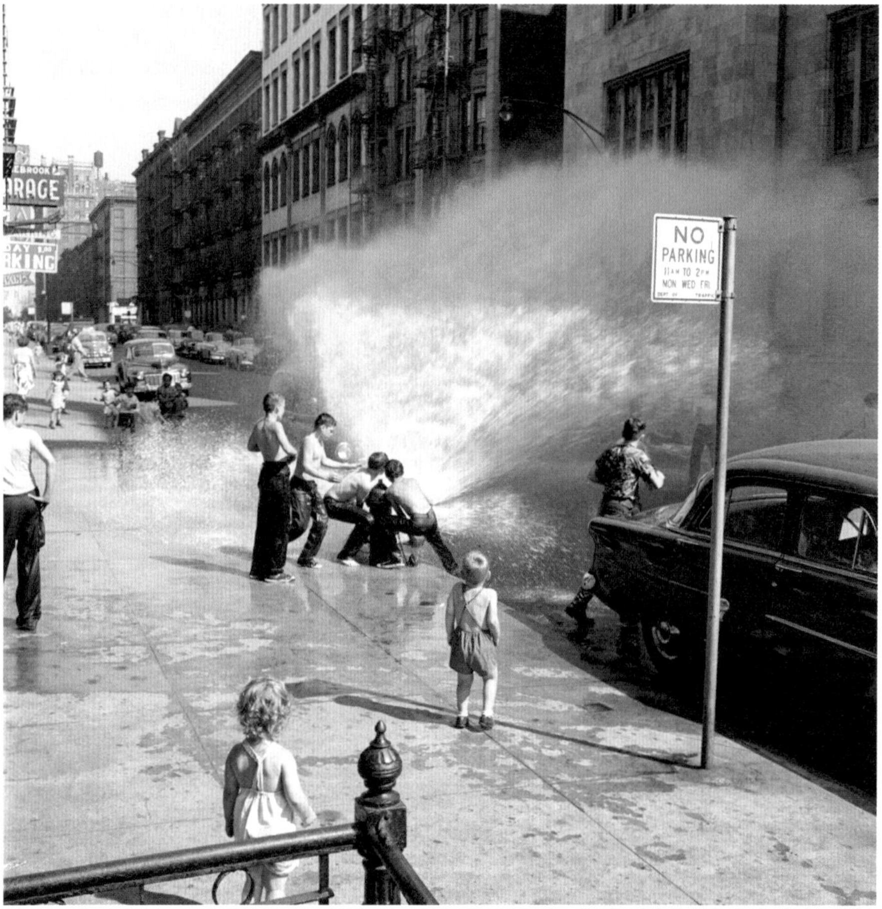

New York, NY, June 1954
Vivian Maier

Extinguishing

Surely among the most joyous images of summer in the city are those familiar scenes of kids playing in the spray of a New York fire hydrant. This pure pleasure, this frowned-upon subversion of a safety device for enjoyment, encapsulates the mischief, the relief from the intensity of the urban heat and the tendency towards (and occasional necessity of) a little anarchy of street life in the big city. Look at the faces and the postures of the figures in Leonard Freed's image of an improvised shower in Harlem. It is almost a religious ecstasy, a group that might have been sculpted by Bernini atop a fountain. Vivian Maier's 1954 photo of kids playing in the spray has a harder working feel, almost military in its effort and organisation, or like workers at a ruptured oil well. This is the hydrant equivalent of Joe Rosenthal's iconic photo *Raising the Flag on Iwo Jima*, but natural, not posed, and still heroic in its enjoyable way.

Fire hydrant showers were a pleasure denied to us British kids, who only witnessed these scenes on TV's *Sesame Stree*t, or later in our lives in films like Spike Lee's *Do the Right Thing* or at the clichéd end of a car-chase scene as a speeding cop car inevitably crashes into a hydrant allowing the protagonist to get away and drenching the cop in water. Many, I suppose, will particularly remember the fight scene in *The Godfather* where a fire hydrant spews water over the victim of the impetuous Sonny (played by James Caan). It stands as a visual reminder that Sonny needs to cool that famous temper.

In Britain, fire hydrants tend to be small concrete paddles marked with a mean yellow enamelled 'H'. Joyless and municipal. The mechanics are underground and invisible - this was a development of an earlier technology in which wooden conduits ran beneath the streets and firefighters would have to remove the cobbles and drill into the water supply to power their pumps. They would then plug the holes with fireplugs; subsequently, firemen who guarded those plugs (often against competing fire brigades) would become known as fireplugs themselves. Stocky and muscular (in order to fight off fellow firefighters, or angry burning-home owners), the phrase became associated with a particular body type and also became gay slang. The phrase 'plug-ugly' comes from the same source.

The US hydrants represented another level. Highly visible and almost anthropomorphic, these chunks of cast metal seem a particularly American item of street furniture. Associated with New York more than anywhere, they are as much a part of the city's street scene and visual branding as yellow cabs and steaming vents. The function of the hydrant is revealed in the cap which crowns it, looking suspiciously (and surely accidentally) like a fireman's hard hat.

There had been hydrant upstands since the beginning of the 19th century. Before then, as is often still the case in Europe, firefighters would bring their own portable standpipes. A rather lovely patent for a design by John M. Jordan of Baltimore in 1839 showed a standpipe which emptied after use to prevent the water inside freezing, and boasted a tapering timber octagonal cover - a blend of lighthouse and carefully crafted traffic cone.

Cast-iron hydrants also appeared around the beginning of the 19th century. In 1804 Frederick Graff Sr designed a hydrant which he had manufactured by Foxall & Richards, a firm better known for producing cannon used by the US Navy. Some hydrants had flip-up tops, some were designed to look like chunky Doric columns (rather elegant). Various versions proliferated across the US until 1869, when engineer and inventor Birdsill Holly patented a design for New York able to cope with the high-pressure water system recently fitted in the city. His hydrants can still be seen - more have survived in the backwaters of the Deep South than in New York City, but the rusting hulks of his 1869 model with its bulbous Victorian vase of a base still survive.

The illicit tradition of citizens using adjustable wrenches to turn on their local hydrants seems to date back as far as the hydrants themselves. The first famous incident came with the heatwave of 1896 when a young police commissioner, Teddy Roosevelt, ordered the fire department to open the hydrants and spray the city's streets to clear them of rotting garbage and animal carcasses. The most famous photos (and there are many), however, tend to show the results of what locals rather than local government have done. And it is almost always African American kids playing in the waters. The residents of poorer boroughs lived more on the streets than in their (often slum) accommodation and rarely would have had air-conditioning, so this activity tended to be indulged in by the more deprived neighbourhoods. The brownstones in the background of those wonderful moments of street photography have mostly been gentrified today; these events are less necessary and far rarer than they once were, and probably would be more frowned upon by increasingly health- and safety-conscious authorities.

Like most pieces of American hardware, the fire hydrant is a supremely practical piece of kit, chunky and slightly over-engineered. In sticking up above ground (unlike those shy British versions) it is easily accessible and clearly visible to firefighters, but it also acts as a very obvious deterrent against parking. During the bicentennial celebrations in 1976, it became fashionable for citizens to paint their local hydrants in stars and stripes or Uncle Sam colours; a few jolly and now slightly faded examples still survive.

The fire hydrant is also a supremely expressive object, the various outlets for fire hoses protruding from the column. If the hydrant can be seen as a kind of safety valve for an overheating city, it can equally be used to control. Photographers seem strangely drawn to its presence as an abstract sculptural object in the city. And when it is not in use, it is just that, a piece of street sculpture. Walker Evans's series of Polaroids of various fire hydrants (1973–74, some of his last photos) has a portrait quality but also a Hopperesque, haunting silence. Lee Friedlander's photograph of a fire hydrant places it centre shot, and allows the viewer's eye to wander around the Albuquerque cityscape from there so that you suddenly become aware of the sheer amount of street furniture of which this is only one, albeit charismatic, constituent (the black dog half hidden behind a pole is a terrific touch).

If those ecstatic images of summer spray pervade the imagination, it is less widely known that one of the other longstanding uses for hydrants is for police to plug their hoses into it to use the high-pressure water to quell riots and disturbances.

The spraying isn't all one way. Hydrants have become the favoured scent centres for dogs relieving themselves and checking out who's been in the area. Spraying water or not, the hydrant's scale somehow imposes itself more on the world of kids and pets than it does on that of adults. Which is perhaps appropriate. They are entitled to their urban markers and the appropriation of street furniture too.

Fading

One of the most striking things about photos of the 19th-century city is the almost insane amount of text. The glazing of shop windows, shopfronts, awnings, offices and pubs - all were smothered in signage, making the city throb with the density of text of a Victorian newspaper, teeming with words and stuffed with advertising. It is hardly surprising that some of this screed of text survives in the form of what have come to be known as 'ghost signs', fading words often on the bare brick walls and flanks of buildings, isolated pieces of advertising for long-gone brands, products and places. They can be profoundly evocative moments of memory which suddenly remind you of the sheer quantity of manifestations that even a century-old building must have gone through.

For most of the 19th century, even the most modest pub would feature dozens of hand-painted descriptions of the beers and drinks sold inside, the brewers, the history of the building, the meals, rooms, prices and class. A grocer or a butcher's would have similarly outlined the goods and brands purveyed. Shop windows were adorned with arches of lettering, copper or brass ledges and plates were embossed with the items sold and the names of the shopkeepers. What's surprising is not that ghost signs survive, but rather that so little text has endured. Even where the buildings themselves survive pretty much intact, almost everything has been painted over.

There is, of course, still signage and advertising today, but it has been separated out from the architecture. Billboards are digital screens applied to façades, acrylic fascias occupy just a small, garish, strip. Applied cheaply and badly, it is not integrated with the fabric but is an add-on layer which doesn't even have the confidence of its own permanence.

Among the survivors there are the usual commercial signs, adverts for Hovis Bread, Bovril or Sunlight Laundries, for barbers or dining rooms, for tonic products and snake-oil potions. But perhaps more interesting are the signs pointing the way to obsolete functions or spaces, such as arrows indicating air-raid or nuclear shelters and bunkers, or remnants of tradesmen's signs and tradesmen's entrances. There is so much to look for and it is always such a pleasure to find it. The traces evoke in us something of the urban archaeologist, stripping away the layers of accretions, in our minds at least, to reveal what once must have been in places otherwise so familiar. The oddness of it, perhaps, is that our city seems so much plainer. Perhaps as ads have migrated on to phones, the city has relinquished its role as a massive screed of text. We are now required to read it in less literal ways.

Fetishising

Street furniture in Britain was not much commented on until it started disappearing. When old, elaborate gaslights began to be replaced by local authorities in the 1950s and '60s as part of modernisation schemes and highway engineering projects, residents suddenly took an interest. These once ubiquitous artefacts suddenly found themselves appreciated, understood as urban antiques, components of a 'townscape'. They were seen to be contributing to the character of a neighbourhood, and a kind of genteel resistance emerged to the homogenisation offered by councils and their contemporary products.

Being Britain, this was all inevitably tied up with questions of class and property values. When much of the finest ironwork, railings, decorative gates and posts were gathered for scrap as part of the war effort (most was of such low quality it could not be used in any kind of arms production and was, according to reports, dumped in the Thames Estuary; this was purely part of a political effort to make people feel 'involved'), many of the most genteel squares and church gardens in London somehow escaped. Something similar happened with street furniture in the great renewal which happened after the war. Old iron bollards, gaslights, signposts and benches were removed from predominantly working-class areas and industrial towns to be replaced by more practical versions, while those in more expensive neighbourhoods and prosperous cathedral towns were left in place as characterful heritage.

Most of the apparently historic street furniture we see today is a sham. Those lamps that look Victorian are almost certainly not. Their lanterns have never held a gas lamp, the bars beneath have been designed to resemble those that might have once supported a ladder but are more likely to be used for suspending hanging baskets. The decorative grills on their tops are not there to ventilate but to make them look *authentic*. If we look carefully at those heritage streetlights, as we rarely ever do, we see that in fact they are oddly ugly, often ill-proportioned, too flimsy-looking. They are there to represent rather than to be, they recall an image of history but do not attempt any real presence or effect for themselves.

Likewise, cast-iron benches with 19th-century foliage come straight out of a catalogue; they may recall the form of Victorian casting but not its mas or presence. Those cannon-shaped bollards will probably turn out to have a black polyurethane coating. Most of the historic street furniture proved too costly or fiddly to convert from gas to electric, complex ironwork was too tricky to paint, councils just couldn't be bothered or items were replaced with newer, better, heritage models, and residents were satisfied because they looked authentic and maintained house prices, serving to distinguish neighbourhoods.

In Paris, on the other hand, many items survived surprisingly well. The city wasn't subject to the same highway engineering modernisations as were British and US cities - until, that is, it was realised there were big profits to be made in street furniture, converting previously dumb devices into billboards or cladding them with smart screens. The J.C. Decaux model, which provided municipalities with free street furniture in exchange for advertising rights, was widely adopted and proved the end for thousands of historic artefacts, from pissoirs to advertising columns. The elaborate cast lampposts which now look so picturesque are mostly reproductions.

As downtowns began to revive and councils began to understand that urban authenticity could be ascribed a real estate and tourist value, historic street furniture began reappearing - a little different, a lot newer, but trying *so* hard to look old. Items like Paris's Morris columns and Wallace fountains and the UK's red phoneboxes might have appeared as commercial prospects but they were conceived as utilities, integral elements in the complexion of the civilised street, weapons in the armoury of the modern city. They were, of course, themselves part of a renewal project, illuminating the streets, banishing dark corners, providing places to piss or sources of pure, cool drinking water. Their elaborate, often exotic architectural forms, with sculpted muses and onion domes, were meant to present them as art as well as utility, to soften the pill of these mass-produced, industrial lumps of iron suddenly appearing on the streets.

Now guidebooks are stuffed with hints at where to find rare survivals. There is the Carting Lane sewer lamp, for instance, one of London's most famous pieces of street furniture, an elegant light which works not on mains gas but on the methane from the drain, burning off the miasma. It is the perfect farcical London story - the fartlight, illumination powered by the darkness of the sewers. It still functions, its orangey flame gently flickering all day and all night. Or the strange London Stone, a lump of rock that was once something, though no-one is quite sure what. Perhaps a coronation seat? A milestone? A zero point? An altar? For years it sat inside a WHSmith store in the City, now it is embedded in a Cannon Street commercial development, in a curious kind of vitrine. Or what I think might be the one remaining pissoir in London, a green-painted shed with relief decoration in Star Yard, Holborn. It is a cult attraction yet is always closed, a reminder of what we once had and can't have any more.

Remaining coal-hole covers outside houses have become more appreciated, as have original phoneboxes and unusual pillarboxes. They are seen as authentic markers, valued, revered, mundane bits of streetscape that have somehow survived and transcended the quotidian to become fetishised as antiques. There is no way to recreate this value so these survivals just keep gaining in value, their survival increasingly a marker of gentrification. Prime property.

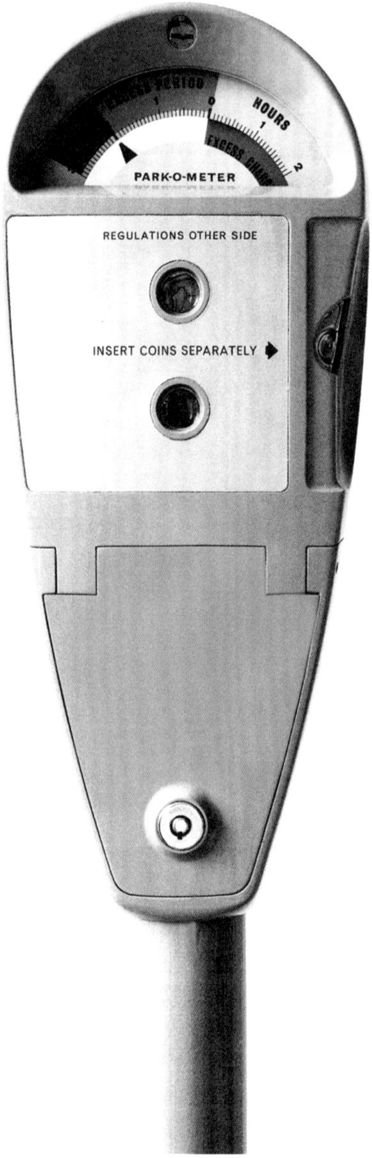

Venner Parking Meter, 1958
Sir Kenneth Grange

Fining

The opening of *Cool Hand Luke* sees Paul Newman's character lopping off the heads of what looks like a forest of parking meters with a pipe-cutter. The way he pushes the cutter round in circles makes it look a Herculean task, or like a sailor with a winding gear - it is heroic, hard work. This, surely, is the most victimless of crimes. Parking meters came to represent a particular aggressive bureaucracy, an attack on the freedom for drivers to possess the city in any way they wanted, to own the road. It is a strange kind of harvest for Newman, drunk, sweating, grinning with his twinkling smile and tassled loafers. But it will be his end. Bizarrely, the filmmakers chose a set of real, working meters in the town of Lodi, east of San Francisco. The cops, who had shown up to watch the filming, stood by. Only in California.

Everybody hates parking meters. Yet they became characters in the city, standing tall and lean with their lollipop heads, symbols of civic grift and legitimators of the insanely inefficient use of public space that is street parking.

In the mid-20th century, news photographer Weegee spent most of his time tuned into police radio frequencies, rushing to crime scenes or car crashes to catch gruesome tableaux of verity noir, but if you take a look at his photo *Street Scene Distortion* (p.94) you catch a little glimpse of the effects on the city of car culture and street parking. The car, one of those chunky, early streamlined numbers, takes up most of the frame. To the right a strange pair of Siamese-twin parking meters poke up, their space-alien heads drawing the eye ineluctably. What you see here is a gleaming hubcap, the meters, the Eppy Corsets neon sign and the fire escapes. It is probably Manhattan, perhaps the Lower East Side that Weegee haunted with his camera, but otherwise we don't know anything at all. What it shows is a city in which the car is king. For a few coins you too could blot out the city with your inky sedan. And the parking meter was the intermediary.

The man who invented the parking meter was, like Weegee, a newspaperman. Carl C. Magee was a colourful character who had already lived one life as an Albuquerque reporter. He uncovered a huge racket in the 1920s which became known as the Teapot Dome Scandal, in which Secretary of the Interior Albert B. Fall was found to have been taking backhanders for leasing government-owned lands to oil companies. Fall became the first US cabinet member to be sent to prison. Like so much of modern US history, everything boils down to oil.

Magee moved to Oklahoma City in 1927 to set up a new paper (*The Oklahoma News*); this was the boom time for print as much as it was for cars. One of the big issues in his new city was parking. Automobiles had become big business, and shopkeepers were complaining that people drove into downtown and parked in a spot all day. Magee's solution was the parking meter, which appealed to businesses because it meant shorter visits by more drivers. Magee worked with engineers to make a prototype and the first model was installed in downtown Oklahoma City in 1935, charging 5 cents an hour for parking. Park-O-Meter 1 was a remarkable-looking thing - an Art Deco, vaguely fan-shaped head with a recessed coin drop for the nickel, and a winder which required customers to operate the mechanism (like an old film camera) after depositing their coins.

The introduction of the parking meter was, initially, seen an un-American, a tax on automobiles and hugely unpopular with drivers, but it became, unusually for street furniture, a huge revenue-raiser for cities. Things that make money tend to stick around. The British version was designed by Sir Kenneth Grange in 1958 (p.92). This was a much more modernist affair, with a half-sucked lollipop head or an oar-paddle top, refined and reduced from the streamlined US original. Grange told me that Westminster Council had originally made a deal with Park-O-Meter but the rollout was vetoed by the Council of Industrial Design, a government body with a remit to promote modern products. 'In a great flap they came to my door,' he said. 'It coincided with my just going on honeymoon, so I took the job with me. Bought all the plasticine I could find in the Italian resort and cobbled the new covers to the US mechanism and came home, made a model and the rest is history ...'

'The whole point of the story', he continued, 'is that the government - Labour - went on and virtually founded our profession'. The parking meter made the career of the designer who would go on to design, among other things, the Kodak Instamatic camera, the Kenwood Chef and the Inter City 125 Train. His design for the meter was an elegant, extremely contemporary piece of street furniture which looks, ironically, far more modern than the chunky black boxes deployed today. It was, as he explains, very much a part of the Council of Industrial Design project to overlay an infrastructure of modernism on the UK's mostly Victorian streets.

The parking meter, like the streetlight, became a motif of modernity, a tool mediating between the metropolis and the automobile, a hunk of metal rooted in the pavement, part barrier, part merging of car body with urbanity. It was accompanied by a vast thread of yellow lines across the country, which have arguably disfigured streetscapes in a web of paint which can look like graphic overkill.

The lines are still there, but the meters have virtually all disappeared. The advent of digital meters and smartphone technology made the coin-operated versions almost obsolete. Their functions were amalgamated into blocky black machines which are now all that survive of this former pavement population.

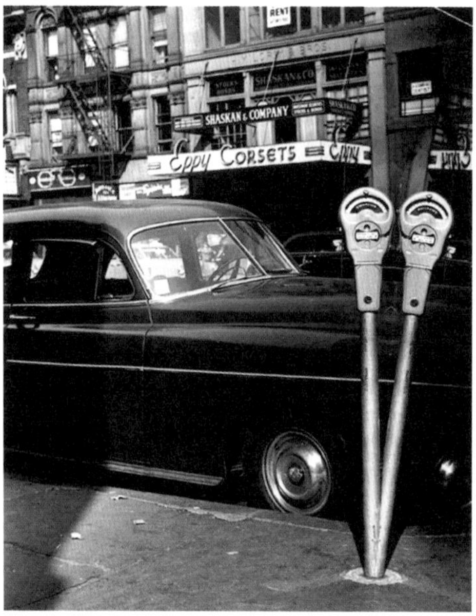

Street Scene Distortion, 1950
Weegee (Arthur Fellig)

Greening

It is a paradox, perhaps, that some of any city's best street furniture is sited not on streets at all. The building of parks proved the perfect display space for coherent new suites of street furniture. Parks became a shopfront for the civilising effects of everything from benches and drinking fountains to public art and public conveniences, creating an urbane effect in a simulation of nature, the best of both worlds without ever quite being either city or country.

From the early 18th century the park became a place apart, a site where social classes could mix, or at least achieve proximity, in a way inconceivable in other settings. These parks, like St James Park and Green Park in London or the Tuileries and Luxembourg in Paris, were likely to have been either former royal hunting grounds or palace gardens, green places which already had a presence in the city. In the mid-19th century new parks began to appear, carved out either from existing sites (such as Victoria Park in East London in 1842, the city's first new park) or planned at the same time as the city's expansion (such as Central Park in New York City in 1857–76).

The 19th-century public park was conceived as an antidote to the city but still within its boundaries, a space intended to be the opposite of everything the city stood for: congestion, density, pollution, intensity, hardness of surface, proximity, noise. In an era when walking in the streets was dirty, muddy and dangerous, the parks were a pleasant retreat, their paths far cleaner than the pavements. Parks were designed to accommodate walking for its own sake, for public display and encounter. They were, ironically, the most metropolitan element of the city and achieved their urbanity precisely through denying their presence in a city at all.

Their arrival of parks as a truly public urban amenity coincided with the proliferation of industrially produced street furniture, part of the same impulse for metropolitan improvement. So it makes sense that they should have become repositories for the finest examples of this emerging public art form. From gaslights in London or Berlin's Tiergarten to benches in Central Park and chairs in Paris, much of the best urban furniture is not on the street but on those elegant faux-rural paths running through the park.

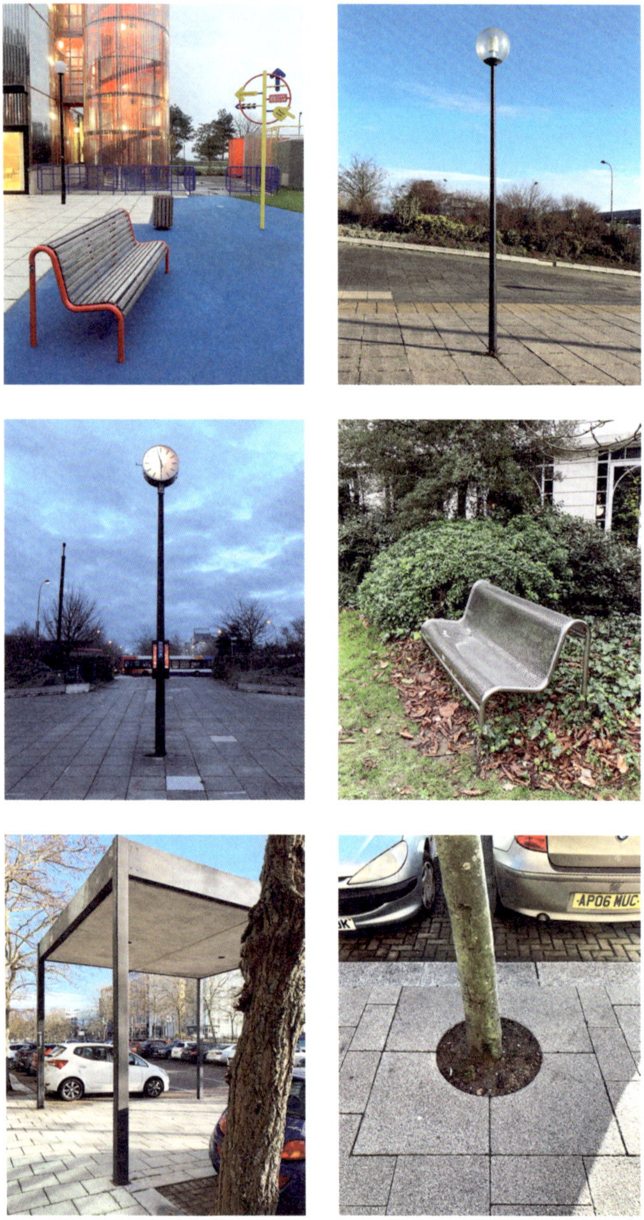

Scenes from Milton Keynes

Gridding

In one town more than any other in Britain, street furniture was fluently interwoven with a language that was simultaneously globally modern and particularly English. Designed in the late 1960s and largely executed in the 1970s and '80s, Milton Keynes was a curious and eclectic amalgam of an Americanised, car-centric grid, of corporate modernity and a fondness for the picturesque landscape, and a curious nostalgia for a hippyish interest in ley lines and stone circles. Architect Sam Jacob dubbed it, perceptively, the 'Electric Pastoral'.

The street furniture was always conceived as an integral element. The architects of the Milton Keynes Development Corporation (a state-run agency founded in 1967) spent a huge amount of time building a vocabulary of urban fittings which were placed precisely at the junctions of paving stones (in the corner perfectly between four slabs) and huge granite kerbs. It was an exercise in creating identity and continuity, ascribing value to the public elements of the plan rather than adding them in as afterthoughts. Gathered together in a series of loose-leaf information sheets, the 1975 *Infrastructure Pack* (now a cult object) included designs for streetlights, benches, signage, paving, playground equipment and much, much more.

The lighting, for instance, was a delight: slender, subtly tapering columns capped by a frosted glass globe - an echo, perhaps, of the 1968 *Earthrise* photo taken from Apollo 8 and used that same year on the cover of Stewart Brand's *Whole Earth Catalog*, often cited as a kind of pre-digital precursor to the internet. The original lights, many of which have been replaced, remain remarkably elegant and easy to distinguish from later, clunkier models. The benches (designed by Brian Milne) were similarly an exemplar of late modern design, the tail-end of Britain as a manufacturing power. Their curving perforated metal and tubular structure has proven durable, with many still dotted around the parks and green spaces of the new town. And then there were the porte-cochères designed by Derek Walker, the architect who laid out Milton Keynes and designed its epic Shopping Building. These Mies van der Rohe-inspired structures created public shelters between buildings and roads - a nod, perhaps, to the canopies of upscale New York apartment blocks, but clearly delineated as public spaces. They ensured a dash of pure modernity amidst the tree-lined streets and large corporate structures, an intermediary between the anonymity of late modern architecture, the intimacy of the street and the space between car, bus and building. Now they seem to have been mostly appropriated as smoking shelters. This golden age of street furniture was surprisingly short-lived. By the mid-1980s campaigns to install more traditional products were in full swing, with modernism now being associated with municipal housing. The meticulously built-up catalogue of modernist street furniture was abandoned.

Today the effect of that carefully conceived and designed landscape of street furniture has been significantly diluted by the insertion of hundreds of off-the-shelf faux-historical items from benches to bollards, illustrating how quickly that coherence can dissipate. But as one of the most concerted and considered attempts to define a new town through the design of its most seemingly unassuming of elements, Milton Keynes remains a fascinating and enduring experiment.

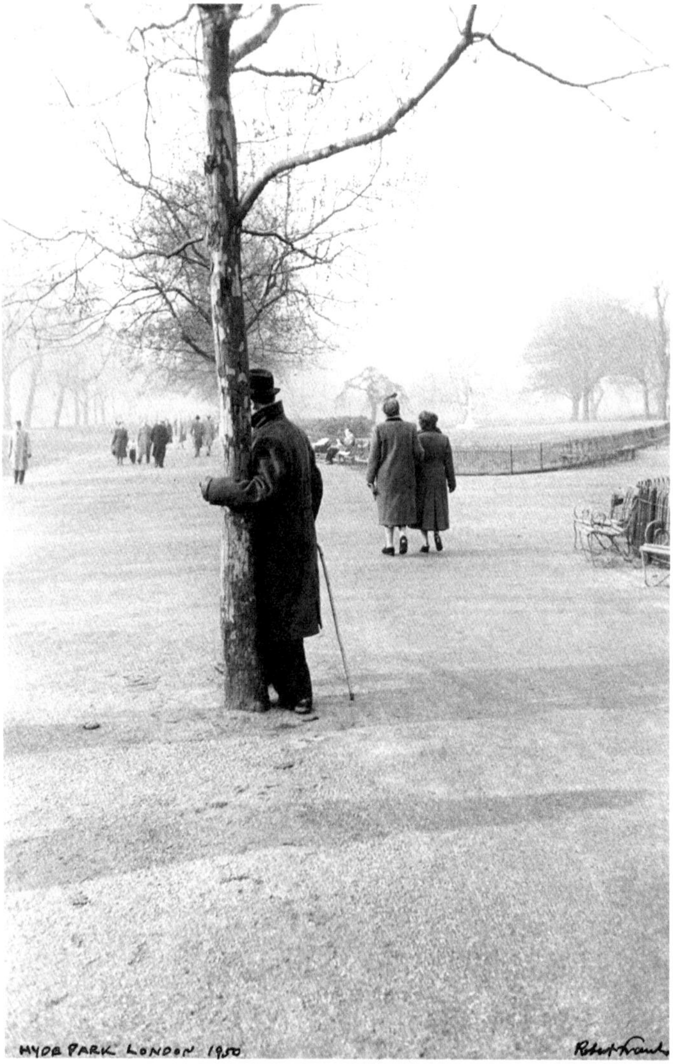

Hyde Park, London, 1950
Robert Frank

Growing

Trees might seem to be a category error here, but the cages that contain them and the cast-iron gratings that allow water to filter through to their roots belong firmly in the taxonomy of street furniture. And trees are here not only because they are, arguably, the most visible of all items of street furniture, but because they are transformative and endlessly beautiful.

Trees are the toughest and yet the most sensitive of urban inhabitants. As spindly youths, they require protection from everything from dogs to cars (some are placed in growing sacks), but as sturdy adults they become hefty urban bouncers, impervious to almost everything the city throws at them and, almost miraculously, cleaning up the air of the streets.

As they grow, trees begin to bulge through neighbouring railings, they envelop postboxes and bollards, swallowing them up in their barky bellies, squeezing through fences and making walls billow like sails and tarmac blister up like lava. Trees are the hooligans of street furniture, unpredictable, unwilling to be contained, always doing damage. Yet, as they blossom, and as green shoots appear and birds nest in their branches, they are also the most magnificent of all street adornments - constantly changing, endlessly accommodating, giving shade from the sun, shelter from the rain, branches for the birds and the rustling sound of leaves you might just hear if the traffic has died down. They are utterly cheering.

One of the earliest photos of a city, Louis Daguerre's *Boulevard du Temple* (p.101), depicts the infancy of Paris's then still precarious street trees. A row of delicate looking examples, some already apparently damaged or dead, creates a diagonal through the frame. At the lower left corner a fellow stands with one foot on a shoe-polisher's box. These figures were among the first humans ever captured on camera, but they represent only a smudge. Instead it's the white flank walls and the contrast of the row of dark trees that constitute the real subject here.

A little less than a century later, Brassaï pointed his lens to create *Winding Stream* (1932), which is, of course, nothing of the sort. It shows a serpentine kerb, and a puddle following it around, which appears to be swerving to avoid a pair of trees. By now the trees are firmly embedded in the Parisian streets as mature, solid, rooted citizens. You see it too in his photo of the shadows they cast on the grim walls of the Santé prison, as if they were inscribed on the most solid structure in the city, intertwined with its mass, intimations of the timber gallows or the guillotine. In other pictures Paris's trees appear as vertical elements, as much a part of the urban street furniture as the lampposts and the *colonnes Morris*. The trees were every bit as much a part of Haussmann's design as the Mansard roofs, the heavily modelled facades and the elaborate streetlights and furniture, and Brassaï captures this in depicting them as vertical elements in the city, always hanging into views, exerting their presence, framing, foregrounding, casting shadows, catching the light. In portraying a bench in the Tuileries Gardens with a kissing couple, the curve of the slats appears as the completion of the sinuous lines of the tree behind them. It's a completely theatrical shot, perfectly framed, almost twee. But the bare, skeletal tree imposes itself with gravitas. In his shot *The Stairs of Montmartre*, the lampposts and the trees march up the steps in parallel columns of light and dark. And occasionally, as in his portrait of a plane tree (*Platane Parisienne*), the trunk is all that is shown, a pillar as robust as any iron post but delicate in its decoration, the complex patterns on its bark creating a dappled black and white Pointillism. The tree has become a Parisian, an inhabitant of the city streets that is as much an organic part as the hookers, the sweepers, the lovers and the drunks.

The mid-19th century streets of Paris and London were often better suited to trees than are the streets of our own day. Cobbled surfaces allowed water to filter down into their roots, and the subterranean realm was less carved up by services than it is today. Overhead cables had not arrived in such a big way and double-decker buses and juggernauts had yet to arrive, so the crowns of the trees remained largely unmolested. The trees were smaller and their roots had not yet spread so far, so the need to pollard them with intense brutality, to artificially maintain them as growth-restricted teenagers, had not yet become widespread. That constant pollarding, incidentally, gives the timber from street trees a wonderful knottiness, almost useless for carpenters but beautiful in its own way with a dense figuring. Contemporary streets of tarmac treat them less kindly, their roots and branches are brutalised by subsequent interventions and excavations. Yet they survive.

Trees inhabit the streets just as do the people, their verticality and reaching for the light a parallel to ours. But their relationship to place is more intimate and more permanent. In 19th-century photos the presence of the trees is more vivid than that of people, who can't help but move and blur themselves over long exposures. Trees stand still and reappear in later photos of those same spots, larger, more spread out, their trunks thicker. In parks the trees might be drawn from across the world, planted from seeds brought from imperial outposts as part of the great colonial project. London's plane tree, for instance, is a hybrid of two trees taken from opposite sides of the globe - the oriental plane and the American sycamore - which came about by accident when two examples were planted in close proximity in the Vauxhall garden of John Tradescant and cross-pollinated, to create the now ubiquitous London street tree. Their hardiness, their relatively modest root systems and resistance to pollution, made them the default urban tree in cities across the world - tough, long-lived, resilient and handsome (if also a bit of a bother to those with allergies). The wonderful plane trees in Mayfair's Berkeley Square were planted in the year of the French Revolution: 1789.

Elsewhere in the world it might be the palms, upright and spiky, which define the streetscape. The appearance of those spindly trunks and shaggy tops is emblematic of warmth, a visual cipher that never fails to jolt. Los Angeles and Florida knew it well, their palms were all part of the real estate sales pitch: look, here you are, at home *and* on vacation. The affecting final scene of John Schlesinger's *Midnight Cowboy* in which, after an endless bus journey from New York, the palm trees of the Florida highways making their first tentative appearance make you understand that this unlikely pair, the cowboy and the con-man, have left their old lives behind. As a child, my first glimpse of the slightly shabby palms on Weymouth's seafront in Dorset convinced me I had arrived somewhere more exotic than might have really been the case. Throughout Asia and the Gulf, palm trees serve a similar purpose - to promote an identity through something instantly recognisable, to bring an archetype into the streetscape. They often need less care than steel poles and road signs, yet they create a skyline where there is precious little else with minimal means. The same goes for the tall cypresses in Italy. Their verticality makes them every bit as architectural as the buildings they punctuate, elements in the skyline able to define a route, frame a view, create a contrast in colour and form, permeate the sun-scorched air with scent.

There is a growing understanding of the ways in which trees communicate, through root systems and fungi and through the release of chemicals. It seems to suggest that we should be planting trees together, in groves or clusters. This was something already being recommended in the 1970s - my Design Council guide (see p.61), for example, suggests it as a way of creating a ‘focus’. Here the designers were probably thinking of visual effect and shade, but we might think of the trees themselves a little too. Why should we leave them alone? Their systems foreshadow the smart, connected technologies of today but with none of the sinister undertones of surveillance, data harvesting and control.

Trees are perhaps the least appreciated of all items of street furniture, but it is time we understood them as the wonderful hybrids that they are - extreme artifice and the organic, urbanity and nature in one.

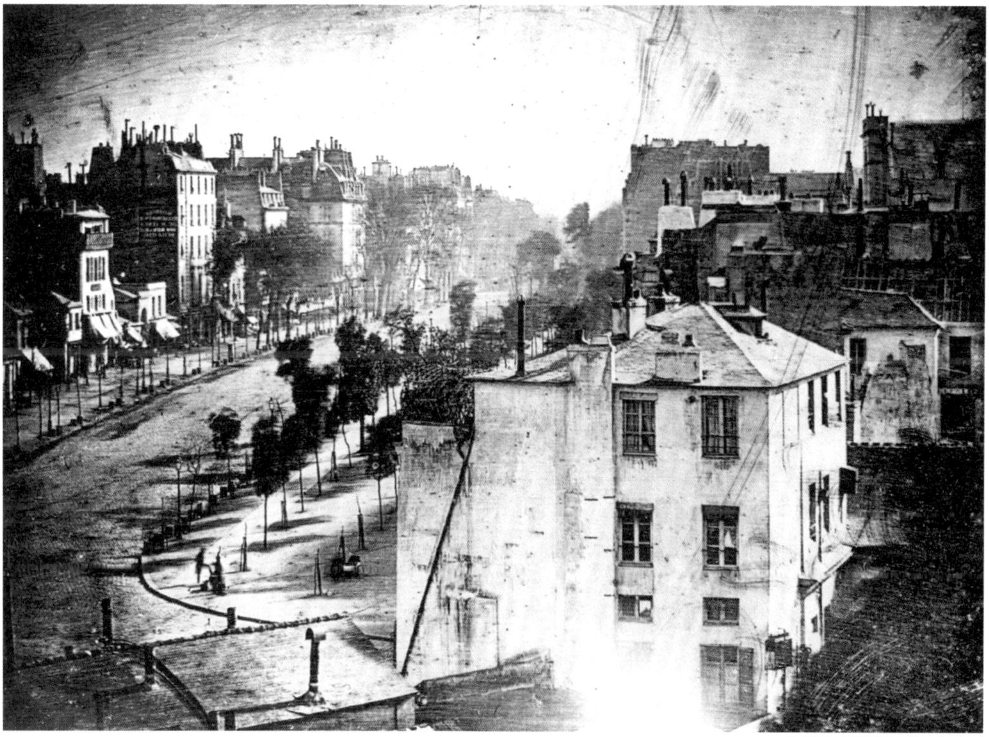

Boulevard du Temple, Paris, 1838
Louis Daguerre

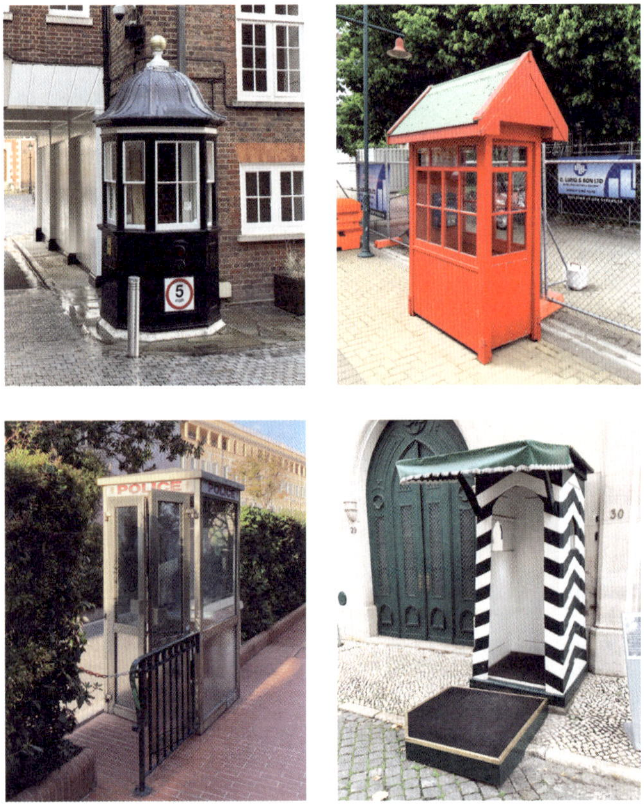

Top row, left: *Temple, London*; right: *Christchurch, New Zealand*
Bottom row, left: *Monaco;* right: *Lisbon*

Guarding

The world of architecture theory was, for much of its existence, obsessed with the idea of the primitive hut, the origins of architecture, the first forest dwelling. Where did it all begin and how can we get back there? What is the essence of architecture? The original language? But it always remained an unattainable archetype, perhaps just a bower of trees, a simple structure of sticks, a shed - too primitive for modern dwelling. There could never be any archaeology for something so impermanent. But that most basic unit, the ur-architecture, appears on the street in hundreds of forms. It is there in the toll booth and again in the sentry box. It is present in the guardhouse and the security guard's cabin, the seaside pier kiosk and the Japanese koban. And just as the primitive hut was all about an idea of security and safety in the dangerous, elemental world of the forest, so these little structures are dedicated to guarding or protecting, although usually they are about keeping you out or charging you to enter, rather than keeping you safe.

There's something slightly absurd about these structures, the miniaturisation, the extreme 'houseness' of something that is clearly nothing like a house. Take the sentry box, usually designed to accommodate a towering bearskin busby or some complicated hat atop a guardsmen with fanatically polished boots, buttons and belt and a sword or a rifle. The whole ensemble looks like a toy, an anachronistic, colourfully uniformed soldier that comes in its own readymade full-size box. The box is tailored to fit, an attenuated primitive hut for a standing form, a kind of upright, preemptive military coffin. It might be decorated in national colours like the odd, red toy box design for the guards outside Copenhagen's Royal Palace or in a dark blue-green and gold with faux marble that is designed, presumably, to look royal and expensive outside London's palaces. Or it might be a complex proto-postmodern golden beach hut, like the Neoclassical versions in Stockholm with their bauble and spike tops. Or they could even have danger stripes like those in Prague Castle (and the Nazi ones in old *Commando* comics, I seem to remember). But they all feature the farcical ridiculousness of the institution and a vivid contrast with the grandeur, scale and solidity of the palaces they stand in front of. They are, quite deliberately, an architecture apart.

This, despite the visible lack of luxuries, is the top of sentry real estate, self-consciously dignified and meant to show off those uniforms and eccentric hats to full effect. The real work is done elsewhere by the hundreds of thousands of low-paid security guards who swelter in guardhouses in front of expensive mansions and private estates in those cities where inequality is at its most extreme. Whether in Johannesburg or Bogota, these guard shacks are prefabricated, mass-produced boxes which create an impression of reassurance and a very visible reminder of crises in security.

There is an extra layer of more formal police infrastructure, some of which survives and some of which is newer. The presence of police was once seen as important, not just to guard against terror or political assassination but in presenting an image of order. One particular structure in London perfectly encapsulates this slightly odd typology. At the south-east corner of Trafalgar Square is a curious lamppost that is more base than lamp. The cylindrical granite plinth is occasionally referred to as London's smallest police station, but it is actually a small lookout post designed so that a single copper can survey the square during protests and, if necessary, call for support. The lamp on top is a curious thing - an almost Expressionist lantern, it was designed to flash in times of need so that other policemen would notice. Elsewhere in the city tall blue boxes, bearing a slight resemblance to the classic K2 phonebox but much thinner, create another kind of infrastructure of police presence.

Related to these miniature guard structures are the toll booths that once stood at the entrances to bridges but have now proliferated outside cities on motorways and turnpikes. There are the streamlined Art Deco 1930s versions of US turnpikes, with sleek stainless steel trim, and the boxy European versions which more closely resemble ticket collectors' booths beneath huge gas station canopies. There is also the panoply of now abandoned Eastern European border crossings (a subject that would make a whole publication in itself) and the former checkpoints in Western Europe, now defunct since the introduction of the Schengen free movement zone. They range from the socialist pick'n'mix modernism of the Central European crossings (lovingly documented by photographer Ignacio Evangelista in his *After Schengen* series) to the mountain shacks and lodges of the Alpine crossings. Every single architectural style is here, from Mid-Century to extreme postmodern, again emphasising the toy-like nature of these structures, as if they had been made for a miniaturised layout to demonstrate the range of possible modernisms.

Architecture becomes more extreme at borders and crossings, gatehouses and front doors of palaces, as if its volume needs to be turned up for emphasis. But it comes from a tiny, tinny speaker, so it rattles and buzzes, lo-fi but high intensity. Flavours, like in a sauce, get more intense as they are reduced.

Hacking

The positioning of street furniture is intended to establish a pattern for how a space should be used. It is free and it is ostensibly well-intentioned and public-spirited, but it is also almost always prescriptive. Street furniture outlines ways of living in the city: do not come through here, do not go this way, sit here - don't lie here, do not throw this kind of rubbish here, only this kind. Signage, for instance, is almost always prohibitive.

Street furniture at its best can be generous - a bench, a water fountain, a shelter - but much of the time it is authoritarian, from parking meters to bollards, signs, CCTV posts, barriers and railings. Much of it is alienating. And even those pieces that appear generous, park benches for instance, tend to be arranged in rows so that it becomes difficult to gather in a group and chat because everyone is sitting beside each other at widely spaced intervals.

The proliferation of POPS (privately owned public spaces, which first emerged in New York as far back as the early 1960s) has exacerbated the deception of spaces which appear to be public - and which may once have been public - being controlled by privately employed security guards who pounce on any infringements of the screeds of rules, from not taking photographs to no skateboarding. The issue came to the fore in London and New York during the Occupy protests of 2011 when protestors set up camp outside the London Stock Exchange and Zuccotti Park in Lower Manhattan. They were removed from the former, eventually settling in the churchyard of St Paul's Cathedral (surrounded, incidentally, by the oldest surviving cast-iron railings in the city), but were allowed to stay on sufferance of the owner in New York. The stone seating and ledges of Zuccotti Park proved particularly hospitable to a convivial atmosphere of conversation and public events. In London the accommodation was more ad hoc, with the steps in front of the cathedral forming a kind of natural raked theatre.

POPS are usually heavily supplied with street furniture, with benches as landscaping, planters that double as truck-stoppers, CCTV, bollards and so on - security disguised as amenity. These heavily defended and surveilled spaces are presented as public but are in fact exclusive, in that they will only tolerate certain behaviours and modes of occupation, tied to consumption. Protest is impossible, photography often banned, the homeless are made unwelcome, as are drinkers and, often, larger groups of young people.

The Occupy protests proved that it is possible to hack these spaces but only if the owners acquiesce. There are instances where people have reconfigured seating in parks or piazzas to make it more convivial, moving benches around or adding a table to a small ensemble of seating. Often it doesn't take much to radically alter a place. There are some striking examples of artists and activists subverting street advertising. These billboard hacks present unbeatable platforms for political statements and Dadaist tricks, often employing the visual language of corporate advertising so that the viewer is initially not aware that these are hacks at all. Now that so much street furniture has been outsourced to private companies (with outfits like J.C. Decaux and Adshel rolling out products across the urban landscape from bus stops and advertising columns), it has become a platform for ads as much as an amenity but, of course, its real raison d'être is profit and not people. And increasingly its real use is data harvesting.

There are subtler methods of subversion than occupying, ways in which street furniture can be used in a manner that was never intended. The most common is the lamppost or telegraph pole noticeboards, with lost dogs, cleaning services, man and a van, English lessons, wrapped around the pole and pasted down. There are temporary, harmless hacks which can be surprisingly effective. I liked the skateboards slotted between the slats of a park bench to make a little table for drinks. I also thought the appropriation of now-defunct and empty newspaper vending machines as planters (by opening the glass door and filling it up with earth) was wittily provocative. There has also been a wave of miniaturisation, placing tiny models in boot-scraper holes or other gaps, little scenarios with figures and plants that easily veer into the twee territory of decorating trees with doors for elves and fairies. There have also been outbreaks - at different levels - of street art, painting communications boxes to look very convincingly like miniaturised panel housing blocks in a hyper-real style (notably the artist EVOL in Germany). These can have an uplifting wit about them.

The fashion for guerrilla knitting or yarn bombing sits somewhere around here too, the practice of wrapping posts or poles in crocheted cardigans or putting wooly hats on bollards or pillarboxes. Often understood as a feminist practice, in which craft is applied to the mass-manufactured, increasingly militarised fittings of the public realm, it presents an interesting and colourful alternative to graffiti. Unlike the latter it is removable and reversible, and not technically illegal. But it does allow for expression through making, and its intimate relationship with street furniture makes it one of the few widely spread hacking practices. At its most extreme it can be visually arresting and thought-provoking, though I am never entirely sure which thoughts are being provoked.

Guerrilla gardening, the appropriation of urban land to plant greenery or even vegetables, has a similar profile, not necessarily vandalism but not quite legit either. It has a long history, arguably stretching back to the Diggers, or the True Levellers, in 17th-century England. The Diggers attempted to grow food on common land, reappropriating for the people what should already have been theirs. The contemporary, often slightly less confrontational, approach does something similar, seeing space as a resource not to be wasted and plants as a common good.

One of the more recent hacks has been of parking space. The setting up of parklets and seating in parking slots has been used to highlight the huge amount of space taken up by stationary cars in cities (see p.197). One appealing hack in France consisted of a cardboard box about the size of a pizza box, designed to convert anti-parking bollards into stand-up café tables.

A number of designers have come up with seats and surfaces to transform bollards and street sign poles into furniture, or even playground items like mini-roundabouts. Others have designed tools allowing poles to be converted into kick-boxing training pads or multi-gyms and there have been projects to create entire ecosystems of tables, chairs and loungers up the sides of broad public stairs.

These work well as temporary events, installations and provocations, with instant appeal to design and architecture students who yearn to make an impact in the public realm and the real world after working so long in the studio. They facilitate moments of joy, participation and transformation, which is always admirable, and they have the added benefit of making people think about the way in which public space is used or, more pertinently, the way it is wasted. But they rarely have a lasting impact, partly due to the lack of uniformity in fittings (which makes roll-outs impossible) but also due to the additional problems they are perceived to cause: concerns about health and safety, responsibility, crowding and so on. They can, of course, be tremendous fun.

Brandalism has emerged as a response to corporate advertising and the takeover of everything from bus stops to toilets by advertising companies. Allowing citizens to buy the tools they need to hack into advertising sites (they're sold as art objects) enables the replacement of generic posters with artistic interventions.

There are quieter appropriations too. I was struck by seeing how in Japan, with its tiny domestic spaces, people began to use the railings outside their flats or houses as extra storage spaces. Gloves were stuck on spikes, scarves wrapped around uprights, socks were balled up and kept on porches or stretched on to the tops of railings. Japan has low crime rates but as testified by lost keys and cuddly toys left on walls near where they're found, the sentiments are universal.

The question is, who does the city belong to and who is street furniture for? If it is a part of the public realm then surely it belongs to us? And if it belongs to us should we not be able to use it in more ingenious and dynamic ways? Is street furniture a layer of things which affirms our right to the city, or is it a stratum which undermines it?

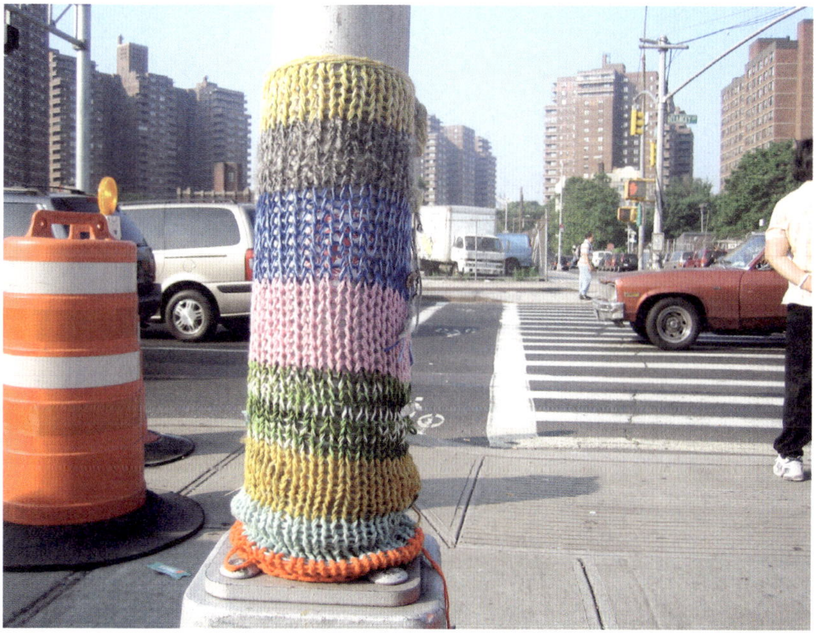

Knitta on Delancey, New York, 2016
Photograph by Noah Sussman

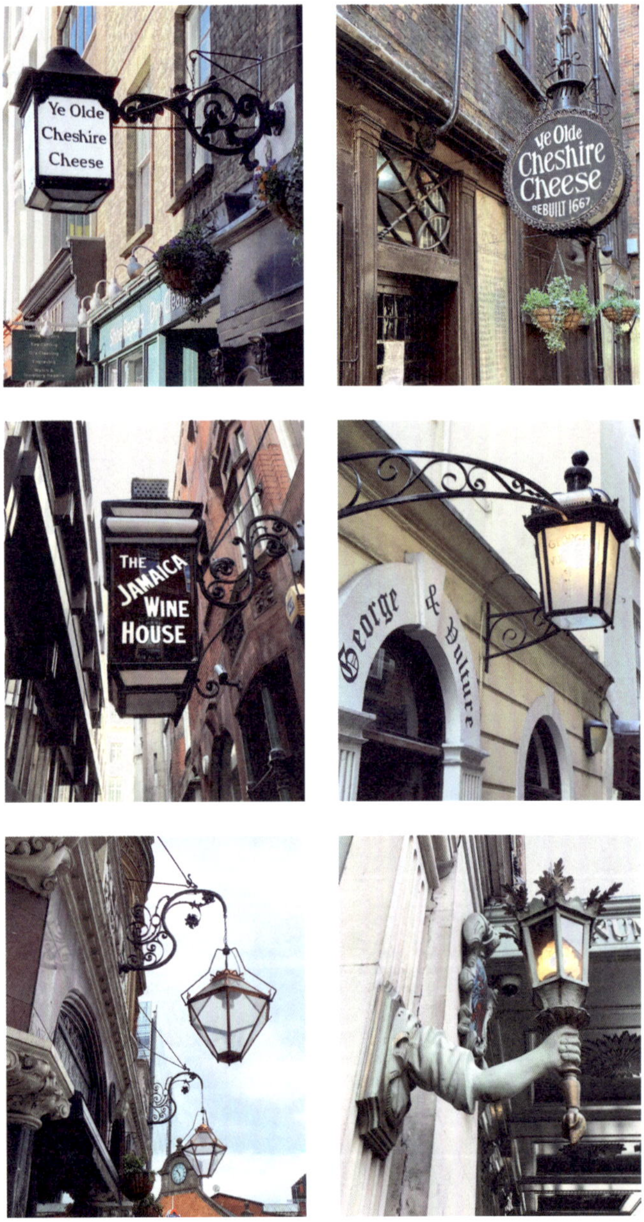

Pub and shop lanterns and signs, London

Hanging

Before there were publicly provided streetlights, there were lanterns. The street was rarely entirely dark. The first streetlamps were on the sides of buildings, private infrastructure illuminating the public realm. In Renaissance Italy only the wealthiest families were allowed to mount 'cressets' on their walls. These were wrought-iron cages or baskets filled with a snake-like coil of rope soaked in pitch and lit each evening. There is a nice 16th-century Italian example hanging, slightly forlorn, in the Cast Courts of the V&A in London. High up on the wall, it seems to be largely unlooked at. Twisted iron uprights and barley-sugar strips coiled around the base all suggest the black rope that would have burnt inside the basket, and flattened leaves lick out like flames. The form announced the purpose almost perfectly, even in its blackened, scorched iron, itself forged in the fire.

For much of the medieval era in Europe's age of walled cities, curfews were imposed at night and people were forbidden to be outside their homes after a certain time, often surprisingly early. Authority always feared the night, and the safest measure was to lock everybody inside. Order and empty streets were maintained by constables or soldiers.

The earliest streetlighting was a status symbol. The palaces of the wealthy were illuminated in a gesture that was both self-aggrandising and a public good, like the benches Italian architects often built into the heavily rusticated bases of their palazzi. In the narrow alleys of Mediterranean towns, lamps remained on the walls as the obligation to light the street passed from the private to the public. Where there was no room to place a post, lanterns were mounted on walls, their wiring adding to the spaghetti of cables and connections threaded across the outsides of houses. The effect is very different, more intimate and domestic. A surprising number of old lanterns with wrought-iron lamps and brackets survive, suspended like fruit just above head height. Anyone walking the backstreets of Venice after dark will notice the effect of lanterns hung above doors, strung between buildings, on shopfronts or at gondola stations. By bringing the light lower down, closer to eye-level and eschewing tall, freestanding lights, the lamps illuminate the middles of buildings rather than their roofs, amplifying the colours of paint and peeling plaster, the russets and rusts, the mustards and ochres. There is a warmth which spreads across the walls.

In Britain, lamps survived in one specific setting. British pubs could be easily spotted in the smog thanks to their huge hanging lanterns suspended, usually from a corner, on florid curlicues of wrought iron. Their outsize dimensions made them impossible to confuse with anything else. Many of these have disappeared, but where they survive they can be stunning, insanely caricatured combinations of aggrandisement and advertising. St Stephen's Tavern in Westminster, still a site of political gossip and intrigue, boasts a beauty with a pub sign lettered above and Ye Olde Cheshire Cheese in Fleet Street has two, one on either side, more modest but inventive. The Swan in the middle of Hammersmith Broadway features lanterns all around, visible from every busy angle.

The rise of cities as entities and identities led, eventually, to councils and public authorities taking on responsibility for lighting, blanketing whole metropolitan areas in night light. But the survival of a few of these huge lamps gives a hints of a more highlighted streetscape.

Hoarding

Advertising is so ubiquitous in the city that we barely notice it. Except, perhaps, for hoardings. Billboards are static and feature a changing array of ads which we can choose to ignore but, when moving through the city, we might suddenly find that a familiar building is wrapped in hoarding, advertising its own demolition or disembowelling and a future as something more expensive. The developer's site hoarding is surely one of the most visible and high-profile contributions to contemporary graphic culture, particularly in London. Yet these highly visible super-graphics, which might define our streetscapes for the many years a construction project can take, are little commented on or controlled. If a culture can be best read through its streets, London could be read through the moronic marketing and numbingly dumb aphorisms of its developers. It is a view of a city constantly being rebranded and financialised. And it is not pretty.

The images used by real estate companies to promote their developments have been a constant irritant and a needling reminder of the churn, the commodification, gentrification and architectural homogenisation of a city. Swathes of cities and their pavements have been given over to a property-porn reimagining of an idealised, globalised city, but mostly this is a story about London and its reinvention as a real-estate safe deposit box for the suspiciously generated spare cash around in the offshore accounts of the global super-rich. Of course there is always going to be top-end property speculation - the city's economy, in large part, depends on it - but to push it in peoples' faces, often those whose families are being displaced, is decidedly uncool.

These hoardings have become more than advertising. They are ingratiating attempts to create a *narrative,* to turn speculation into a story. This is not the simple selling of a product but the marketing of a lifestyle, fully formed and simpering. There is no single approach, but it is worth looking in detail at some of the more popular tropes. There is, of course, the glamorous young couple on their balcony, champagne in hand, looking over the twinkling lights of the city below. He will be wearing a tux, bow tie nonchalantly undone (this is the cypher for real wealth, not a sticky dickie but the real thing, Rat-Pack style). He will have slightly floppy hair, a post-yuppie of unspecified employment and patronising demeanour somewhere between Patrick Bateman and Christian Grey. She will be flawless in her backless gown, satin or silk, perhaps wearing a simple diamond pendant, sparkling just a little. They will be smiling. Smug at their own superiority. This typology can be employed by any aesthetically challenged development in even the least glamorous part of town, because the building itself remains invisible (expect for the glass balcony front, a dematerialised cipher for an anonymous non-building) and because, from that height, any piece of the city, even one dominated by railway sidings or concrete road infrastructure, can look spectacular. This is Google-Earth architecture, a city stripped of grain or detail or (real) people, a place to be *overlooked.*

Then there is also the opposite approach. This is characterised by beards, tattoos and leather aprons. This style will feature hairy men and, perhaps, at a push, mixed-heritage women (an embrace of diversity). They will be working hard, treating a top-end espresso machine like a multi-gym, flexing their biceps and working their retro tats to manufacture a serious flat white. This is the hipster Stakhanovite end of the thing. Real work for creative workers, creative industry. These ads attempt to embed the development (almost certainly invisible in the generic pics) in the area, to build on the characteristics which have made this once-mixed and now rapidly gentrifying neighbourhood popular with the young wealthy who now cannot afford where they would have actually wanted to live. Shoreditch gives way to Hoxton which gives way to Dalston which gives way to Walthamstow, Peckham... you get the picture. This place, the place going up behind the flattened-out pictures of flat white artisanship, is the next big thing, *authentic*. It is also, of course, part of the thing that will make this place too expensive and squeeze out the last vestiges of what made it a real piece of city. This trope is a non-ironic representation of the authenticity it is itself killing.

One other noticeable type is the market-shopping couple. These urban pioneers (probably heterosexual - remember hoardings must not offend the sensibilities of Saudi princes or the families of African autocrats) laugh and hug their way through smiling stallholders and assorted beefy butchers, meat curers and cheese artisans. This is frontline consumerism, buyers buying into as yet non-existent traditional businesses with long lists of provenances.

Then there is what we might call generic luxury. This is a place which has nothing going for it, no height, no neighbourhood, so it needs to convince consumers that what looks suspiciously like a South London traffic island will be *the* place to be. Having failed to produce convincing imagery of authenticity, artisans or architectural elegance, these hoardings will rely on faux-luxury branding. The hoarding becomes a wraparound emblazoned with a vaguely familiar monogram created by a marketing agency to be reminiscent of something else: the 'C' for Chanel or the interlocking 'LV's of Louis Vuitton for instance. But there is always something wrong with it. The effect is a little like smiling at a 'Channel' bag or 'Hike' trainers in the old Mong Kok market. In the wake of One Hyde Park becoming a byword for oligarchitecture it will have some spurious designation, often made to sound vaguely Manhattany like 'One Central Park', 'One Hundred City Heights' or 'One Midtown'. And then there is the bullshit. The meaningless words and superlatives hastily conjured up by marketeers in cafés and plastered in spindly, sans serif fonts across pastel shades: 'Live life to the full every day of the week', 'It is more fun at the top', 'A world class outlook', 'Luxury in the heart of the city', 'Natural beauty taken to new heights of sophistication', 'Massive icon, intimate place' (these are all, by the way, real).

It isn't all bad. There are a few witty interventions. Sometimes there is the odd phenomenon of a huge 1:1 rendering of the building about to go up (or be restored) behind, which can be visually arresting, an architectural trompe l'oeil. Then there are the more sculptural efforts. There are 3D book spines, pencils and classical colonnades. There are green walls and fake green walls, and developers who invite street artists to daub their boards, a move which always seems to sterilise an art that should be illicit. Of course, you don't want the hoarding to be better than the building so that the unveiling is a disappointment, so there are limits.

Victorian engravings and photos of London's streets show a city in flux. Hoardings were everywhere, plastered in playbills, freakshow and circus posters, quack ads and snake-oil product promotions. Paris had its *colonnes Morris*, city-sanctioned pillars for pasting advertising, London had its construction sites, the scraggy edges of which became a way to read the city and understand its critical commercial undercurrents: one, an ideal city designed to last, the other a site of endless churn, expressing itself through the framing of change.

The wrapping around a construction project tells us as much about the nature of the contemporary city as the development itself. So what do these vacuous, irritating and smug promotional images say about the state of the city? And do we want to know? In fact hoardings are intensely architectural, they represent the genesis of a building and could be used inventively as a means to embed a site into a city's consciousness. Beautiful wrapping can be more than half the pleasure of a present. These hoardings could be that. But they are not.

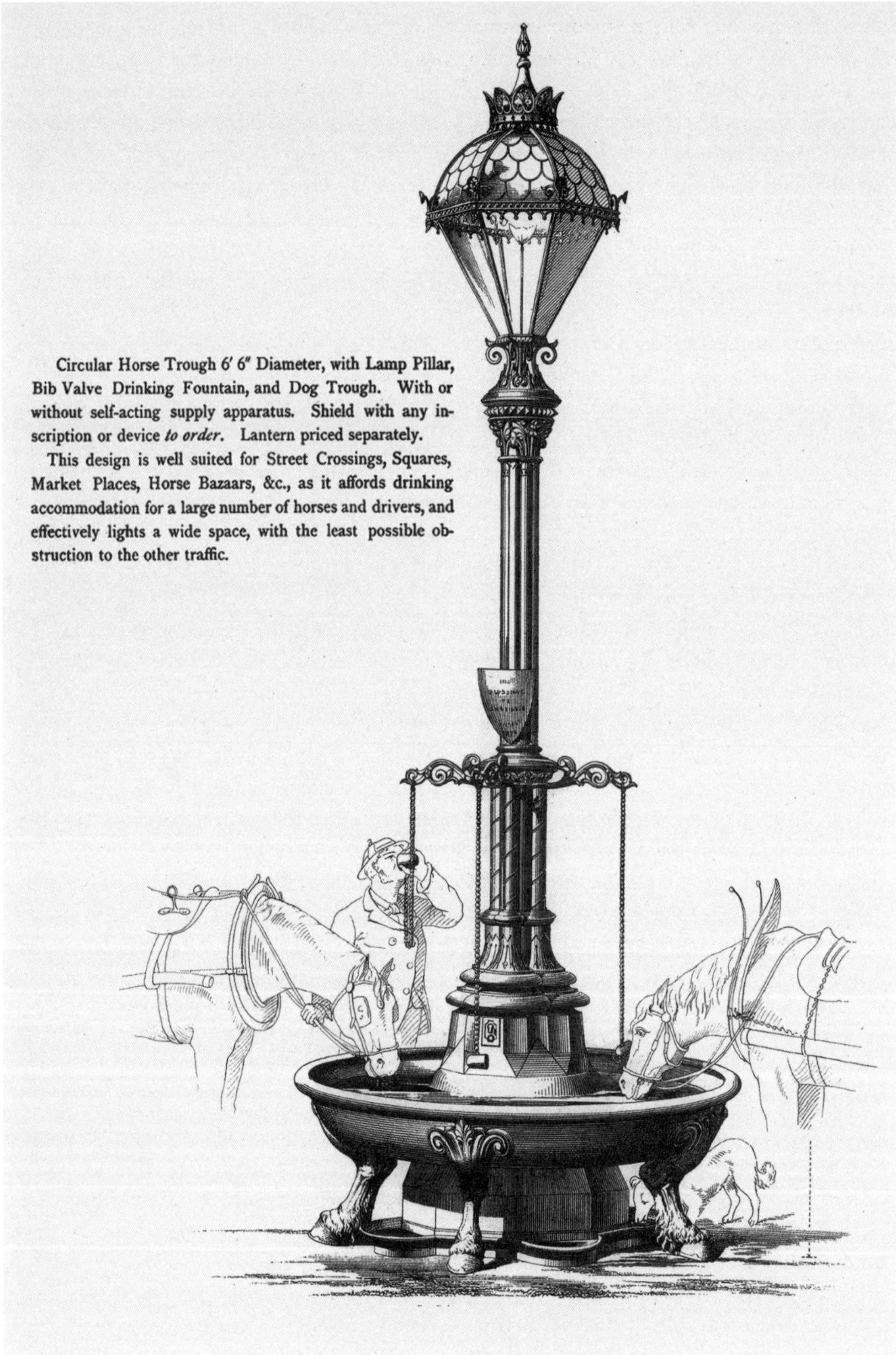
Circular Horse Trough 6′ 6″ Diameter, with Lamp Pillar, Bib Valve Drinking Fountain, and Dog Trough. With or without self-acting supply apparatus. Shield with any inscription or device *to order*. Lantern priced separately.

This design is well suited for Street Crossings, Squares, Market Places, Horse Bazaars, &c., as it affords drinking accommodation for a large number of horses and drivers, and effectively lights a wide space, with the least possible obstruction to the other traffic.

Multi-functional water trough design, from catalogue published by Walter MacFarlane & Co. Saracen Foundry, Glasgow (Volume II, 6th edition, c.1882)

Hybridising

Occasionally, an item of street furniture will pop up as the Swiss Army knife of the genre. Most you would hardly notice: traffic lights with signs sticking out of them, lampposts with traffic lights cantilevered off them, signposts with cigarette butt collectors added on, multi-directional signs with dustbins strapped on, planters with benches around them. The intent is hardly new. Gordon Cullen's drawings of the visual pollution of the British landscape in the *Architectural Review*'s 'Outrage' issue (see p.139) are indignantly ripe with examples of overburdened street furniture. Photos of Breezewood, Pennsylvania (dubbed 'Gas Vegas') do something even more extreme, standing in as a cipher for the visual chaos of the US interstate landscape. Edward Burtynsky's are probably the best known, but there are dozens of others, popping up to illustrate everything from climate crisis and traffic to planning and exurban sprawl.

This half-mile strip of filling stations and fast-food outlets could hardly be a more perfect illustration of clutter and the hybridisation of signs, with no steel post wasted when it could be supporting another piece of advertising. But it also, in its own ways, communicates something of the essence of the contemporary landscape. The mongrel mix of multi-functional fittings can generate its own unselfconscious beauty and clarity, as does a crowded urban backstreet in Tokyo or Seoul - the sheer intensity of stuff, the overhead cables, signs, paper lanterns, neons, fascias, streetlights, everything you might imagine. It can exude a steampunk sci-fi Futurism, like the sets for *Blade Runner*.

At Shibuya in Tokyo there are traffic lights cantilevered over the crossing which double up as street signs and traffic directions. One street back, there are telegraph poles with convex mirrors, streetlights and shop signs. Nothing is doing only one thing, there is too much to be done in these cities for purity. The hybrid is increasingly common on streets as advertising companies attempt to grab pavement real estate through spurious provision of charging points, benches or free Wi-Fi, in return for putting up illuminated advertising in the middle of the pedestrian path. It is not all bad: the new bus stops in Paris, at the time of writing, have water bottle refill stations strapped on to their posts alongside, of course, all the ads. Lampposts now find themselves with an extra fitting, a spherical CCTV camera hanging like rotten fruit, its dark, black eye countering the witness of the glass globes of light. Rays radiating outwards, images being sucked in.

There is nothing new in streetlights being called upon to do more than one thing. Victorian catalogues were full of multi-functional designs including lamps that doubled-up as drinking fountains, gateposts or sewer vents. But in recent years there has been a hyperinflation in the additions to their shafts which might find themselves with spiky collars, cameras or pollution-measuring devices. As big tech embeds itself ever deeper into the landscape of the street, the fashion for hybridity will inevitably accelerate producing, predictably, a few mangy mongrels and, perhaps, occasionally, something of actual utility and value. There is simultaneously something sinister about a fitting that is inscrutably trying to do too many things at once, and a touch of slapstick about a landscape of products which appear overwhelmed by all the things they are expected to do.

Imposing

There are streetlights designed to light the street but there are also massive lamps intended as urban sculpture, as something in between street furniture and a monument, something that aspires to *architecture*.

These monumental lamps create a new layer to express a hierarchy of space. Huge space needs huge lamps, objects of mass and substance able to stand their ground in the representational places of the city. The best are in Paris: the lamps, for instance, outside the Opera, where an array of excessive designs marks the zenith of urban aggrandisement. The Opera, or Palais Garnier (named after its architect Charles Garnier) was the apex of the theatrical city plan and, not incidentally, the place where Yablochkoff candles, the brilliant arclights which were the first form of electric streetlighting in the city, were first installed. These lamps had to compete with the elaborate architecture of the opera, to express something of the wonder of the new technology and to celebrate and encapsulate the City of Light and its new public space. They needed to become the external expression of the brilliant chandeliers and footlights inside, the essence of artifice embodied in the Opera as *Gesamtkunstwerk*.

The results can be quite mad. The most extreme examples merge with the architecture, their shafts stone (not cast iron) columns. With noticeboards for programmes built into their bases and dark iron capitals crowning them, they feature three galleon beakheads with vicious-looking spikes (presumably for ramming other warships), on top of which are balanced spiky-topped glass lanterns. Besides these are nude female figures cast in bronze carrying lanterns on their heads. As you get further away from the Opera, the lights get toned down a little but remain extravagant, their delicately cast forms still featuring galleons and crests until, finally, a few more steps away, the lamps become a little more restrained. These are the versions captured by photographer Charles Marville in his documenting of the new city street furniture in the 1870s (see p.78).

The same motifs appear again in the Place de la Concorde. The vast architectural inventions here, in which the lamps seem to be little more than an afterthought, were designed by Jacques-Ignace Hittorff, architect of the Gare du Nord. Exquisitely cast in bronze with incredible details of acanthus leaves and sea horses, gilded and painted, these too feature those galleon beakheads, here rendered in gold. Outside the Hôtel de la Marine, once the HQ of the French Navy, they make a little more sense here than at the Opera, but the whole design is worthy of a little consideration.

At the centre of the Place de la Concorde is the Obelisk of Luxor, one of two needles which stood outside the Temple of Luxor (the other one is still there) - a gift to the French of Muhammad Ali Pasha in 1830. In its erection in Paris's most ceremonial square, the city is representing itself as a successor to the great empires of classical civilisation. The streetlamps then had to somehow embody the grandeur of those civilisations. Hittorff chose Rome rather than Luxor (after all, the Romans had subsumed the Egyptian Empire); his design features a fluted column with a composite capital with a sculpted head (looking a little like that of the Statue of Liberty, or arguably, late Elvis) at the centre of each face. Atop is a ball wrapped with a golden band

and a spike on top of that. The spike seems to predict, rather uncomfortably, the German *Pickelhaube,* the spiked helmet worn by German soldiers who would later humiliate the French in the war of 1870. The ball represents, surely, the world and French connections and culture spanning the equator, embracing the globe. The galleons, sea horses and shells represent the seas, the acanthus, oak and laurel leaves the land, and an anchor appears, if you look long enough, between the two lamp brackets.

It merges the form of the rostral column (the Roman moment of victory) on which Rome would display the captured beaks of captured warships with a streetlight, the form for which was still emerging. It has a lot of work to do which, presumably, is why it also needs to be expressed as a column.

If street furniture is a language of objects which exists between architecture and pedestrians, this is a rarefied world of things mediating between the various scales of the monumental, between the statues and fountains, the porticoes and flagpoles. They can seem beautiful or, in another mood, wonderfully ridiculous.

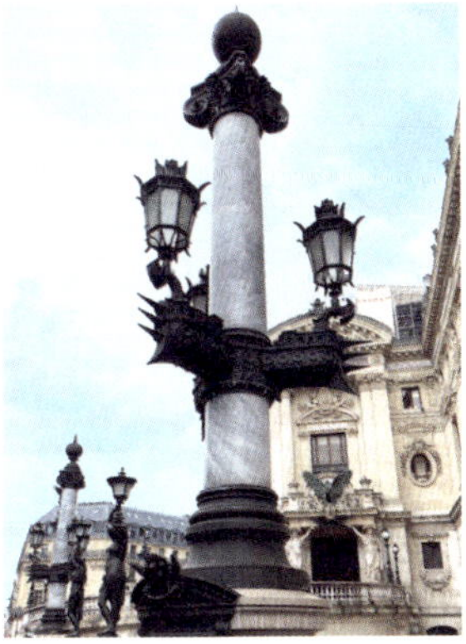
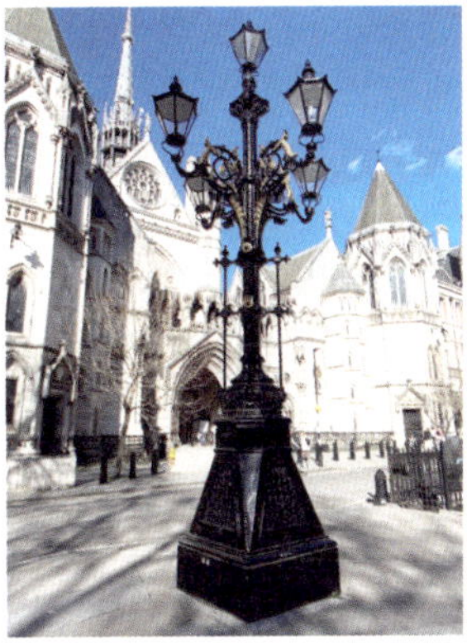
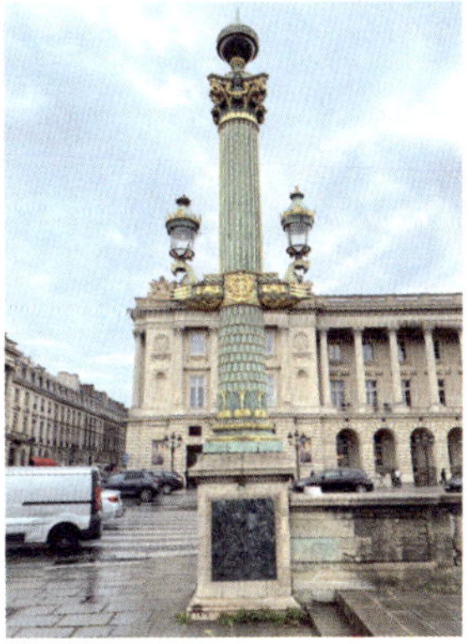

Left: *the Paris Opera*; middle: *the Law Courts, London*; right: *Place de la Concorde, Paris*

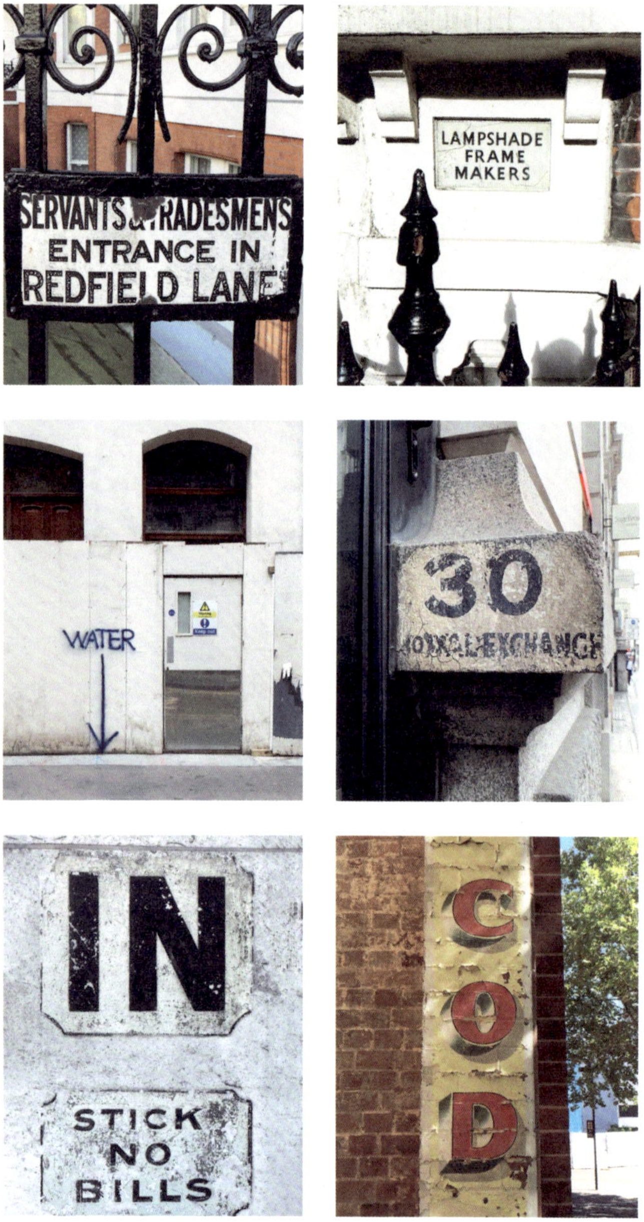

Lettering and ghost signs, London and (bottom right) *Sydney*

Lettering

To look at a photo of old London is to see a scrapbook of a city of descriptions. Every surface seems to be adorned with script, the windows, the walls, the lanterns, the signs, the doors. Seemingly everything sold in the shops on the ground floor was advertised on the façade, and what went on in the upper floors was demarcated in the windows and on the walls. Goods were seen filtered through layers of text.

There were signs for rooms to rent and offices to let, bed-and-breakfasts and services. Iron fittings had makers' marks and foundry locations cast into their bases, and shops and mansion blocks had their names spelt out in terrazzo and mosaic thresholds. Houses had their historic names alongside numbers that were only given later. This cacophony of text has faded from façades. Some has migrated on to street signs which have become their own discrete screed of directions and instructions in modernist type overlaid on the older city. But most of it has shifted from the street to the screen. The city seems a less legible place in its own terms but we read it now through our phones, through the maps and routes, the ads and location services, social media and messages. Our gaze has shifted from the city to the simulacrum, the signified to the sign and the sign to the sign of the sign.

This is not a book about signs or about lettering; there are plenty of words in here without more words about words. But the surviving text haunts the street, the ghost signs and terazzo demarcating long-gone businesses - the outline of breweries' names atop pubs which have long stopped serving, the rare survivals of architectural lettering in metalwork or in 1960s Egyptian slab serif fonts on apartment blocks and council estates. Fascia boards are periodically removed, revealing old hand-lettered shops signs beneath, the wares delineated in detail with long defunct brands and pungent memories. Posters are stripped back to reveal flyers for gigs you might remember or bands that ring a bell. Graffiti lingers, its message now long lost and becomes more poetic because of it. The words and letters which survive impart a slightly eerie feeling of continuous inhabitation, that these rooms and walls have contained countless lives and moments and have lived through so many iterations that even old neighbours are unable to recall what was there a few decades ago. Much is made about how a city can be read through its architecture, its material, but it is far easier to read it through its words, so many of which survive, albeit disjointed and incoherent. But isn't that exactly the nature of the city?

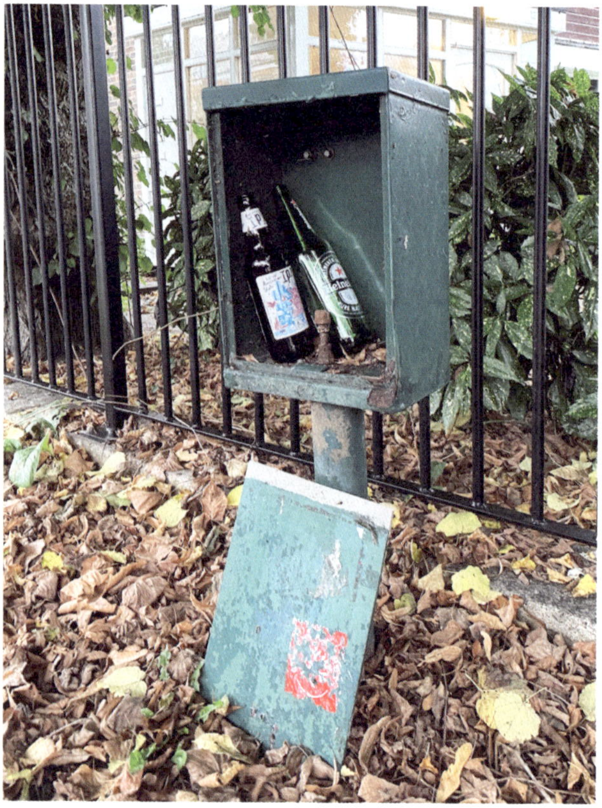

Never quite empty junction box, Putney, London

Littering

Cities are messy places. But humans are not all naturally - or at least necessarily - messy creatures. They are, however, often lazy, and cities are not as full of bins as they once were. The detritus and packaging of modern life is however far more extensive than it ever was (with the exception, perhaps, of cigarettes and the paraphernalia that came with them). The result is litter. It is also evident that many people who litter also feel uneasy littering. The result of this paradox is a very human kind of mess: creative littering.

The term may not be familiar but the phenomenon will be - a cup impaled on the spike of an iron railing, a cigarette stubbed out in a hole in the wall, a beer bottle left on top of a parking meter, a sandwich packet stuffed into the gaps between seats at a bus stop, a box of chips placed carefully on a gatepost. There is an empty, dark green junction box near me with its wiring stripped out and its door left mostly open. I don't ever see it without a beer bottle or some carefully placed disposable inside. Another spot, a gap in the bottom of a fence, has an artful arrangement of neatly placed cigarette ends, their filters protruding like little logs.

In all these cases the effort has been made to not just chuck the thing away but to find a place for it, off the surface of the street. Once you become conscious of it there is something in creative littering that can be quite comforting - not, of course, that it should necessarily be encouraged. There is effort here, and a recognition of the surfaces of the city which might otherwise be invisible. Having something to throw away, it seems, makes us see the city at a microcosmic level, to suddenly pick up on places we would never otherwise have noticed, all in order to make that small gesture.

Richard Wentworth, in his series *Making Do and Getting By*, has been documenting this kind of thing for decades, exposing the effort that can go into not wanting to just throw something on the ground. In looking for a place to stow unwanted stuff, people expose odd gaps in the urban fabric, cracks in the city surface. These are the interstices, invisible until they are suddenly exposed by rubbish, by becoming useful in an odd kind of way.

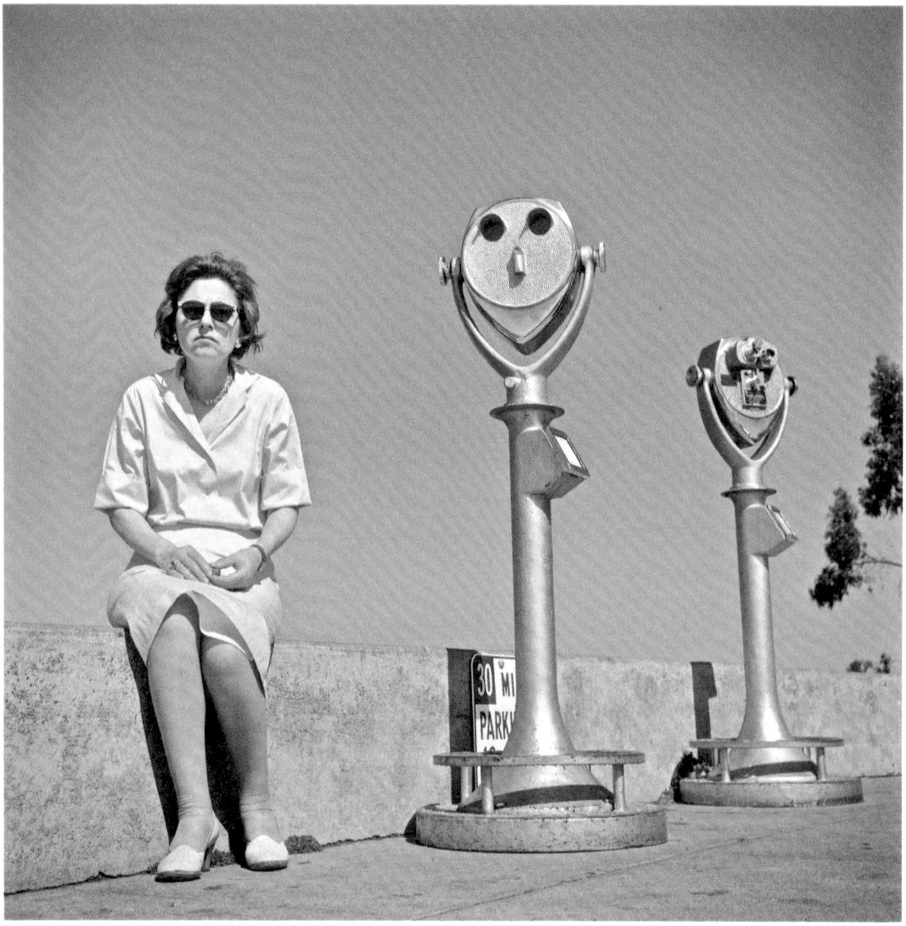

Woman with Binocular Viewers, San Francisco, 1964
Arthur Tress

Looking

In a 1964 shot from Arthur Tress's *San Francisco* series, a woman in sunglasses sits looking directly at the camera, as does a fixed pair of binoculars. Another set of binoculars stands a little further away, looking slightly askance. The congruence between the woman's glasses and the dark disks of the viewing apertures in the binoculars makes clear the anthropomorphism of the fitting - it even has a kind of rudimentary nose.

These machines for looking were commonplace when I was growing up, placed on almost every seafront, clifftop or panoramic outlook. I rarely got a chance to use them and, when I did, found myself scanning the horizon for something to look at, a ship, perhaps, for so long that the time usually ran out and the blurry filters went back up leaving me looking through the lens at something much less clear than what I could have seen with my own eyes. But there was still something exciting about it, the sense, perhaps, of looking through a submarine periscope, or a sniper-rifle sight.

In retrospect, these things were a complete distraction, a way of focusing children's minds on entirely the wrong thing - although perhaps it was to focus them on at least something. The reason they were there, I think, is that authorities felt a need to validate the notion that this was a place from which something could be seen. The thing that should have been obvious, the view, which was virtually unavoidable (think of a promenade looking out to sea) was somehow not enough; it needed to be signposted. So these once ubiquitous telescopes and binoculars were sited to validate its importance. That function is now fulfilled by the selfie, the mobile phone snap. In each case some mechanism is needed for affirming the sublime, the view itself is never enough. As is the case with so many other pieces of street furniture, the mobile phone has killed this fitting and I guess they will not be much mourned.

Tress, however, is perhaps suggesting something else here. The shot was taken at Coit Tower, the Pioneer Park landmark with a panoramic view of the city. The tower appeared as a phallic McGuffin in Hitchcock's *Vertigo*, a symbol that the mysterious Madeleine uses to orient herself to Scotty's apartment. But Tress's series was about change - about the protests of the civil rights movement, the arrival of the Beatles, about political protest as well as the everyday in the streets of San Francisco. We are always, in a way, he suggests, looking at the wrong thing. But sometimes that is where the most interesting things are happening.

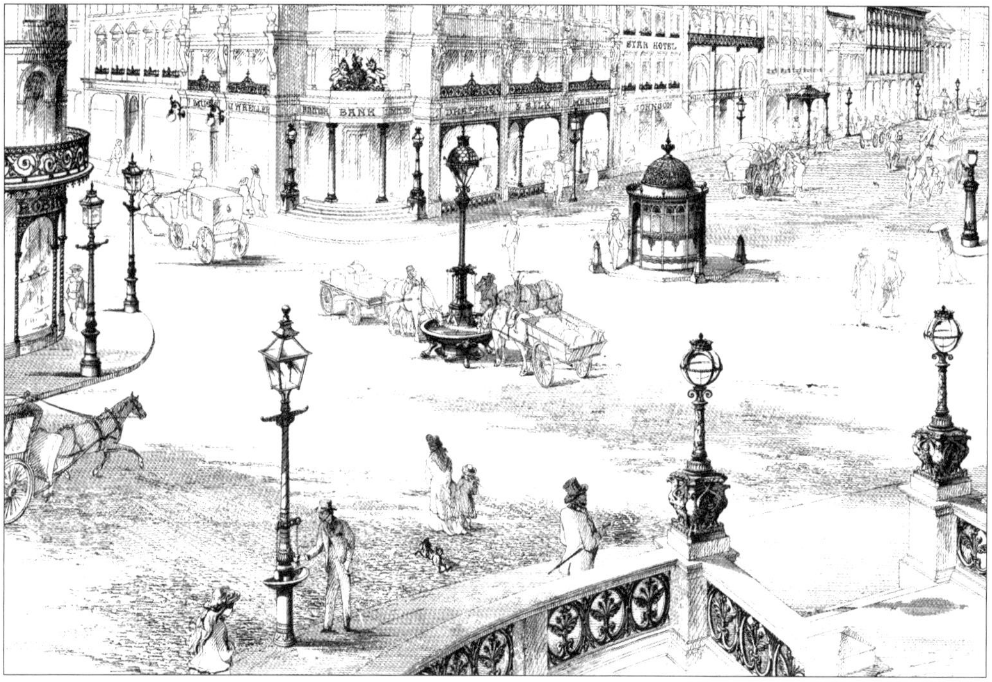

Street scene from catalogue published by Walter MacFarlane & Co. Saracen Foundry, Glasgow (Volume II, 6th edition, c.1882)

Manufacturing

The catalogue of the Saracen Foundry, otherwise known as Walter MacFarlane & Co. Ltd, is an almost perfect record of the Victorian city. The 1885 edition opens with a street scene in which the Saracen products are represented with a slightly heavier line. It's a clever device which begins to illustrate quite how ubiquitous iron casting was in the city and how it created, effectively, the new public image of urbanity. Among the more prominently rendered items are columns and shopfronts, balustrades and balconies, but most striking is the sheer amount and variety of street furniture. This was, without a doubt, the zenith of its presence in the city and its use as a marker of urban identity and civic amenity. At the centre of the scene are two items: a hybrid streetlight, horse trough, dog bowl and drinking fountain, and an elaborately ornamented and domed W/C crowned by a similar light. Both are amenities intended to relieve and refresh; both are so often conspicuously lacking in the modern city.

The catalogue itself is, for lovers of detail, taxonomy and industry, a thing of wonder. Its pages embrace every scale from finials for railings to demountable market halls and exhibition buildings. The range of types and styles of street furniture is astonishing. From curlicued brackets for hanging pub lanterns to solid classical columns and grand lamp bases for the streets in front of opera houses or gentlemen's clubs, this was an entire language of public infrastructure for an age of eclecticism. From this one catalogue you could build a world's fair using the vast greenhouses, arcades and pavilions. Proto-prefab. Contemporary engravings of the firm's showroom at their vast Possilpark works illustrate a kind of condensed public world of benches, fountains, pissoirs, lamps, railings, grilles, grates and gates beneath, of course, a selection of cast-iron and glass domes. At this time, Britain was the manufacturer for the world (producing a greater percentage of the world's industrial goods than China does today), a status assisted by this moment being the apotheosis of its empire and possessing a captive market. Colonial capitals were filled with the fruits of Glaswegian industry: the Rondebosch drinking fountain and horse trough in Capetown or the Elder Park bandstand in Adelaide. They reached beyond the empire too, such as the famous drinking fountain in Paraná, Argentina, and in stations, libraries and greenhouses from São Paulo to Bangalore.

During the Second World War, government drives for scrap iron saw tens of thousands of elaborately cast MacFarlane items stripped out of the streetscape and melted down. Our cities are much poorer for their loss; nothing comparable replaced them. As work waned with the diminution of empire, other archetypes arrived. It was the Saracen Foundry that cast the K6 telephone boxes.

Theirs, though, was just one foundry among hundreds. As a record of material culture and industry, street furniture provides the most perfect traces. Cast into the elaborate upright forms of lampposts and pillarboxes (usually at the base) you might find the names of foundries in Derby, Worcester, Edinburgh, Falkirk, Clyde, Birmingham or Bristol as well as London locations such as Finsbury, Borough, Old Street. The names of the manufacturers - the Lion Foundry, the Eagle Ironworks, Vulcan Ironworks - make the work of production sound legendary: epic products from the realm of fire and the forge of the gods. The dates might well be there too. Tom Emerson pointed out to me how the row of cast lights along London's Embankment bear marks indicating the dates of their manufacture, ranging from the 1880s to, slightly surprisingly, the 1980s - the same, complex, decorative lamps with their fishy bases being made using the same techniques and the same materials over a century of almost unimaginable change. You can find the same marks on postboxes in New Zealand or balustrades in Hong Kong, a vast web of iron and heavy industry connecting the world back to Britain. Walking in New York recently I saw a manhole cover with the characteristic bluntness of the city inscribed in its pattern 'NYC SEWER', but below, in equal-sized capital letters, was 'MADE IN INDIA'. The seemingly local and parochial can be surprisingly global.

Street furniture is a marker not only of transformations in technology but in industry, trade, transport and manufacture itself: from the stone of Renaissance cities pocked with occasional wrought-iron rings or lamps made by the same smiths who shoed the horses that would be tethered to those fittings to the appearance of cast-iron railings and gas lamps in Georgian London, to the concrete fittings of the 1950s, to the plain lamp and sign poles of today as complex casting gave way to cheap-to-produce and easy-to-maintain unpainted extruded steel tubes. For a while in the mid-20th century, concrete arrived in all its knobbly, aggregated glory, only to fall away again. Before these there was timber, the thick bollards and pillars now all rotted away, while plastic appeared in the 1960s, in the bubble-hoods of phone booths and the vivid pop colours of seats and bins. Perforated metal had its moment too, bum-freezing in the winter, toaster-hot in the summer.

Politics, too, is inscribed in their forms. Cities sought to express their values through the provision of new technologies: gas and then electric lighting (the 'gas-and-water' municipal socialism of the late Victorian era), manholes for telegraph cables, postboxes and phoneboxes, drinking fountains and advertising columns. The cast items of street furniture were the visible manifestations of public amenities, conceived as branding and visible not just for practicality but as the identity of a city transformed through technology and communication.

That pride in these objects cumulatively creating a public commons has disappeared, along with the clarity of understanding of ownership as networks and utilities are privatised, globalised and acquired by off-shored private equity. The combination of this anonymity and the overlaying of a modernist mode of convenience, which stripped out the detail and the more awkward-to-maintain elements, has conspired to create a more mundane world of things, for better and for worse. Street furniture is perceived as a purely functional item, designed almost to disappear - unless it is designed to deter, in which case its mass and immobility will become part of a deliberate language and coding without the relief of any delicacy or elegance. Concrete, once disdained as the flavour of mass social housing is now back as a manifestation of mass, craned into place in big cast blocks, tough enough to stop a truck.

The roads of two centuries ago were heavily punctuated with iron, from coal holes, bollards and railings to pub lanterns, signs and mud scrapers. Today that same landscape is littered almost entirely with pressed steel and welded tube, wiring boxes and endless poles for signs and lights, all smooth; less labour, more mechanisation. The items themselves have become anonymous, their makers uncelebrated, their origins untold except for an occasional sticker on the side of a communications box. The age of rich ornament enabled by foundry casting and a desire to create urban identity through everyday items has given way to galvanised blankness - light, cheap, easy to transport, easy to export, featureless, friction-free. A few retro products appear - historicising bollards, heritage streetlights - often reduced in both scale and material. They suggest an idea of a remembered thing rather than the thing itself. The monsters and dragons have disappeared along with the vast smoke-and-fire belching foundries and the ironworks that cast them. Street furniture, that most local and particular of things, is now, as that NYC sewer cover illustrates so eloquently, globalised. Just as it was a century and a half ago.

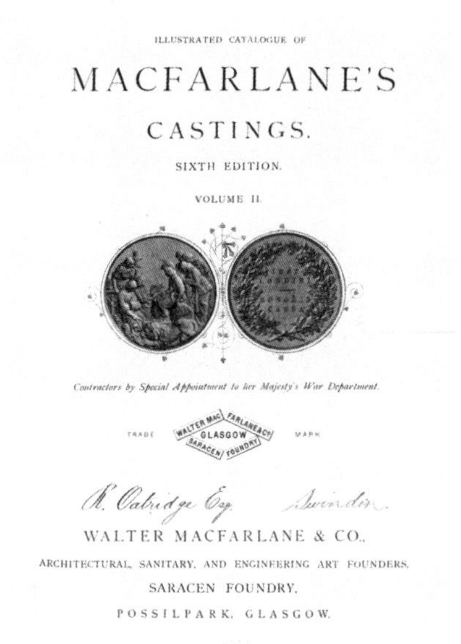

ILLUSTRATED CATALOGUE OF

MACFARLANE'S

CASTINGS.

SIXTH EDITION.

VOLUME II.

Contractors by Special Appointment to her Majesty's War Department.

TRADE WALTER MACFARLANE & Co GLASGOW SARACEN FOUNDRY MARK

R. Oatridge Esq. Swindon

WALTER MACFARLANE & CO.,

ARCHITECTURAL, SANITARY, AND ENGINEERING ART FOUNDERS.

SARACEN FOUNDRY,

POSSILPARK, GLASGOW.

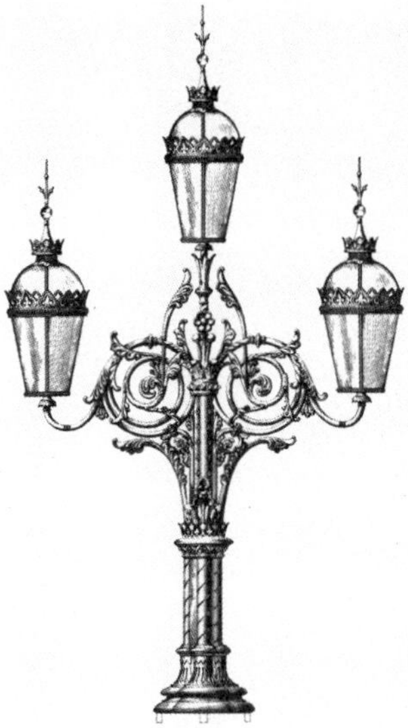

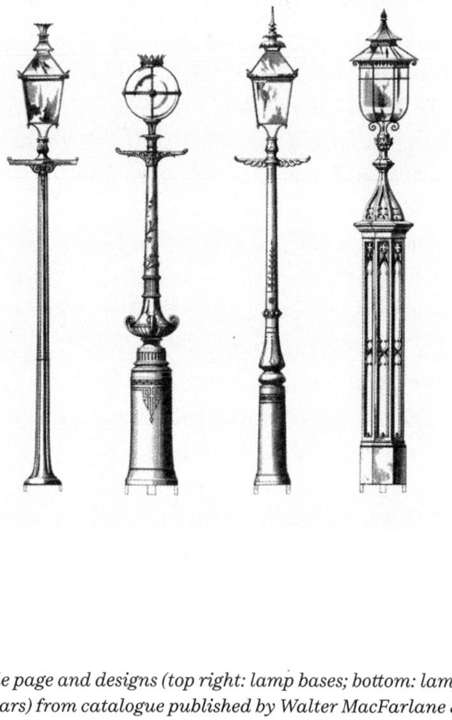

Title page and designs (top right: lamp bases; bottom: lamp pillars) from catalogue published by Walter MacFarlane & Co. Saracen Foundry, Glasgow (Volume II, 6th edition, c.1882)

Measuring

All roads lead, as we know, to Rome. In fact, they lead to a stumpy stone column in the middle of the Forum, the Milliarium Aureum (the 'Golden Milestone'). This was the centre of empire, the centre of the world and the point from which all distances were measured. From here radiated lines of stones stretching as far as modern-day Libya and Egypt, to York, Lisbon and Budapest.

The Romans took their milestones seriously, marking every thousandth marching double step on routes used by marching legions. They obsessively surveyed the landscape, surveying itself being an act of colonisation. To measure and to map was to acquire. They imposed upon the landscape not only their infamously straight roads (an astonishing quarter of a million miles of them), but also aqueducts, cities, camps, walls and temples. The stones were the first points of reference they set down, marking the landscape as something acquired, domesticated. The seriousness with which they took their milestones was indicated by the threat of execution against anyone found attempting to move one. To move a milestone, to deface it or alter it, is to unsettle something fundamental: the understanding of the landscape and attempts to privatise the land. This is the battle with nature and geography, the frontier of civilisation.

It is not entirely certain what the original Milliarium Aureum looked like but it is assumed, from other surviving milestones (notably those many, many stones on the Via Appia) that it was a truncated column possibly of gilded bronze or perhaps of stone with its inscriptions picked out in gold. The Romans had extremely rigorous rules and regulations on the physical structure of milestones. They were carved as columns, like the one at their origin, a universal language always relating back to Rome. The idea of establishing and marking a centre has endured - it can be seen in Washington DC's blocky Zero Milestone (1923) or in Buenos Aires' Kilometre Zero (1935) and in inlaid bronze pavement plaques across the world (London's is in Trafalgar Square). But the form of the milestone itself, the road marker, went through a series of transformations and its legacy is a hearty mess of myth and meaning.

The Romans might have been its master, but the milestone predates them by millennia. The Ancient Egyptians seem to have had cairns (piles of stacked stones) to mark points along routes, the Ancient Greeks certainly had milestones, and the Inuit had *inuksuk* - cairns or standing stones which acted as way-markers or milestones. Sometimes shaped vaguely anthropomorphically, these *inuksuk* may even have had a practical function; their name, apparently, means 'a thing performing the function of a person' and they were about human-sized, a rare vertical presence in treeless landscapes. They have become a bit of a cult in Canada, a kind of landscape logo for events, artists and graphic designers, a shorthand for the survival of indigenous culture and the tenacious presence of humans in even the harshest of landscapes. One appears on the flag of the Nunavut people, another was used as the logo of the Vancouver Winter Olympics in 2010.

In Britain the earliest 'pudding stones' (named after their material in which pebbles set in a silica matrix resemble the fruit in a plum pudding) have been dated to around 5000 BC and were also used as way-markers.

Legends and myths can attach to things of this age which appear in the landscape yet of which the origins are only sketchily known. There is, inherent in the rocky form of the milestone, a reminder of death, an intimate relationship with the tombstone. And there is something in it which suggests an in-between world, between the ground and the sky, darkness and light, between the traveller's origin and destination. Positioned on roadsides and crossroads, milestones inhabit a kind of no-man's land like boundary-markers. These locations suggest a realm of superstition and angst, think of the highwaymen hanged by the side of the road or Robert Johnson's *Cross Road Blues*. That most old English milestones were carved into the shapes of obelisks, as were war memorials in the 20th century, reinforces this link with history and with death.

Take a look at London's Edgware Road. This was an ancient track which was incorporated by the Romans into Watling Street, connecting the capital with Dover. If you walk along the road (itself since incorporated by traffic engineers into the A5), past the Joe Strummer Subway and across the road to the looming Hilton London Metropole Hotel, take a peek into the porch to the left of the revolving doors and you'll see an obelisk-shaped milestone, the Tyburn Stone. This once marked a toll gate but also the location of the infamous Tyburn Gallows, London's most famous place of public execution. The stone has been moved - the gallows were closer to Marble Arch - yet the whiff of death hangs around this stone, a curious welcome for even this rather grim hotel.

Milestones might also mark a particular way. Those carved for the pilgrimage route, the Camino de Santiago for instance, are inscribed with the scallop shell that is the symbol of St James. As cast iron replaced stone as the street furniture material of choice in the 19th century, the formal vocabulary of milestones exploded from a simple stone marker into all kinds of tablets, triangles, tombstones and plaques with the destinations and distances cast into their iron surfaces and painted and overpainted until the letters become almost too indistinct to read. The translation from stone to iron ironically made many milestones look even more like gravestones, with a particular shape with an arched top and two slightly angled sides. There's a good one, most appropriately, outside the Royal Geographical Society on Kensington Gore dating from 1911 and featuring a rather reduced version of the classic Victorian pointing fingers.

During the Second World War in Britain, thousands of milestones were removed or defaced in an oddly British and commendably eccentric effort to confuse potential German invaders. Most were not replaced, nevertheless the Milestone Society (of course there's a Milestone Society) estimates there are still around 9,000 left alongside the nation's roads and paths.

In an age of Google maps, the milestone is functionally defunct. But its enduring importance in culture remains at least in language. A 'milestone' has become one of those personal development and corporate clichés. The odd thing is that the ephemeral nature of GPS mapping has made milestones seem almost more tangible and somehow mystical. Iain Sinclair described milestones 'ground down like ancient molars' and their very irrelevance has made them more mysterious. Perhaps, like the London stone sitting forlornly in its fake-fireplace vitrine in the City, their inscriptions will wear down and become illegible - and we will be left with a legacy of stone stubs that probably once meant something.

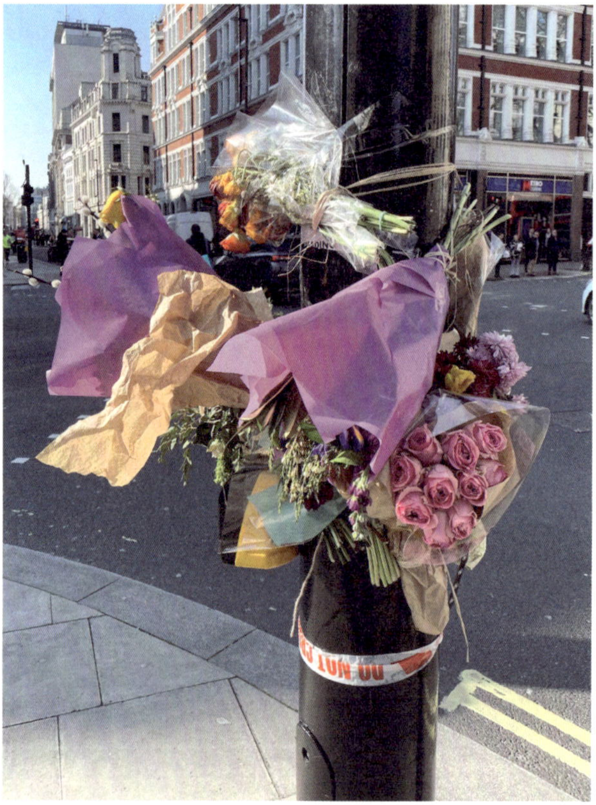

Roadside memorial, London

Memorialising

A bunch of wilting supermarket flowers taped to a lamppost. A fading, laser-printed portrait. A rain-soaked fluffy toy tied to a traffic barrier with a message of condolence in a plastic wallet, its coloured letters leeching into each other and creating pastel auras around them in the damp drizzle. The pathos of floral tributes to stabbings, shootings, disappearances and traffic accidents is amplified by the banality of the objects they are taped to: smooth metal stems of lampposts or anonymous, utilitarian traffic barriers, occasionally bent out of shape by the very accident they are commemorating, a park bench, the stripy stem of a Belisha beacon, the cracked, dirty, fried-egg plastic of an illuminated traffic island bollard.

I don't know when these roadside memorials began. When I was a child, tributes were reserved for the funeral, the cemetery and the pub. But not far from where I lived, Marc Bolan was killed in a car accident in 1977 and the tree by the crash site became a shrine. The paraphernalia of glam rock proved the perfect medium for making commemoration visible in a green suburban lane. The gold lamé scarves, the badges, plastic flowers, the photos, tiny T-shirts and pink cuddly toys created a landscape of mawkish merch, unmissable on the muddy, weedy embankment. It was the year of the Silver Jubilee and, to me, they somehow merged a little, the flags and the bunting, the fluttering crisp packets and the feather boas, each versions of their own royalty, their own glam rituals, crowns and platforms. The shrine is still there. It somehow seems to keep changing, I don't know what happens, whether some visitors take souvenirs and replace items or whether bits just get blown away or taken by magpies.

But the real turning point came almost exactly two decades later, with the death of Princess Diana in 1997. Tons of bouquets and thousands of candles were left outside palace gates and other sites around the country, in an explosion of what seemed to me then very much like mass hysteria but which proved a portent for a subsequent sentimentalisation of the streets. This was a bottom-up expression of grief, solidarity and recognition, the arrival of a secular, post-Christian, consumerist ritual. It dumbfounded the authorities, who remain unsure exactly how to handle the remnants of floral tributes, caught between an inclination to neatness, an unspoken desire to overlook the dangers of motoring, cycling and being young, and nervousness around tampering with the people's manifestations of raw emotion.

The urge to commemorate is powerful. In a more-or-less secular society the desire for ritual has not disappeared, rather it has become disassociated from the physical structure of the church and spilt on to the streets. In a church there are dedicated languages of mourning and remembering, the votive candles and effigy limbs, the building itself which forms a carapace for commemoration. On the streets, however, there is no shelter, only the sky. The architecture, which might otherwise form an armature, is private property; what is left is the public infrastructure of street furniture. On these emotional occasions, it becomes a matrix of memory, a framework for the attachment of cellophane-wrapped forecourt flowers, fluffy teddies and football scarves, cards and mementoes. The contrast of the colourful items, rich textures and the determined municipal monotone is perennially striking, and it represents a popular appropriation of what is, after all, the most public of provisions.

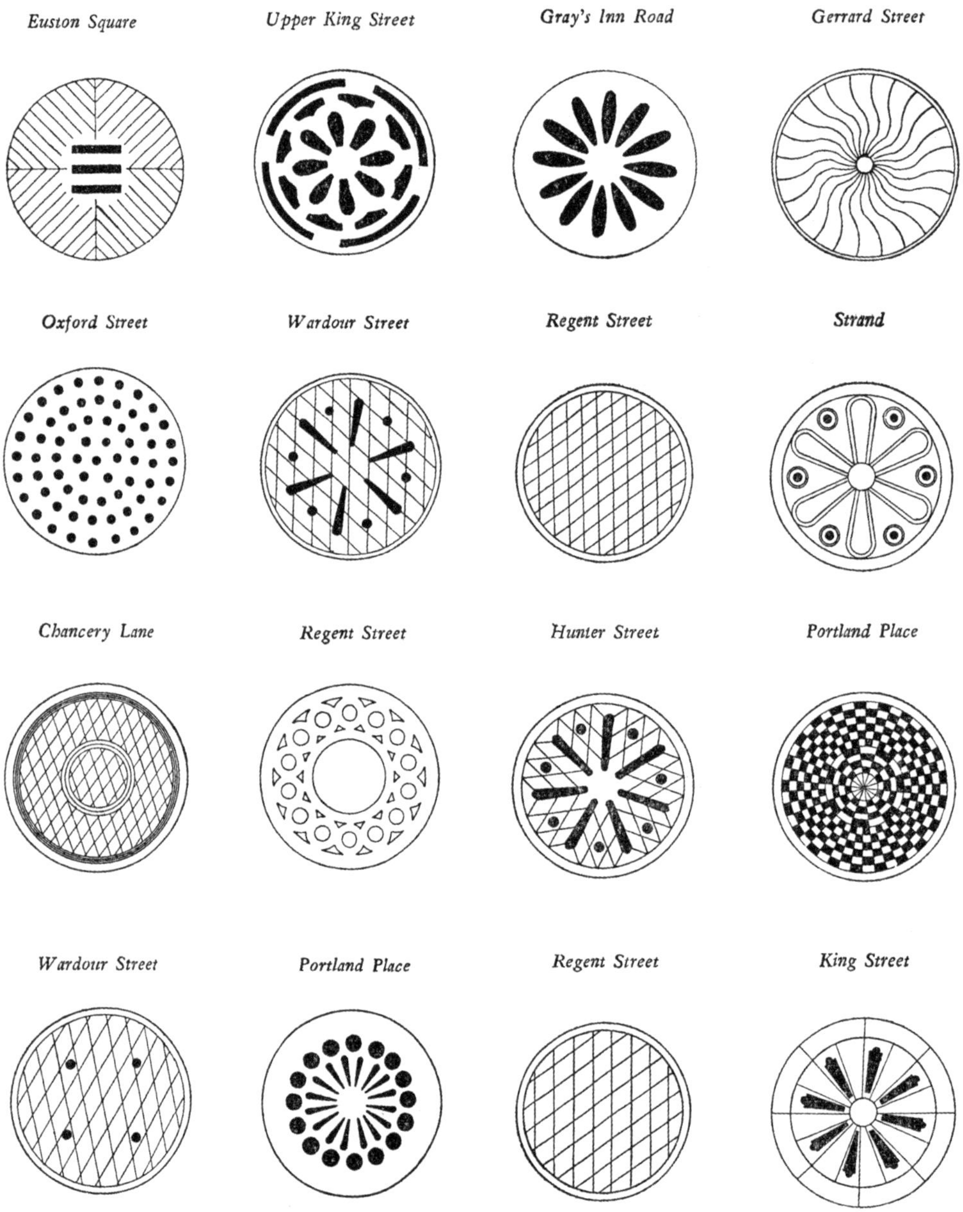

Coal Plate Sketches from the 1965 edition of Opercula (London Coal Plates), 1929
Illustrations by Shephard Taylor (aka Aesculapius Junior)

Mining

Take a stroll around Thurloe Square in South Kensington, more or less opposite the V&A, and look beneath your feet. You'll see a selection of round, cast-iron coal-hole covers in an incredible array of patterns - some purely abstract, others big on branding, yet others extolling their own self-locking technologies.

Each of these iron disks is 12 inches in diameter, the exact size and more or less the colour of an old vinyl LP. They were designed to allow coalmen to deposit the contents of their sacks from the pavement without having to take their filthy, blackened boots and bodies anywhere near the interiors of the elegant, white-stuccoed terraced houses. Instead a maid would open the hole from the inside (they can only ever be opened from the inside), and the coal would be poured into the vaults beneath the pavements.

They mostly date from around the mid-19th century, some a little later, and they represent a little glimpse into the moment when Britain was the world's biggest producer and exporter of coal, and the greatest exporter of manufactured goods by such a margin that it is almost difficult to conceive for us today. We might now think of the incredible domination of Chinese manufacturing which, at the time of writing, stands at around 14% of manufactured exports. Great Britain in 1870 had a 40% share. The coal and the iron covers were emblems of the wealth of the nation, but the evidence of heavy industry was always placed at the margins of the dwelling; the coal in a vault outside the house and under what appears to be public space (in an echo of coal's underground origins - a public resource privatised) and the iron railings which demarcated the boundaries.

Like coins set into the pavement, the coal-hole covers have attracted their own brand of numismatists. Already in 1869 (more or less at the height of coal-plates' popularity), a medical student named Shephard Taylor sketched dozens of designs he found on his walks, taxonomised them and later published the drawings as a book, *Opercula*, using the medical pseudonym Aesculapius Junior. Taylor coined the phrase which had been a biological term (a cover, for instance, for the gills of a fish). It is an eccentric little publication from 1929 (by which date Taylor was 90 years old) which was then republished in 1965. It features Taylor's basic but perfectly adequate diagrams which begin to express the seemingly endless variety of the covers from severely functional versions to elaborate Gothic designs and others that seem to presage 1960s Op art with swirls and checkerboards. The covers are stripped here of their advertising. In reality, most of the designs you'll find (certainly most of those in Thurloe Square) feature prominent lettering, usually either advertising the manufacturer or the ironmonger who retailed it (which explains why some seem to suggest they were made in unlikely locations like Regent Street or Chelsea). Occasionally the lettering trumpets the technological achievements or the patents of the locking mechanism (self-locking seems to have been a very big deal). They represent a rare moment in which advertising is used to enhance function. The raised letters, like the raised patterns on all of the designs, are there to make the plates less slippery underfoot.

In Thurloe Square, for instance, you might come across an exquisite floral pattern surrounded by little disks and a zigzag, almost Romanesque border. You might encounter one design consisting of seven circles with radiating petal patterns which seem to foreshadow the Japonisme of the Aesthetic Movement in the 1880s (R.H. & J. Pearson's Patent Automatic Action, Notting Hill) or, perhaps the four interlocking circles of Jas. Battle and Co.'s Western Iron Works (also Notting Hill). There are examples of glass disks (Howard's of North Woolwich is very elegant) and perforated versions (Hayward's Patent Self-Locking). There were both ventilating and illuminating coal-hole covers; ones which allowed air into the cellar and others which allowed light in (it was dangerous to wander around in combustible coal dust with a naked flame).

There was one major manufacturer in London, Hayward Brothers, whose address in Borough is often found cast into these covers: 187–189 Union Street. They had a foundry there, which was later expanded into Orange Street and then to Enfield. The Haywards had originally made their fortune in glass, a patented prismatic design which threw illumination from pavement lights further into the basement where there might often be workshops or warehouses. They used similar glass on some of their coal plates.

The dimensions of the disk, that 12-inch format, was a compromise between being able to funnel sacks of coal down the chute efficiently and being a little too small for a body to enter - either deliberately or accidentally, in case one plate might have been left unlocked.

These coal-hole covers are, it turns out, a bit of a cult. Jeremy Corbyn, one-time Labour leader, is a fan, frequently snapping coal plates on his mobile ('people think it is a little odd' he was quoted as saying). My friend Christian Küsters, a London-based graphic designer, has turned coal-hole plate designs into a series of prints, badges and even T-shirts. There's something so strikingly graphic about their form that they lend themselves to everything from Tumblr, Twitter, Facebook and Instagram sites to beer mats. I particularly like Christopher Howse's account (@BeardyHowse, #Opercula). The internet, with its huge reach and affection for easy graphic devices (much like Taylor's original and very graphic booklet), has proved fertile ground for coal holes, but the idea of treating manholes as medium is nothing new. Already in 1962 art dealer, poet and curator Victor Musgrave (who was the first to show Bridget Riley and Yves Klein in London) put on a display of cast-iron manhole covers in his Soho gallery - the ultimate urban found objects.

Despite their one-time ubiquity and seeming indestructibility, these coal plates are vulnerable. Unlike the utility and manhole covers maintained by local authorities and power and telecoms companies, coal holes have become redundant, and as private fittings in a public footpath they are not always respected when paving is relaid. When terraced housing was built in the Georgian and early Victorian eras, the responsibility for paving lay with developers, who would put in pavements as an inducement to potential homeowners. In the same way that the garden squares (like that in Thurloe Square) were very private, fenced off and locked shut, the pavements were part of the private property (which is partly how the vaults could stretch under what seems to be public land). Streets and pavements were later entirely adopted by local authorities. The curious anomaly endures that these odd private baubles remain embedded in a now-public pavement yet are functionally redundant. They are, however, a constant supply of small delight if you care to look, a little disk of industrial and design history.

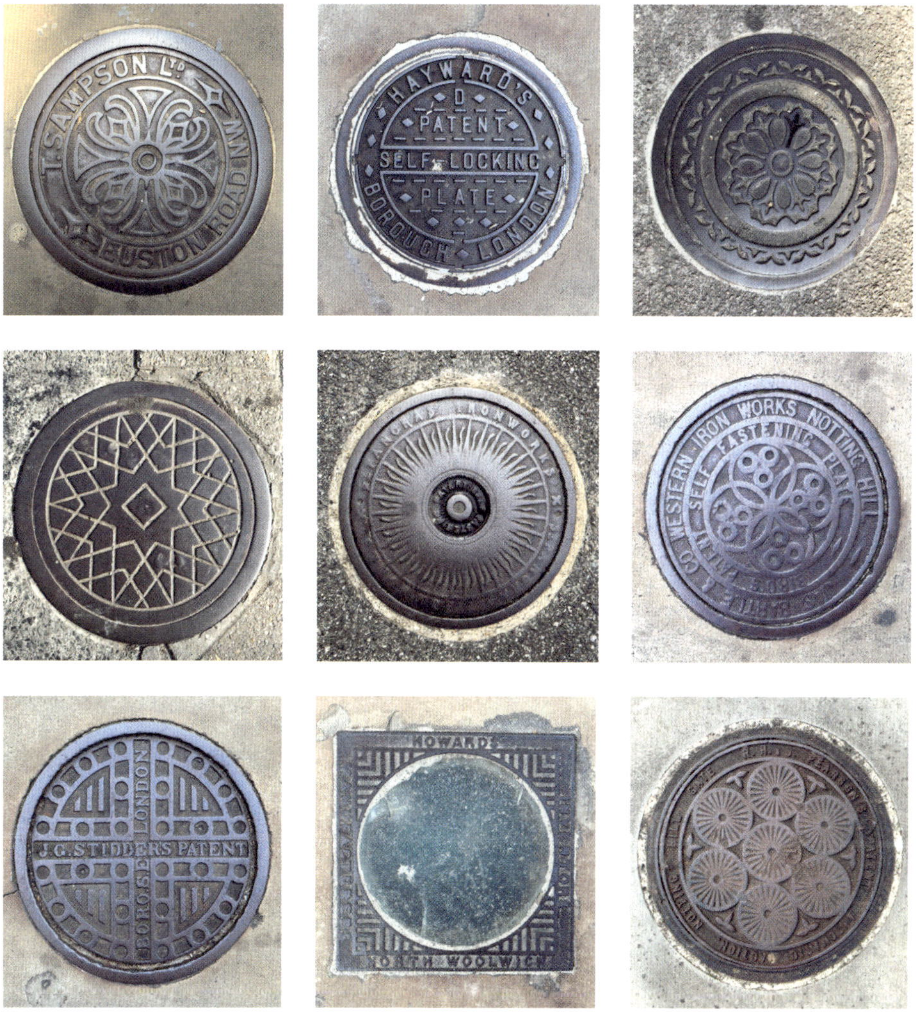

Coal-hole covers, London

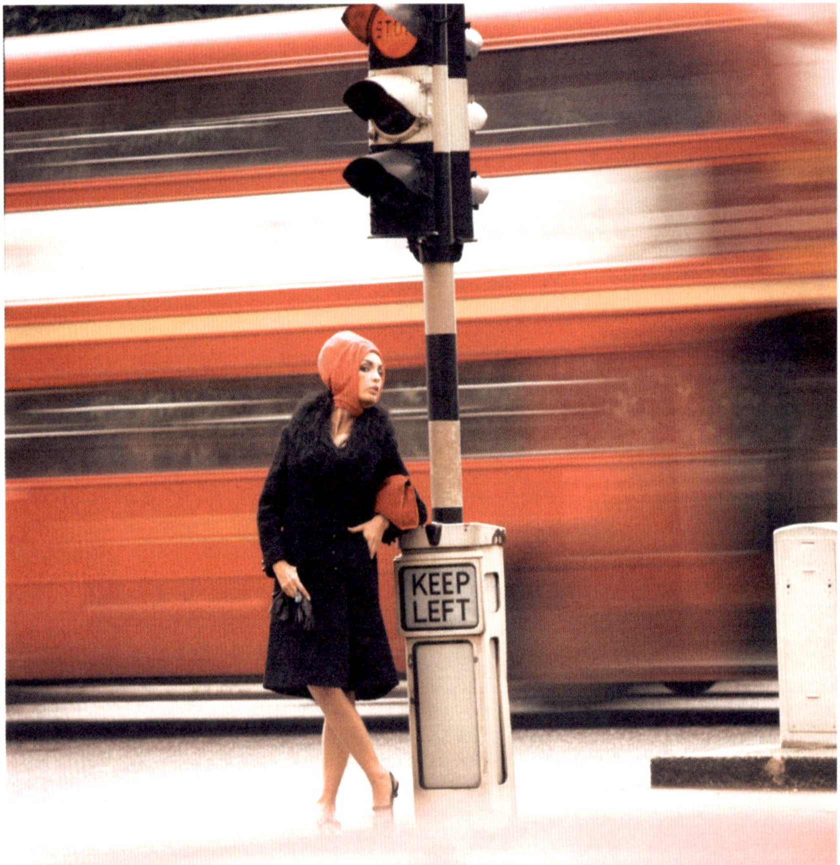

Capital Chic, 1960
Norman Parkinson

Modelling

The postwar fashion media, like the movie industry, seemed conflicted between the studio and the streets. There were directors who desired the gritty authenticity of filming in the streets and there were directors who relished the control and artifice of the studio. For photographers who created images for the fashion industry, the split was the same: the texture and reality of the street, or the endless possibilities and options of the controlled studio environment? And just as the directors of film noir in the 1940s moved out into the city, fashion tentatively stuck its toe into reality too.

The settings for some of its most memorable images were the war-torn cityscapes of Europe. Lee Miller's striking shot of a model in a Digby Morton suit (p.137), for instance, shows a figure standing beneath a hanging lamp in an archway with the ruins of the city beside her. Or there's Cecil Beaton's famous photographs of a model posting a letter against the rubble of London (p.176). After the war, the shoots stayed on the streets, such as Dior's famous New Look shoot (1947) on the streets and quays of Paris against cast-iron Metro stations and cobbled surfaces. For Richard Avedon the patterns in the Parisian paving, the railings of the Eiffel Tower and the geometry of the granite kerbs from which the models so famously leapt into the air (which he ripped off, albeit acknowledged, from Martin Munkacsi) are the armature against which the lines of the tailoring are displayed.

Fashion is exactly what pavements were for. The first paved streets of the modern(ish) era were in Paris, as courtiers and their hangers-on began to move from the court of Versailles to the city after the death of Louis XIV. The palace had been an architectural stage-set, on which the court had performed, its costumes and wigs a key component of its theatricality; the street was then required to assume that role. Around the same time London began laying paving after the reconstruction following the Great Fire and the westward spread of the city. Mayfair and St James became fashionable quarters, and paving stones allowed women in elaborate dresses and men in expensively buckled shoes to traverse the streets without ruining their look. The development of paving and the cultivating of fashion went hand-in-hand, and the result was city as backdrop to style. Cobbles and kerbs, flagstones and granite setts, resembled stitching and patching, the new roads appearing as a layer of fabric connecting the neighbourhoods of the city. The stone surfaces were a membrane, uniquely patterned so that they could tell the viewer about the place much as the feel of a fabric might reveal the quality of a garment.

The formal gardens of Paris, the piazzas of Venice and the pleasure gardens of London became, in the 17th and 18th centuries, stage-sets for appearing in public. They were about parading, the *passeggiata*. Here, with hanging paper lanterns and candles, a nighttime world of fashion emerged to match the twinkly chandelier and sconce-lit interior worlds of the theatre and the ballroom.

The arrival of gaslight in the early 19th century metastasised the evening economy of appearance with the simultaneous arrival of arcades (their pavements lacking in horseshit and beggars), large, illuminated and elaborate shop windows which reinforced the status of the city's streets, and squares as an urban ballroom accommodating a ritual dance of display and attraction. The phantasmagoria of consumption viewed through glass became the set for aspiration.

Stifled by the transformation of the city into a place of work as well as entertainment and its attendant accessibility and crowds, the street came roaring back as a backdrop for fashion when it was rediscovered as a found landscape. A London bomb site depicted in the background of a shoot suggested endurance and a fashion for practicality, utility and resistance, while a Parisian backdrop suggested haute couture and haut bas, and of Rome the *sprezzatura* and passion. The clichés were built into the streetscape as readymades, doing the editor's work for them.

There was a period of Paris photoshoots in which the city itself appeared almost incessantly as a character and the elements of the street became props: the *colonnes Morris,* the bridges, sculpted lions, Metro stations, ornate lampposts and the park benches. They were conceived as supremely staged scenarios, striking but stiff. Marilyn Stafford's work exemplifies this kind of vicarious tourism, with the street furniture appearing as self-conscious characters framing the models.

During the 1950s the street was adopted as a far more effective background, adding a layer of interest to fashion shoots, grounding the fashion in reality even if the effects were pure theatricality. William Klein's *Nina + Simone, Piazza di Spagna* for *Vogue* in 1960 used the zebra crossing as a geometric backdrop for the models' striking black and white dresses (and caught a motor scooter, the perfect cipher for the Italian street, buzzing by), presaging the Op art aesthetic of the coming decade through the tones of the street surface. The 1960s saw an incredible revival in the street used as fashion theatre, as the desirability of authenticity once again usurped the artifice of haute couture's historic dressed studio backgrounds and the cities shifted, from Rome to Paris, Manhattan and Milan to London and back again. Georges Dambier, for instance, transplanted Parisian chic to the unlikely setting of a London phonebox in his 1959 shoot featuring Lucinda Hollingsworth.

More than any other, though, it was Norman Parkinson's shot, *Capital Chic* for *Queen Magazine* (p.134) which foreshadowed the advent of Swinging London and its moment in the fashion limelight. A model leans nonchalantly against a traffic light while a bus zips by in the background, a blur of red, white and yellow. She is wearing a red headscarf and has a red clutch bag beneath her arm, her black coat chiming with the black and white stripes of the traffic light. The speed and the colour (fashion photography was still largely black and white) seem to suggest this is where it is all happening.

Françoise Hardy was photographed in London from a low angle by an unknown photographer in the 1960s, against a backdrop of Nelson's Column and an elaborate (and slightly Parisian-looking) cast-iron lamp. Photographers used street furniture as props, partnering them with the chanteuse's white boots or bohemian blouse as indicators of place and the earthiness of the street. Another photograph, by Doreen Spooner, shows actress Martine Beswick in her sister Laurelie's flowery minidress beside a parking meter. The form of the meter, perhaps, anticipates models like Twiggy, with the distinctive London lollipop shape of skinny body, big head - models morphing with street typologies.

In a way the model here appears as perpetual tourist, the backgrounds always a set and the set is the city. The street furniture frames the clothes but also acts as a kind of supporting cast, betraying the exact locations, an easy visual shorthand. We see here, perhaps, how the pillars, posts and kiosks inhabit the streets as well as the imagination. They are characters in their own right in the fashion parade - sleek, static models, always ready and willing to be photographed.

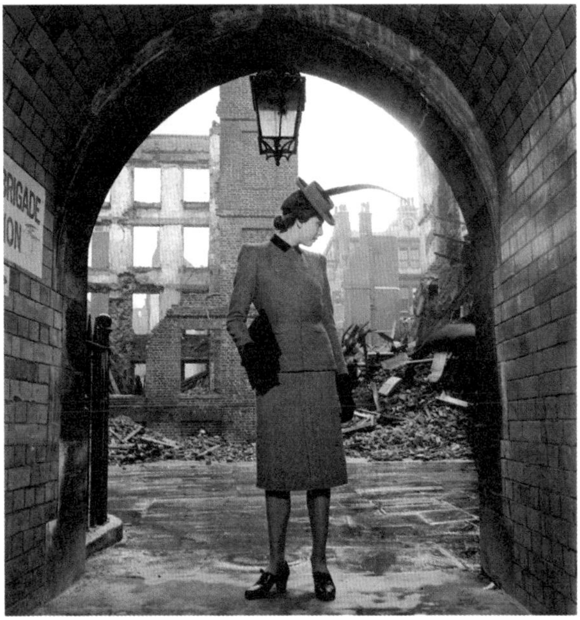

Model [Elizabeth Cowell] Wearing Digby Morton Suit, London, 1941
Lee Miller

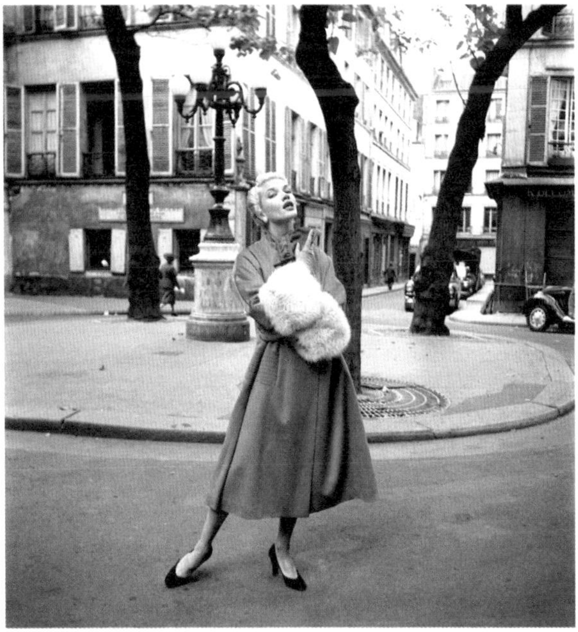

*Model in Ready-to-Wear, Place De Furstenberg, Paris, c.*1955
Marilyn Stafford

Modernising

For a brief moment in the 1950s, street furniture found itself at the centre of British architectural discourse. The removal and scrapping (for no useful reason other than propaganda and dubious morale value) of the nation's fine Georgian and Victorian wrought- and cast-iron railings and gates to assist the war effort had sparked a kind of repulsion, a sense of waste and a sudden, renewed appreciation of the beauty and workmanship of what had been lost. Some, including George Orwell, welcomed the removal of all those barriers and the opening up of garden squares and parks to all, at all times of the day, the ending of the 'Keep Off the Grass' culture. Others saw only decline.

Amid the postwar reconstruction that slowly asserted itself on the nation's tired, soot-stained and bomb-damaged cities came a nostalgic realisation that the historic language of the street was being lost along with the old cast-iron gas lamps, bollards, cobblestones and pumps. The debate happened at local level, often escalating into very English and slightly farcical protests with residents chaining themselves to Victorian lampposts to stymie their replacements with newer, modern concrete models. But the concerns were genuine and the voicings vociferous. Fearful of losing the 'character' of their neighbourhoods, people clung to the familiar markers of place. Whether George Formby leaning on a lamppost, Gene Kelly embracing a streetlight to sing and dance in the rain, or a gaslight emerging from the fog in Sherlock Holmes's London, streetlamps in particular had reached a paradoxical status where they were simultaneously almost invisible and hugely symbolic.

It was mostly the middle classes who protested, upset by the change in the nature of a streetscape over which they felt some ownership yet which they now found they were powerless to influence. The principle theoretical forum for that very middle-class debate was the *Architectural Review*, a specialist professional magazine which, at the time, exerted an outsized influence. From around the 1930s onwards, wistful photos began appearing in the magazine showing clusters of street furniture, picturesque, winding streetscapes and peculiarly English scenes with police phone booths, pillarboxes and other items with a slightly surrealist aspect in their grouping, even a humanity in their anthropomorphic uprightness. There were features about coal-hole covers and paving - all part of a building consciousness of what was beginning to be called 'townscape'.

Artists began looking at street furniture; there was a notion that the street might be akin to a public sculpture gallery displaying the unselfconscious three-dimensional expressions of the evolution of the civic realm. If there was an English sensibility, might it be found in these everyday things? It was part of a moment in which the picturesque and the textures of the historic city were being rediscovered. Steen Eiler Rasmussen's *London: The Unique City* (1937) and *Experiencing Architecture* (1959) explored a world of cobbles and York-stone pavings, of bollards and the shadows of London railings on brick, of worn steps and aged sooty walls, the texture and grain of the city. Nikolaus Pevsner wrote about the picturesque and planning. A new generation of modernists was beginning to acknowledge the complexity of the cityscape, reacting in part to the tabula rasa approach of Le Corbusier and the utopian visions of the first generation.

A group of writers, architects and historians - including the *Architectural Review*'s editor J.M. Richards and also Pevsner, Gordon Cullen, John Betjeman and Osbert Lancaster - coalesced around a very English idea of a charming, picturesque streetscape which had developed over time in an apparently ad hoc but actually humane and responsive manner, catering to civic and public needs but also to a desire for markers and symbols of place and time. It came, I think, from the same impulse as the historic British fondness for antiques, for an idea that an inherited set of furniture and pictures was superior to anything that could be bought new. There was, of course, a class element to all this, as there always was in British culture. Collecting antiques, after all, was also a way of accumulating the markers of taste and class for those who had not inherited them. It was a display of taste and refinement. The curious thing for many readers, however, might have been the platform for this position. The *Architectural Review* was an otherwise dependable proponent of modernism, often found decrying the sad and timid state of British architecture and design when compared to Germany or Scandinavia. Yet here were these apparently determined modernists picking a fight with councils over their attempts to modernise street furniture.

The June 1955 issue of *Architectural Review* was titled 'Outrage' and its cover (by Gordon Cullen) depicted a vision of 'subtopia', a confused and cluttered landscape of non-complimentary things: an Art Deco-inflected road sign, ominously hunched streetlights (their lamps described by Betjeman as looking like bodies hanging from a gibbet) and, in the distance, a line of electricity pylons disappearing into a bleak horizon. The issue was written mostly by Ian Nairn, a perceptive architecture critic who, in his guidebook *Nairn's Paris,* proved to have a fine eye for the French capital's outdoor seating, café chairs, bollards and so on, the collective stuff of city life which he termed 'trim'. The contention was that the British landscape was being despoiled by planners, municipal officials and traffic engineers who were unaccountable and lacking in *taste*. You might argue that this was, at least in part, an attack on the planning profession, seen as less established and less educated than architects (at least, by architects and the architectural establishment). A huge success, the 'Outrage' issue was subsequently republished as a book. It even spawned a sequel, 'Counter Attack: Against Subtopia', also edited by Nairn. An odd mix of town planning, picturesque urbanism, examples of likeable historic street furniture, memorials and signage, this was not a manual and not really a proposal – it was, rather, I think, intended as an inspiration.

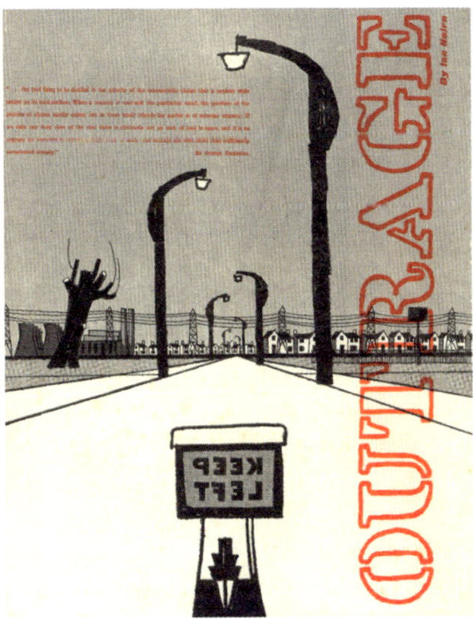

Cover of 'Outrage', special number of the Architectural Review, *June 1955 (reprint)*
Cover by Gordon Cullen

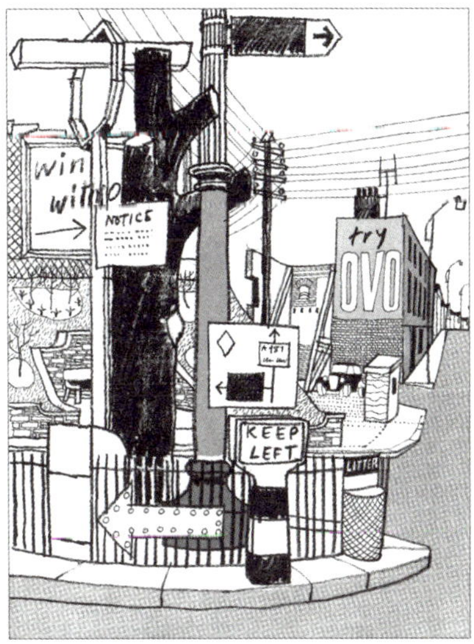

Page 70 of 'Outrage', June 1955 (reprint)
Illustration by Gordon Cullen

There was no call here, as you might expect from a modernist magazine, for a harmonisation or standardisation of well-designed street fittings but rather the exact opposite, a plea for the retention of quirky and varied originals and a more disparate, tolerant and eccentric approach to new designs. It represented a rather surprising proto-postmodern moment of tolerance and heterogeneity.

In reality, outside the rarefied organs of the architectural establishment, the landscape was changing dramatically in the 1950s. Streetlamps designed for gaslight and often only relatively recently converted to electricity were being taken down and replaced with concrete versions billed as lower maintenance, as they didn't need to be painted. Old iron bollards were replaced by bulky concrete phalluses, cobbles were being ripped up or covered in tarmac, and manhole covers replaced by newer versions with new archetypes like the GPO's telephone access covers made from concrete and iron. Drinking troughs, water pumps and fountains fell into disrepair and were often removed. New typologies - from Belisha beacons, traffic lights and seemingly endless new traffic signs to, most controversially, parking meters - began to appear, a whole new landscape, in fact, of what was condemned by the *Architectural Review* writers as 'visual clutter'.

Britain's working-class neighbourhoods, often near targets such as docks, railways and factories, had been disproportionately affected by bombing. Combined with a postwar drive to replace 'slum' housing with new council estates, this meant that entire quarters were razed. There was no time, energy or inclination to discuss the niceties of street furniture when your whole neighbourhood was being demolished. Instead the debate was played out in middle-class strongholds, where residents were keen to maintain the 'identity' of their streetscape. This defensiveness was part of a growing awareness of what was being lost in terms of historic fabric, a move towards conservation and a creeping distrust of 'faceless' municipal officials. There were awards for civic conservation schemes and then the introduction of conservation areas (perhaps surprisingly an import from the US and then France) as late as 1967 - measures which acknowledged the 'character' of townscape and embraced the layer of street furniture that was once considered dispensable by officialdom.

As ever in Britain, property values were at the heart of the debate. The moves might be interpreted as an attempt to maintain property values, with street furniture an element in defining character and, consequently, desirability of a place to live. Old artefacts increasingly differentiated middle-class from working-class neighbourhoods, which were now more and more associated with municipal modernism. But there was also an effort to address new items of street furniture. Official bodies including the powerful Council of Industrial Design attempted, mostly unsuccessfully, to harmonise street furniture and ensure better (by which they meant 'more modern') design.

Britain's brightest and best industrial designers were engaged to create new forms, with seemingly simple street furniture conceived as a kind of beachhead for modernism, stakes in the ground setting out a new territory for design. Jack Howe designed streetlights from spun concrete and perforated metal litter bins, Ernest Race and Misha Black designed public seating, David Mellor (later known for expensive cutlery) designed tubular steel streetlighting, bus shelters, traffic lights and pillarboxes, and Kenneth Grange (designer of the Kenwood Chef, Kodak Instamatic and later the InterCity 125 train) designed parking meters and bus shelters. While these figures were designing the new landscape of consumption, the products and machines which defined the postwar, post-austerity world of stuff and their street furniture might be seen as a continuation of that realm of things. It was catalogued and taxonomised and printed in expensive-looking brochures illustrating how *modern* a municipality's townscape could look.

Modern street furniture became a stratum of modernity in what was mostly still a historic environment. Like a series of modernist punctuation marks, it proposed a new grammar of infrastructure, a grid of points setting out a new language.

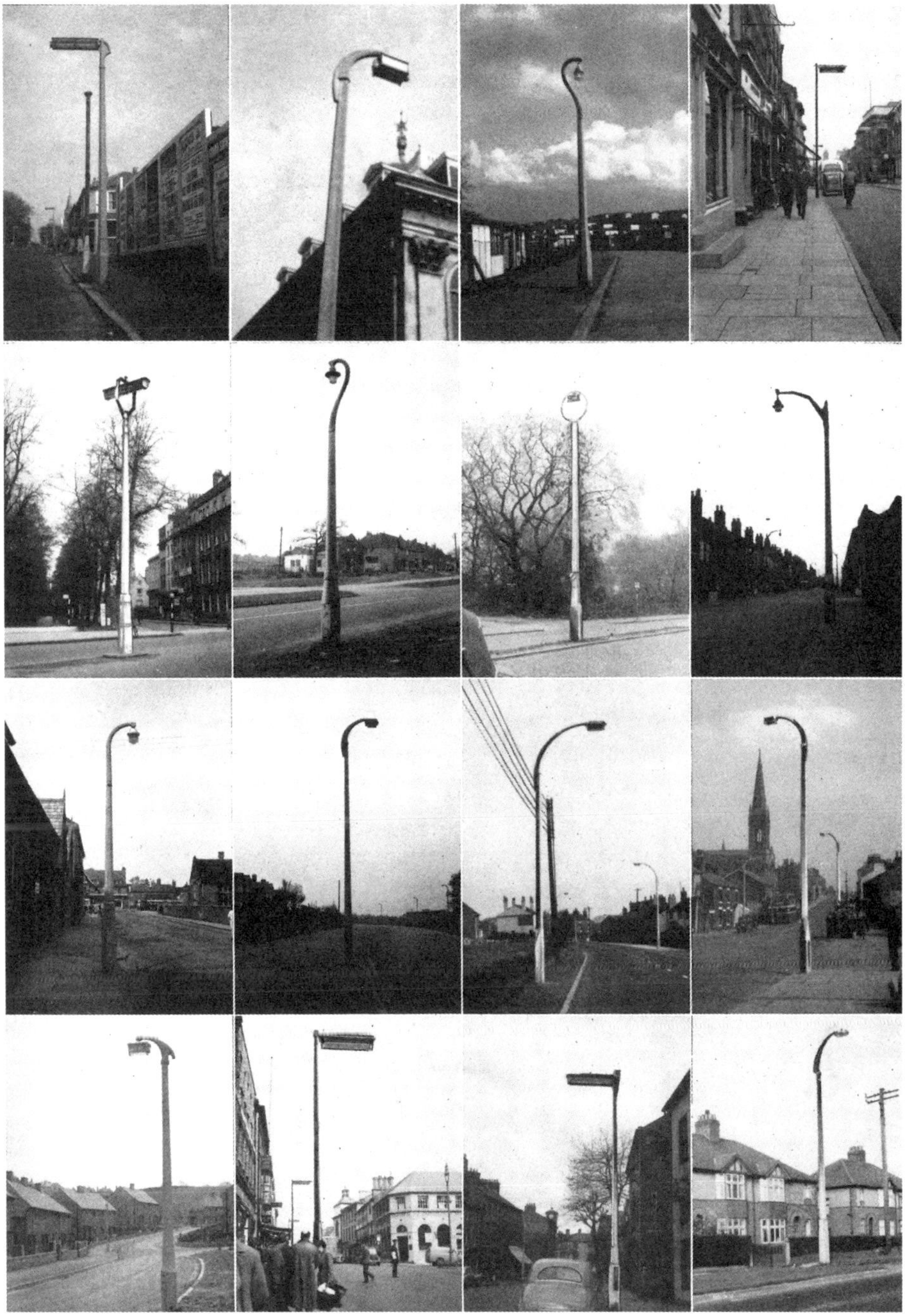

Page 373 of 'Outrage', June 1955 (reprint)
Photographer(s) unknown

Mooring

The heftiest, the heaviest, perhaps even the earliest street furniture sat at the edge of the water. The huge mooring bollards and capstans, the cranes and cleats used for securing ships, represent an entire world of fittings which were once scattered along the quays of almost every city but which, if they remain at all, have become curios, artefacts of industrial archaeology and urban ornaments speaking of a history which can seem impossibly distant.

The docksides of our cities, almost all now converted to some kind of leisure and amenity use, linger on as skansens of nautical history. The solid, cast pieces were once wrapped in rope, creaking at the effort of retaining the ships by the quay. Many have been worn smooth by decades of friction, of nights holding boats back from the tides as the vessels strained at their moorings.

The warehouses which line the docks and that once held goods from around the globe, now repurposed as upscale housing or restaurants, have hanging from them the chains and cranes and pulleys which give their history away. The docks, once probably inaccessible to all but sailors, stevedores and customs officials, now find themselves a landscape of consumption in which the product is the view - the water converted from highway to spectacle.

Of course there are the huge cranes that survive in some locations as curios, proto-skyscrapers outside our remit here too big to be street furniture. But there is also an entire taxonomy of mooring bollards of every type. Their sheer mass, their authenticity-value and their ability to contain a world of memory and allusion in the specificity of their form has enabled some of them to survive. It is a huge category of types. There are tee bollards and kidney bollards with flattened, flared heads like squashed bicycle seats. There are pillar bollards with a rim around the circular top like the hypertrophied head of a nail, and there are single-bitt bollards with domed heads and what look like handlebars sticking out to either sides. There are double-bitts with two heads tilting gently away from each other like legs and shoes sticking out of concrete, there are stag-horn bollards with all kinds of odd configurations at strange angles, and there are cleat bollards, some perhaps adapted from nautical fittings, little mini-anvils or faucet heads.

Once more organic, the shapes in contemporary versions have been flattened out a little, their gentle contours made sharper. What were once huge castings are now fabricated from welded and capped tube, so while they are recognisable they have lost the charismatic forms, the swells and curves, the mushroom tops and head-shaped lumps. They survive, somehow, as memories of former forms, co-ordinates fed through code to become digitised ghosts of themselves.

Where these old fittings and fixings survive, they might be used as seats, by people or by gulls. They have become street furniture in their dotage. So huge are some that they might appear to be mooring the quayside to the land as they once held fast the ships, creating that sensation of looking out across the water and feeling almost buoyant, as if on a raft. It can seem as if these huge iron fittings are the last bolts stopping the quay from drifting into the sea, now that its docks have been dematerialised into real-estate marketing.

Moralising

The mass manufacture and deployment of street furniture in the 19th century is usually understood as part of an effort to improve physical conditions in the city. But it was much more than that. It was as much a moral as a functional imperative. Water fountains were sponsored by Temperance Societies, bandstands were built to provide wholesome free entertainment (music shorn of suggestive lyrics or bawdy content) for the masses in the fresh air, streetlighting was introduced to deter prostitution and al fresco nighttime sex, pissoirs were erected to maintain decency and so on. Street furniture was conceived as an infrastructure of rectitude, a framework of redress to the iniquity of the big city.

The 19th-century metropolis was both a wonder and a nightmare. Revered and reviled, it was a place of technological, architectural and cultural marvels but also of slums and rookeries, brothels and boozers. While some streets were paved in stone, most were caked in mud. The arcade emerged (notably in Paris and London in the early 19th century but then everywhere else too) as a partial solution to the problem of where to walk and talk in your finest clothes, to see and be seen sheltered from the weather, to stroll on clean, paved ground and under the illumination of skylights and the oil and gas lamps of the stores and cafés. It was a new kind of public space, internalised, continuous, but effectively private and secure. But even these surveilled spaces soon became seedy, their upper floors filling up with brothels. It was not until the mid-century arrival of department stores that women on their own or in small groups had anywhere they could be in the city outside their own homes without causing moral indignation.

The layer of street furniture which began to appear in the 19th century may have been part of an effort to make the streets safe, to reclaim the night with lighting, to provide drinking fountains and to improve paving and make pavements safe from traffic. But you might also suggest that it was part of an urban enclosure equivalent to the enclosures of the commons which so unsettled British communal life and accelerated inequality and precarity from the medieval age to the present day. The fear of revolution led to a transformation of the streets. In Paris, where revolution had become a kind of popular festival, celebrated every few years, the entire centre of the city was rebuilt by Baron Haussmann's administration in an effort to create streets less easy to barricade, alleys less easy to disolve into and slums less easy to foment revolution in than the new bourgeois apartments with their informer/caretakers and expensive rents. Elsewhere the moves were less extensive, but nevertheless pervasive.

Chief among them was streetlighting. The authorities feared the chaos of the night. It allowed criminals to go about their business but also seditionaries, revolutionaries, anarchists and others to assemble and discuss their furtive plans. Darkness facilitated the sex trade and moral decay, enabling the bourgeoisie to take disease and turpitude back to their prosperous homes. Thomas Rowlandson's 1809 cartoon *A Peep at the Gas Lights in Pall-Mall* (p.144) depicts a group staring at the newfangled lamps. A prostitute on the right (a muff indicates her profession) is saying 'If this light is not put a stop to - we must give up our business. We may as well shut up shop'. Lighting was far from universally welcomed; in some cases glass lanterns were smashed, lampposts vandalised.

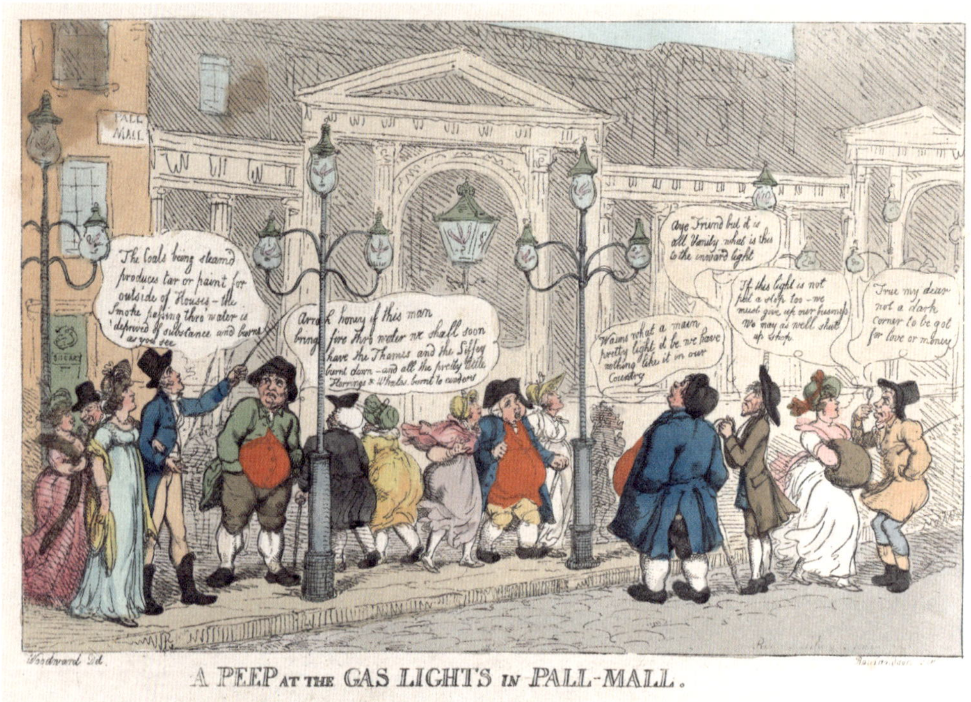

A Peep at the Gas Lights in Pall-Mall, 1809
Thomas Rowlandson

During the 19th century clocks began appearing on public buildings and, in Britain and its colonies, at crossings and on towers. Presented as purely practical these were actually reminders of responsibility, framing the working day, promoting punctuality and regularity. Clocks are a prompt to start work, to make that last train in time. They imposed another rhythm of order on the streets, reinforcing physical improvements with a temporal framework.

The most visible manifestation of morality expressed through street furniture was the water fountain. For most of the city's history water was filthy and dangerous, so its inhabitants drank beer or other fermented drinks. In the UK, its colonies and in the US, the Temperance movement burgeoned in the mid-19th century. An often curious alliance of Christians, Quakers, women's groups, friendly societies, working class and self-improvement interests and politicians, it became hugely powerful, its success culminating ultimately in the great failed experiment of prohibition in the US (1920–33). Alternatives to alcohol were promoted: hot chocolate (backed by the Quakers, who founded so many of Britain's most famous chocolate brands), tea, carbonated drinks and, most notably, water. If the others were all commercial ventures of some sort, water was to be free, a genuine alternative to cheap, free-flowing beer.

John Snow's demonstration that a cholera outbreak in London's Soho had spread through contaminated water from a pump in Broad Street in 1854 was one of the most momentous discoveries in public health, but unsurprisingly it did little to encourage people to drink water. The solution was provided by the foundation of the Metropolitan Drinking Fountain and Cattle Trough Association in 1859 and the proliferation of public facilities in the city, often pointedly positioned outside pubs.

During the Second World War when a blackout was imposed, criminality soared. The emergence of a thriving black market in response to rationing, and an explosion in prostitution and outdoor encounters made authorities nervous, reviving fears of moral decay. The postwar boom in street furnishing and a switch to abundant modern electric lighting was, at least in part, a reaction to this – a fear of renewed protest and rebellion by a newly returned and battle-hardened army and newly liberated women now used to paid work and independence.

The appropriation of public lavatories by gay men when homosexuality was still outlawed was a perfect illustration of the potential for the subversion of street furniture introduced to counter one moral outrage (people pissing in the streets) for purposes other than intended. The practice of cruising public toilets became known as 'cottaging' after the often cutesy domestic designs of low-rise public lavatories in parks and other faux-pastoral settings. An entire language of codes and signals emerged to attract the attention of the users of adjacent stalls. Many of the facilities in British parks were closed down due to 'moral panics' (often entirely invented by the popular press) and the deliberate conflation of gay sexual practices (then described as 'public indecency') with threats to children. It presented a convenient excuse for cash-strapped councils to shut down council lavs which were costing money to run. The end of the public toilet is partly attributable to the official reaction to gay sex.

More recently, the proliferation of CCTV has its own moral dimensions. Combined with the ubiquity of mobile phones and the ability to track individuals through cellular masts, it creates a web of surveillance. Attacks on women have been used to justify and expand this web. New layers of street furniture, digital ticket barriers, bike rental stands and so on have also emerged as part of the surveillance capital network, co-opting street furniture into an unavoidable network of tracking. Moral panic over terrorism, sexual assault, abduction, knife crime, gangs and immigration is being assuaged by a hyperinflation in the gathering of data. Street furniture has become profoundly complicit in that ambition to control, just as it has always been.

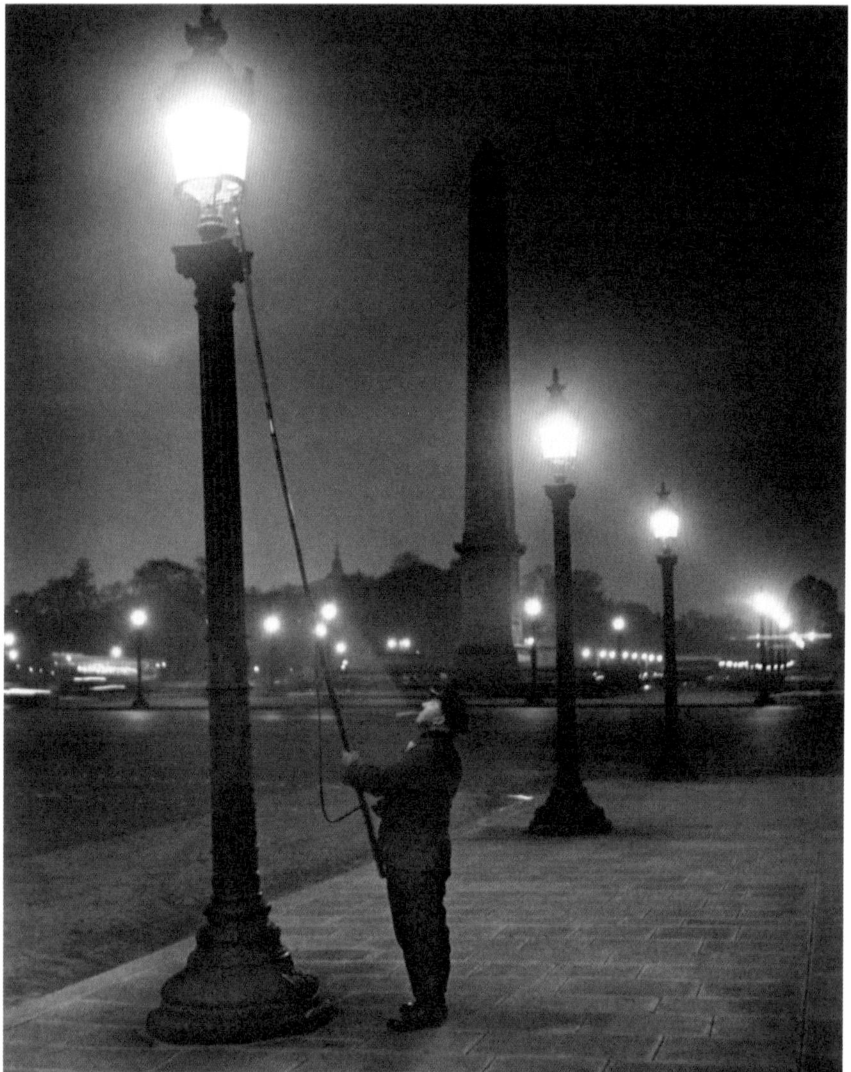

Lamplighter, Place de la Concorde, 1933
Brassaï

Nightwalking

Two photo books - Brassaï's *Paris de Nuit*, and Harold Burdekin and John Morrison's *London Night* - defined an image of the two cities after dark which, though maybe romanticised and a little fanciful, has proven stubbornly enduring. Brassaï published his work (thought to be the first photo book of purely nocturnal scenes) in December 1932, and its images of rain-soaked cobbles, *colonnes Morris*, illuminated adverts, pissoirs and lovers on benches and beneath streetlights, of brothels and bars, drunken crowds and loneliness have encoded our perception of the City of Light after dark. Brassaï was known for wondering the city at night, observing and depicting the radically different character of the nighttime city, a set with a different cast to the one lit by the sun. His was a city in which the street furniture emerges as a frame for urban life, things that seem almost invisible during the crowded daytimes suddenly spotlit by the new electric lights that had been installed in Paris and which gave a new, sharper illumination. Brassaï picks up on the brightness, on the reflected light on the cobbled streets, in the puddles and the way it creates an aura in the evening mist.

Inspired by Brassaï, British photographers Harold Burdekin and John Morrison published the much less known but similarly seductive *London Night* just over a year later in 1934. Burdekin was killed by a falling bomb a decade later and Morrison remains almost completely unknown, yet their book remains not only an incredible record of the nighttime city but a fascinating contrast to Brassaï's depiction of Paris. Whereas the Hungarian-born Brassaï focused mostly on people, whether in silhouette or shadow and used the city's street furniture as an armature, Burdekin revelled in the emptiness of the city streets. His is a city inhabited chiefly by its fittings, the bollards and streetlights, the sculptures and benches, the trees and chimneys. When he photographed a park with benches, the benches were empty, when he photographed an archway into an alley it resembles the Venice of *Don't Look Now,* foreboding, deeply shadowed, perhaps just vacated.

London, traditionally seen as a far less elegant capital than Paris, begins to look beautiful in the dark. Burdekin's aerial shot of Regent Street is astonishing (p.148). You have to look twice to check it isn't a painting. The graininess looks like a fizzing cocktail of fog and particles, the miasma of industrial urbanity. But he captures the sweep of a street inhabited only by lamps and a single postbox. The only other illumination comes from the shopfronts while Air Street, by day a grand, Piranesian archway, here appears as a channel of light emerging into the street. You can tell that there were cars but that the long exposure has blurred them into pale smudges. Even Leicester Square is empty. When was Leicester Square ever empty? The benches are uninhabited and the streetlamps and the lone warm glow of the phonebox become the focus, with the background firework highlighting the Hippodrome's illuminations. The photos suggest the beauty of a city which we somehow do not now see, watched over by iron sentinels, black bollards and glowing lanterns.

In 1938 German-born Bill Brandt (who would later deny his German roots and claim to have been born in South London) published *A Night in London*, another response to Brassaï's book from over the channel. Although there are photos of streetlights and bollards, blank brick walls and dark courts inhabited by nothing more than washing on a line, this is mostly much more in the vein of Brassaï, with crowds and waiting women, policemen and prostitutes (or, at least, women looking a little like sex-workers, one of whom was modelled by Brandt's wife). One of the most chilling of his photos, *Deserted Street in Bloomsbury,* taken in a bombed area during a blackout, is so effective because it fails to show any damage. Instead the nighttime scene centres on a streetlight which is not illuminated, symbol of a city switched off in the blackout, a city waiting with apprehension, fear embodied in the lone lamppost.

Brandt's are arguably the better photos, but in attempting to address Brassaï's vision of a very different city he fails, perhaps, to capture the city's essence in the way that Burdekin did, instead mostly imposing a Parisian template on a colder and, in many ways, more inscrutable city. All, however, illustrate perfectly how at night the street furniture comes into its own, defining and refining the cityscapes, radiating light and casting shadows, inviting and blocking, suggesting shelter and yet remaining empty.

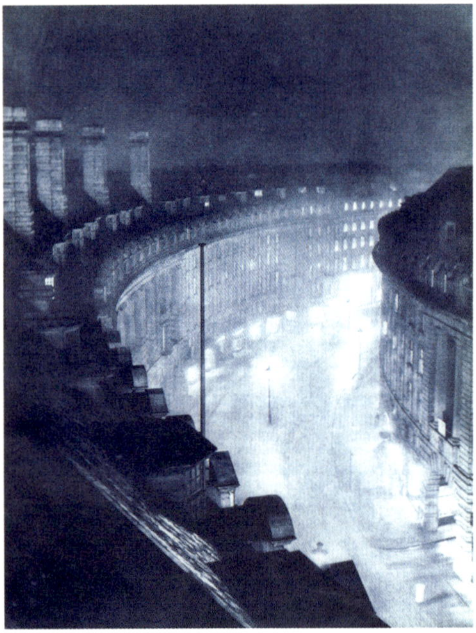

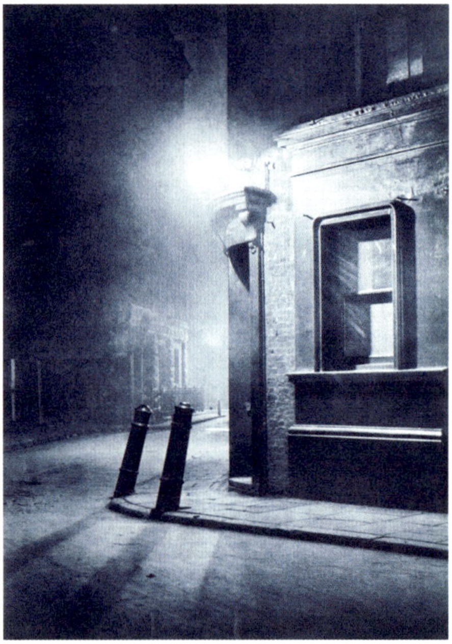

Left: *Curve (Regent Street, Piccadilly)*; right:
Beyond the Pavement (A City Street), 1934
Harold Burdekin

Deserted Street in Bloomsbury, 1941
Bill Brandt

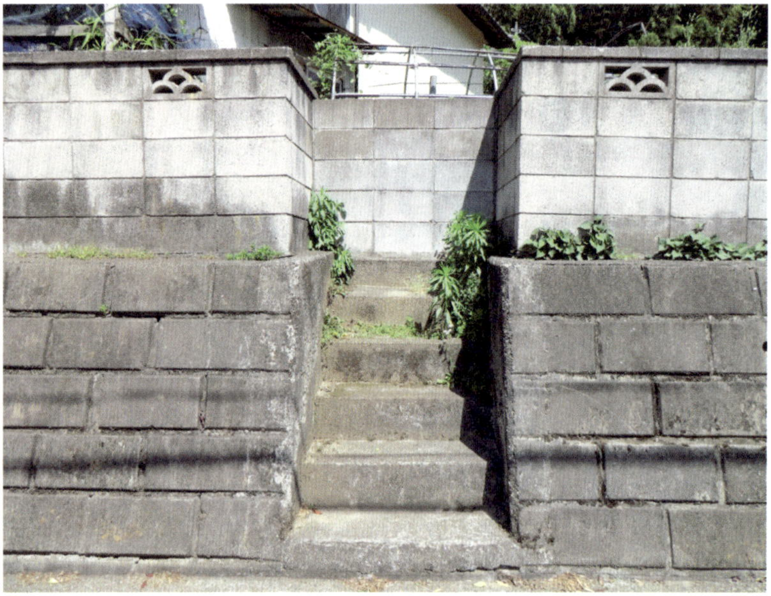

Thomasson in Ozakura, Japan, 2015
Photograph by heriheri

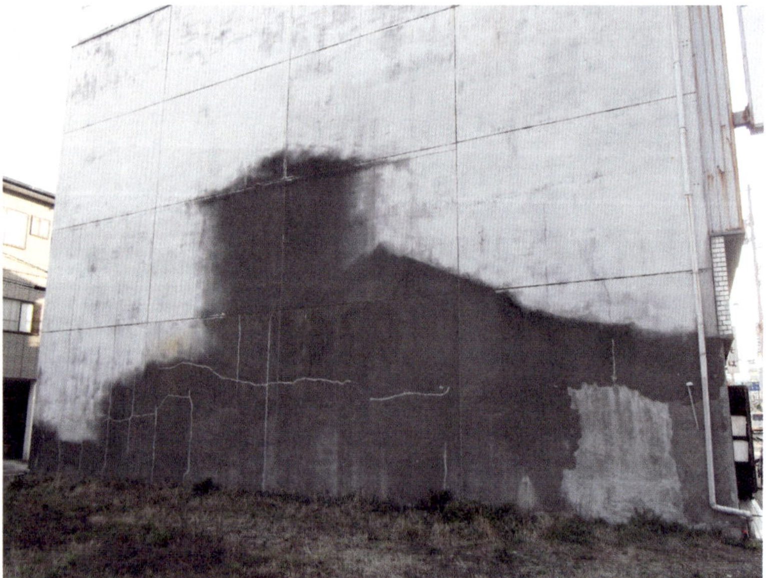

Genbaku Type Thomasson in Suruga Word, Japan, 2014
Photograph by Halowand

Observing

> However, a truly pure street sensitivity can recall the profound pathos of the city in a weather-beaten cast-metal manhole lid ... in the stump of a roadside telephone pole, feel the sweet innocence of human society in flyers stuck on a wall, imagine the entire world in the melancholy chickweed that sprouts inside a disused, rusty hand-pump - it is those kinds of sensations. Such trivial things can't be used as weapons of consumption.

With these words, Japanese architectural historian and designer Terunobu Fujimori attempted to explain the attraction of street furniture and fittings, not as art objects, or even necessarily readymades, but rather as containers of a kind of history, the remaining traces of an older manifestation of a townscape which may have been long superseded. The words come from the 1986 manifesto of The Street Observation Society, an informal organisation dedicated to investigating and recording the odd corners and strange survivals which studded the Japanese city and which somehow survived the relentless renewal and instability of Japan's urban fabric.

It was the natural next step for a figure who, while a student in the 1970s, had founded the enigmatic-sounding Architecture Detective Agency. This loose organisation had been dedicated to finding and recording neglected (and rapidly disappearing) western-style modernist buildings on the streets of Japan. It was a deliberate riposte to the kind of architectural anthropology which focuses on the historic and the vernacular, instead finding beauty in banality much as Georges Perec was doing in Paris at around the same time. Like Perec, Terunobu Fujimori and his friend Genpei Akasegawa (a pseudonym used by Katsuhiko Akasegawa) were documenting the infraordinary. This attitude to the things and survivals embedded in the city was deeply indebted to 'modernology', the study of the material manifestations of the modern city which emerged after the Great Kantō Earthquake of 1923.

Modernology had been pioneered by Wajiro Kon as a branch of sociology adapted to urban modernity and the effects of rapid and radical modernisation on populations. Kon's studies of this emerging landscape of modern things - a world and a moment described through everyday items of use, drawn and labelled on crowded, visually intriguing pages - remain profoundly inspirational. As a method it refused to impose a hierarchy on the world of things, treating high and low cultural products from children's clothes and stationery to house plants and eating utensils with the same sociological seriousness. The remarkable results sit somewhere between an ethnography applied to the familiar: comic books, police notebooks, architectural surveys and choreographic notation.

By the late 20th century, modernology had morphed into something else, a more debased notion of the study of the commercial landscape - the products in Japanese stores, the packaging and colours, the brands and logos, documenting the endless varieties of instant noodles or the subtle differences between cult sports shoes. The Street Observation Society was, as Fujimori suggests, a reaction to this commodification. 'Consumption', he wrote, 'is BAD, observation is GOOD. In a shop is BAD, on a street is EXTRA GOOD'.

One of the fundamental objects in the observation of the city was the 'Thomasson'. These were architectural elements that had remained in place despite having lost their intended function. They were named after major league baseball star Gary Thomasson, who was signed from the Dodgers by the Yomiuri Giants in the Nippon Baseball League in 1980, becoming the league's most expensive signing. He spent two hapless seasons in Japan as one of the lowest scoring players, his record-breaking signing becoming a byword for ignominious failure, but also for the pitfalls of cultural transfer and, in a way, a kind of cult.

It was Akasegawa, a conceptual artist and writer, who first applied the name 'Thomasson' to the stray architectural elements left over from previous incarnations of a building. In the rapidly changing landscape of urban Japan (where the architectural culture is not of continuity but of constant demolition and rebuilding) there were frequent anomalies, and the Thomasson Observation Centre's project was to document these rather pathetic, occasionally slightly surreal, hauntings of defunct functions. Typologies and taxonomies were created which suggested reverence and artistic significance. There were 'Useless Doors' and 'Useless Stairs': openings which had been blocked up or steps which had once led somewhere but now didn't, or that were just built in the wrong place and left there as it was cheaper and easier to not remove them, testament to a culture of speed in building. There was the 'Abe Sada', the stump of a chopped-down utility pole (its name deriving from a notorious incident in which a geisha killed and then castrated her lover, carrying off his genitalia in her kimono). There was 'The Boundary', a fenced-off area which seems to have no purpose, and 'The Live Burial', a bollard or piece of street furniture which has become partially submerged in a structure or in the road surface. There was 'The Devouring Tree' where a railing or fence had become subsumed into the trunk of a tree as it grew. There was 'The A-Bomb Type', a hauntingly named phenomenon where the silhouette or profile of a building is retained on a neighbouring flank wall after the original building had been demolished. There was 'The Uyama', a sign in which some of the letters had dropped off or gone missing (Uyama was the word left on one particular sign and it came to denote the type). And, among many others, there was 'The Atago', a bollard or stump which had no clear purpose.

These leftover traces were regarded as notably pure, precious things. Like art they had no function and existed only as archetypes, almost Platonic suggestions of things as if existing in a higher realm, beyond function. Like Gary Thomasson, these perfectly formed objects existed in the world and might once have performed a function but now had no discernible use.

The Thomasson is instantly understandable, in the sense of a kind of pathos, the lost child, but also in the sense of Walter Benjamin's understanding of the modern city as an accumulation of clues. Benjamin suggested that the detective novel was the key to understanding the modern city, a place of alienation in which events leave behind traces. Each of these traces implies a world that was different as well as an understanding of other worlds that might have been. There is a fine line though between observation of these lonely leftovers and sentimentality. As I understand it, the project of the modernologists and the observation societies was not to mourn the passing of the worlds that these traces imply, nor to sentimentalise or anthropomorphise the Thomassons as lost souls in the city - rather it was to objectively document the object. It is predicated on an understanding that we comprehend the city and the landscape not, as architects would often like us to, as *space* but that our eyes are drawn to *things*. Fujimori calls it 'object sensitivity'.

The problem, of course, with this attachment to objects and traces of incidents is the potential for a fetishisation of these events. Fujimori is careful to avoid this trap: To explain why I am emphasising this point', he writes, 'the reason our eyeballs have bulged on to the streets is that we have become sick of intentional things. In art intended to produce beauty, in avant-garde art intended to demolish beautiful art, in parodies intended to get a laugh, and in products intended only to be purchased, it is the intentional part that we don't.'

So the difference between appreciation (or fetishisation) and observation is made abundantly clear. And that observation, which may be accompanied by a sense of discovery, a joy in finding the traces, allows us to reconnect with the city and regain a sense that 'the city has somehow come to belong to us'. There is something here of the Situationists and their drive, the intention to subvert the nature of a city intended to impose an order on the world through wandering seemingly aimlessly, taking back control through walking, seeing and revelling in the imperfections. This is not, as it could easily be interpreted, a sentimental assessment of the streets, celebrating its rare survivals and quirks and turning them into art objects. Rather, it is a clear-eyed assessment of the street and the way in which it preserves, quite neutrally and without judgement, moments and deviations, traces of incidents, events, mistakes and carelessness, the world in which we live, the world of things.

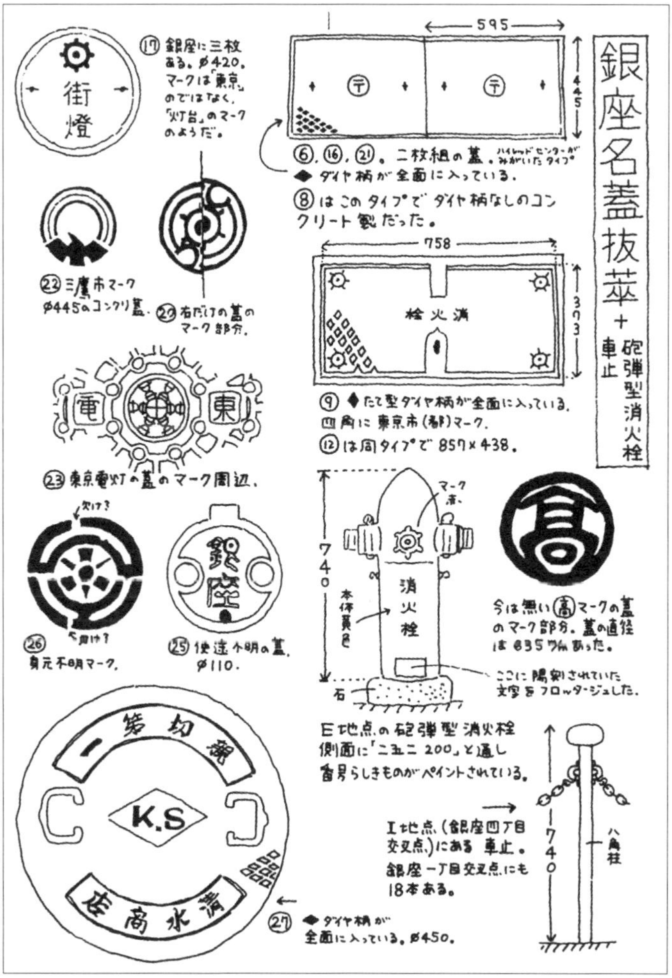

Manhole Covers, Hydrants, and Other Objects Observed in the Ginza District, 1986
Illustration by Joji Hayashi

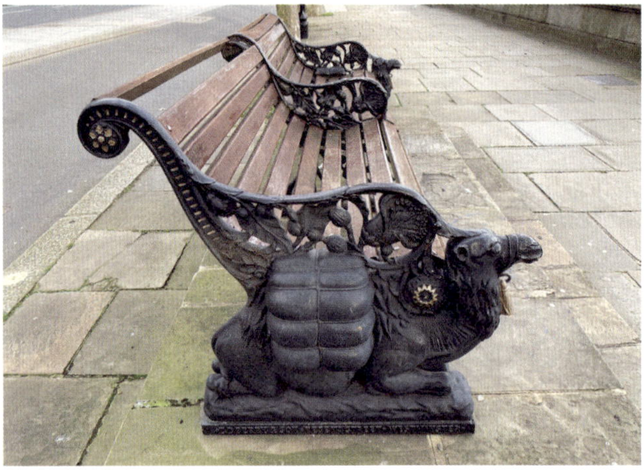

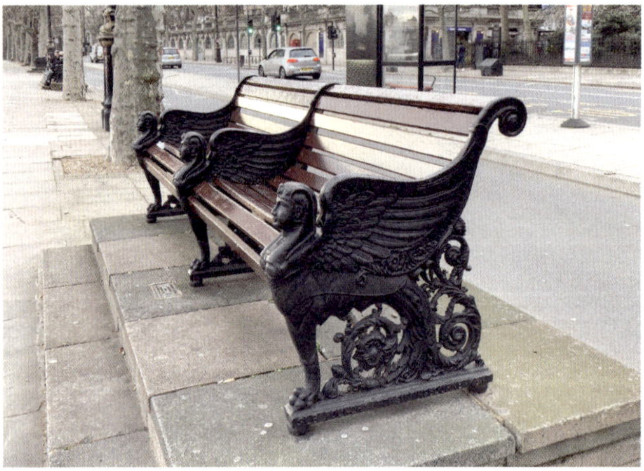

Two cast-iron benches, London Embankment

Orientalising

If you walk down the London Embankment you might be struck by a run of remarkable benches. There are two types: one features a cast-iron camel, the other a cast-iron sphinx. These exotic creatures form the brackets of the benches, their arms, ends and legs. The wings of the Sphinx sweep behind it to form the back in what looks a little like a kitschy sleigh. The camels meanwhile are sitting, their legs folded up beneath them, their humps heavily laden with booty, above them a screed of exotic flowers and plants. There isn't much mystery about them - Cleopatra's Needle, an Ancient Egyptian obelisk, rises on the Embankment close by, flanked by huge bronze sphinxes (still pock-marked and pitted from a First World War bomb). Another, similar obelisk sits in Paris's Place de Concorde, though there it is the grand bronze lampposts which are left to create an exotic impression with their anachronistic blend of Roman and Egyptian iconography.

If these items of bespoke street furniture attempt to address and amplify the antiquities, they also express an orientalism which pervaded the development of municipal street furniture in the 19th century. Partly it was the inspiration taken from the Persian and Ottoman kiosks which influenced the designs of everything from *colonnes Morris* to pissoirs and cabmen's shelters. But partly it was the culture of empire, using the presence of municipal objects to remind the populace that these were imperial capitals with global reach, inscribing colonial power in the fabric of the street.

The kiosks, advertising columns, fountains and even urinals of Paris, Berlin, Vienna, Budapest and dozens of other cities featured onion domes, fretwork arches and panels decorated with vaguely oriental designs. This was not a specific architecture. It had elements of Mughal, bits of the Alhambra, perhaps touches of Fez or Istanbul. The stamped panels of the prefabricated toilets which once sat on the streets of European and colonial capitals often featured Islamic-inspired ornament to go with domes that could have come from a hamam. Surely, these must feature among the grossest aesthetic insults to a Muslim? A damning confirmation of Edward Said's condemnation of orientalism as a primitive, debased form of cultural appropriation with little understanding of meaning beyond surface.

To some extent this exoticised language of material and ornament was a response to the emergence of new typologies which architects and designers had to conceive and decorate from scratch. That period, broadly the second half of the 19th century, coincided with a genuine curiosity and interest in decorative culture from across the globe. The publication of Owen Jones's hugely influential *The Grammar of Ornament* (1856) was concurrent with the boom in mass-produced street furniture and was surely used as a source for appliqué designs. The Asian-inflected park kiosk comes from the same impulse as the Japonisme at Liberty's or the Arab Hall at Lord Leighton's House in Holland Park. In the Battle of the Styles all aesthetic treatments were game, regardless of their derivation. Is it worse to use Islamic-inspired forms rather than those of a Gothic cathedral? Well, yes, because one was already the culture of the place whereas the other is unknown and misunderstood, but that isn't necessarily the point.

The proliferation of street furniture as a mass-produced cosmopolitan consumable resulted in odd hybrids of style and suggestion. While designers were looking to Iznik tiles and plates, and architects to hamams and mosques, for inspiration, industrial designers were searching for a new form of expression which had neither the solemn solidity of classical architecture nor the ecclesiastical associations of the Gothic. They found that, by hybridising both of these and adding a dash of Mughal ornament or Moorish detail, they were able to create something new and distinctive but still recognisable.

These mongrel forms, much used in British seaside and colonial architecture, were adopted by the manufacturers of street furniture as a kind of spice, a flavouring, a small dash of which was enough to give a hint of the exotic in what were often the most banal of buildings. Take, for instance, the remarkable water fountain in Newport-on-Tay, Fife (a resolutely non-exotic place). Its octagonal form, the shape of its columns, the capitals, the frills on the arches and the pierced dome with a kind of Aladdin's lamp on its crown, all suggest something Moorish, yet nothing here is explicitly Islamic. There is no literal borrowing. Something similar might be said of the Gents' lavatories in Thorne Park, Plymouth, and Blackboy Hill (yes, I know) in Clifton, Bristol. Designed by George Jennings in the late 19th century, they both feature pierced screens of distinctly Islamic patterning. Or you might look at Brighton's bandstand, designed by Philip Lockwood in 1884, with its onion dome and filigree Ibero-Moorish columns, or at the Mughal-inflected dome of the bandstand on Clapham Common (1890). Lavatories and bandstands were seen as close relatives of Turkish baths (Victorian public and municipal baths often featured steam rooms) and Ottoman kiosks, exotic public goods in a kind of *One Thousand and One Nights* manner. The cabmen's shelter preserved in Ripon's market square bears the traces of the late 19th-century craze for chinoiserie in its delicate iron frieze.

Orientalist decoration represented an attractive language, appropriate for new urban typologies with no real precedent. These mass-manufactured things, entire new languages of public amenities, were conferred a meaning through their expression as something other, something different. Their status as public goods was conferred a little luxury by exotic associations. Our values have changed, but their value as public amenity remains, albeit, occasionally, a little tarnished by weather, time and culture.

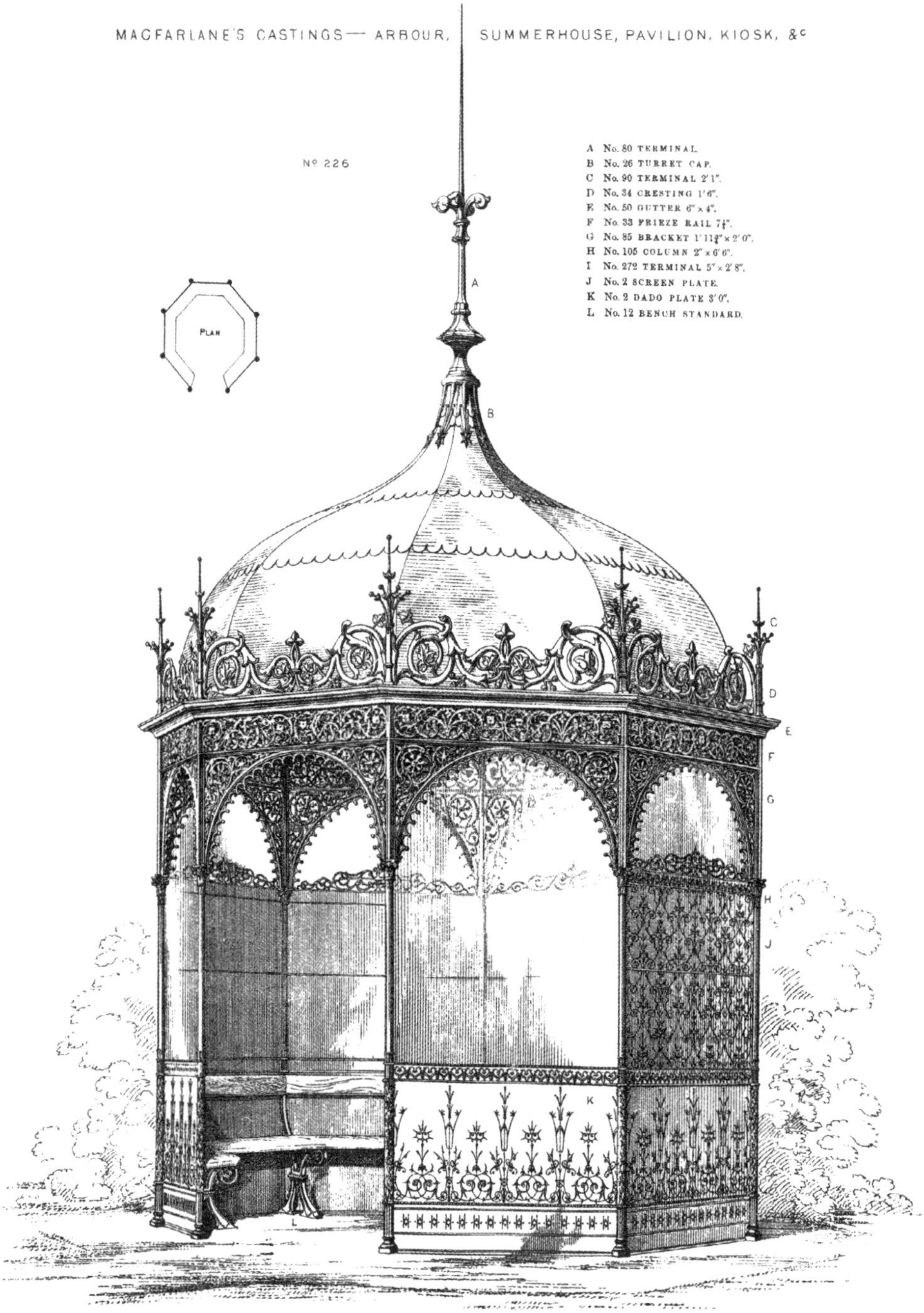

Design for arbour, summerhouse, pavilion or kiosk, from catalogue published by Walter MacFarlane & Co. Saracen Foundry, Glasgow (Volume II, 6th edition, c.1882)

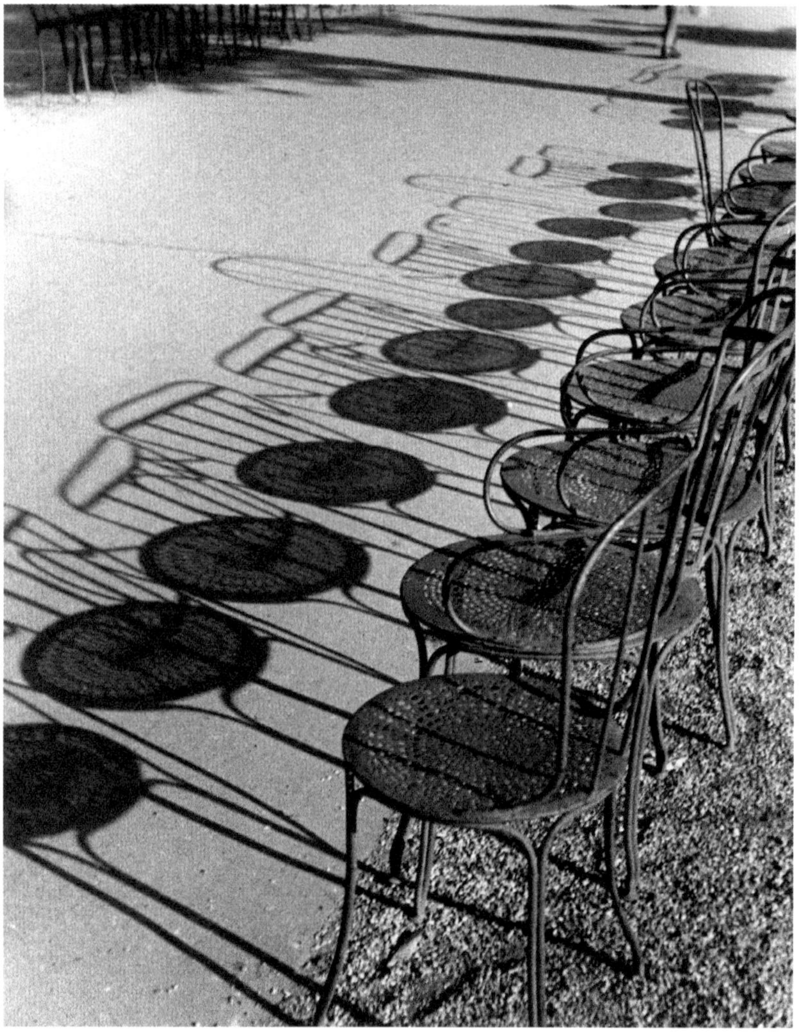

Chairs, Champs Elysées, 1929
André Kertész

Parking

Walter Benjamin referred to Eugène Atget's documents of a disappearing Paris as resembling photographs of 'the scene of a crime'. The crime is the eerie emptiness, it looks like an aftermath, charged, though never entirely clear with what. But it is also the subsequent disappearance of so many places, of the vestiges of the old Paris. In Atget's photo *Café, Avenue de la Grande-Armée*, Paris, 1925, the chairs and tables of a very Parisian pavement café stand empty. We're used to seeing these places populated, to looking at customers now long dead, but here it seems as if it is the city itself which has died.

If the unsat-on café chairs evoke a sleeping city, the empty chairs of Paris's parks seem to have become a kind of photographic cliché of the city in which chairs stand in for people, populating the city while there is no-one around. André Kertész's *Chairs, Champs Elysées* depicts a group of wiry chairs on the gravel. At first glance they look identical, the kind of fin-de-siècle garden chairs that were ubiquitous on the Continent at the time - the form of which appears to have been inspired by the bentwood café chairs of Thonet, easily translated here into bent metal. But the longer you look, the more you realise that almost every chair is unique. Subtle variations in the designs of the backs, the line of the curve, the spacing of the bars, one crossbar or two, the splay of the legs. Like people, each chair exhibits its own characteristics and stance. This is what makes the photo a little haunting; the female figure walking by in the background seems to be almost disturbing the scene, as if interrupting a moment. Their informal layout and the ways in which they are turned toward each other or placed next to each other in different attitudes and spacings seems to suggest a conversation, a social scene. Chairs have a degree of freedom of movement, in contrast to benches fixed in place. The lightness is expressed in their wiry form, the compromise between mobility and comfort, letting the rain and wind right through them. But because they so clearly suggest the human body, or its absence, they become ciphers for use and there is something almost unsettling in their congregation.

Kertész returned to chairs in his 1963 shot *The Big Pond in the Tuileries* (p.160), in which the chairs appear to be looking out to the water while a pigeon picks its way beneath them. In his much earlier (1924) photo of chairs in the Jardin du Luxembourg, the photographer plays with the long shadows cast by three folding chairs which make a kind of dance diagram on the gravel, as if suggesting a delicate choreography and rhythm. In another, taken in the Champs Elysées in 1929, the shadows of a row of chairs appear as a series of disks, almost like coal-hole covers, with their delicate pierced patterns. But then a glance at the reflections of their varied backs recalls a kind of static orchestra, each with its own strange instrument. In its anthropomorphised subject it is Surrealist, in its composition Constructivist, and in its geometry almost Op art.

The architecture critic Ian Nairn, who took his own photos for his guidebook *Nairn's Paris* (1968), titled his picture of a pair of chairs in the Tuileries gardens *Rendezvous*. These are two very different chairs, the one on the left a folding version with a timber slat seat and on the right a bent metal chair with arms and circular metal pressed disk for a seat. It is a conversation not only between imaginary bodies but between the forms, the material language, the masculine folding chair and the feminine curves of the bent metal version. Or perhaps vice versa.

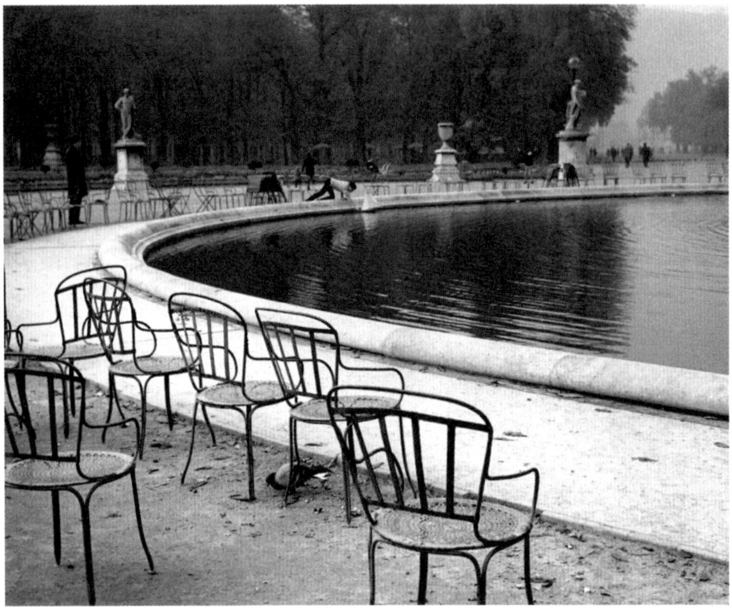

The Big Pond in the Tuileries, 1927
André Kertész

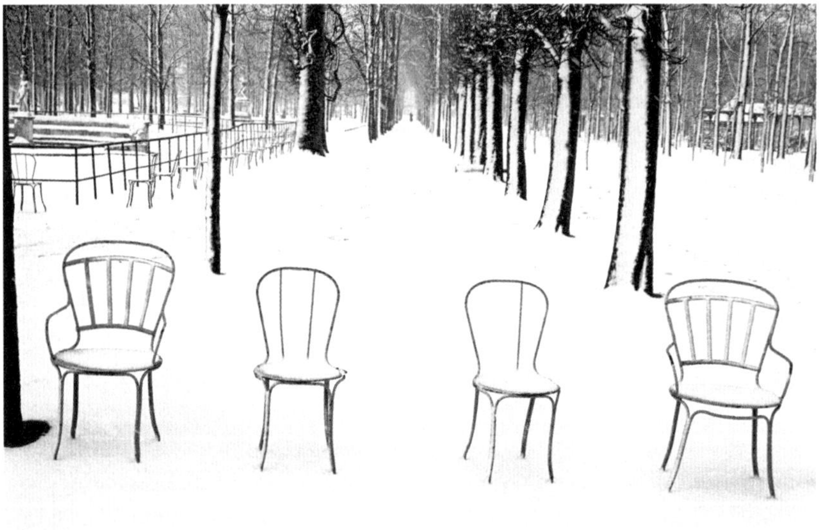

Snow in Jardin des Tuileries, 1978
Martine Franck

A decade later photographer Martine Franck took a beautiful photo of four chairs in the snow-covered Tuileries. They might have been placed, so perfect is their formation, though the lack of traces in the snow suggests this is how she found them. Two identical, broad, armed, bent-metal chairs flank the middle two which are more slender models, one with a vertical in its back missing. They appear clearly as a group, almost like a pop group. But the line is odd. Were they facing towards a performance? It certainly isn't a set up for conversation. Each of these arrangements of chairs has its own character, suggesting social situations. Kertész suggested he didn't know what he was doing at the time was art, he was just taking a photo. Does that then suggest that the placing of the chairs themselves is art?

Actually, the attraction of these groupings is that they capture a moment of togetherness and conversation. After they have been left in a particular configuration their placement embodies the memory of an encounter. They are like silent memories of words spoken in which the conversation is still present although the words themselves have long faded away.

The Paris park chairs were a municipal amenity but they were not free. Until the 1970s a fee was charged for their use, as it was for deckchairs on British beaches (though of course the Paris versions, this being France, were subsidised). So class enters the equation again. Chairs, the symbol of the individual, are classy; the bench, for everyone, was common. Chairs could not be slept in. Chairs could be arranged to be convivial, benches force people to sit side-by-side and to contemplate the park rather than each other. Benches are the city, chairs are the individual.

The parks department of Paris had its own workshops in the 19th century and made its own chairs, which were mixed in with others from commercial suppliers. The now classic, sage green stacking Luxembourg Chair (designed in 1923) was the result of an effort to harmonise the chairs across the city's estate.

At one point, during the 19th and early 20th centuries, parks were full of wiry café chairs as beer gardens, tea pavilions, kiosks and restaurants spread through the cities. Paris, Vienna, Budapest, Berlin, even London, populated its parks with mass catering and civilised cafés, all of which came with endless phalanxes of chairs. The chairs photographed in the 20th century can seem like the ghosts of those huge collections, wiry reminders of a pre-war Europe. It must have been a world of bonhomie and conviviality in which the city played its part as background and which, perhaps, seemed as if it would never end.

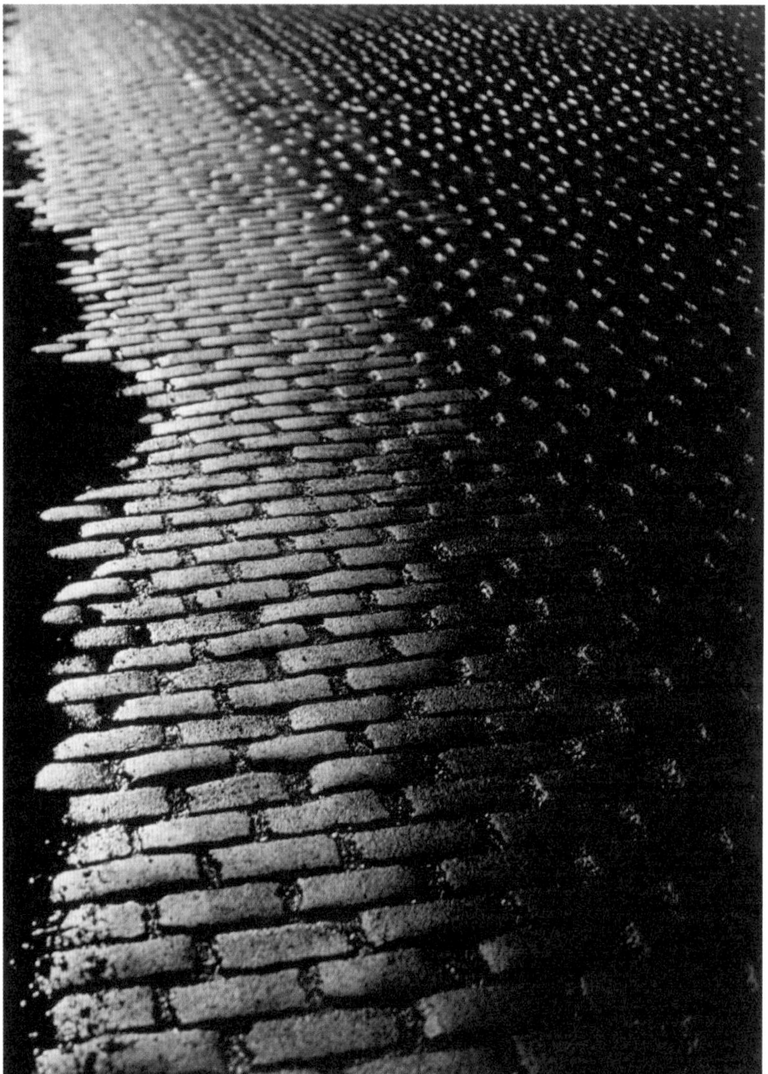

Paving Stones, c.1931–32
Brassaï

Paving

The pavements of Paris have been the world's most dug up, not by the utility companies (that's London) but by successive generations of protestors, communards and students. 1968 was the year the authorities finally had enough. After the protests that shut the city down, the cobbles were replaced by tarmac, robbing the city of the texture and complexity that made its streets an Impressionist's delight and a high-heel-wearer's nightmare, making them the smoothest in Europe. That had its own repercussions. It made the streets of Paris perfect for rollerblading and groups would gather, gliding through the city in a contemporary version of the *dérive*, the famous *flâneur*'s walk - a way of subverting the patterns of power inscribed in the city's streets through aimless wandering. It was not the first time the authorities had attempted to address the problem of paving a revolutionary *matériel*. Earlier in the 19th century, efforts had been made to replace cobbles with wood blocks, to address both noise and adaptation as barricades or weapons. Events overtook their efforts.

The pavement is the skin of the city, a membrane which separates the veneer of civilisation from the darkness of the earth. Below it are nestled the viscera, the tubes and cables, the gas, sewage, water, drains and electric cables, the arteries, veins and guts which keep the city alive. Each excavation is an operation, a surgical intervention which requires plastic surgery on the surface, a stitching and patching back together. But, for a thin surface, the pavement can have a hugely powerful effect on how the city feels, how it looks and how it behaves.

The story of the modern pavement starts not in Paris but in London. The Westminster Paving Act of 1762 led to the provision of pavements to either side of the road as a safe and clean place for pedestrians to walk. Georgian London became an exemplar of civilised streets in which walkers could avoid the mud, filth, butchered guts, blood and manure which covered the 18th-century road surface. Voltaire, visiting London, had been so impressed that he wrote the *Projet sur L'éstablissement de trottoirs* for Paris, arguing that the pavement was a method of democratising the city. The argument was that the wealthy could avoid the *ordure* in their carriages but the poor were destined to walk ankle-deep in shit. Pavements would allow the masses to enjoy a civilised city in purity and parity with the aristocratic elite.

This in itself was the result of a shift in fashion from the court to the street. In 18th-century Paris and London, fashion was set by the courtiers who spent their days in and around the well-tended grounds of the royal palaces. The growth of an affluent middle class in both cities, grown rich through trade and empire, and the advent of bigger, more elegant shops and streets and later hotels and restaurants, underscored a shift from royal precincts to public places. Once the shoes of the powerful and the wealthy needed to tread the pavements of the city, resources were found to improve them.

In the wake of the French Revolution, pavements were laid in Paris and became seen as an urban symbol of the Republic. In Britain, however, they were understood not as the pavements of power to the people but rather as a mechanism for hygiene, for protecting people from the filth of the streets (a metaphor for the moral corruption of the city). In Paris paving was funded by taxation, a public good; in London it was landowners, an enhancement of property value.

The introduction of pavements transformed the streets. Where shopping arcades had once been necessary to engender a sense of security and cleanliness, now shops could spread along the streets. Bigger and more spectacular stores began displaying their wares in windows, illuminating the sidewalks and making them places of fashion, food, phantasmagoria and longing. What was once a utilitarian thoroughfare became an avenue of consumption - streets of desire.

The pavement is a paradoxical thing. It begins as a symbol of civilisation and liberation but also becomes a kind of final resort, the domain of the homeless, of beggars and of defecating dogs. In New York the streets are given an extra dimension by the vents which funnel steam out from the pipes below the city, giving a glimpse of what appears to be a hot underworld. The coal holes and manholes that punctuate its surface all suggest the unknown underworld, the coal and gas, the water and copper wires, the fossil fuels and fruits of the earth returned to their subterranean state.

Small differences in paving can create wildly different impressions and experience. The cobbled streets of the industrial north, rain soaked and sooty, gave a grain to the town, a tightly knitted coherence which echoed the bricks in the walls which frame them to either side. The stone paving slabs of London can give an even, grey finish slightly sparkling with quartz. The feel under our feet can change from one street to the next. Thin leather soles on cobbles or trainers on tarmac give two distinct impressions of the city.

In Europe we can become complacent about the pavement. It is only when we encounter situations where it is absent that its importance becomes apparent. On the edges of US cities or when trying to traverse Gulf capitals on foot, in the informal settlements and after torrential rain when the roads are flooded, we suddenly see the beauty of the sidewalk.

We have come to perceive the pavement as something slightly dirty, something we only notice when it is dug up or when a slab has come loose and protrudes. But there are joyful manifestations too, places where the pavement makes the city. The black and white, tessellated pavements of Portugal, decorated with geometric shapes, stars, waves, labyrinths or curlicues, make the city something different. Public space becomes a huge decorated carpet.

The Brazilians took it an extra mile with Roberto Burle Marx's mosaic paving along Rio's Copacabana Beach becoming one of the unadulterated joys of tropical modernism. They made an explicit link with the former colonial capital across the Atlantic but expressed something of the geometries, the waves and dunes of freedom. What in Europe and the US was a utilitarian landscape of rigour and austerity became a swirling riot of Op art movement best seen from the swanky apartments above, but also seductive from street level where it transforms a surface into a shimmering landscape. He repeated the trick, to slightly less effect, at Biscayne Boulevard in Miami.

'I think that our bodies are in truth naked,' wrote Virginia Woolf in *The Waves*. 'We are only lightly covered with buttoned cloth; and beneath these pavements are shells, bones and silence.' The beach or the cemetery, the pavement separates us from a fantasy of life and a dream of death and it is the surface on which we walk and on which we fear we might end up sleeping. It embodies the life and death of the city.

Performing

The bandstand arrived as a product of Victorian morality. These delicate-looking structures started appearing in British and colonial parks in the 1860s (the first in the Royal Horticultural Gardens, now Kensington Gardens, in 1861). Their origins lie in the music pavilions scattered around the Pleasure Gardens of the 18th century. Visitors wandered around the paid attractions while music played gently in the background. These were themed spaces, with supper boxes and places to picnic, and grottoes and dark corners suitable for assignations. The Victorians stripped any sense of sex out of the pavilions and put military brass bands beneath them, transforming a magical, seductive idea of sylvan romance with their muscular municipal publicness.

Victorian parks were conceived as a relief from the slums, a way of getting the working classes out of their parlours and pubs for fresh air, wholesome nature and perhaps sunshine to counteract their children's rickets. The proliferation of tea rooms in parks was part of the same impulse, removing alcohol from the equation. Bowling greens, tennis courts and perhaps a paddling pool completed the picture. But bandstands were the architectural highlights. They came in a variety of forms and yet somehow all looked the same: an octagonal base with slender cast-iron columns which in turn supported a slightly exotic roof, perhaps in the form of a vaguely oriental dome, a squished Chinese pagoda or an Ottoman tent. Over 1,500 were built.

In London the LCC erected 22 bandstands in its parks and sponsored a number of bands to perform in them. Hundreds have survived, despite the kind of edifying music that they were designed for having long disappeared from the agendas of cash-strapped councils. At one time the musical programmes were astonishingly popular, with thousands gathered around in chairs and on the grass to listen to brass bands damaging delicate classics with their oompahs.

Now mostly unused and empty, though often well-maintained, the uselessness of bandstands almost seems to enhance their appeal. These purposeless platforms, sometimes fenced off, sometimes completely accessible, have become follies, as exotic in their own way as the grottoes, peacocks and floral clocks that once inhabited parks. Their ubiquity reveals their nature - early pre-fab pavilions, adopting mass-manufactured parts and customised slightly to their settings by, perhaps, a subtly different roof or some added ironwork details. They were part of the same architectural landscape as seaside shelters and seaside piers, as ornate railings and lampposts, ordered from catalogues from foundries geared to mass-production and long runs.

The ornate, orientalising, sometimes slightly Moorish, sometimes slightly Gothic or Renaissance ironwork was to symbolise culture and pleasure. Or perhaps we should say leisure - it was more about providing spaces in which to fill a Sunday off (still then a new phenomenon) than to create a place that would necessarily be hugely enjoyable. But they do represent a way in which the Victorians attempted to provide an infrastructure for *being* in the city, a place for those who had no access to gardens or concerts of their own. They refer to the romantic garden, the concert hall, to travel and to a kind of formal inhabitation of a nature of artifice without ever quite achieving any of it. It is worth noting, however, that the first bandstand in Kensington arrived a decade before the Albert Hall opposite it. Whatever its failings, it was an attempt to introduce culture to the masses for free via an elaborate piece of street furniture.

Persuading

When billboards were placed on top of buildings, around them, on street corners or intersections, you might have argued that they were a kind of street furniture. Certainly with the *colonne Morris* or the bus shelter as ad space, they exerted a certain physical presence. But when the city itself becomes a brandscape, a confection of corporate identity, then there is an argument that billboards cease to become distinguishable from the urban fabric, that the whole curtain-walled container becomes a billboard.

The reconstruction of Potsdamer Platz in Berlin in the early 1990s and the 'cleaning up' of Times Square in New York in the 21st century blurred the lines between advertising, corporate branding and architecture. The Potsdamer Platz of the 1920s with its cocktail of modernist architecture, stolid classicism, looming neons and advertising pillars and columns, or the seedy Times Square of the 1980s with its peep shows and cheap hotels, were distinctive places. Their rebuilding as surfaces for marketing and expressing corporate identity has seen a transition from architecture to advertising, tangible urbanity to digital information. It is no longer possible to draw a line between one and the other. Architects have long been attracted to advertising, from Robert Venturi and Denise Scott Brown's *Learning from Las Vegas* and their excitement at discovering a pop-architecture in which form is function but that function is advertising, to Jon Jerde's malls as production-design urbanity, reproducing the experience of the city within the privatised realm. But the advent of digital signage and the LED billboard in the 1990s blurred the lines still further, with architecture clad purely in signs, appearing as surface only.

All of this, it turns out, is nothing. The next phase is the subsumation of bodies into the brandscape. As our data is harvested, we are advertised to directly, at the moment via our devices, but soon, surely, via responsive advertising on architectural surfaces too. Street furniture, almost since its inception, has been used as branding, as information, as signs and, more recently, as advertising. As the marketing comes more directly to us the question might be, do we replace it? Are we all, now, wandering, internalised signposts consuming the fruits of our own search engine activity and browsing history?

Pissing

In Paris, the *colonne Rambuteau* was a free-standing structure for male urination - better known as a *pissotière* or pissoir. Claude-Philibert Barthelot, the Comte de Rambuteau, was the préfet of the Department of the Seine who laid the foundations for the renewal of Paris which his successor Baron Haussmann would complete. Rambuteau did not invent the pissoir - early versions had begun appearing on Parisian streets in 1830, and were almost immediately appropriated by revolutionaries as handy additions to their barricades. Rambuteau was responsible for the next wave of urinals in 1834, and these strange, curiously (and appropriately) phallic urban interventions became ubiquitous in Paris, with around 1,200 dotted around the streets of city by 1900. So much so that authors and artists suggested the pissoir was as much a constituent of the image of Paris as the Eiffel Tower.

It is an honour to have something named after you. But, Rambuteau must have thought, not *that*. It was almost certainly him, then, who lobbied to rename the pissoir as the *vespasienne*, taking as the patron saint of pissing the emperor Vespasian. In the late 1st century AD, the emperor had imposed a tax on urine collected for tanning and toga bleaching, placing pots around cities to make collection easier.

Reeking of and leaking urine, speaking of sexual discrimination (there was no female provision) and notorious for gay assignations, the *vespasienne* was about so much more than pissing. The designs themselves could form the basis of a fascinating history of architecture, albeit one that lasted barely a century. The earliest examples were vertical kiosks, miniature spires with hybrid functions often with a streetlamp perched atop, advertising panels beneath that, a central double-sided urinal of elaborate cast-iron design and curving screens to protect a little modesty (though feet and heads and shoulders remained mostly visible). One photographed by Charles Marville in 1865 is a fine early example (p.288). Some even earlier examples were more exposed, with no screens, solid-looking central cores with an alcove carved out and posters all around; others looked more like stable stalls, lined up in a row. Some had highly ornate screens, others had simple perforated metal sheets. At their most elaborate, the cast-iron details were remarkable - delicate columns and intricately wrought capitals, orientalising cupolas and finials, or onion domes. Sometimes they featured glazed lanterns and backlit ads, as depicted in Brassaï's enigmatic *Une Vespasienne, Boulevard Auguste Blanqui* (1935), showing a gently glowing pissoir, a tree and a streetlamp standing out against a light sprinkling of snow pocked with footsteps and inscribed with tyre tracks. There were larger versions too, whole buildings built from prefabricated cast-iron panels and pitched roofs (the type which became popular in Berlin in the late 19th century).

No matter what the form, all were painted in the dignified dark green which characterised all of Paris's plethora of new civic furnishing and fittings. A kind of class system was made implicit in the design of the pissoirs, with upmarket neighbourhoods being adorned with elaborate models and less salubrious quartiers being fobbed off with utilitarian-looking bent and stamped metal sheet fabrications. After the war, concrete replaced iron and some late Art Deco examples started appearing, with bathtub plan forms and curving ends.

The *vespasiennes* quickly became meeting points for gay men. Within a short time of their introduction, glory-holes appeared (recorded in police reports from the early 1860s) and an entire sub-culture emerged complete with its own language and bizarre fetishes. The structures became known as *tasses* (cups), due to their curving sides and the fact that the activities which went on inside, which might have seen men thrown in prison, were referred to as 'taking tea'. One particular specialist sub-culture involved dipping crusts of bread into the piss on the floor and eating it. The reputation of *vespasiennes* was redeemed, a little, by their new-found status under occupation in the Second World War, when they found themselves venues for resistance fighters exchanging messages, for dead drops and stashed weapons.

The conservative backlash came in the form of police surveillance, frequent arrests and also entrapment. The religious right's reaction was, eventually, responsible for the slow decline of the *vespasiennes*. The ostensible objections were to the smell and the despoliation of the streetscape, particularly in expensive quartiers. But the whiff of homophobia was always present and they were ultimately swept away by right-wing mayor Jacques Chirac in the early 1980s. They were replaced by the unloved *sanisettes*, the factory-built toilet pods better known over here as 'superloos'. These curiously Brutalist-looking mini-buildings have everything that the pissoirs lacked: closing doors, self-cleaning mechanisms, washbasins and privacy. But they are not free. They operate with a coin and, generally, open automatically after a fixed time. These too have been subverted by drug dealers and sex-workers, but they have seemingly engendered none of the affection and nostalgia of the *vespasiennes*.

One solitary pissoir remains in Paris. Standing on the Boulevard Arrago in the 13th arrondissement, its dark green metal sides now scuffed and graffitied without much conviction or ambition in marker pen, the little structure is dwarfed by the massive wall of the Santé prison, the only prison left in the centre of the capital. These two ends of the line, the last remaining examples of their type, make a sad, uneven pair, but one story unites them. In December 1876 a policeman discovered an encounter at the pissoir between a clearly well-to-do individual and an '18-year-old labourer'. The offence against public decency was documented as 'indecent exposure', but it was the identity of the older man which made it a sensation. Eugène de Germiny was a reactionary Catholic politician who ran on a platform of family values, anti-secularism and restoration of the monarchy. Attempting to explain away his encounter as 'research', he became the target of fierce satire and ridicule. He was sentenced to two months in Santé prison and a 200-franc fine. Paris's last *pissotière* is a piquant little memorial.

Planting

Like fish in a fishbowl, plants in pots represent a translation, an attempt to bring the earth from the ground and place it in a container on the surface. It is both a miniature representation of the garden and a transition of the private (garden) realm into the public (urban) realm. Occasionally you come across a street in which the residents have nurtured barrages of plants and trees in pots and placed them outside their houses to create a green, softened public place. Usually the only blurring of the boundary between public and private in the street in this way is with parked cars, effectively privatising public space in a manner which it is surprising that more people do not object to. But no-one objects to plants, even if they take up a large proportion of the public space.

That planting is seen as a public good represents our particular sentimentalised attitude to nature. Plants are, in themselves, understood as *a good thing* - which of course they are. So their multiplication in the curiously artificial environment of pots and planters is similarly understood as a benefit, even if they create obstructions. They are perhaps unique in this way as an item of street furniture which is largely accepted and appreciated with few qualms, even from the authorities.

Civic planters, a public rather than a private initiative, have a different profile. These municipal items (which most definitely fall into the category of street furniture, even if it is the plants rather than the planters which we tend to notice) enjoyed a period of prosperity in the postwar era. The world's cities filled with concrete troughs in odd shapes and raised brick areas filled with trees and, perhaps, surrounded by benches. They were decorative, perhaps indicating that this was a pedestrian plaza (they were hugely popular in the 'shopping precincts' of mid-century Britain, both outdoor and indoor malls). In other places they might be used as a visual signal to block traffic or as a way of filling too-large public plazas. Then, in response to an increased threat of terror in the early 21st century, they were reconceived as disguises for defensive mechanisms. Truck-stopping barriers were dressed up as planters to make public spaces look a little less fearful. What had begun as terracotta pots ended up as steel-lined concrete roadblocks. In private developments which boasted public spaces (known as POPS: privately owned public spaces), they became part of the branding. Planting has become a branch of greenwashing, the subversion of this communal good by big business to divert from the scale of what it is actually doing to the city.

Where once planters might have been public property, understood as a gesture of civic identity and municipal generosity, now they might be interpreted as tools for increasing and maintaining value and eliminating certain behaviours. They might feature sad-looking trees, reluctantly removed from the earth, or fussily coiffured bushes. The latest fashion is for a kind of meadow planting with wildflowers and grasses, which contrasts a natural look with the most artificial environment imaginable, perhaps all placed in a shabby-chic timber crate with self-conscious signs about all the insects they might attract, drawing attention to their goodness. The pretence at what is now understood as nature can be striking.

Playing

There is a particular kind of photo of children playing in the streets. You'll recognise it when you see it. In fact there's almost an entire genre just of kids using lampposts as swings. Mostly black and white, they are the kind of mid 20th-century products of an age of picture magazines when exotic and erotic subjects might be tempered with a smudge of social realism, but kept quite cheery. The working classes, these images might suggest, are fine, their scruffy but cheerful children inhabiting and appropriating their shabby, sooty streets.

You might look at Marc Riboud's 1954 shot, for instance. Here a little girl is swinging away, getting pushed from both sides, on a cobbled street somewhere in London. Or you might try Paul Popper's joyful, kinetic shot of two Dublin kids swinging in tandem from a cast-iron post, the lamp cropped out, or at Karl Morris Hughes's picture of a couple of children swinging around a Victorian lamppost in Liverpool as if it was a Maypole. David Lewis-Hodgson repeated the trick in his 1969 shot of two girls spinning around a streetlight, and Nigel Henderson's *Street Play* depicts a boy at the top of a tall lamppost, hugging it like a koala. There are probably hundreds of others with subtly varying backdrops from bomb-sites to barricades, each treating street furniture fun as foreground while telling the real story through the background: the dirty, slate-roofed terraces, the wet cobbles, the damaged houses, the bunting, the war, the working-class solidarity. The images are often now dragged out as some kind of tabloid condemnation of today's kids who don't play in the streets like they used to. But a quick glance reveals streets almost entirely devoid of cars. This is a public realm while it was still public, before it was effectively privatised by parked vehicles or traffic.

The real subject, however, is play - and the ingenuity of adaptation, the hijacking and hacking of a functional object for use as something else. Children will find other uses for items in a street. They might leapfrog over a row of bollards or use a barrier set up to stop cyclists as a piece of gymnastics kit, swinging on it and hanging from it. Paving stones become a canvas for chalk drawings, a fire hydrant is a free water feature on a hot day. They may use railings as frames or benches for parkour. Any steep slope becomes a slide (especially in the snow), and slim low walls are there to be balanced on and walked on, high-wire style, even if they are only a few inches above the ground. And, of course, they might adapt barriers or gates as goalposts. Products designed to imply exclusion might become something entirely more playful and hospitable. But much street furniture now is designed precisely not to be used in any creative way. Smooth shafts on tall streetlights to which nothing can be attached or grim barriers coated in anti-climb paint display a complete lack of joy, an alienating blankness.

Play in the city should not be limited to children. The project of the Parisian Situationists was to reconceive the city as a playground, in which to wander aimlessly and subvert its order through drifting. This was in contrast to the city of consumption in which leisure is a commercial transaction and part of the same world as that of work. To continue to consume corporate culture is to be subsumed into the world of capital and control. Instead they sought to subvert the city in its sleeping state, at night, at dawn, in between. The anti-colonial struggles which had preoccupied the Parisian left and its intelligentsia, and which scarred the nation so brutally in the Algerian struggle for independence, came back to haunt the mother city. Capital and commerce was understood as a colonisation of the city, and the struggle for independence from its structures and strictures as analogous to decolonisation. Situationist sympathiser Constant Nieuwenhuys even designed an entire city for play - New Babylon - a ludic modular megastructure that could be reconfigured to accommodate an endlessly adapting, post-work world of leisure.

Play, then, was not seen as leisure but as a critical part of freeing the body and mind from control. The challenge was to understand the urban fabric and its furniture not as the structure of control envisaged by Baron Haussmann but as its opposite, the tool-kit for unlocking freedom. That parkour emerged in the Banlieues and streets of Paris, then, is not accidental. This dangerous but incredible subversion of the city through free-running is, in its way, an extreme realisation of the Situationist understanding. Here, all urban fabric, from the rooftops to the park benches, the low walls and terraces, lampposts and electrical switch boxes become elements in a landscape of continuous movement. The point is not to suggest that parks are built for parkour, but rather that the ingenuity lies in finding choreographic connections that the rest of us would not see because we are understanding the city through our eyes rather than our bodies. Skateboarders, too, revel in the appropriation of benches, edges, boundary walls, railings, ramps and stairs, understanding these architectural elements in entirely new ways as vectors of movement rather than, as they so frequently are conceived to be, boundaries. The new privatised city of course, frowns on ideas of its subversion. It has been designed for one use and one use only, the accumulation of capital and value. The introduction of anti-skateboard studs and fittings is a direct expression of the unease felt by landowners about what appropriation can mean.

The recent spate of outdoor gym equipment comes with its own agenda - that citizen health is a social good. There is little to argue about in these installations, except that it would be a misunderstanding to understand them as play. They are improving machines, physical as well as social engineering, and distant from the freedoms and fun of play.

So while there is a compunction for cities to build in spaces for play for children - designed spaces for playgrounds, and green spaces for less structured entertainment - there is also an obligation to create a city open enough to welcome subversion, a city which welcomes creative adaptation. If a city can acknowledge play and accommodate it, it will be a good place to live.

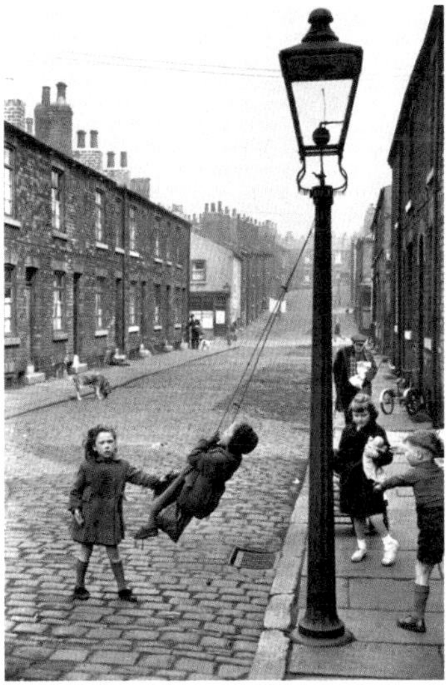

London, 1954
Marc Riboud

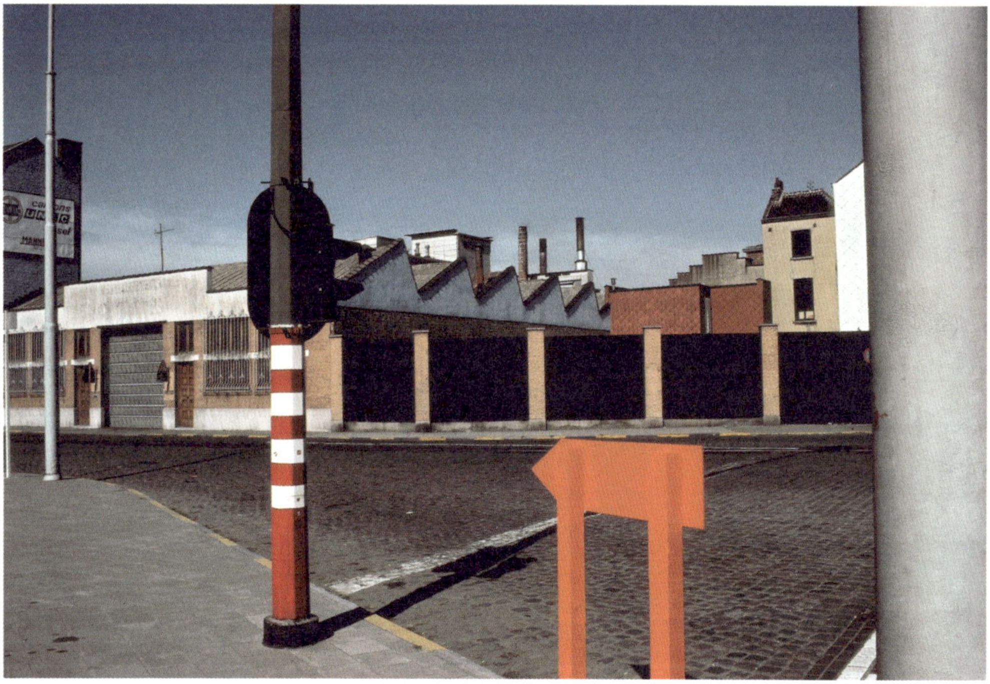

Midi Train Station District, Brussels, 1981
Harry Gruyaert

Poleing

Sometimes it takes a photographer to reveal what is otherwise invisible. When we see a sign we look, not surprisingly, at the sign, at what it says. We do not look at the pole, at its armature.

Harry Gruyaert teaches us to see a city subdivided, punctuated and framed by those anonymous, almost invisible poles. From Ginza via New York, Brabant and Galway, Gruyaert finds street scenes in which the poles act as figures in the landscape and as structures for containing the view, constantly subdividing, creating diptychs, triptychs and devices which centre a townscape otherwise so eerily empty its elements might not hold together without them.

His 1981 shot, *Midi Train Station District, Brussels,* evokes for me a fictional landscape by architect Aldo Rossi, a city of archetypes. A traffic sign forms an orange arrow which points towards the heart of the picture, the red and white striped post. Stripped of their legibility because we only see the backs, the signs ironically take on much more graphic meanings, pure symbol. The shot is bookended by two anonymous, grey-painted steel poles, the one to the right so close we could touch it, the one to the left more distant and attenuated. Three factory chimneys in the background recall the city of industry, a little hint of De Chirico or Lowry. The whole ensemble looks eerily perfect and empty, unpopulated except by the things left behind, the scene of the crime. Here it is the poles which populate the landscape but, devoid of people, what are they communicating?

There is a beautifully understated photo, looking like a moment of urban ennui, by Roy DeCarava of a hand gripping a pole. But then, if you look a little harder, you see another figure on the opposite side of the road. Blurred but clearly casual, in an untucked white shirt, the two figures are locked into the scene by the poles, almost communicating, feeling the city's vibrations through the metal dowsing the streets.

The contemporary city is punctuated by thousands of poles, barely full stops in the urban ground plan, unmarked on maps, negligible in the abstract, yet, as dogs can testify, physically very present in the pavement. Poles might be zebra-striped with a yellow lollipop head or they might be painted and dressed like palm trees. They might have signs atop them or lights, directions, traffic signals, 5G masts, CCTV cameras, even speakers. The smoothness of their metal shafts is supposed to make them friction free, to allow the life of the city to flow around them, but their accumulation is inhibiting the pavement. The scarce strips left to pedestrians are being increasingly populated by poles which are, in themselves, almost insignificant but which, when accumulated, create a galvanised forest of canopyless trunks.

Sometimes we need to photograph the city even to see them but when we do, it becomes clear how rapidly and effectively they have proliferated. Japanese street photographer RK captures a scene in Tokyo of an urban jogger. She is running through a city of poles, an artificial avenue, an arcade, almost, the static spectators on her route. There is barely any street left. Only furniture.

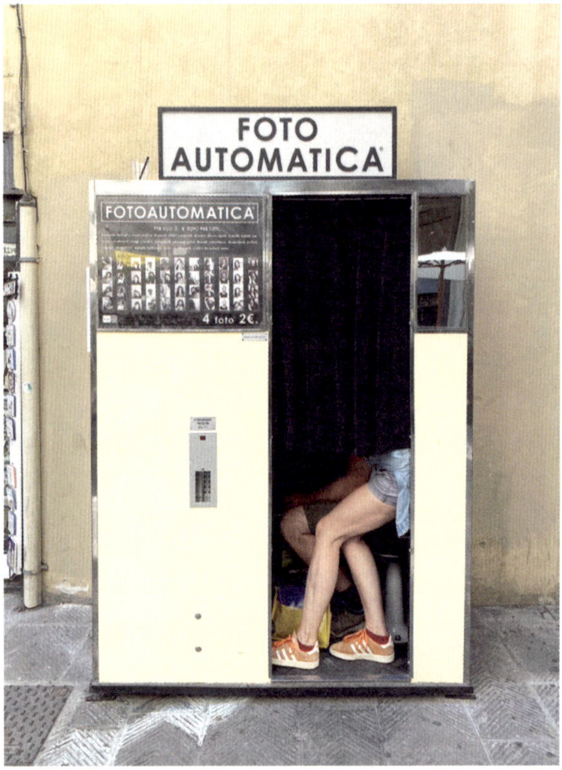

Photo booth in Florence

Posing

Before there were selfies there were photo booths. In an era when photography was an expensive and long-drawn out process – buying and loading film, unloading, waiting and developing – these curtained kiosks represented a moment of transformative instant magic. Often in station concourses, arcades and malls, there were also examples on the street. They were both practical and playful, for passport photos, ID cards and snaps of flirty first dates.

The photo booth also, perhaps inevitably, became a hugely successful popular cultural trope. It represents a moment of stillness in the city, of people awkwardly posing and waiting for the strip of (almost inevitably grim-looking and disappointing) film to emerge from the slot. Architecturally the booths embody a slightly weird, hybrid language of vending machine, kiosk and private studio. A strip of curtain hides the identity of the user, but the feet or legs remain visible (so any assumed privacy is never quite what it seems). The camera flash, the frantic adjustment of the stool to get the height right before the clicking starts, the jostling for position when a couple giggles themselves into place – all create a slightly theatrical air of expectation.

Photo booths have a surprisingly long lineage. The first example, the Photomaton, appeared on the street at Broadway and 51st Street, near Times Square in New York in 1925. They quickly became a favourite of the Surrealists when the first one arrived in Paris in 1928; they admired its automatic nature, the lack of a human eye, the pure mechanical nature of its art. André Breton, Max Ernst, Luis Buñuel, René Magritte, Yves Tanguy, Paul Éluard and Louis Aragon all experimented with the format. Later it proved irresistible to pop stars and Pop artists: Andy Warhol used to take his muses and hangers-on around New York and feed them quarters from a roll to take pictures in the booth, the perfect 20th-century form of popular art.

It also became a staple of the movies. Christopher Reeve's Superman got changed in one, the Beatles hid from charging fans in one in *A Hard Day's Night*, Billy Liar hid from his boss in another. A strip of photo booths even appears in *Dawn of the Dead*. More fruitfully than any other though, Jean-Pierre Jeunet uses it as a motif at the heart of *Amélie*, in which the target of the eponymous protagonist's affections loses a scrapbook of torn passport photos with which she is utterly entranced. They end up being pictures of the photo-booth engineer testing the machines. It is a smart twist of what appears to be an act of alienation and symbolic self-destruction. There is even a curious film called *Photo Booth*, about a group of soldiers who find a lonely, out-of-place kiosk which evokes deeply personal memories for each as they enter.

As a machine, the photo booth presented the perfect combination of public and private, accessibility and technology, blandness and a recognition of celebrity. The anonymity of the brightly illuminated but dull interior and a naff curtain masked the wonder of the technology. Just as it was impossible to know quite what was going on behind the curtain, it was impossible to understand that there must be an entire photographic developing lab inside its bowels.

The idea of the photo booth has survived remarkably well, into the age of the front camera and the insertion of the self into every scene. The photo kiosk is an almost perfect representation of the notion of the inextricable bond between photography and street furniture, though not, perhaps, in the way I had intended.

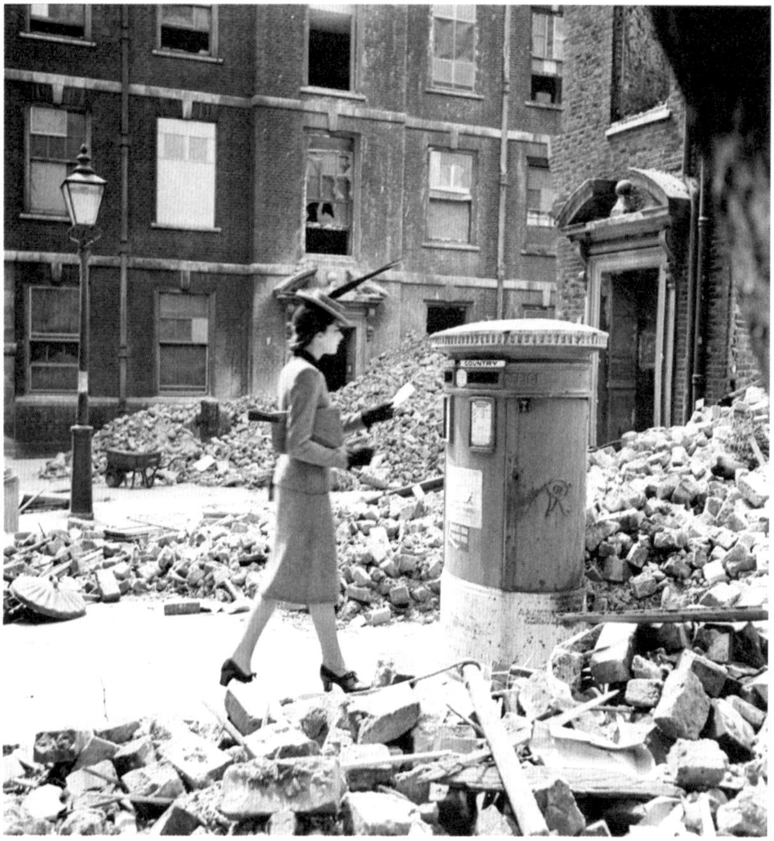

The Letter, 1940
Cecil Beaton

Posting

A postbox is the opposite of a dustbin, yet the form of the two objects inevitably converges. Both are public receptacles into which the public can throw specific items, but one has to confer value and the other to imply disposal. The British postbox presents a fine example of how to successfully develop an enduring language to imply value and confer distinction.

The red pillarbox is an object clearly designed to last. A huge lump of cast iron it is given status by a royal crest and monogram, mass by its material and a black base to imply its solid anchoring to the ground. Importance and visibility are imparted by its red livery and a strange kind of pagan presence through its slightly phallic form.

You can see something of the self-consciously symbolic nature of the British pillarbox in Cecil Beaton's photo *The Letter* from a 1941 issue of *Vogue*. The setting is the bombed-out city, the message is that life is carrying on, calmly. But also elegantly. The model pops a letter in the box, her slim form framed perfectly between a lamppost, an elaborate door architrave and the postbox. This is a twin-slot pillarbox of oval form with a VR (Victoria Regina) monogram. The sun is shining. Life goes on. Beaton was a set-designer as well as a photographer, and his eye for a visual story is employed here to the full. The lamp and the postbox appear as theatrical props, ciphers for a resilient system. The cast-iron pillarbox really does look like it could survive the Blitz, perhaps even a direct hit. It probably did.

Of all items of street furniture the postbox, or at least the British pillarbox, is the most determinedly architectural in form. Some early examples from the 1850s were actually cast in the form of a fluted Doric column, architecture without a building, extremely elegant hollow bollards with added functionality.

Postboxes as a typology are surprisingly archaic. There were examples in Paris from the 1650s, a full two centuries before they appeared in Britain. Yet the longevity and solidity of the British red pillarbox (they were green for their first couple of decades) does seem to have made a lasting impression. There is a popular story that Anthony Trollope invented the postbox and it is true, certainly, that, in his role as clerk to the Post Office surveyor, he introduced them to Britain, beginning with an experiment in the Channel Isles in 1852. Early models had vertical letter slots and granite bases. By the 1860s they had evolved into a fairly familiar form, a hexagonal pillar with an elaborate dome and a knob on top, a horizontal slot, hinged front door and black-painted base. Functioning as both sign and signified, instructions and lettering were cast directly into the iron. A couple of decades after that, they had morphed into the yet-more familiar form of a cylindrical pillar with a shallow-domed top, dentilled frieze, and with the collection times typed up in a sign stuck into a noticeboard on the front.

The name and location of the foundry is often cast into the base, lest we forget that these were products of the world's greatest industrial power. It is a curious conjunction of royalty, function and manufacture, celebrating the hierarchy but recognising the workers. That location - Falkirk, Hoxton, Carlisle, Derbyshire, Madras or wherever it might be - cropped up all over the world as these huge chunks of iron were exported to the colonies and dependencies and beyond, including to Argentina and Uruguay. They became, like milestones, markers of a carefully calibrated global network of power and control and communication, tying the empire together. And just as the removal or vandalisation of milestones was, to the Romans, punishable even by death, postboxes became sacrosanct in Britain. To interfere with the mail remains a serious offence, a particular kind of treachery and can attract a two-year custodial sentence. It undermines the system and trust, the fundamentals of civil society.

These brightly coloured and highly symbolic items of street furniture were also called upon to act as signposts. Few survive, but signs on top of many pillarboxes pointed the way to nearby post offices or, occasionally, to telephone boxes with which many were later paired, creating a kind of conversation between these two red iron objects in competing and complimentary communication networks.

Other nations, meanwhile, adopted yet more elaborate forms for their postboxes, from the convoluted cast sculptural versions of the French system (and their more recent yellow plastic versions) to the yellow bird boxes of Vienna, the convoluted Baroque boxes of Budapest mounted on cast-iron sewing-machine-type legs and the wall-mounted Rococo aedicules of Rome. It is striking that the US early-on adopted a more utilitarian model, the pizza oven-shaped, blue, barrel-vaulted box on legs which has, in its own chunky, functional way, proved remarkably enduring. Another type, a similarly barrel-vaulted, key-lockable relay box designed so that mailmen would not have to carry their entire load for the full round, is now disappearing, victims of vans.

As the emanations of national, rather than municipal self-image, the mailbox became a repository of national and cultural identity. But while, for instance, French designs passed through various fashions from Belle Epoque through Art Deco to severe modernist, the British rarely deviated from their classical ideal; the pillarbox remained, more or less, a standalone column, a slightly absurd object. There were fatter elliptical versions with slots for domestic, local and overseas mail, but these too were stolid and failed to fall victim to fashion. There were also inevitable efforts to modernise the form. David Mellor was commissioned in 1966 and came up with the fridge-shaped F-Type. Constructed from welded sheet steel, it was a striking failure of a functionalist object, rusting and reacting badly to dog's piss which made some models corrode so badly they became unstable. The Post Office tried again with a design by Tony Gibbs in 1980, a purer cylinder, returning to cast iron. It often came with an odd-looking hoop on top, so that it could be easily craned into place. This one was not a great success either, though plenty survive.

The traditional British postbox has, however, endured to become a strange kind of national symbol. As a child I had a piggy-bank in the shape of a postbox, and you can find postbox biscuit tins, jigsaw puzzles, keyrings, fridge magnets and torches. It is a slightly bizarre fetish and one that failed to stop the Conservative/Liberal coalition government privatising the Royal Mail in 2010. Even these lovely, symbolic things do not belong to us any more.

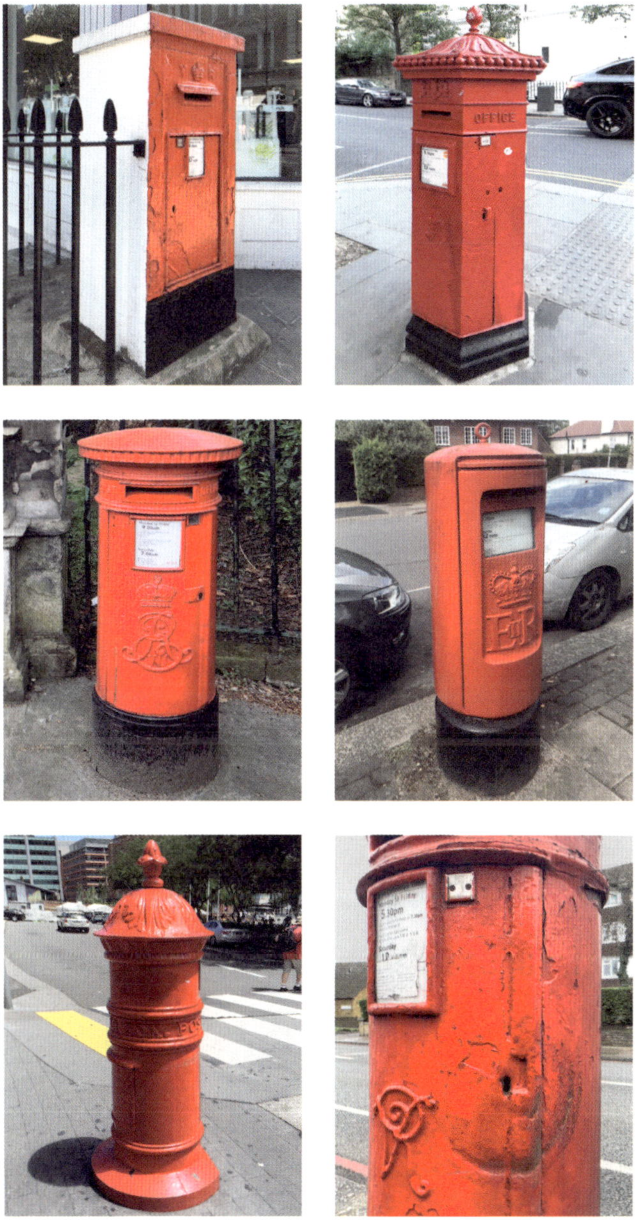

British postbox designs

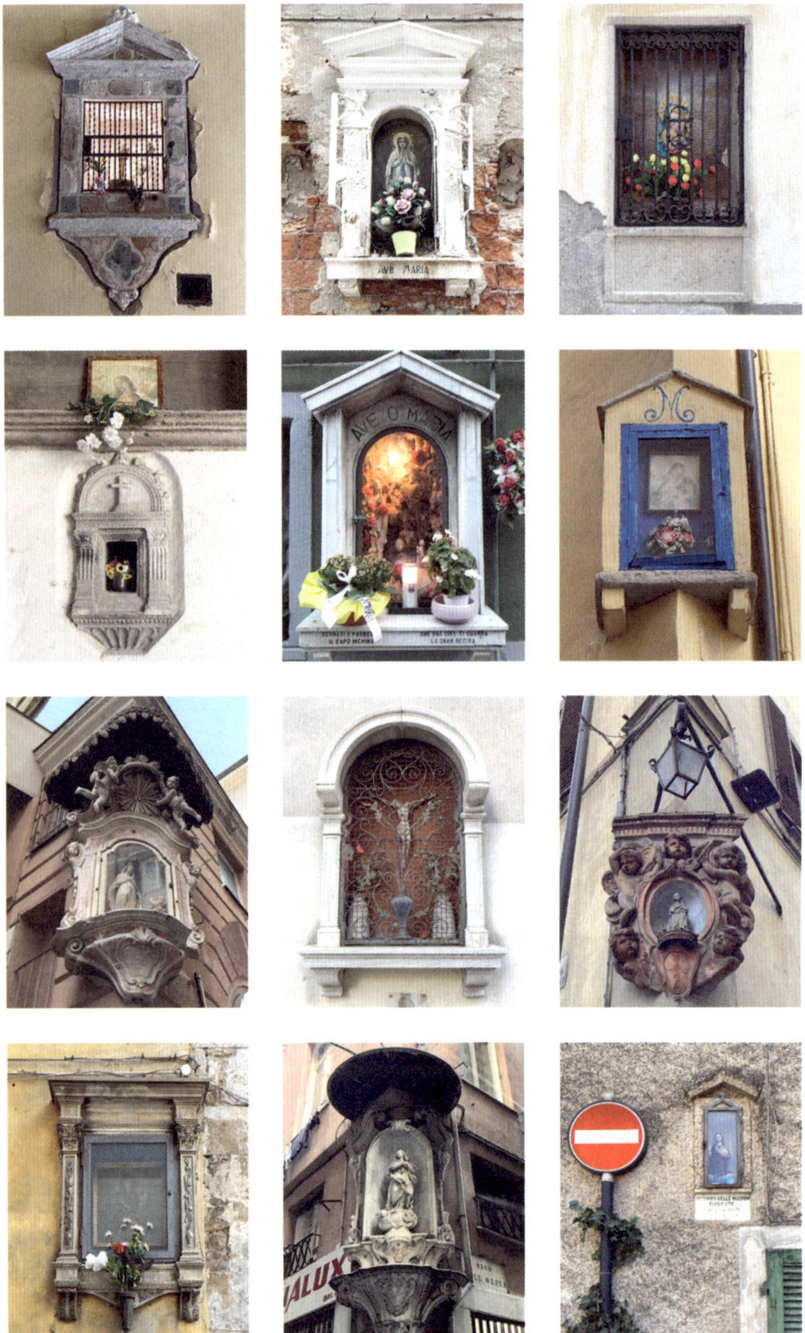

Italian madonelle *(street shrines)*

Praying

The cocktail kitsch of Rococo, Baroque and church-porch souvenirs that are the *madonelle* are among the most eye-catching features of a walk through the backstreets of any Italian city. They might be Rococo aedicules framing painted Madonnas, mosaic Marys in roundels, or elaborate Baroque angels flanking a serene figure with a filigree copper or cast-iron and zinc roof to protect them from the rain. Or they might be little figurines in old glass vitrines - plaster virgins with fairy-light halos and faded fake flowers, or plastic Madonnas arranged with sea shells and red glass candle holders in holes-in-the-wall. The weak glow of a fairy-lit virgin in a dark alley is both a warming and a slightly unsettling sight. They are the most public affirmations of Catholicism in the secular townscape, but they are simultaneously strangely pagan in their origins and their affect.

They evolved, it seems, from the Roman tradition of shrines to the *Lares*, gods of good fortune, which were placed in homes or at crossroads to bring safety to those who prayed to them. Crossroads have always been seen as places of danger or demons, potential wrong roads taken, presided over by evil spirits. It is a tradition which survives from the classical world: the Greeks had Hermes and Hecates, guardians of the crossroads which were seen as liminal zones, uncertain places fraught with danger; offerings and sacrifices were made to appease the gods. Perhaps those customs carried through into Northern European traditions, in which gallows were erected at crossroads. Bodies were left to rot above them and suicides buried beneath them - the idea was that any ghosts would be lost, uncertain where to go, remaining stranded at the junction. In African American hoodoo, similar myths about crossroads appear to have survived from Kongo culture.

The Italian *madonelle* (there are similar versions elsewhere in Europe, notably France) embody all these anxieties, but they are also an attempt to inscribe sanctity into the city with the very practical side-effect of becoming an early form of streetlighting, urban way-finding and the expression of local identity and piety. Candles and votive lamps placed in the shrines or around them (some even had wrought-iron candle holders and lanterns) subtly lit dark streets with tiny points of light, enough for orientation. Coming across a lit shrine in the dingy, misty winter alleys of Venice still gives a little thrill, a sense that you are not entirely alone in a seemingly deserted city. Just occasionally they might appear above a vitrine, a showcase for a nearby store. I noticed one such juxtaposition in Florence, a very particular mix of consumption and devotion.

With some of the shrines behind glass, others in aedicular structures like miniature temples, there is an impression of the doll's house or even the miniature theatre. Like the votive disembodied body parts which stud the velvet panels of southern Spanish or Mexican churches, there is a drama, a foot-lit glow. Even the most modern of the *madonelle*, with their cheap plastic statues and strings of One Euro store lights, exude something ancient, a curious mix of intrigue and discomfort. These shrines still do their job, to remind the walker that dark streets are not always safe, in the city you are never alone, and that it is always good to say a little prayer and perhaps cross yourself, just in case.

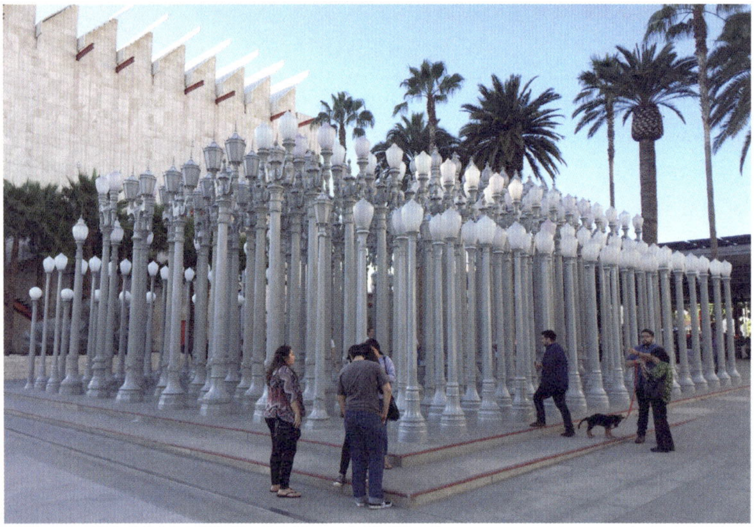

Urban Light, Los Angeles, 2018
Chris Burden

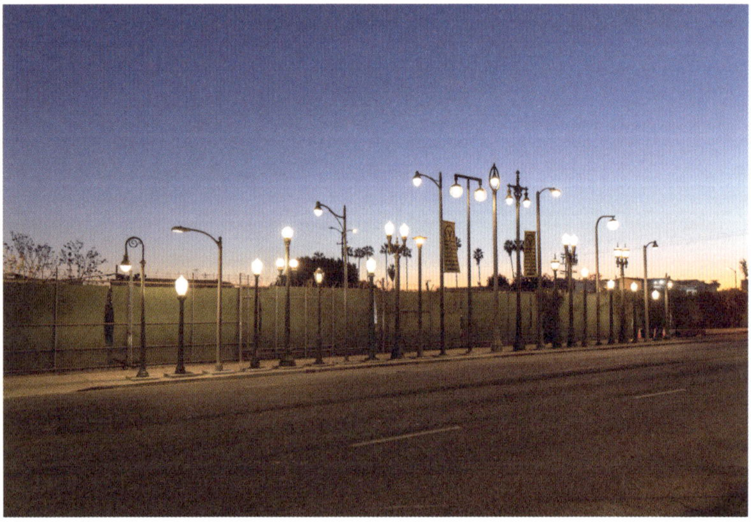

Vermonica, Los Angeles, 1993–present
Sheila Klein

Producing

Street furniture is not art. It is almost the opposite - barely visible, utilitarian, functional, largely uncelebrated and unnoticed. Yet when Chris Burden gathered together 202 salvaged streetlights produced in the 1920s and '30s and clustered them together in a kind of illuminated forest, the result became one of the US's most popular and totemic public artworks.

Urban Light outside LACMA is a striking installation by day, and a hypnotic one at night. One of Los Angeles's default spots for selfies and social media moments, it achieves its effect by the grouping and grading of lights by height and style - anything gathered together in sufficient numbers can look like art. But it also brings attention to the elegance of the lampposts themselves as objects, and the richness of their styling and variety. There are gaslight lantern-style heads, globes and elaborate twin tops. There are lamps that look like cabouchon gems mounted in a Baroque brooch and others that resemble an ice-cream sundae cup. The range of decoration is delightful, from fluted columns and acanthus to turned tops and twin torches. These salvaged relics commemorate a streetscape that was once home to the most widespread and beautiful suite of streetlights. Paris may have patented the name 'City of Light' with its ambitious and extravagant streetlamps, but perhaps it was Los Angeles which, in its 1940s heyday, more fully embodied and deserved the title. Burden's artwork is just the cherry on top.

Mike Davis christened Los Angeles the 'City of Quartz' with its implications of the crystalline, the sparkling and the brittle. Attractive, seductive but also hard, uncaring. LA is simultaneously the utopia and the dystopia of the modern age. Davis illustrates it brilliantly, as does Thom Andersen in his stunning visual essay *Los Angeles Plays Itself* (2003), constructed entirely from movie clips depicting scenes of the city.

Light is the medium of the movies and it is the material of Los Angeles. The brilliant sunlight (which made filming easier) is why the movie studios moved there in the first place, the sunshine was how it sold itself to those fleeing freezing winters. At night the light becomes something else, equally vivid, the neons and the storefronts, the movie theatre marquees and drive-in canopies, the illuminated ads and flashing lightbulbs. Then there is the carpet of flickering lights, the city grid seen at night from Mulholland Drive or the Griffith Observatory stretching as far as the eye can see in every direction. The city transformed into an electric spectacle. And the movies themselves are, of course, pure light.

This new and constantly reimagined city suffered from what Davis describes as a perception of 'counterfeit urbanity', a sense of inauthenticity. The way it was so often recreated in the studio, on the lots (which were themselves as old as much of the city itself, their sets occasionally even older and more urban than its buildings), added to this sense of unreality, the confusion between the real and the unreal. In a way the streetlamp acted as an anchor, an artefact of authentic urban life transplanted to the studio and bolted to the floor. So when *Singing in the Rain* tries to convince us it is suddenly outside the studio, the motif is a rainy street and the scene centres on a lamppost. Gene Kelly jumps on it, using it as a prop to connect himself to the city, as if drawing power from its electricity for his elastic dance routine. But it was shot, of course, in Metro Goldwyn Mayer's Culver City studio.

Streetlights play a similar role in film noir. European emigré directors like Fritz Lang, Billy Wilder, Robert Siodmak, Michael Curtiz, Otto Preminger and the others, had been brought up with Expressionism in their veins and a desire for deep, dark shadows. We think of lamps giving light but perhaps even more importantly for the movies they cast shadows, they enable the darkness to be translated on to the screen as a cipher for evil and corruption. The first scene of Robert Siodmak's *The Killers* sees the eponymous hitmen arrive at a sleepy town and, as they wander into view in the darkness (under the credits), the streetlight slowly flickers on. It does not bring light but darkness, shadow and threat, something from the past.

The filmmakers' streetlight becomes a paradox, a symbol of urban authenticity constructed in the studio, and it appears in Burden's *Urban Light* infused with all that confusion. It is also, for LA, the nighttime parallel to the palm trees which define the city's public spaces. The streetlight's halo is the opposite of the palm tree's fronds, the city of sunshine and shadow, nature and artifice. And down those palm-lined boulevards are the cars which have characterised the city since its first starring role in the movies. Just as it was the automobile and its fierce industrial lobby that killed off public transport and the old-fashioned main street in Los Angeles, it was the car which finished off the streetlight. Those ornate columns and decorated bases were brutalised by the bumpers of endless autos mounting the kerbs. Or, you might argue, they caused too much damage to the increasingly elaborate bodywork, the chrome fenders and tail fins of louche, streamlined cars of the mid-century. The solid, exquisitely cast and complex lamps had to go, and they were replaced by smoother, taller, more anodyne versions which made Los Angeles a little more like everywhere else.

Chris Burden was not the first to make an artwork of LA lights. Whether he was aware of it or not, Sheila Klein had got there first. Her installation *Vermonica* (1993) featured a row of salvaged historic streetlights of all types set on the Santa Monica Boulevard (though it has been moved a couple of times). There is something almost perfect about these itinerant artefacts which were once all about anchoring a sense of place, of making the famous anti-city more urban. They introduce a touch of Paris to the city where there is, famously, no 'there'. Both Burden and Klein came across these symbols of a lost urbanity and moved them, and only in their transplanting did they become appreciated. The studios moved to Hollywood because of the light. But the lights are still moving, disappearing, reappearing, flickering, fading into the distance.

Protecting

During the golden age of picture magazines, the middle decades of the 20th century, there was a great demand for photos which captured the country's class divide. Most famous is the shot that has become known as *Toffs and Toughs*, taken by Jimmy Sime (often erroneously attributed to Bert Hardy) outside Lord's cricket ground in 1937. It portrays five boys, two in the Sunday best of Harrow with top hats, waistcoats and buttonholes, and three in shabbier schmutter, dad's tweeds, too-big-trousers, tatty tennis shoes. The taller of the Harrow boys has his hand on a bollard. The stained stone street furniture does exactly what it is supposed to do, it represents an insurmountable barrier, both physical and social. The boy's hand grips the bollard in what looks like an act of ownership and entitlement. Yet, ironically, it is the grinning, open-collared kids who own the street and look most at home.

There's something a little ridiculous about bollards: vaguely phallic extrusions of solid stuff sticking out of the street. But, along with corner protectors, they are perhaps the oldest pieces of street furniture, forbidding in their mass and defensive in their attitude. That blend of offence and defence is perfectly expressed in the remarkably resilient story that, after Napoleon's defeat at the Battle of Trafalgar in 1805, the Royal Navy requisitioned the cannon from French ships and planted them as bollards in London and the docks, inscribing British military superiority into the fabric of the city and its streets. Convenient, romantic, patriotic and half-believable as it sounds, that particular tale turns out to be mostly myth. However, from the 17th century redundant guns certainly were used across the British streetscape.

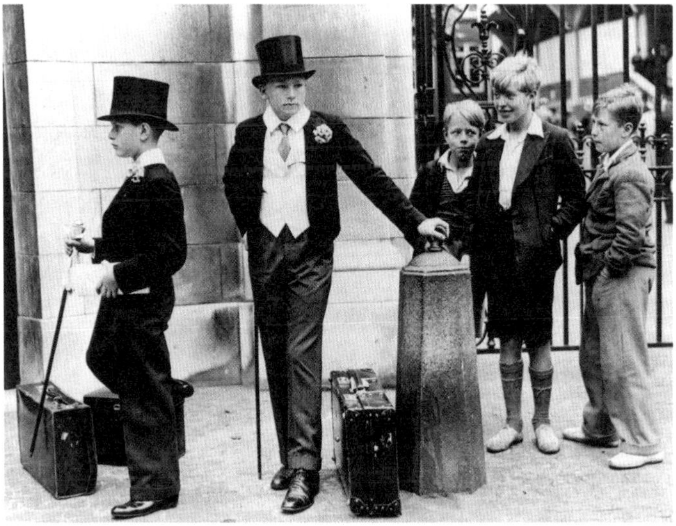

Toffs and Toughs, 1937
Jimmy Sime

Half-buried in the pavement, breech first, they might often have a cannonball brazed into the muzzle. That shape, of a found object, a Duchampian piece of art, has curiously survived to become a streetscape archetype. The traditional cast-iron form of the cannon muzzle remains the most popular shape for street bollards. The standard bollard profile may have become a little anorexic in reproduction versions, but the ghost of the form remains oddly intact.

Almost all cannon-shaped bollards visible in British streetscapes, as well as its former colonial strongholds across the world, are imitations of that archetype. Huge, pitted and chunky examples can be found at all the naval strongholds: outside the gates to Chatham's naval dockyards, in Gosport, in Portsmouth. But they can also be seen in Cannon Lane (of course), in Hampstead and Borough Market as well as at St Helens, Bishopsgate. There's one on the Embankment in Southwark near Shakespeare's Globe, and wonky versions scattered around London's Docklands. It isn't entirely a British phenomenon; the canals in Utrecht feature similar types. The surprise, though, is the survival of that form. New York's Federal Plaza features cannon-type bollards, as do the streets of Caracas and many others beyond.

The earliest cast-iron bollards were used on docksides and wharves for mooring ships. Often plain cylinders with a flared rim, these massive objects could also serve as seats or as places to rest a load. There were also more shapely versions, bollards with iron plates bolted to the wharf which looked like giant, official rubber stamps, and others with flattened heads like elephantine sash window lifts. The adapted naval cannon just reinforced that nautical connection.

Before iron there was stone: bollards as round balls, flattened bells, lumpy, domed shafts and hundreds of other variations. There were huge lumps of carved stone around the edges of Renaissance Italian piazzas, and bell-topped types surrounding fountains like Bernini's in front of St Peter's in Rome or the pith-helmet-topped types by the Spanish Steps. There were big bollards like those in Siena's Piazza del Campo, bollards with a mass and presence that act like a magnet. It is rare that someone is not leaning with their back against the faceted sides or has placed their forearms on the top. And when there are no people, they populate the square, to give it structure, shadow, texture, articulation.

These stone bollards might be linked with finely wrought-iron railings or chunky, spiked iron chains. Their solidity and seeming permanence make historic bollards appear very much part of the townscape; at their best they can be strikingly elegant. The streets of central London are punctuated by the occasional historical example: the polygonal Gothic inflected version, the 'Norman' style with zigzag inscriptions and a crown like a spinning top, and the urbane William IV types which start off with a rectangular footprint and taper to an octagonal head with incised bands and a prominent Royal cipher. In Amsterdam the bollards are marked 'XXX', indicating a row of St Andrew's crosses. The saint was a fisherman, and the city began as a fishing port with its patron's X-shaped crucifix as its emblem. Brazilian artist Paulo Bruscky alighted on its ridiculousness in his work *Erotic Amsterdam* which shows the artist lying on his back, the triple-X inscribed bollard sticking straight up between his legs like a huge phallus.

More, perhaps, than any other item of street furniture, bollards trace the history of material and industry, power and trade. The Romans, of course, made bollards of stone, the material of the city and the same stuff they used for their sacred milestones and temples. They were superseded by the wooden stumps of the Dark Ages; the English word 'bollard' derives, perhaps, from the Middle English *bole* (tree trunk). In the 18th century, as we have seen, excess cannons were redeployed as bollards. These in turn gave way to cast iron as the industrial revolution transformed the nation. A malleable material, it proved perfect for mass-producing newly decorative forms, moulded in multiple forms to trace the competition between Gothic, Classical,

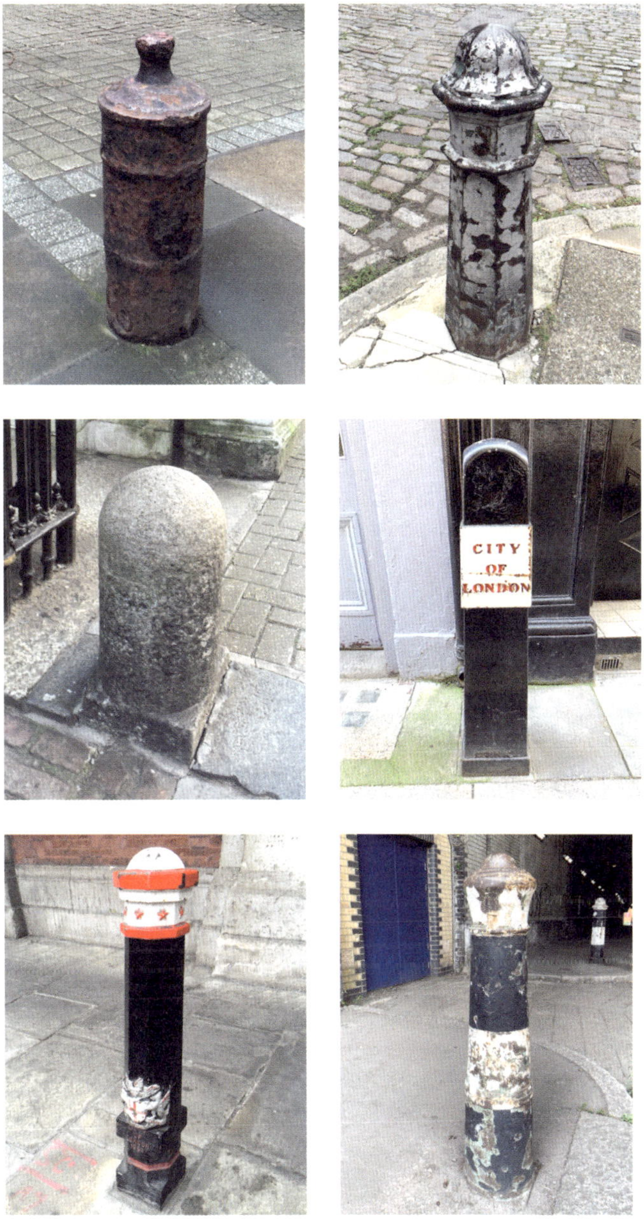

Selection of London bollards

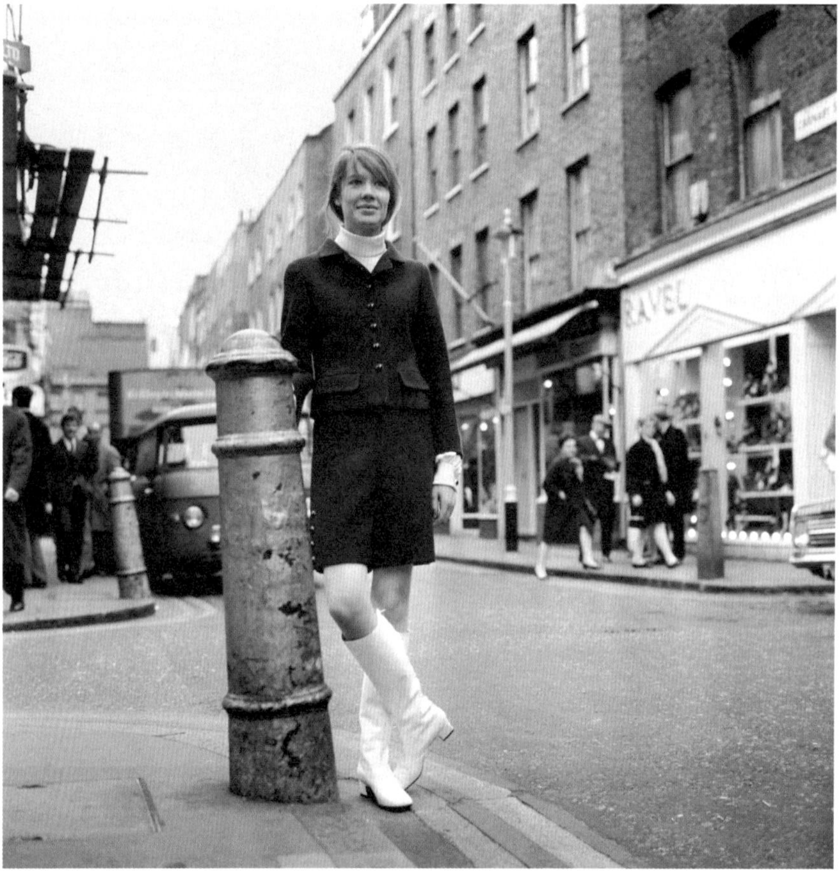

Françoise Hardy, Carnaby Street, London, 1967
John Pratt

Romanesque and Regency. They became, like the classical column, a self-contained and autonomous expression of aesthetics and culture, of allegiance and taste. In the 20th century, of course, makers turned to concrete, that ultimate promethean material. Concrete bollards popped up all over the streets, part of an architectural language of Brutalism. And what better vehicle for the brutal than a bollard, the ultimate elemental symbol of defence and defiance?

Their aggregate showing like nuts in a Lion Bar, bollards, once the preserve of grand squares and huge waves, went suburban. Then, in reaction to the concrete versions, came heritage. Historic forms were rediscovered and these bollards became the perfect cipher for a historic neighbourhood – a mass-produced commodity inspired by a debased, emaciated version of the naval cannon. They now stand scattered through the cities, most versions with some kind of polyurethane coating so that, when they are smashed into, the plastic cracks away to reveal slowly rusting steel and a profile that looks like Darth Vader's helmet.

That plastic-coated, debased form might have been the perfect symbol of the search for characteristically modern taste for economical authenticity, were it not for an even newer generation of anti-terror bollards, the massive stainless steel stumps capable of stopping a truck bomb in its tracks. Bollards were always about protection, but these new objects are brutal, unsparing in their intent and unwilling to alleviate their sense of purpose through any attempts at expression. If they are going to disappear into an underground steel sheath, then their sides must be smooth. There is no room here for dissembling or double coding. These new disappearing bollards have been mechanised, militarised and digitised, they have become part of a machine, the dumbest object in the internet of things, the stupidest component of the smart city.

But most of all, perhaps, bollards are a bit silly. Even the word can trigger schoolboy sniggers. The rather beautiful ribbed cucumber-shaped bollards that occasionally appeared in the British townscape took this gentle humour to an extreme. The urban lingam, the dangerously crotch-height urban dildo. Perhaps its suggestive form led to the bollard becoming a permanent presence in London's fashion and pop iconography. John Pratt's terrific 1967 shot of Françoise Hardy in Carnaby Street is stiffly posed and self-consciously smirking. Hardy doesn't seem to know quite what to do with her hand, and the way her white boots are crossed echoes the jaunty angle of the bollard. I think the bollard directly behind Hardy was the same one being leapfrogged over by Cat Stevens in Pratt's 1967 publicity photo. One of the women in Paul Popper's photo *Two Women Chatting and Smoking on a Street in Soho* looks a little more comfortable, which then makes you wonder what she's doing in Soho on the street at night, which then brings the bollard back into the picture.

Thanks to its autonomy and its vaguely embodied proportions, the bollard has also been taken up by artists attempting to inject a little joy into the city. Antony Gormley's range of bollards was designed to be employed across Peckham but only one set ultimately survived (although they were employed again outside a Maggie's Cancer Care centre in Cardiff, designed by architects Dow Jones). Gormley implicitly understood the ridiculousness of the type.

Few items of street furniture have proven so durable and so capable of provoking humour. Few have survived so well and yet have been so debased. And, for the dumbest piece of urban design, few have enjoyed such a remarkable revival and urban ubiquity. The future is endless and absolute bollards.

Pumping

Street furniture inhabits the realm of the barely visible, the often overlooked and the everyday. Often brutally utilitarian, its municipal, functional nature often obscures its critical nature - indispensable things which contribute to the smooth running of the civilised city. But for wells, probably the oldest items of street furniture, this was not the case. Celebrated, revered, sometimes worshipped at, public wells and springs were attributed with their own spirits and, later, their guardian angels. In every urban culture wells were associated with deities. For the Romans it was Fontus (from which, of course, derive the words 'fountain' and 'font'). Fontus's mother, Juturna, had been in her time the goddess of wells and water, and his father Janus the god of gateways, doors and beginnings.

Archaeologists have consistently found devotional objects and coins in wells, tributes to the gods of water in a tradition that still continues in a diluted form today. Our abundant, piped supply has perhaps made us blasé. I remember as a child that strange interlude in the 1970s of blackouts and fuel shortages which forced us to gather at the standpipe in the street to bring buckets of water home, an odd blip in our otherwise complacent urban existence. Water, you suddenly became aware, is a precious thing. And we use bucketloads.

Roman and medieval cities used to fanatically celebrate their water. Think of the aqueduct, that most incredible of Roman feats of engineering: a city like Segovia in Spain is still in thrall to its structure, this huge celebration of the arrival of water imposing itself on the landscape.

Any stroll through the intimate piazzas of Venice will eventually include an encounter with a beautifully carved stone well-head (*verre da pozzo*). These look like huge, repurposed column capitals (which is exactly what the first ones were) with foliage and occasionally a lion's head or four. It is an intriguing example of adaptive reuse subsequently formalised into a familiar form, retaining the memory of the capital. The etymology of the word 'capital' derives from the Latin for head - that it should be used to decorate a well-head appears perfect. In fact, these weren't really wells at all but heads for cisterns, as the water in the Venetian lagoon is salty all the way down. Instead they gathered rainwater and, when there was none, imported fresh water by boat.

Outside the strange, preserved world of Venice, most well-heads have disappeared. In medieval towns and villages they often appeared as mini-monuments with elaborate stone carvings and sometimes a Gothic spire or miniature tower. In the British Isles, wells were 'dressed' on particular days (particularly in the north of England), with an elaborate wooden structure built over the head and decorated with flowers and garlands. Superstitions and fairy tales cleave deeply to wells and pumps, such was their centrality to everyday life. In London their locations are inscribed in the names of neighbourhoods and streets: Clerkenwell, Sadler's Wells, Well Walk, Spa Fields, Stockwell and so on.

During the 17th century, wells began to give way gradually to pumps. A surprising amount of these have survived in the British streetscape. There is a very fine pump at Cornhill just outside the Royal Exchange, dating from 1799. Its form indicates its status, a dignified tapering monument resembling an obelisk. Pumps were designed to be visible. A later version stands in Bedford Row with a similar one in Queen's Square. Both have been surmounted with a streetlamp - why waste a good, solid iron base? The best and most concentrated selection can be found by wandering around London's Inns of Court, ranging from the strictly utilitarian to the vividly Gothic (a lovely example of these can be found in Gray's Inn Square).

Pumps became popular gathering places because they were critical infrastructure; they were usually the only way the poor, or servants, could fetch fresh(ish) water. They became a focus of small public spaces, queues would accumulate and they became a conduit for local gossip. They also became a locus for disease. One of the great scientific breakthroughs came in 1854 when physician John Snow attempted to prove his notion that deaths from cholera were not being caused by bad air or 'miasma' but were being carried through the water. He charted deaths in London's Soho and identified a particular water pump in Broad (now Broadwick) Street as the source of the disease. He had the handle from the pump removed, and deaths fell drastically. His theory of 'germs' was, eventually, accepted. A fake pump in Poland Street now commemorates the momentous discovery.

With a history at least as rich, the Aldgate Pump still stands at the junction of Aldgate High Street, Fenchurch Street and Leadenhall Street. Stories and myths are as engrained in this curious piece of street furniture as the bands of rustication which seem to suggest the rocks from which the springs rise. Mentioned in Stow's 1598 *Survey of London*, the site is traditionally the spot where the City gives way to the East End and marked, in the 19th century, the point from which distances from London to the surrounding counties were measured. Low down on the structure is a bronze wolf's head, rubbed smooth by generations of hands, that commemorates the slightly spurious-sounding story that this was the spot where the last wolf left in London was hunted down and killed. It even has its place in Cockney rhyming slang: 'to get the Aldgate [pump]' is to get the hump. Photos from the 19th century show it with a gas lamp on top, which was apparently knocked off when a bus ran into it in the 1920s. This was more recently replaced by an electric lantern. It has an absolutely beautiful, slender, serpentine pump handle and, above the wolf's head and to the left of the old water button, you can see the blob of lead to which was once attached a cup. The most gruesome story of all dates from the 19th century, when the water from the pump was reputed to be very fine tasting, fresh and slightly sweet. It was found that the water, which arrived via springs rising in Hampstead, was running through graveyards and being filtered through the bones of bodies, the calcium from which gave it that sweeter taste. Unsurprisingly it was found to be responsible for hundreds of deaths from its contaminated flow in the 1870s, and was converted to water from the New River in Clerkenwell.

Punishing

There is, perhaps, an expectation that street furniture exists to somehow improve civic life. Its mission is to provide a conduit for some ordinary, possibly even unseen, utility or infrastructure to enhance our being in the city. This was not always the case. For most of history the streets were punctuated by reminders of life's fragility and the consequences of crime.

Most visible were the gallows and the gibbets. Often erected at crossroads or in city squares, these might display the decomposing bodies of criminals, traitors or pirates hanging from them in iron cages. The practice survives in the name of Execution Dock at Wapping and in a few schlocky fake gallows still scattered around. There were also stocks, pillories and whipping posts. Often set on a platform so the crowds that gathered to jeer, taunt or pelt the miscreants could get a better view and a better shot, these devices were part of the street's language of social control. This was popular justice as urban spectacle. The prominence of these punishment pieces was intended to act as deterrent but not necessarily as an indication of the power of the state. The real pain was inflicted by the mob, the pelting with rotten vegetables, faeces and (a particular favourite) dead cats. These were symbols of vengeance, of the uncontrollable rage of the citizens.

There may have been heads on spikes scattered around the city as there were on London Bridge. These were maintained, if that is the right word, by the Keeper of the Heads, whose job was to boil and then coat in pitch the severed heads and ensure they stayed intact, if not necessarily recognisable, for as long as possible. Public executions were huge events, with people often being given a day off work to enjoy them. Although the acts of violence - the burning of witches, the hanging, drawing and quartering, beheading and whipping - were often short-lived, the aftermath was very deliberately left on show.

The contemporary city, of course, displays none of these barbaric installations, but the language of deterrence and pain is rife. There was a furore in 2014 when supermarket Tesco's installed a fakir's bed of spikes on the granite window ledges of its Regent Street store in London. These 'anti-homeless' spikes were intended to deter people from sitting or sleeping on the ledges, off the ground in an architectural nook that seemed perfectly placed to provide rest and respite from the city streets. There was a minor media storm, a good dose of social media opprobrium, and the supermarket responded by quietly removing the spikes. They were not the only spikes in the city. London is peppered with barbs and sharp stainless steel cones, one more weaponised piece of public realm in the increasing hostility of the city to its public.

'Anti-homeless' spikes have joined CCTV cameras, anti-skateboard studs, high-frequency whining to deter teenagers from hanging around, deliberately uncomfortable benches and a plethora of other devices meant to make the city more hostile to those who are not consuming but rather using the streets as public places. It is a radical remaking of the ideal of the city as a civic space, a vicious and persistent erosion of the public realm.

Benches, which had disappeared from many cities, suddenly and surprisingly reappeared in the post 9/11 streetscape, not as the cast iron and timber archetypes but as big stone blocks. These were designs less to do with sitting than with stopping truck bombs and suicide drivers. Occasionally, they are absorbed into what seem like curious landscaping features - the clunky faux Victorian balustrades in Whitehall for example, which are actually steel plates disguised as heritage, to deny speeding vehicles access. Elsewhere rows of tightly spaced bollards have appeared as defences, urban henges. The City of London has its 'Ring of Steel', implemented in response to IRA bombs but now repurposed as an anti-Islamist fortification. There are the cameras which have become ubiquitous in the streetscape, looking down from above as Britain has become, after China, the most surveilled nation on earth. Each of these features takes up a little more of the street, keeping the public space safe while also reducing it. Meanwhile the few spaces of public amenity and the few nooks and corners that gave refuge to the tired, the homeless or the transgressive, are being closed or cordoned off. Dustbins, once a ubiquitous symbol of a civilised city, have disappeared and only a few have been replaced in London with transparent plastic bags flapping in the draught beneath a yellow plastic hoop. Of course we understand the danger of bombs being placed in bins, but none of this compensates for the sense of loss of civic amenity.

It can seem as if the streets themselves are bristling with deterrents, their complexions stubbled with steel. The poles and posts, the private security guards and barriers make for an urbanism of pseudo-militarised alienation. The encroachment of the BID (Business Improvement District) has seen an increasing 'mallification' of the city's streets. This effective privatisation of the urban realm is intended to push the 'undesirables' and the economically unproductive out but mostly just succeeds in making them more uncomfortable. Where else, after all, will they go? Is a sanitised city still a real city though?

It is easy to romanticise the historic city as a place of publicness. It is less remembered that London's garden squares were once fiercely private, that spiked iron railings were everywhere, that the amenities we think of as inviolable - the benches, the public baths and libraries, parks and so on - were almost all Victorian introductions. On the other hand, there was an architectural language of relief. Churches, for example, had lychgates and porches to provide shelter for the needy and refuge for the criminal.

But churches have long since clammed up, and the amenities introduced by the Victorians are being eroded or disposed of altogether. If we ornament what is left of the public realm with spikes and deterrents, what do we say about what the contemporary city wants to be? There is little discussion in the US or the UK about what kinds of cities we want. Are they friendly to children or to the hard of luck? Are these innovations actually making us more secure or do they amplify an underlying atmosphere of dread? Our cities have rid themselves of the gibbets and the stocks only to find themselves reintroducing an architecture of apprehension and judgement. This is an architecture of escalation, of fear and apprehension, whereas a city wants liberty. As the medieval Germans said, *Stadtluft macht frei* - city air makes you free. At the same time as Tesco fitted its spikes, Toronto installed a series of benches in its parks and bus shelters which transformed into simple nighttime shelters for the homeless. It was part of a striking ad campaign for a homeless charity and the benches only appeared for a few weeks, but the generosity inherent in the design suggests an alternative. With a simple gesture the street can be made a less hostile place and the city can regain a little of its humanity.

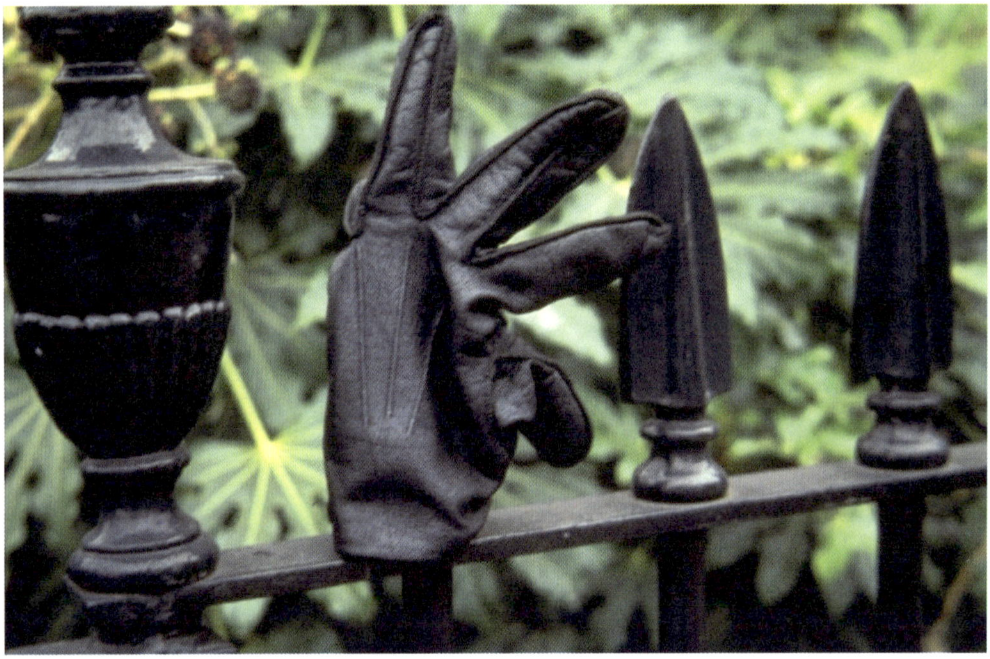

Islington, London, 2001
Richard Wentworth

Railing

A funerary urn, a spearhead and a glove - an enigmatic detail of a London street. The image of the shiny painted ironwork and the slightly sinister matt black of a leather glove, its forefinger pointing towards the heavens like that of John the Baptist in a Renaissance painting, is also a record of creative littering at its finest. A gesture of goodwill, a found glove fitted on to a finial so that its owner might easily find it if she returns. It is something we might see, maybe register, but not really notice. It is typical of Richard Wentworth's eye for the way in which people interact with the static framework of the city, the way in which people improvise and invent, constantly, but often almost unconsciously, reimagining the physical world. His photos beautifully capture the fleeting traces of those encounters. The glove alters the composition: the softness of the leather, the implication of the shapes of the fingers, the impaling of the simulacrum of a hand radically shift the death-like stiffness of the finials. It allows us to see the strangeness of the language. A spearhead? An urn? That most funerary of symbols?

These are the most common finials, but there are plenty of others: acorn, thistle, anthemion, pineapple, artichoke and the simplest, spiniest spikes. The language is Ancient Greek, a classical, mythical inflection to communicate class, culture and keep-outness. During the Gordon Riots in London (1780), the iron railings of Sir George Savile's Leicester Square house were torn apart by an angry anti-Catholic mob to make weapons - the symbolic metamorphosing into the tangible.

There is also a lovely London twist to this transformation of material into *matériel*. If you walk around a few housing estates in South and East London, you may come across railings with mesh panels in between and curious indents in the horizontals which look like they ought to curve around the uprights, but don't. These were originally stretchers intended to carry victims of the Blitz to makeshift medical centres - the indents in the frames are actually kinks in the tube which allowed the stretchers to be more easily picked up off the ground and kept the patients a little above the rubble. After the war thousands of stretchers were left over and, as there was a shortage of metal, hundreds were repurposed as railings around local authority housing.

The park I used to play in as a child used to have the most fearsome-looking railings imaginable. The finials appeared as a medieval weapon, with huge spikes protruding from the top. What were they meant to be protecting? It was a park with a playground, there was nothing valuable in there and the only building was a public lavatory (now converted into a café, one of my first jobs, incidentally, as an architect). At some point, perhaps when it seemed the local authority might get sued by the irate parents of an impaled child, workmen came round with angle grinders and cut and filed the spikes away. It now looks emasculated, like a weapon made safe but still with the ugliness of violence implicit in its impotent form.

One of the comedy tropes of my childhood was the image of a child getting his head (it was, inevitably perhaps, always a boy) stuck between the railings. In fact it seemed to be one of the fire brigade's chief occupations, greasing children's ears to free them, or grinding away the uprights when that failed. It was all very Beano or Ealing Comedy, like kids with saucepans stuck on their heads (saucepans were also taken to be melted down during the war). But the kid with his head stuck in the railings does illustrate something about the nature of this thing which is not quite street furniture because it is not public, yet which is not quite private either. Railings inhabit an interstitial zone, demarcating the private but precisely because of this having also to exist in the public realm.

The curious disposition of the British Georgian townhouse with its basement area creates a kind of dry moat in front of the house (services and servants had to be kept out of sight, and the terraced form did not allow wings or annexes, or the extensive mansard attics of Paris). Its railings demarcate private property and stop people or things falling into the hole. While other nations have their own traditions - heavy rustication, raised ground floors which allow workshops or bars in the basement, the stoops of the US which create a more convivial engagement between public and private - the railings in front of the Georgian house create a very specific condition. They are there to separate the chaos of the street, with its mud, dust and horseshit, from the restrained neatness of the flat-fronted house. The barrier itself is transparent (railings and not a wall), but the material is the defining element of the industrial revolution: the wrought and cast iron from which Britain's wealth derives. These were houses for landowners who made their fortunes from coal on their land or industrialists who created the iron industry. The iron of the boot scrapers, the finials, the railings and the elaborate gaslights found on some houses are all part of a language of separation and an expression of wealth through material means rather than shows of conspicuous consumption. These are not palaces, and their restraint is, like the Savile Row suit, expressed in a quiet way through the quality of material and a kind of specialist tailoring. Railings are like the hand-stitching on a lapel, you can see the distinction if you know the signs. They often extended to create a gateway, too, with an arc of iron and a lantern at its centre. There may even be a conical snuffer attached like a little iron megaphone.

All this is why the leather glove is such a perfect symbol. Carefully stitched to fit the hand yet preserve functionality and a kind of anonymity, it is a piece of craftwork from that same world. And just as the black of the spikes and funerary urns suggests a kind of fetishistic sadism, so the leather glove is here as the German officer's face-slap, Darth Vader's remote strangulation, an S&M conception of spikes and leather, membranes and the materials of dead things. It is elegance, self-effacement and class alongside cruelty and perversion, the fetish for private property, for separating out the private from the public, for speaking in a language that can be read at some subconscious level that this is expensive, valuable, tastefully restrained - and not for you.

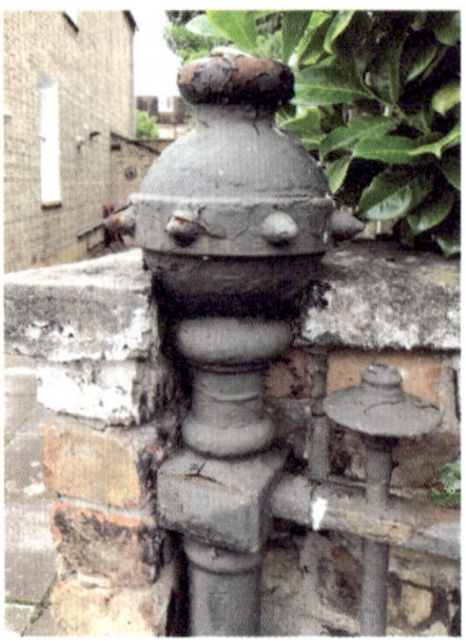
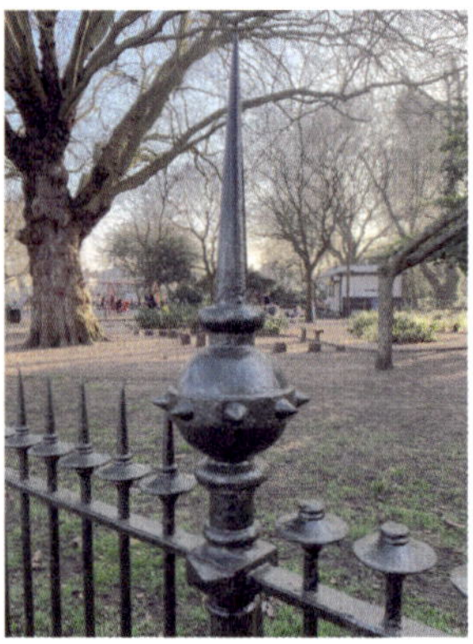
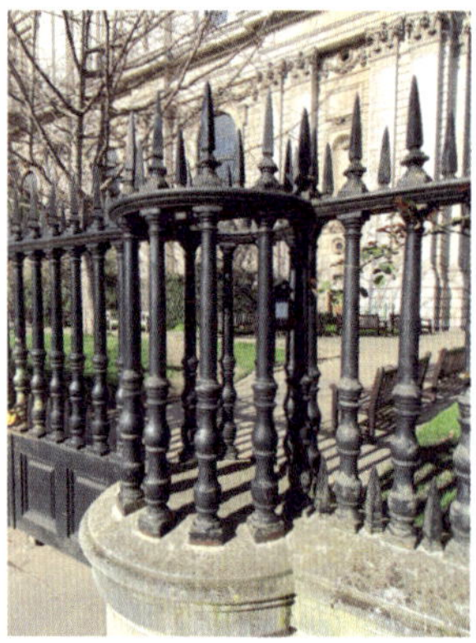

Railings in London

Reappropriating

Most new items of street furniture are connected to technology, with surveillance, traffic or signal coverage. But one new piece of decidedly non-technical kit has arrived in recent years (though its name seems to deny its status as street furniture in favour of something grander). Beginning as a gesture of guerrilla urbanism, the parklet represents a very rare type of street furniture which emerged from the bottom up. The idea was to reappropriate parking space for pedestrians by rolling out fake turf and setting up seating, thereby expanding the pavement but allowing traffic through. It was a practical demonstration of the life and conviviality that can be brought to the city streets through a simple street furniture intervention. It started in San Francisco in 2011 but quickly spread around the globe. The idea was such a success that its originators inaugurated a global Park(ing) Day for cities to experiment with their own temporary transformations.

Its inventors - John Bela, Blaine Merker and Matthew Passmore - were inspired by artist Gordon Matta-Clark's interventions into the leftover spaces in the grid of New York City, spaces created due to errors or irregularities in surveying. Searching for what they termed 'unscripted spaces', they came across parking bays. To claim temporary ownership all they had to do was stuff the parking meters and the space was theirs. It is well-understood that on-street parking is a colossal waste of space, but it appears to be a convenience that citizens are unwilling to forego. Cars remain stationary for 95% of their lives; around 30% of traffic in inner cities is said, incredibly, to consist of drivers looking for parking spaces. So permanent a presence are cars in the street that you might argue for including them as street furniture, but they offer no public amenity. During the pandemic years of 2020/21, with traffic reduced in city centres and the need for parking diminished, the parklet trend went globally viral. Cities attempted to outdo each other, increasing Covid-safe outdoor urban spaces where they had somehow forgotten to do so for the past century.

The typology became codified into a patch of decking with planters and benches, a unit ready to slot into spaces left by evicted automobiles. The designs so far have been unassuming - welded steel sections and cheap timber - but no worse for it. The more look-at-me they appear, the less they would be able to fulfil the quotidian job of street furniture existing as background. But, as with so many successful urban phenomena, the parklet is on the brink of commodification. As cities struggled with the demands of the ill-named social distancing (it was actually physical distancing), they turned to pavements as restaurant and bar extensions. What had been conceived as a free public amenity and a transfer of power and agency from drivers to pedestrians was handed back again to big business. Of course al fresco dining space makes for an enjoyable city, but it also creates an apartheid between affluent diners and other users of the street, those with buggies, those in wheelchairs, those with impaired vision who find themselves in newly restricted and unfamiliar environments and, of course, those who cannot afford to eat or drink in these places and find themselves excluded from this new version of public space. Street furniture should create amenity for all.

Nevertheless, the parklet is a deceptively simple intervention loaded with potential and one which is already developing into an entirely new typology. They have been adopted in a big way by fast-food delivery riders and cycle couriers alongside the homeless and the heavier drinkers. At their best, they provide a genuine public amenity in civilised circumstances.

Recording

In his 1948 photo of the Place Saint Sulpice, Édouard Boubat depicts a scene blurred by rain, a scene of a city full of things. We see a building as a kind of backdrop, a decorated theatre flat; depth is provided by the layering of street furniture: the ledge of a fountain pool, the newsstand, the Morris column, the trees, the W/C, the streetlight. There is one dark figure scurrying with an umbrella but, with the privilege of peering at the view without getting wet, we see a city of objects and surfaces rather than architecture. It is a scene of public space and its inhabitants are mostly inanimate. But that does not mean they do not change. The news vendor puts out the papers each morning, each with a new headline; the streetlights, unlit here, slowly burn into a glow; the pool of the fountain is a blur of rain and water but still a few minutes later; the trees, still bare here, will fill with leaves becoming something very different, giving shade and sound from their rustle; the illumination on the advertising column will come on at twilight.

It was this scene that inspired Georges Perec to write *An Attempt at Exhausting a Place in Paris* over a long weekend in October 1974. The scene looked much as it did in Boubat's 1948 photo, though with more parked cars and traffic. Today it looks very different.

Perec was fascinating by what others might have classified as the boring. He found himself depressed by the daily newspapers which reported everything *but* the daily, the cascade of disasters and outrages which populated the pages, he sought not the extraordinary, which made the news, but what he termed the 'infraordinary', the stories of the everyday, familiar, comforting, often uplifting, often depressing, but nevertheless the fabric of most peoples' experience of life. In his characteristically playful obsessive way he attempted to do this by simply noting everything he observed from the café tables in the Place Saint Sulpice. He called it 'recording what happens when nothing happens.'

At first he struggles a little. The pace is jerky, a list of the obvious and the pointless. But the pointlessness is the point. This *is* life in the city. Patterns begin to emerge. The pigeons who populate the square play a large role, their seemingly random movements creating a choreography, flapping up to roofs and circling the square. The same people begin to return, the ads on the buses begin to become a kind of concrete poetry. Perec succeeds in finding beauty in the banal. 'Make oneself into the court stenographer of reality,' he wrote, 'let reality impose itself without intervening... and thereby found our anthropology.'

When the Covid pandemic began I, along with millions of others, found myself in an almost empty city. It was a world in which the everyday had disappeared but its armature - the landscape of street furniture, the pavements, the shuttered shops and the transport - were still present, only the people were largely absent. This was not the everyday, the emptiness *was* the news. But it did present an opportunity to look more carefully at that dense and historic layering of objects which populates the city. I attempted to go one further than Perec, even more boring, just a straight list of what there was, an inventory. It proved, to my surprise, difficult. Firstly because of the sheer density. The number and purpose of manholes and telecoms boxes defeated me and the age and history of most of the things themselves was unclear. I went to Clerkenwell Green, a very familiar place which was now different, its pubs, offices and cafés, closed, the throng of people entirely absent. This is a very old place, a part of London which was once a stronghold of printing, clockmaking and communism. Physically it was once the leftover space between two monasteries, and it has a famous history of radicalism from the proto-Protestant Lollards to the Chartists and communists. The editorial offices of Lenin's paper *Iskra* were here in 1902 and Charles Dickens has Fagin and the Artful Dodger teach Oliver Twist how to pick pockets at the market which was then held here. The other side of the sleaze was its status as a place of public punishment. As well as the Middlesex Sessions House with its courts and cells it had a pound, a pillory, a lock-up and a watch-house into the 19th century.

There is a sense, or rather I had a sense, that some of that history would be inscribed in the streets and in their taxonomies of things. But it isn't really the case. Looking at historic photos there was once a fountain at its centre, then a public toilet which was seemingly about to be demolished when I visited. Occasionally you might see cobblestones peeping through the black skin of tarmac on the roads but almost everything here, the streetlights, the benches, the bollards - with a very few exceptions - proves to be relatively new. It does all adhere to a certain language though, a recognised vocabulary of historic street furniture filtered through modern economy of production. London, very clearly, is not Paris. In the latter's major rebuilding programme under Baron Haussmann in the 19th century, street furniture was a clearly considered and coherent component. The new typologies which appeared were understood as a language of public amenity, painted in Parisian green, a web of infrastructure made to make urban life more comfortable and amenable - albeit with an underlying system of control and policing. Despite big slum clearances and rebuilding programmes by the still-embryonic LCC (London County Council) at the end of the 19th century (including the creation of Farringdon Road on one side of Clerkenwell Green), there was no comparable system of infrastructure installed. Bits of the old survived (a few bollards here are genuinely Georgian), but most stuff was slowly replaced with an incoherent succession of new fittings dictated by changing fashions; modern, heritage reproduction, pseudo-Parisian, tech-generic and so on.

Like Perec who ran out of steam after three days, my survey sputtered out too. But I lasted just a few hours before the rain turned from spitting to downpour. My notebook got so wet I could only read a fraction of what I'd written. But I thought it might still have a certain value if only that it demonstrates the sheer amount of stuff in our streets and its intimate relationship with changing fashions and technologies.

Once the lockdown was over I thought it might be interesting, as I was in Paris for a story, to revisit Boubat's scene too. It wasn't too hard to identify the place, the architecture of the buildings in the background is unchanged. But, apart from the fountain, everything else in the picture is gone, the whole panoply of street furniture; the newsstand, the toilet, the advertising column. There are booths in the square but they connect to an underground car park, remaining mostly inactive all day. The Café de la Mairie from where Perec took his notes is still there, the buses still pass by and the pigeons are as active as ever. And it still gets cold on an October morning, although the outdoor heaters under the awning help. *Plus ça change, plus c'est la même chose.*

Clerkenwell Green, 2021, Inventory

Two red phoneboxes. K2 design, 1927. Very clean inside.

Stone horse and cattle trough (with daffodils growing in it). Installed 1870s by the Drinking Fountain & Cattle Trough Association. Rounded corner protectors to one end.

Signpost ('fingerpost') with directions to various parts of the city. Faux heritage style, black with gold painted crown.

Two black plastic dustbins. 'Litter'.

Two metal dustbins, black. 'Litter'. Plaque on top of one reads 'Stub it & bin it'.

Bike hire racks, row of 21.

Sixteen heritage-style bollards, painted black.

Four old bollards, chunky cannon style.
Raised lettering cast into iron reads 'St James, Clerkenwell'.

Nine heritage-style fake gaslights with electric lighting. Black painted.

Ten anti-traffic bollards in the roadway, two hinged.

Three benches, cast iron and wood. Faux-antique in style and double-sided they have elaborate cast-iron ends resting on animal-paw feet. In the centre is a curly wrought-iron section, presumably intended to stop the bench from being used to lie down on. On one of the benches this central section is missing. Based on a Parisian model.

Noticeboard, black plastic on steel legs. 'Guided Walks'. One side of the illuminated panel is missing.

Eleven mature trees.

Two yellow plastic bins. 'GRIT-SALT'.

Transport for London pylon with details of cycle hire scheme and local map.

Two communications boxes, knee-height. Black.

Bench outside The Crown Tavern. Cast iron and green-painted wood.

Water dispenser for refilling bottles. Green-painted steel. 'Supported by the Mayor of London'. Hazard tape wrapped around it. Presumed out of use due to Covid.

Nine bollards, straight sides, tapering and ribbed. Cast iron.

Two bus stops/stands (end of route).

Four bike racks, bent steel tube.

Underground W/C. Now disused. Hoardings around the site, painted black. The hoarding appears to have absorbed two cast-iron bollards.

Four temporary bollards, slender steel shafts on concrete bases. Uncertain whether these are for fencing off an area for the use fo the pub or for crowd or traffic control.

Lantern on corner of The Crown Tavern. Steel plate, tube and brass-effect.

CCTV camera below the lantern.

Small green communications box.

Three chunky bent-steel tube bike stands.

Four benches. Cast iron and wood. New-ish looking. No central anti-sleeping fitting.

Pair of recesses for boot scrapers on Sessions House. Cast-iron fittings missing in both.

Surfaces

Mostly paving. Cobbled area in parking bay. Cobbles (granite setts) also visible beneath worn away tarmac on some areas of road surface.

Various cast-iron, cast-glass and concrete pavement lights. Luxcrete, among others.

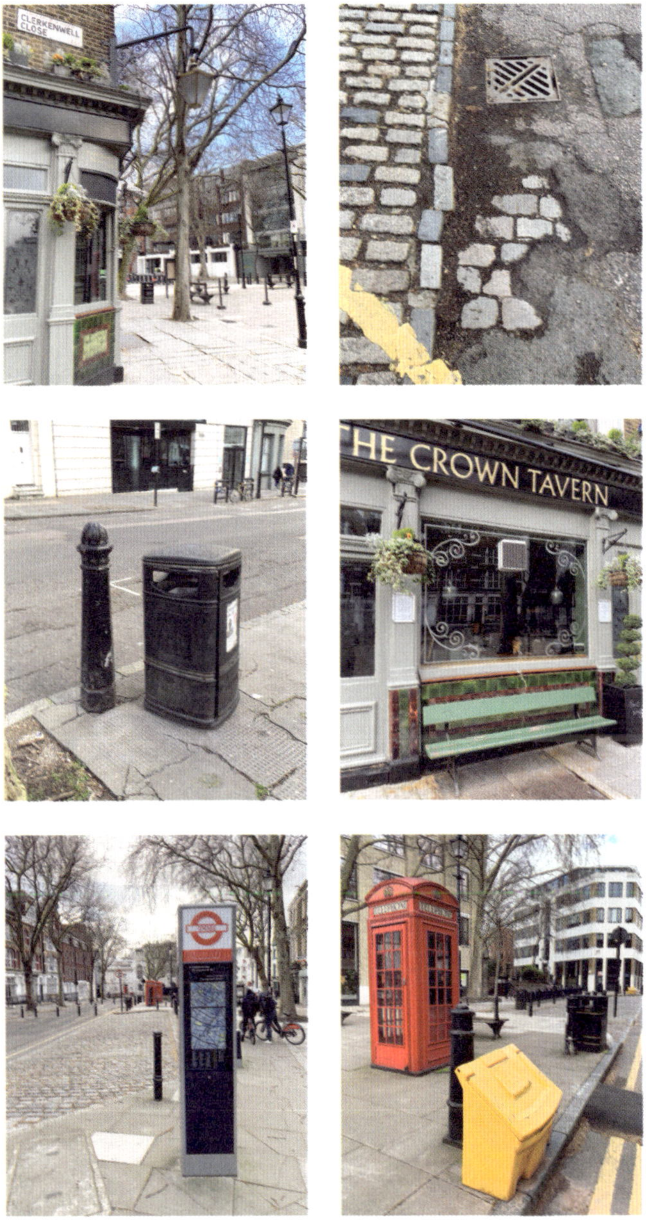

Scenes from Clerkenwell, London

Relieving

Some time around the 1880s there was an explosion in public lavatories in Britain. The subterranean had recently been rediscovered - the London Underground was being built and rapidly expanded, and Joseph Bazalgette's sewer system was becoming a wonder of the world. Suddenly, the space beneath the streets, and particularly in London, was reconceived as a network to create more real estate for the modern city. Prolific Victorian city builders excavated plots in the middle of roads, on traffic islands, on the edges of bridges, on pavements and at crossroads. The public lavatories would be contained in a cage of cast and wrought iron, often with a double entrance with stairs leading down beneath the road - one for Gents, the other for Ladies.

Most were designed and manufactured by the prolific George Jennings, who had presented his lavatories at the Great Exhibition of 1851 to much fanfare and opened them as the world's first public flushing toilets. They varied in design and luxury. Trimmings might be in marble, slate or in dark, varnished wood, as were the stalls - the use of which originally cost one penny, hence 'spending a penny'. There were cream or white tiles on the walls, with elaborate bands in more prestigious settings. Light was supplied by prismatic glass blocks set into the pavement above or, occasionally, from a lantern set within the urban iron cage above. A lamp was originally suspended above the iron entrances, a beacon in the fog and smog.

These subterranean toilets barely changed, even into my childhood in the 1970s. There may have been a little more graffiti, and certain locations got reputations as cottaging hotspots or drug-scoring venues. But in the 1980s, with swingeing cuts on local councils and the Thatcherite hatred of any kind of subsidy or public provision, they began to be slowly whittled away. The few that remained were upgraded by being made worse, their beautiful, antiquated urinals and marble-lined washbasins replaced with generic sanitary-ware, the cream tiles stripped and laid over with dull, cheap, square versions. A few survive to testify to an age of public grandeur in even the lowliest places. The 1899 example in Rothesay is spectacular, though mostly closed. More have been converted into unlikely uses: cocktail bars, homes, cafés. Occasionally, as with the filigree ironwork and curlicues of the former toilet in Foley Street, Fitzrovia, you get a momentary glimpse of Victorian pomposity and utilitarianism. For years I lived in a flat opposite an underground W/C elegantly set into the approach to Putney Bridge, an integral part of the structure. For all the time I lived there it was shut, leaves and litter accumulating behind its padlocked iron gate.

That this infrastructure already existed and was allowed to rot or be sold off should be an embarrassing testament to a country which seems happy to have become less public and far less amenable than it once was. Often the excuse of accessibility was used (the stairs were non-negotiable to the less abled or those with buggies or other impediments), but rather than adding accessible toilets elsewhere, councils just closed everything without replacing anything. A truly shameful legacy.

Remembering

The warm glow of a phonebox on a cold night.

The shade of a tree on a hot day with the slight rustle of the canopy above and the dappled light dancing on the street.

The dense, scrambled text of a newsstand. Scanning the world of words right there on the street.

A bench in a park in the sun on a spring day.

Finding a ledge to put a pint on after work.

The way in which the pattern cast in an iron coal-hole cover has worn away with hundreds of thousands of footsteps.

The actual smell of the interior of a phonebox.

A figure reaching into a dustbin on a warm evening to take something out.

The residual warmth of the rail of a stone balustrade felt on the forearms while overlooking the sea in the evening, the memory of the sun.

The concave dip in a set of stairs worn down by millions of footsteps.

Streetlights emerging from the fog, the last things left visible.

A sun-warmed stone ledge to sit and eat a sandwich on.

We can never love a lamppost as much as a dog does.

The absurdly oversized lantern suspended over the corner of a pub on a Rococo frame of wrought iron.

A piece of rubbish discarded not carelessly but meticulously in an unexpected place.

A forgotten object that was once for sale displayed in a vitrine, a relic from the museum of commodities.

The strawberry, orange and lime of a traffic
light. Who really likes lime? But go. Go.

A hand-written note stuck on a bus shelter and torn into a lacy
doily with tickets to tear off with a contact number on. Man and
a van. Reliable cleaner. Workers wanted. Guitar lessons.

The colours and patterns of fruit and
vegetables arranged on a market stand.

The beautiful hand-lettering on the labels. And the punctuation.

A municipal clock tower with four faces, each showing a different time.

A drinking fountain that works.

The rancid smell of a Gents' toilet and the
shiver of delight once the flow gets going.

The chill of a bench by the river in autumn.

A spindly tree imprisoned in a steel cage.

A worn timber handrail to lean on and look out.

The sinister slit of a postbox. Did I put
a stamp on? Did I get the address right?

A couple kissing on a bench.

Tram tracks in the cobblestones.

The smell of an avenue on a hot summer's day after
a sudden downpour. Earth and trees and traffic.

The acid scent of two people sharing a bag of hot
vinegar-soaked chips on a windy day in a seaside shelter.

The dull sheen of a cast piece of brass worn down by thousands of hands.

The diesel generator smell of a coffee cart late at night.

The windsock stripes of a New York steam vent spewing heat into the
night and leaving a residue of vapour on your glasses.

The last free bench in a park.

Pigeons flapping around an elderly woman
feeding them from a bag on a park bench.

The quilted aluminium of a vendor's cart like a diner turned inside out.

The elemental shelter of a bus stop.

The inhumanity of a bench designed to not be able to lie down on.

The beauty of a once-delicate cast-iron finial on
a railing which has been painted over so many times its
original form has been blurred, coarsened and deformed.

Cool water from a flowing drinking fountain on a hot day.

An elderly couple eating homemade sandwiches in
a seaside shelter in silence, looking straight ahead.

Moving in and out of sun and shade on the pavement in the spring.

The breath of the subway as a train passes by in the grate below.

The flicker of a streetlamp as it comes to life at twilight.

Having something to throw away and immediately coming across a bin.

The first papers, still warm from the presses, delivered
to a newsstand the evening before the day of the news.

The sparkling halo of light around a streetlamp in the drizzle.

The upside-down reflected city disrupted by a ripple in a puddle.

The gush of a culverted stream beneath a manhole.

Cobblestones after the rain.

The bulge of a tree as it grows through a railing.

The sizzle of a cigarette stub as it hits a puddle.

The deformed bars of a traffic barrier as the memory of an accident.

The intense fragrance of a pile of Christmas trees
stacked up on the street corner on January 1st.

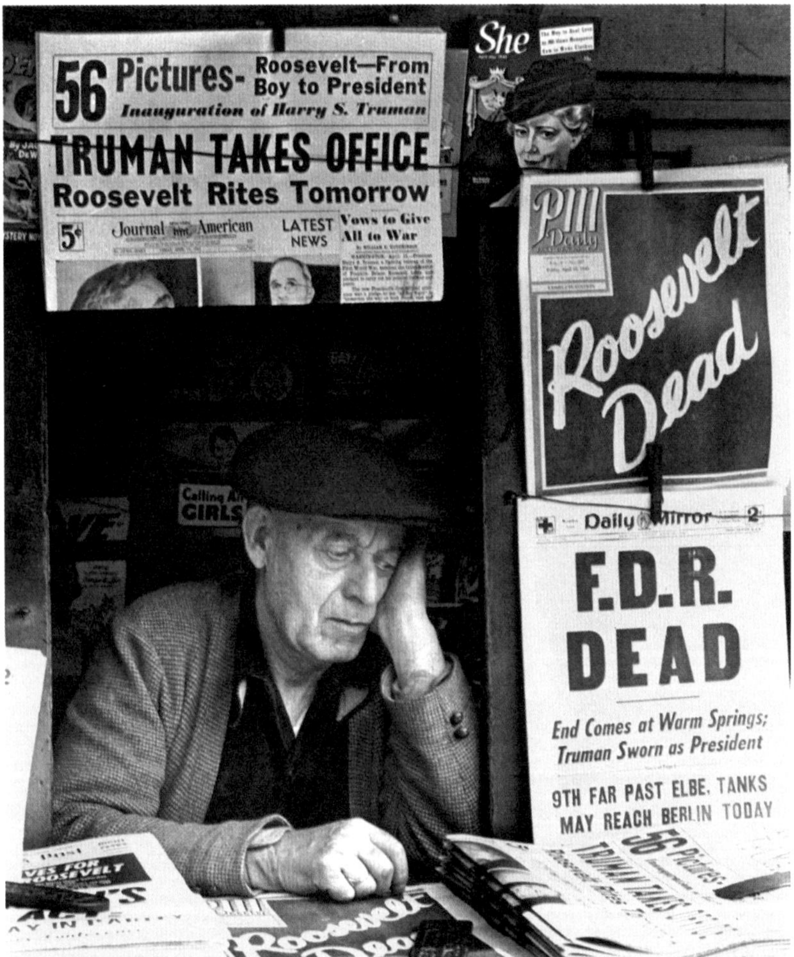

Man in Newspaper Stand, 1945
Stanley Kubrick

Reporting

The first photo Stanley Kubrick ever sold was the mournful-looking vendor in his newsstand, head in hand, looking down towards the headline 'F.D.R. Dead'. Kubrick started off at *Look* magazine, a keen-eyed 17-year-old in New York City. In Vivian Maier's photo of a vendor asleep at his kiosk nine years later (p.209), the eye is drawn to the titles on the newsstand which seem in such exclamatory contrast to their vendor's ennui: *Variety*, *Life*, *Horror* and, of course, *Look*.

Every great photographer of the 20th century seems to have had a stab at shooting a newsstand. In Eugène Atget's beautiful picture of a young boy in characteristic newsboy's cap at his stand in Paris's Rue de Sevres, the boy is perfectly still while the papers, fluttering in the breeze, have become blurred, reversing the usual pattern of people appearing as ghosts and the material world sharply in focus. Berenice Abbott, who rediscovered Atget and bought up his archive to save it shortly after his death, shot her version (New York, 1935) as a simple wall of print: no vendor, just a till. The wall of words is powerful, text as architecture. André Kertész concentrates, unusually, on the browsers: a couple, the woman in cloche hat and furs and the man having just bought a paper blurred in motion as he takes it away. Alexander Rodchenko's 1927 shot from Moscow also features readers, but the eye is drawn away by the child and woman at the small, rather pathetic-looking stall next door. The papers here are presented almost flat, as a screen, a two-dimensional image like the photo itself. Brassaï's 1930 shot of a Paris newsstand is more dramatic, more theatrical. The vendor is avidly reading his wares, illuminated in a box of light, surrounded by darkness. Weegee's daytime shot captures something of the same staginess, despite not having the benefit of artificial light. But, with the main headline as 'VE Day', we also get something of the surrealism of the juxtaposition of the serious news and the funny papers, the celebrity mags and *Air News*. Saul Leiter too makes the booth a kind of shrine, capturing a little moment of warmth in one of his early colour photos from 1955, which allows the yellow glow of the bulb to shine like the streetlight behind amid the snow and ice (p.4).

The reason newsstands appear so often in the visual record of the city is that they are, or at least they were, the embodiment of a particular kind of modern urbanity. They are dependable places of permanence within the flux of the street, yet they embody change in the form of the headlines and covers of the papers and magazines that make their architecture. Because they represent the street life of the city, newsstands and kiosks appear as readymades, backdrops to fashion shoots with famous photos like Brian Duffy's image of a model in Florence, or in magazine spreads and the movies (particularly gangster films with their need to create period detail like *The Godfather* or *Once Upon a Time in America* - headlines have an ability to capture a moment, showing without telling).

Newspapers were once synonymous with their cities. Their headquarters were prominent buildings with big signs and clocks towering over the cityscape, and their mastheads would surround the openings of newsstands while the myriad competing morning and evening papers shouted for attention with sensational headlines. Speed of delivery was the essence, with presses in the buildings' basements and stands spread through the city at points of maximum impact and footfall. The paper kiosk became a way of reading the city, a blown-up newspaper, all its pages and pictures opened simultaneously, a publication of the pulse of the city at urban scale.

In the movies they were the final phase of the trope which began with spinning printing presses, spinning headlines and front pages. Distribution was shown as bundles of newspapers being thrown from trucks and finally finding themselves on the newsstand, their headlines ingrained in the city.

These little freestanding booths arrived with the modern city, the age of cheap newsprint and the mass media. Paris was the first city to codify their design. As part of Baron Haussmann's radical plan for modern Paris in the late 1850s, cast-iron-framed kiosks were designed to harmonise with the rest of the city's street furniture: the benches, advertising columns, filigree pissoirs and lampposts, all painted the same dark green as part of a discrete urban corporate identity. Each newsstand featured a little dome which linked them visually to the advertising columns on which ads for new theatrical shows and often newspaper pages would be pasted. The kiosks were part of a system of public amenities, a hyperlinked information system. Look at any of those old photos and you'll see citizens browsing, not necessarily buying, but peering at headlines or front pages.

Less elegant and often extremely ad hoc versions arrived more or less simultaneously across the world. For most of the 20th century they were a ubiquitous presence on the city streets, dispensing not only newsprint but often also snacks, cigarettes, drinks, postcards, lottery tickets and much else. They quickly became (like New York's food carts today) a way in to work for newly arrived immigrants and the war-wounded. The vendors themselves became permanent presences on the street, often the first call for cops inquiring after local crimes. They became part of the pavement. Photographer Trevor Traynor's colourful global odyssey documenting the news kiosks of the world is a remarkable record of newsprint as a medium of construction as well as communication (p.211).

New York's newsstands have been perhaps the most dynamic, the most varied and colourful, with those inside railway termini often adopting a luxurious, streamlined Art Deco architecture. New York was particularly engaged with the appearance of its newsstands. *The New York Times* of 1923 ran an editorial asking:

> Why should the sidewalk newsstand remain in the architectural class of the squatter's shanty and the chicken coop? Why shouldn't it be beautiful or at least not offensive to the eye? The Municipal Art Society asks these questions and replies: 'There is no reason why the newsstand should not be in artistic harmony with the splendid skyscraper at whose feet it nestles.'

Despite the pleas, not much happened. But with their lack of a self-conscious architecture the city's newsstands did become a pivotal part of the city's identity, most notably at night when their gentle glow provided relief from the encroaching darkness, a refuge of words and culture against the relentless asphalt. Flanked on all sides by paper, the vendor in an illuminated booth took on the appearance of an actor on a stage, or at least a puppet show, a slightly unreal, almost dreamy appearance which photographers like Leiter and Brassaï knew exactly how to exploit.

There is now a concerted effort to save newsstands in New York, which in a city of incessant change have become beacons of continuity. There is an irony in this most ephemeral of architectures trading in the most ephemeral of media becoming a point of reference, a target for preservationists and urban nostalgia, but if you see some of the sidewalk survivals you can't help but be affected. Mike's Newsstand and Candyland was a Harlem fixture since 1932 (I'm not sure if it is still there), growing almost parasitically in between the iron railings of an old brownstone. When he was mayor of the city, Michael Bloomberg replaced many of the newsstands with a generic model by Spanish manufacturer Cemusa, destroying decades of a sense of place. Kiosks once owned by their operators became corporate leasing deals; many vendors subsequently gave up.

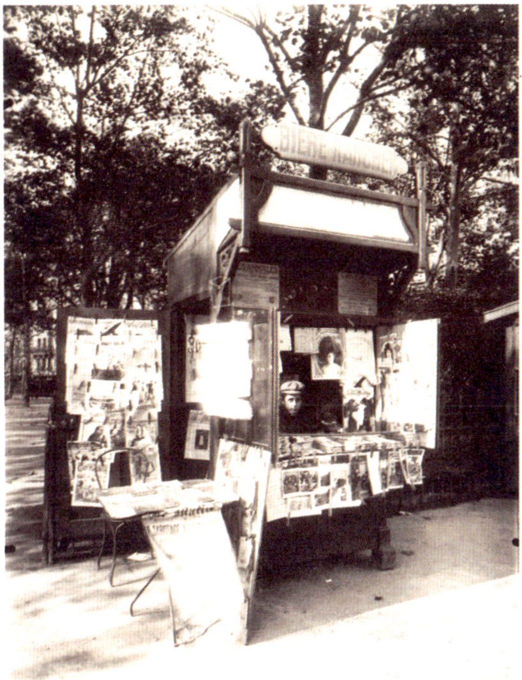

Newspaper Stand, Rue de Sèvres, Paris, 1910–11
Eugène Atget

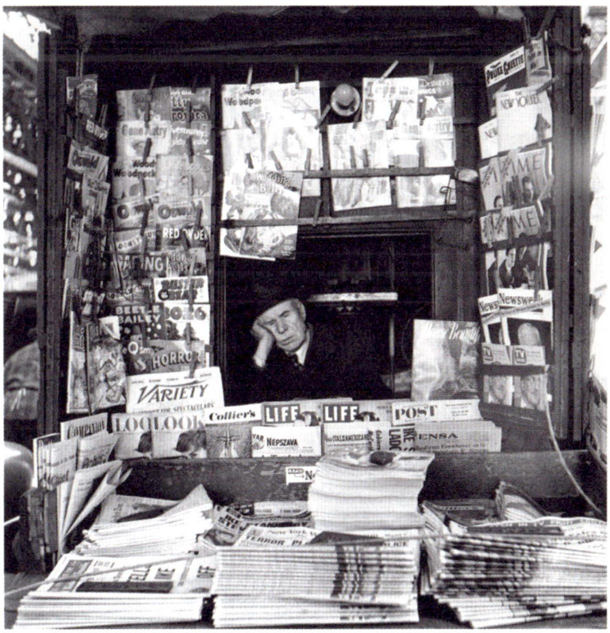

Untitled, March 1954
Vivian Maier

London's newsstands similarly never developed a real architecture of their own, each a kind of ad hoc innovation of tenacious survival. My local version was an astonishingly unattractive box, although when it opened out each day there was something almost butterfly-like in its transformation as the pages became the architecture and its ugliness melted away behind screaming tabloid headlines and glossies. The stand became a mobile phone repair shop, then closed entirely and has now been removed.

The exception to this informal architecture of news was the railway station. Beneath the complex iron and glass canopies of the grand termini, the newsstands came to magnificent life, a panoply of advertising hoardings and hanging titles. This was a universal phenomenon - from Boston and Buenos Aires to Bombay, station newsstands were the pivot of life in what were still 24-hour hubs. Now they have retreated into generic storefronts, branches of chains identical to those in airports.

Occasionally, newsstands survive to become landmarks in themselves, for example the Harvard Square kiosk in Cambridge, Massachusetts, originally built in 1928. Like many newsstands it is integrated into the architecture of urban transport - together they express the dynamism of the city, movement and circulation, commuters and the news. And like almost all historic newsstands, Harvard Square's is under threat.

The architecture of headlines made headlines itself recently when Paris mayor Anne Hidalgo, like Bloomberg before her, decided to replace Paris's existing historic newsstands with generic new versions. The new stands are simple and practical, walk-in pods rather than a kiosk. They are heated, protected, more efficient and more secure than the older versions, but the mayor seems to have missed the point here. Imagine if we were to convert the city's cafés into corporate coffee chains? The outcry would be unimaginable, yet those would be similarly more efficient. Her proposed removal of the city's newsstands was condemned as an attempt to 'make Paris as ugly as London' (thanks for that), and there is, of course, something in it. A certan degree of sleaze and shabbiness is at the heart of the idea of the urban newsstand - that's why *characters* like Tom Waits have themselves photographed next to them.

Newsstands seem to have been particularly unlucky in their commercial options. I was told that, as newspaper circulation started dwindling, much of the revenue from news kiosks, particularly the late-night versions, came from selling porn magazines. They offered a kind of urban anonymity which suited buyers. Printed porn has been even more affected than the papers by the internet. Many one-time news vendors have switched to selling sweets and souvenirs. The magazines and newspapers might still be physically present but they are more decoration than commercial reality - print as advertising and visibility for the news brands and mastheads, more than expectation of sales.

The urge to standardise isn't new. There have been periodic attempts to create new archetypes. Jean Prouvé, the French master of prefabricated modernism, also had a go with an elegant design for a booth in 1930. Another was Kensington's commissioning of a then-fledgling Thomas Heatherwick. The resulting layered pod (which reminds me of Arnold Schwarzenegger's exploding-head disguise in *Total Recall*) was a good effort, but its bulk reminds us why often less design is more.

Newsstands are, almost certainly, on their way out. The consensus seems to be that print media has been replaced by digital and online copy, but I think that's a misconception. There will always be an appetite for print, perhaps it might switch to books or small magazines or formats we haven't thought of yet. The newsstand is the physical manifestation of copy in urban form, the expression of media as architecture. The city would be infinitely poorer without them.

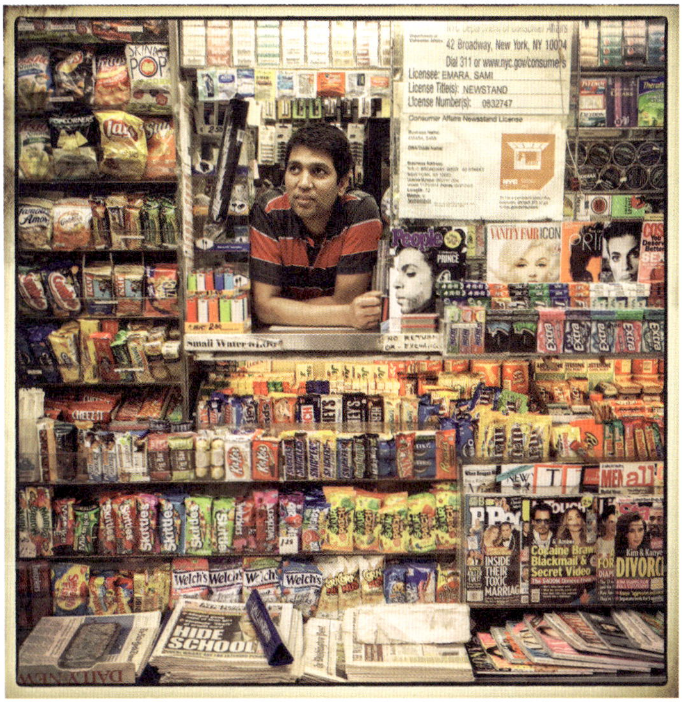

The Newsstand Series, 2012–19
Trevor Traynor

Resting

On the Green Park side of Piccadilly, not far from Hyde Park Corner, there is an easily missable, utilitarian-looking but slightly obscure piece of street furniture. Two steel columns with restrained lotus-leaf capitals support a wooden shelf. It looks like the kind of thing for resting a pint glass - in fact it is a 'porters' rest', dating from 1861. Or it was. The original seems to have been stolen; a replica was put in its place in 2016. As far as I know it is the only one in London, a rare survival (or rare revival). Its function was for porters to rest what they were carrying, probably on their backs, probably in a sack, without putting it down in the mud and dirt.

There are a few more survivors from another genus, the cabmen's shelter. These are scattered throughout London with a few further afield (a lovely wheeled one in Ripon, for instance), and mostly date from the 1870s. These charismatic survivals, painted in pissoir green (the same colour used in Paris for *colonnes Morris* and the default 19th-century hue for chunky street furniture) were places where cabmen could get a hot drink and food, as well as some company and conviviality. Sitting on a cab in the open air was cold and lonely. The structures are only as wide as a horse and cab as they were placed in the middle of the road at cab ranks and could not impede traffic. Like so many other forms of Victorian facility they had a moral dimension: they were not allowed to serve alcohol and were intended as an alternative to pubs. The Cabmen's Shelter Fund was established in 1875 with the purpose of providing 'a place of shelter where [the cabmen] can obtain good and wholesome refreshments at very moderate prices'.

Their form was municipal-domestic: chamfered oak frames, tongue-and-groove boarding, with a steep-pitched park-lavatory roof and, usually, a little flèche for a flue which acted as a chimney for wood-fired stoves that sat in the centre. Inside they were tiny, with benches around their edges and an inevitable intimacy in the huddle. Although they were mandated to serve only cabmen and still adhere to that rule, some now serve takeaways through a serving hatch or door to the winder public. They originally had marble troughs for horses too. Designs progressed from quite basic to rather ornate towards the end of the 19th century; architect George Aitchison was commissioned to design a more sophisticated version in 1879. Around the same time, he was designing a house in Holland Park for the artist Frederic Leighton. The orientalising interior is one of the most gorgeous interiors in the city, a Moorish fantasy of tiles, screens, peacock blue and fountains. I like to think of Aitchison mulling over this decadence while thinking about the welfare of cabmen with the most minimal means imaginable.

The porters' rest and the cabmen's shelter, along with the public toilets popping up all over the city at the same time, represent a gesture toward the service classes, an acknowledgement of the hardship of their labour. They provoke the question of what, exactly, we are doing for our contemporary porters and cabmen, the bike and cycle couriers, the internet delivery people, the Uber drivers and so on. They are increasingly critical cogs in the contemporary city, yet their needs are utterly uncatered for. There are few public toilets, nowhere to rest their loads and no time to rest. I occasionally come across clusters of bikers gathered out in the cold and wonder what the street furniture designed for them might look like. And wonder if anyone in authority really gives a shit.

Sanitising

The pandemic catalysed an entire new genre of furniture for the 2020s. Created in response to concerns about cleanliness and hygiene, fittings appeared rapidly from seemingly ad hoc materials - yet, over the course of Covid, they barely seemed to change or develop. Public hand-sanitiser dispensers, a typology probably unthinkable before the coronavirus outbreak, began to pop up outside stations and stores, on shopping streets and in public buildings. Usually constructed from some kind of folded steel they tended to be basic housings for an off-the-shelf plastic dispenser with a press-down top. Some were refined into more hygienic pedal-operated versions with varying degrees of success. At the same time, the few traditional drinking fountains that had survived the ravages and neglect of recent years were shunned because of the fear of contagion and were replaced or supplemented by bottle-filling stations. These were usually some variations on a metal tube, stunted cacti with awkwardly protruding arms and indents.

As restrictions hit restaurants and bars, hybrid dining sheds began to pop up in cities around the world. Sitting somewhere between covered pavement café terraces in the Parisian mould and smoking shelters or garden sheds, they were an expedient development to exploit loopholes in the regulations. This 'solution' often created even more unsanitary conditions in enclosed spaces without the ventilation, air-conditioning and spacing in the restaurant interiors they were intended to replace.

The pandemic created the conditions for a complete reassessment of street furniture and what we require from the public realm, provoking the arrival of a new layer of public goods for our new, more anxious age: mask dispensers, sanitising stations, the marquees and tents of testing points, endless bottles of gel shoehorned into ill-fitting pumps. It has arguably been the single greatest acceleration of street furniture since the arrival of electricity, as radical in its way as the reconnection of street furniture in Haussmann's Paris as a unifying municipal public good and a mechanism for urban branding.

Yet I have seen not one design emerge from this moment to match the products of the Belle Epoque. In fact, you might argue that the response has revealed the abject failure of the modern age to respond to a health crisis through design and manufacture, at least not to match its response in terms of the vaccine. It has highlighted an inability to think through design, to create lasting items of quality and utility. The same might be said of other new typologies, from car-charging points to interactive signposts. More different types of street furniture have appeared in the last few years than, perhaps, at any time since the advent of streetlighting. It was an incredible opportunity. Yet municipal authorities globally have largely failed to improve the public realm or to create new moments of interest, humour, dignity or delight. It is an unhappy indictment of a decline in civic design.

Scraping

When the movement of goods and people depended on horses and donkeys, and cattle and sheep were herded through the city streets on their way to slaughter, the roads were, frankly, covered in shit. Pavements, sometimes of timber, occasionally of stone, constructed above the level of the road made some difference in the 18th and 19th centuries; walking became a little more fashionable as it became possible not to have to wade ankle-deep through ashes and rubbish. But public highways remained filthy until the internal combustion engine dispensed with manure and embarked instead on the complete destruction of our climate and ecosystem.

As long as there were big beasts about, footwear, inevitably, accumulated layers of dirt - the solution was the boot scraper. Although not quite public street furniture, as many examples were built into the walls of houses or inside their front gardens or atop their stoops, they have nevertheless survived in public places: churches, police stations, libraries, civic buildings, on the pavement outside houses.

At first boot scrapers tended to be wrought from iron, a single blade on two legs, freestanding and often leaded into a front step. Then, around the middle of the 19th century, they began to be incorporated into the architecture. Set into small openings, often arched, they resembled miniature fireplaces with cast-iron grates. Most of these have survived, even if many have lost their iron fittings to become odd, oversized cartoon mouse holes.

In the UK and the US, even the best examples tended to be mass-produced items, elaborate but rarely particularly elegant. But there was a brief golden age in Belgium at the end of the 19th century. And the most fantastical were in Brussels. The architects and artisans of Art Nouveau would never have left any part of their buildings, no matter how mundane its purpose, to mass manufacture. The result is a panoply of extravagant designs with organic openings replete with tendrils and whiplash lines, Rococo flurries and complex iron designs that resemble lilies or acanthus leaves. Much of the ironwork has disappeared from these too, and recently there has been a trend to repopulate these odd holes with little figures and twee scenes, sometimes even glazed in and illuminated to resemble little shrines.

In the big cities of the east coast US, many boot scrapers are ingeniously concealed in the cast-iron railings on either side of the stoop. There might be a flat blade and ankle level which you'd barely notice, except that it seems to fill a little too much space in the pattern or a gap in the decoration that might just accommodate the width of a boot.

Having almost entirely lost their original purpose (albeit some beasts do still shit on the streets), they currently languish unused and mostly unnoticed. In my childhood they tended to be employed for storing empty milk bottles for collection and replacement by full ones by the milkman. They have also, inevitably, become a magnet for creative littering, an irresistible hole for not-entirely disposing of beer bottles.

There is something a little odd about those openings. By placing your boot in them you are already entering the space of the house, putting your foot beyond the boundary without going in. They represent a curious in-between zone, acknowledging the filth of the city without quite accepting it.

Sculpting

‘There is nothing in this world’, wrote Robert Musil, ‘so invisible as a monument’.

Seating

Almost anything can be seating. It just takes a little ingenuity. William H. Whyte's influential 1980 film *Social Life of Small Urban Spaces* was concerned in large part with how people sit in cities. It begins in the Seagram Plaza - not, perhaps, the place you'd most associate with successful and humane urbanism. Yet Whyte (a sociologist, urbanist and the creator of the term 'groupthink') shows how Mies van der Rohe's seemingly stark, highly rational modernist space is appropriated through the day with people arriving to sit on its ledges and steps, often following the path of the sun as it moves between the buildings and over the ground, occasionally dangling their feet towards the water, seated on the steps or even lying on the low walls to sun themselves. Whyte's point is that this space is central enough in the city to be a place for people-watching and flexible enough for them to find the right space and the posture most comfortable to them. They cluster around the edges so that they stay, effectively, part of the life of the street rather than removing themselves from it. People enjoy proximity. Whyte calls for ledges and seating 'two backsides deep', not necessarily so that users can sit back-to-back but so that they can choose how to sit, or spread out.

Another part of the film focuses on the way people adjust the positions of freestanding chairs. The shots become almost reminiscent of Jacques Tati in their choreography. People arrive and move the chairs, often to no discernible effect, but the fact that the chair is unfixed allows them a degree of agency, the impression of choice, a kind of customisation. And they use it, making their mark, taking ownership through temporary, personalised appropriation. Others drag chairs across the space so they can sit together; one fellow sits in it exactly where it was, an almost eccentrically rare occurrence.

Freestanding chairs are often a locus of anxiety over theft, yet in most spaces - parks, cafés, plazas - few disappear, and fixed street furniture is itself replaced over time thanks to wear or changes in fashion or security. Whyte's point in all these situations is that street furniture and hard landscaping need to be able to accommodate various modes of inhabitation and appropriation without dictating how they should be used. It is a slightly surprising validation of a certain kind of much-maligned modernism and the potential it offers. It is a very watchable paean to street furniture, and a careful and useful analysis of how easy it is to get it wrong.

Selling

The Tiled Kiosk in the gardens of Istanbul's Topkapi Palace is a colonnaded structure of astonishing beauty. Dating from 1471, the interior is an intensely rich blue-tiled domed space. Entering it on a hot day is like bathing in a cool pool with the starry heavens above. The architect is thought to be Persian (the word 'kiosk' itself is derived from Persian via Turkish) and there are Central Asian influences in the decoration. This is the beginning of an exotic, globalised architecture drawing influences from across Eurasia. The K67 is a plastic box. Designed by Slovenian architect Saša J. Mächtig in 1966 as a mass-produced pop kiosk, it was a versatile, ingenius, modular, candy-coloured street stand which would pop up in public places across the world from New Zealand to MoMA, but mostly across Central and Eastern Europe. It was put into production almost exactly 500 years after the completion of the Tiled Kiosk.

These are the twin poles of the culture of the kiosk and both, in their own ways, agents of globalisation. The Topkapi's Tiled Kiosk became the inspiration for 18th-century architects and landscape designers looking for features for their clients' new romantic gardens. The follies and grottoes of grand new gardens were completed by open kiosks for talking, taking tea or trysts. These in turn inspired the bandstands, seaside shelters, information booths and newsstands that exploded across the burgeoning infrastructure of public entertainment in the 19th century. On many of these examples - from the Parisian *colonnes Morris* to Victorian bandstands and Lisbon's delightful coffee kiosks - the orientalist architecture survives: exotic domes, Islamic fringes, octagonal plans and shady awnings. Those in parks, and there are still many across the world, retain some of the intent, perhaps, of the Palace Pavilion, a place of refreshment in the gardens, though now reimagined as mass entertainment and catering rather than sultanic luxury. And that is the essence of the kiosk - the promise of a moment of relief, luxury for all in the most public arena.

Kiosks are very different from shops, which are embedded in the architecture. By being directly in the public arena, kiosks are more a part of the life of the street or a park, they exist as autonomous objects, an architecture dedicated to service, and they often express this hospitality by facing all ways at once. Octagonal, circular, hexagonal or cubic forms often have windows and ledges around all their edges so they do not discriminate against a single direction; they are open to the entire city.

The Yugoslav K67 was in this vein, but its exoticism stemmed not from a faux-orientalism but from its vivid pop-modernism. If the Persian-inflected kiosk was a symbol of louche luxury, the K67 was a marker of the future in a half-realised landscape of modernity. The streets of Eastern Europe had been stripped of much of their colour by dour communist storefronts, the march of panel-built housing and a lack of maintenance of the (often still war-damaged) historic architecture. These reinforced polyfibre booths were designed not as pop-up interventions but as urban design nodes in their own right. Mächtig understood the kiosk as a critical element in the cityscape, an implement which could influence what happened around it and how citizens used and understood public space. He regarded street furniture as a tool for shaping civic life. The success and spread of the K67 underlined the remarkable range of uses in the city, the resort, the village and the factory, for which there was no real accommodation beyond ad hoc solutions.

The uses to which the K67 kiosk has been put include border-guard's huts, florists, ski-rentals, greengrocers, information booths, shelters for security staff, ticket inspectors and factory foremen,

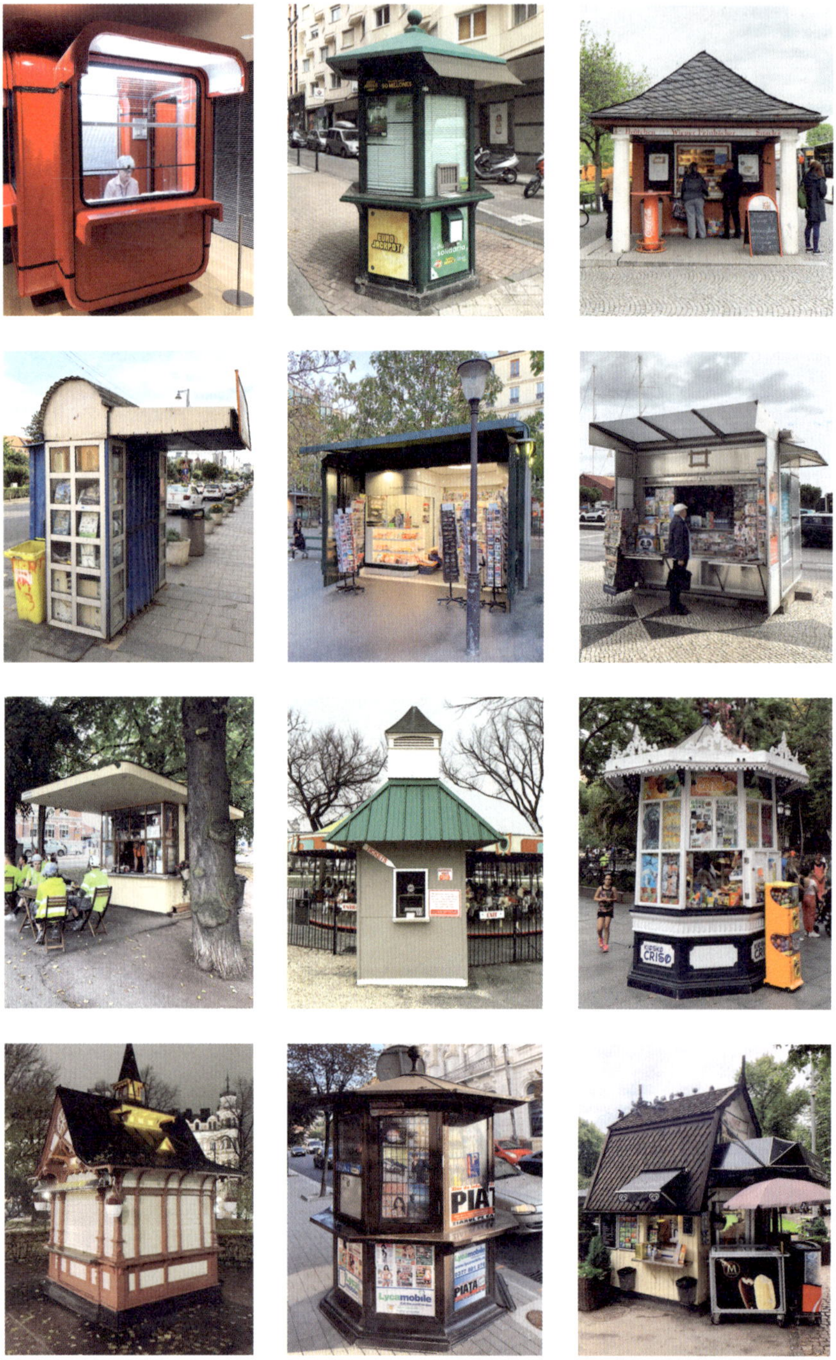

Top row, left: *MoMA, NY*; middle: *Bilbao*; right: *Weimar, Germany*
2nd row, left: *Târgu Mureş, Romania*; middle: *Paris*; right: *Lisbon*
3rd row, left: *Helsinki*; middle: *Washington DC*; right: *Cadiz, Spain*
Bottom row, left: *Helsinki*; middle: *Cluj, Romania*; right: *Helsinki*

chicken coops, ice-cream stands and car-parking attendants' booths. They became almost ubiquitous, particularly around tourist hotspots where there was only seasonal demand, staying shuttered for half the year. They have also proved remarkably enduring. Some have been incorporated into buildings and plastered into place, others have been clustered so that they are robust enough to survive as a group. Others have become the cores of shacks, improvised structures built around them so that only the distinctive curved corners of the windows are visible. Others remain in place because, frankly, no better solution has come along.

Mächtig's was a mass-manufactured modernist notion, but in its way very attuned to the thinking of his contemporaries in London, Cedric Price and Archigram, as well as in Los Angeles, Tokyo and beyond - the idea that the city would need to become a more adaptable place through an architecture of lightweight, modular, responsive pop-up structures able to respond to changing demands. But although it has become a globally recognised artefact of high design (and a rare acknowledgement of a successful commercial design from outside capitalism), it did not survive to become the norm or to inspire later variations.

The collapse of communism from 1989 onwards led to an explosion in entrepreneurialism and an outbreak of ad hoc structures across the former Eastern Bloc, as citizens attempted to establish new businesses with minimal means in an unfamiliar and emerging economic environment. The kiosks of Moscow (many clustered around Metro stations) became an intriguingly cobbled-together infrastructure of strange units using anything from corrugated iron and plastic cladding to garden sheds and trailers. They became a kind of folk architecture, colourful, lively, constantly engaging. As Moscow became wealthier these were suddenly perceived as eyesores and demolished, so that by about 2016 most had been torn down by the authorities, often at night, against their owners' wishes, usually with all their wares still inside.

There was an irony in these Russian kiosks becoming the visual language of transition from communism and the collective to capitalism and private enterprise. The Soviets had extensively explored the language of the kiosk via some of the great Constructivist architects. Gustav Klutsis's designs for agit-prop booths are among the most memorable and graphically striking (as well as influential) products of early modernism. Conceived as easy-to-assemble and easy-to-transport kits of parts able to reach the furthest reaches of the fledgling Soviet Union, these were multi-media platforms for spreading propaganda. His most famous design (Screen Platform Kiosk for the Fifth Anniversary of the Great October Revolution, 1922) includes a bookshelf and pamphlet stand, a vertical board for propaganda posters, a platform or podium for a speaker and a screen for projecting films on to. A statement in itself, it was designed to appeal to the literate and the illiterate alike through its presentation. It was an idea still being peddled by architects in the 1960s and through to the Pompidou Centre in Paris and its proposed (though never realised) information façade.

The main ring road of Budapest, with its wide pavements, fared a little better, with elegant florists' kiosks popping up in the 1990s, brightening up the still uncertain streets and looking like early modernist survivals. Spain's streets are punctuated by the little kiosks of the Lotto sellers (the ONCE, raising money for the charity for the blind), while the Ramblas in Barcelona has become a kind of built taxonomy of kiosk culture.

There are subsets of kiosks in zoos and urban theme parks, often in exotic forms, and there are modernist pavilions left over from the self-consciously modernising efforts of municipalities like Helsinki's beautiful functionalist examples, the superb Lippakioski designed by Gunnar Taucher in the 1930s. There is, of course, a blurring between stalls and food carts, kiosks and *imbiss* and sausage stands, but as a typology the kiosk has survived remarkably well. If we think of its palatial, exotic and exclusive origins it must, surely, represent one of the great democratisations of architectural form.

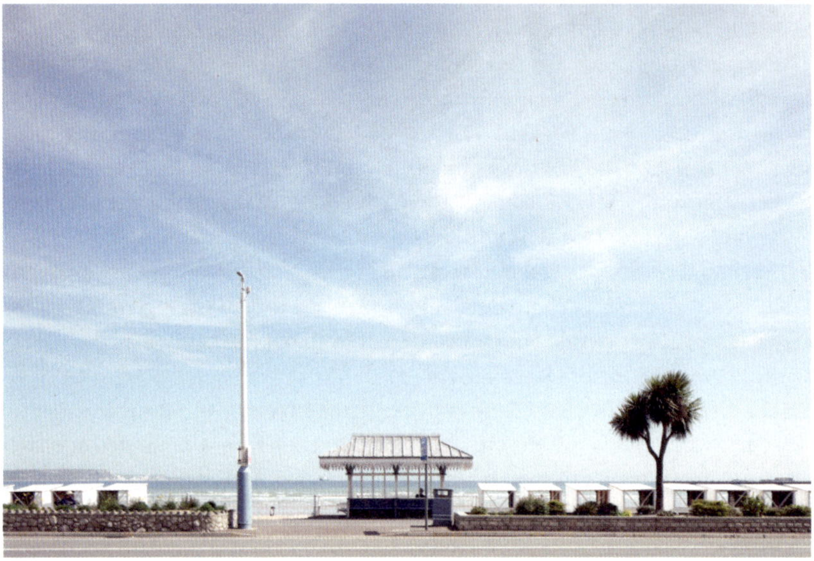

Seaside Shelter: Weymouth, Dorset, 2015–18
Will Scott

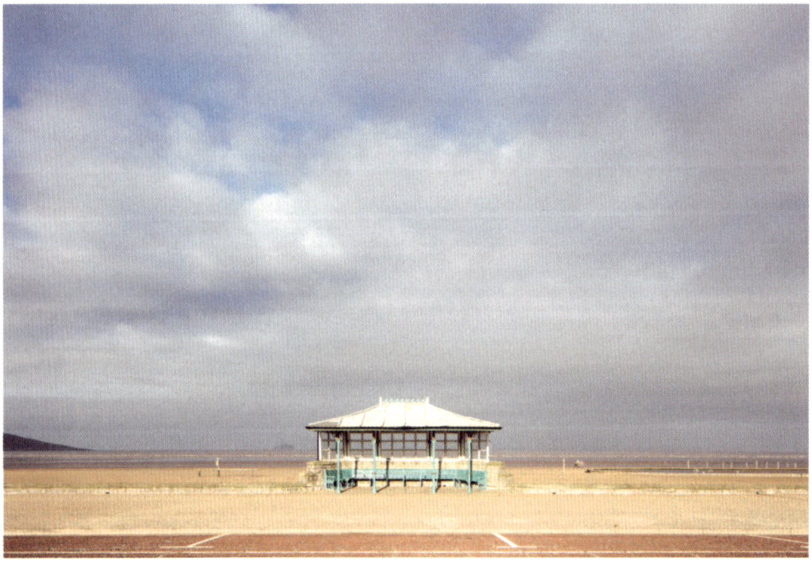

Seaside Shelter: Weston-Super-Mare, Somerset, 2015–18
Will Scott

Sheltering

Situated in the vague space between street furniture and architecture, the seaside shelter is the structural embodiment of the paradoxes of the British summer. The idea ought to be tautologous - you travel, after all, to the seaside for the summer sun, the sand, the sea, the weather. But this particular piece of architecture, situated not on the actual beach but the pavement above it (usually with a busy coastal road behind it) is an expression of the peculiarly British experience of a summer holiday beneath clouds that are constantly threatening to burst while sheltering from gales blown across the steppe from Siberia. Other northern European countries have similar climates but different coping strategies. The Germans and the Danes, for instance, have their remarkable and rather lovely wicker chairs with fold-down canopies protecting the beachgoer from all but the very worst Baltic or Northern weather. They are self-contained, cosy and individual. The Belgians and the Dutch developed bathing huts rather like the British, but these are all private architectures, personal spaces. The British seafront shelter is one of the rare instances in which the British have developed a true public architecture better than anyone else.

The typology is not old. It dates to the mid-19th century, a symptom of the arrival of mass transit in the form of cheap railway travel. If you look at the architecture of the seaside shelter you can see it is closely related to railway buildings, as if the tendrils of Victorian railway engineering reached to the very edge of the sea. But they are also part of an explosion of resort architecture which includes bandstands, piers, boardwalks, pavilions, promenades, lidos and amusement parks. All these new building types employed structural cast and wrought iron (the archetypal materials of the Victorian technical imagination) to create an architecture of exoticism and frilly kitsch. The heavy decoration, the exotic, organic brackets, the oriental columns, the almost colonial timber fretwork, Mughal onion domes and the cast Neptune's head and mermaid bench details represented a deliberate attempt to differentiate the resort from the city, to create a fantasy of dreamy otherness. Which makes it more than a little ironic that the seaside shelter became perhaps the most English archetype imaginable.

Probably the most distinguished of Britain's seaside shelters is the rather large one in Margate in which T.S. Eliot, recovering from a nervous breakdown, wrote some of the most famous lines of his epic modernist poem *The Wasteland*:

On Margate Sands.
I can connect
Nothing with nothing.
The broken fingernails of dirty hands.
My people humble people who expect
Nothing.

The shelter is now listed. Eliot's existential angst seems at odds with the cheery architecture, the optimistic outlook of a shelter designed to lift the spirit, cleanse the lungs and send the viewer's soul metaphorically out to sea, but it is the flip-side of the resort. The off-season chill and the deep, bleak emptiness of the summer resort in winter-time encapsulates a kind of crisis, much as Thomas Mann's mountain sanatorium did for central Europe. It explains why the film version of Kazuo Ishiguro's almost unbearably dark *Never Let Me Go* features a wistful scene in a wind-blown shelter, and why photos of old, tired couples wrapped up against the cold are such a staple of the Martin Parr end of patronising British social realism. They seem to have run out of conversation, to have used it up over long lives lived mostly elsewhere. It is there in an episode of *Steptoe and Son* where the bickering father and son end up eating chips out of a bag in a seafront shelter instead of the planned Spanish package holiday. And it is there in *Brighton Rock*, the ubiquitous background to a flirtatious evening. The shelter is a waiting room for the weather, but it is also a kind of waiting room for death, a kind of architectural limbo in which the endless expanse of the sea in front of you can overwhelm and overpower.

On a happier note, with the sun shining, those same shelters are also intimately tied up with the flavours and sounds of the seaside: the melting whippy ice cream, the stick of rock or the limp sandwiches in tinfoil brought from home. The sounds of the hypertrophied herring gulls greedily eyeing your lunch. These are, in a way, dining spaces as much as they are waiting rooms (more echoes of the railway). They are also, perhaps surprisingly, spaces of sex, or at least what used to be known in seaside swimming pool signage as 'heavy petting' (as in 'No heavy petting'). They are the sites of half-remembered drunken fumbles and first kisses. And they are spaces of suspension, of boredom and the long off-season when nothing happens.

The seaside shelter boom lasted less than a century, roughly the 1860s to the 1930s, but it coincided with arguably the greatest historical shifts in architectural style. They always employed the newest materials and styles - from the slender cast iron of the Victorian versions to the Art Deco of the more glamorous 20th-century types, right up to the reinforcing concrete now decaying in the salty seaside air. The rust stains showing through the paint and the reinforcement bars poking through the crumbling concrete are now as much a part of their character as their distinctive design.

Those built in the 1930s embodied an Art Deco glamour which often far outshone the buildings standing around them. Brighton's streamlined shelters are a delicate delight, straight out of Miami. Some of the shelters in Hastings look as well suited to a modernist stadium as they would be to a beachfront, and those in Bournemouth have an almost Bauhaus air about them. Those in New Brighton meanwhile look like they might be stops for a Greyhound bus and there are a few, dating from a little later, that seem to have digested West Coast Googie architecture, with disc roofs and flaring mushroom columns like something from a 1950s drive-in diner (there's a lovely example of one of these in Deal, Kent). There are hundreds of types, from neo-vernacular to ice-cream-moderne and thatched-roofed suburban to 1930s municipal classical. It is an almost endlessly inventive catalogue, one beautifully documented in photographer Will Scott's series (p.220 and opposite) which shows the little shelters against often glowering skies, always a little overwhelmed by the potential of the British weather.

The shelter pretty much died out after the 1950s, as British resorts suffered widespread decline in the face of package tourism to resorts where shelters weren't needed. But in recent years there have been a few interesting architectural experiments, very much in the vein of their exuberant forebears. Bexhill held a competition to design a new shelter in 2009 and the winner was an elegant, angular timber structure. Littlehampton has become a bit of a nexus of contemporary seaside architecture and features a rather lovely white wave of a shelter while Studio Weave's undulating bench sits beneath a harsh, Corten steel structure, a kind of surreal post-industrial riposte to the Victorian cast-iron version. Despite these occasional revivals, the seaside shelter is an archetype from another age. Democratic, open and free, with no barriers, doors or even real defined purpose, this is perhaps among the most generous, joyous and genuinely public municipal architecture ever.

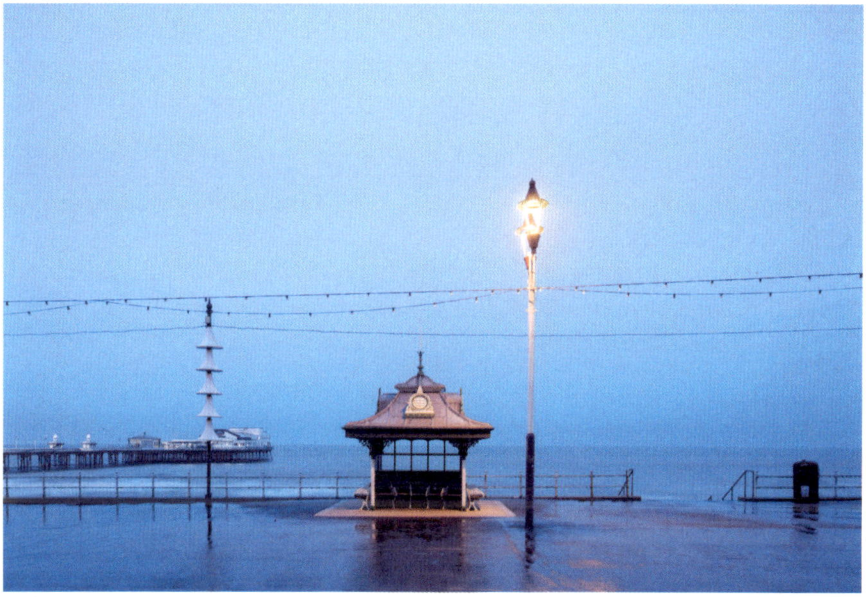

Seaside Shelter: Blackpool, Lancashire, 2015–18
Will Scott

Shelving

If you've ever tried to put anything down in the city, you'll quickly become aware that the city is short of surfaces. It is an absurd proposition, of course - what else is a city but a vast accumulation of surfaces? And yet, if you need to put a bag down, or a cup of coffee, or a pint, or try to find a surface to write down a number on a phone call or to take notes (perhaps this is only a particular problem for journalists), you quickly see the problem. If you are lucky you might come across a broad window sill or a low wall. They may have slightly sloping surfaces so a little judicious balancing might be needed. You might try to balance something on a bench and realise, as I often do (though I just as easily forget) that slightly angled slats are entirely useless for balancing things.

If you are extremely lucky you might find a ledge constructed for exactly such a situation. Pubs are the best. They often feature slim external wooden shelves designed for putting a drink on, shelves which stick around even for the times when the pub is shut. If you're lucky you might find a ledge in gleaming, polished brass. Fantastically useful. Toilets and benches are indispensable, but it seems that it might also be one of the simplest and most civilised of gestures to build more public shelves.

Signing

The streets are full of signs, signals and symbols. The whole cityscape can be read as a system of communication. But the layer of literal signs is significant. The round metal discs on steel poles and the endlessly proliferating directions for traffic are both present and absent. They are physically present in the street (increasingly), often impeding the pavement, cluttering up the streetscape. But they are absent in that they remain part of the system of traffic, mostly aimed at drivers in their autonomous and private bubbles rather than at the pedestrians who co-exist uneasily with them in the physical space of the street.

The abstract nature of the sign, its existence as a code (think of the 'No Entry' sign as a barrier across the circular face) places these things firmly in the realm of the unreal, the symbolic. They appear to drivers as if floating in space, dislocated from the tangible reality of the city. Occasionally the placing of a temporary sign - a 'Men at Work' triangle or a 'Diversion' panel - can become part of the street momentarily through juxtaposition or via a kind of significance through adjacency. It might become a trip hazard or get blown over, or have a sandbag draped over its legs to stop it getting blown over. Even street signs, which you might consider as street furniture, belong to this layer of things which do not belong entirely to the physical. They are flat and coded, existing more in the realm of graphics than objects. Much, also, can be read from a street name about history and intent. But these things are the map, not the territory.

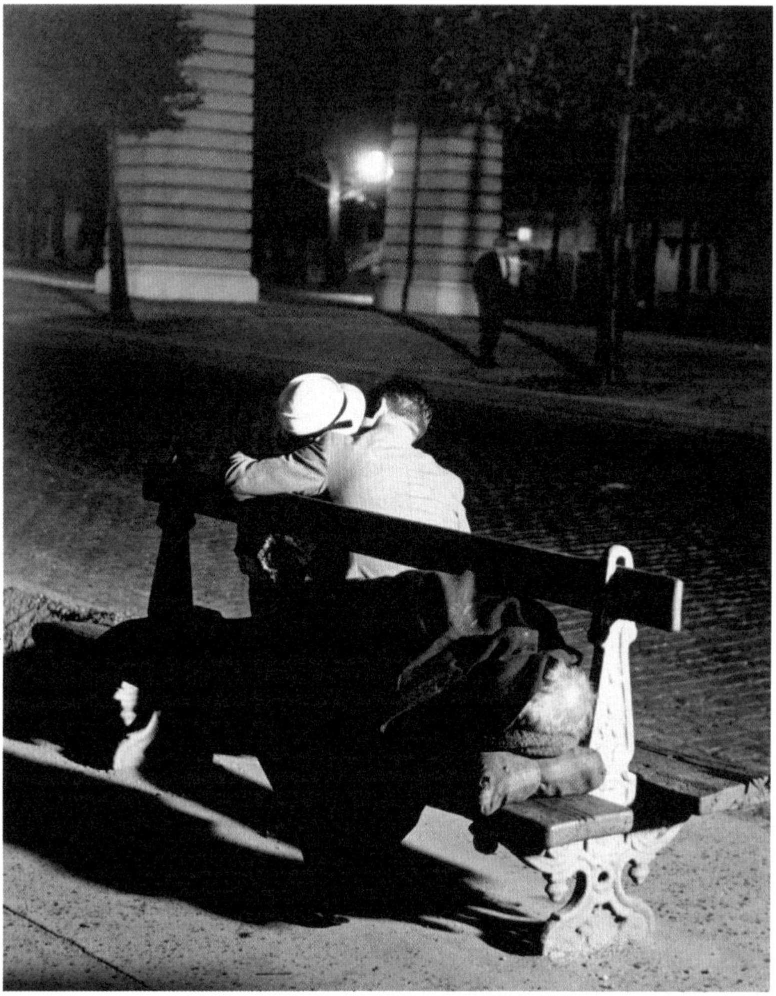

Lovers on a Bench and a Tramp, Boulevard Saint-Jacques, c.1932
Brassaï

Sitting

'We spend our life', said Samuel Beckett, 'trying to bring together in the same instant a ray of sunshine and a free bench.' There's something hugely attractive about the mere idea of a free bench. It suggests pleasant idling, the enjoyable whiling away of a few minutes. Perhaps that freedom is accentuated by the bench's own immovability, the nature of it being fixed to the ground. It is something about the contrast between our own usual motion and accommodating to a fixed point. In England people tend to be quietly disappointed if someone sits beside them on a bench, it spoils their solitary moment (being English, of course, they would never in any way express this disappointment). In Mediterranean countries, on the other hand, benches are social spaces, places where the elderly sit and talk and watch the rhythm of urban life. The bench can address a paradox, that of deliberate isolation in a crowd as well as enabling a presence in the public arena, becoming part of the life of the street.

The bench is the most archetypal item of furniture, street or otherwise. Before there were chairs or even tables, there were benches. The very name flows through our language: a judge sits at the bench, quality is benchmarked, the word 'bank' derives from the benches (*banca*) once used to trade from, Parliament has its front, back and cross benchers, while football subs might come off the bench. But the bench we're concerned with here is a very particular type - the public bench.

Seats have been around in cities for as long as there have been cities. There are benches built into the bases of houses in Pompeii, places for residents to sit outside and mingle with the world, gestures of publicness creating a little fuzzy territory between interior and street. The builders of Renaissance palazzi set stone seats into their walls as a gesture of (very visible) generosity towards the public, while church porches and lychgates had benches which provided shelter and refuge to the homeless, the lawless and to travellers. But it was only as recently as the 19th century that the public bench became a publicly provided symbol of civic life and the civilised city. The bench suggests the city is a place in which we can belong, without having to consume, that it is not the alienating metropolis of myth but a place capable of gestures of welcome and generosity.

That openness to all has made the urban bench one of the most unerringly popular subjects for photographers. Like the bench itself, those occupying it are fixed enough to become a kind of captive audience for the observer of urban life, the observers of urban life themselves observed. The entire range of the human condition and emotion seems to have been captured on benches over the last century or so.

A good place to start might be Brassaï's photo, *Lovers on a Bench and a Tramp*, because it captures both sides of the story. The (unusually) hatless man has his arm around the woman, of whom all we see is her hat. At first it seems an intimate embrace, but the more you look the more one-sided it seems to become, a suddenly slightly awkward encounter with the ardour mostly from one direction. What makes the photo, though, is the man sleeping on the other side, our side. With his overcoat pulled up around his ears, his head resting on an improvised pillow, we see his scruffy white hair. The three people on the bench represent various stages of life and various uses of the city at night. The nighttime bench is unquestioningly accommodating to those with something to hide or nothing to lose, a refuge from polite society. But nothing in the city is ever truly private, attested to by the blurred, burly figure in a flat cap walking by and looking toward the photographer and, in consequence, at us.

From there we might move to the same photographer's 1936 shot *The Riviera*. Here we find a single seated man, his head obscured by a white umbrella raised against the sun, separated from the sea by delicate railings in similar white-painted cast iron to the legs of the bench. The bench is in a summer suit, light linen as opposed to the dark worsted of the Paris version. It should be a more cheerful scene than the dark, nighttime shot, but somehow, it is not. This man appears just as isolated against the vastness of the sea. He has found his bench in the sunshine but then has to shelter from it. Between these two shots we have the forms of publicness embedded in the bench. But not all of its possibilities or combinations. There are also Diane Arbus shots of teenage couples on benches, all attempting to look grown up in their curiously middle-aged clothes, kids in the city grown prematurely mature, the girls in headscarves, the boys in greased quiffs and cardigans. Her wonderful shot *Teenage Boy on a Bench in Central Park* captures a little of the cool and the cold and the child; the desperation to be seen to not care and the clear penetration of the cold air through to the bones.

Walker Evans captured dozens of images of people sitting on benches, some in comfort, others in drooping desperation. Together they form a painful record of the effects of the Depression but leavened by others embodying the crowded buzz of city social life. The always brilliant Vivian Maier also seemed to delight in scenes on city benches, park furniture as urban stage. Often with her young charges (she was working as a nanny) she would be in the parks anyway, using the opportunity to snap sleeping men or women, their heads leaning slightly back to catch a few rays of sun, their eyes closed against the glare.

Or we might look to Garry Winogrand's famous crowded 1964 shot *World's Fair, New York* which, despite its title, is a photo of a bunch of people on a long bench. If most bench shots display a kind of stasis, this one is full of movement and an almost stagy sense of drama. One young woman covers her mouth as she appears to whisper to her neighbour who, in turn, is cradling the head of what appears to be her sleeping friend. Two other women are looking intently at something out of shot, one putting on her glasses, the other putting up her hair. On the far left a white woman is in conversation with a black man, while on the far right a besuited fellow is reading the paper. The two men who frame the shot appear calm, in contrast to the heightened states of the women. It is a wonderful composition around which you might weave almost endless stories and scenarios. And the bench, which stretches from one edge to the other, its ends unseen, is the armature supporting the whole thing.

Others from André Kertész and Stanley Kubrick to Weegee and Martin Parr have used scenes on benches to express something of the city from every side, from the melancholy appearance of a broken, empty and unusable bench to the wry scene of dozing pensioners. Sleeping, horizontal or seated bodies appear particularly irresistible, surely because the subjects are unaware and unselfconscious.

In Edinburgh's Princes Street there is a bench with a brass plaque stating simply: 'Remembering J.C.H. Who was often tired.' It is a moment of small pleasure. For others, the tiredness might be more profound, the bench closer to a home. It has always been a haven for the homeless, the last refuge. Laurel and Hardy, the indomitable losers of the Great Depression, articulate this idea in their 1932 film *Ladies of the Jury*. The pair are charged with vagrancy. They plead not guilty. 'On what grounds?' asks the judge. 'We weren't on the ground,' replies Laurel, 'We were on a park bench.' It might not be desirable to the authorities, but one of the critical roles of the bench is that it offers this refuge. While there is a bench, you haven't yet reached the rock bottom level of the ground.

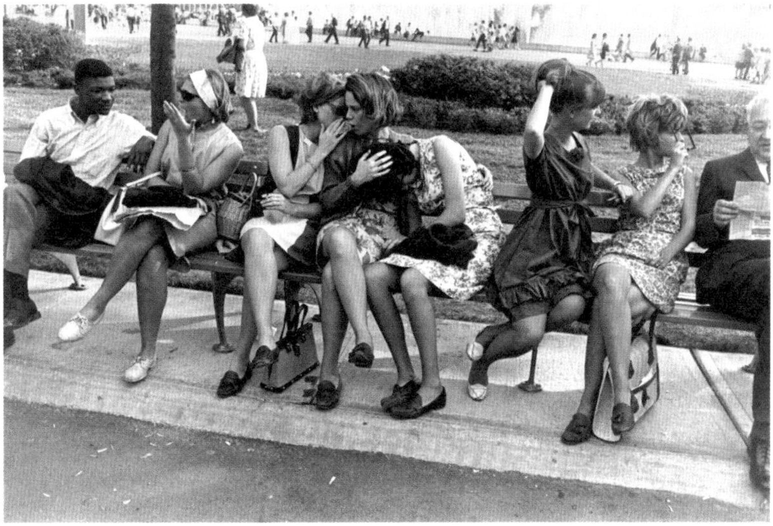

World's Fair, New York, 1964
Garry Winogrand

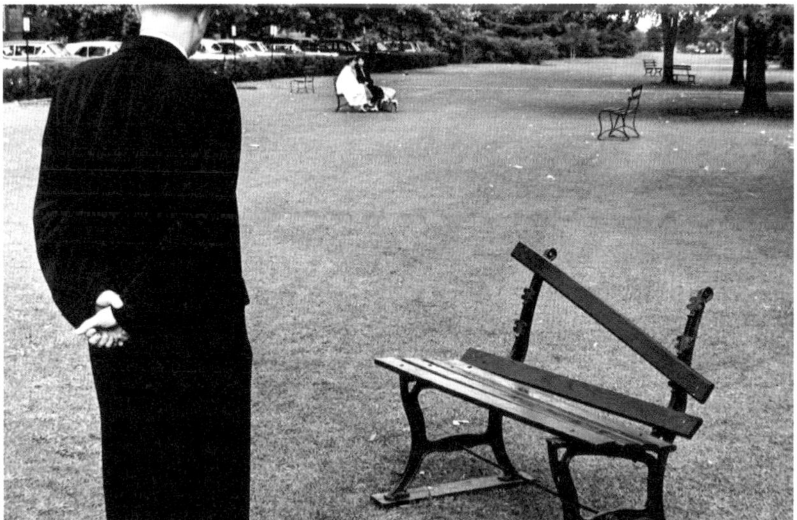

Broken Bench, 1962
André Kertész

The bench is a versatile thing, supple enough to embody both that ideal of a welcome place to sit in comfort for a few quiet moments in the park as well as its possibly very different meaning to someone whose last resort it is at night. It is able to change radically from day to night. Increasingly, though, that is itself changing, and benches are being designed and built to discourage rough sleeping, with extra arms and dividers, the kind of thing seen in airports and stations. Huge amounts of thought has clearly been applied to ways in which benches can be made hostile to horizontality. But sleeping does not necessary mean lying down. Jack London, more famous for his novels than his photography, recorded the poverty that so astonished and dispirited him in London at the very beginning of the 20th century. His photos documented the homeless sitting, rather than lying, on London's benches. One, showing four men on a bench on the Embankment portrays the camel-sided bench still present today (p.154), another captures a pitiful group of women asleep on benches beside a Spitalfields churchyard.

There are estimated, incidentally, to be over 100 homeless people effectively living at Heathrow airport. Airports may be private spaces and exemplary non-places, but they are also the contemporary city's gateway default civic space in the way that stations were once. Whole lives are being lived there.

The curious universality and classlessness of the bench has also made it a synecdoche of contemplation in the city. The memorial plaques on benches effectively anthropomorphise them, suggesting that when we park ourselves on a bench we are sitting with the ghosts of all the others who have sat there before us.

Once you start looking in literature and the movies, benches appear everywhere. It is an extraordinary thing, for example, to sit in the Victorian seaside shelter at Margate, on the bench on which T.S. Eliot wrote *The Wasteland*. You feel the harsh sea wind and a chill penetrates your bones while you peer out at the sea and the big Thanet sky. John Lanchester's novel, *Mr Phillips*, features an executive who has been laid off and, unable to face his wife with the news, spends a day on a bench in Battersea Park contemplating the meaning of life and encountering a tramp who may, or may not, be a performance artist. From the magical surrealism of Bulgakov's *The Master and Margarita* to the exploitative dim sentimentalism of *Forrest Gump*, from Samuel Beckett's own *Watt* to *The Fault in our Stars*, the bench is a ubiquitous device in popular culture. Michelangelo Antonioni's existentially deep film about shallow people, *L'Avventura*, ends on a bench. The spy genre too is replete with benches. Here, the park bench in particular becomes the default venue for the surreptitious meeting, the dead drop or the treacherous encounter. It is a public place, difficult to bug. Safe. Which is precisely the essence of the bench, a moment of respite.

In Woody Allen's *Manhattan*, the bench looking over at Manhattan through the looming web of the Queensboro Bridge had to be brought in by the production team as the view from the actual pocket park wasn't quite right. But that is the film's defining moment, the comprehension of the grandeur of the city from the humble park bench - it became the poster. Perhaps it was inspired by Walker Evans's shot of a man sleeping on a bench with the Brooklyn Bridge behind him.

The bench is so often a vantage point for the city and, in a way, it melts into the metropolis, a small piece of cityness. So much so that its actual form becomes anonymous. Try to draw a park bench from memory and it is surprisingly difficult. There are myriad bench designs, each vaguely different but each also vaguely similar. That, I suppose, is the point of an archetype. That is not to say there aren't wonderful exceptions. New York's Central Park, for instance, provides a wonderful survey of changing tastes in benches. They start with the 19th-century rustic timber log examples conceived by the park's designer, Frederick Law Olmsted (attempts to create a romantic version of nature tamed with civilised fittings) and carry on through to

Robert Moses's more functional but still elegant 1930s designs (with their iron-hoop ends) and on to the more self-consciously heritage versions of today. Each carries with it their own idea of modernity: nature and artifice, deliberate modernism, nostalgia for a better era.

Boom time for benches, though, was the mid-19th century. The industrial revolution had made the manufacture of cast iron cheap and easy. The material lent itself to the outdoors and to the complex, florid modelling adored by the Victorians. The extraordinary Egyptian-themed examples inspired by the neighbouring Cleopatra's Needle on London's Embankment, with seats resting on camels and sphinxes, are among the most enjoyably overblown public benches anywhere. On the opposite side of the river stands another set of benches, their cast-iron ends formed into the shape of swans (although with the very strange modification of lions' feet).

My favourite design is one from Bishop's Park in Fulham. It is a deceptively simple design with wooden seat and back and a bent metal frame. Its legs describe an S-shaped curve, its arms a sweeping bow, a little like the chairs in some of the old photos of Paris parks. It looks old, but I don't think it is. Unselfconscious but elegant, it has few pretensions and is largely comfortable, although its back could have a little more curve and, perhaps, an extra slat. It looks like it belongs in a park. As such a ubiquitous product, the bench has been popular with designers, architects and artists, but few have come up with anything that good. The more designers attempt to design, the more awkward the bench becomes. The generic versions seem to be the best.

Critically, the bench is classless. Particularly a park bench. From well-dressed ladies to homeless men, from horny teens to elderly people-watchers and pigeon-feeders, they come out to just be in the world a little. It exemplifies a certain kind of publicness, a truly democratic intervention and a place to be private in public, a small space in the melee of the metropolis where it is acceptable to do nothing, to consume nothing, to just be. Truly, a free bench is a wonderful thing.

Smarting

The urban layer of street furniture is a landscape of things. So, of course, when the Internet of Things arrives, it immediately alights on it as a source of revenue extraction and data mining. Streetlights, benches, bus stops, phone kiosks and the rest, once apparently benign artefacts, are currently being subverted into high-tech surveillance machines and tools for harvesting our data.

It might be argued that much of the history of street furniture was already driven by a desire for control, to make them safer for the bourgeoisie and introduce an element of surveillance. Streetlighting is the most obvious example. But the fanaticism with which the Romans treated the removal of a milestone, for instance, points to the role of these things in maintaining a sense of decorum and imposing order on a city which might otherwise naturally veer towards anarchy, entropy and chaos. This landscape of things marks out a territory, it represents in some ways a colonisation of space by power.

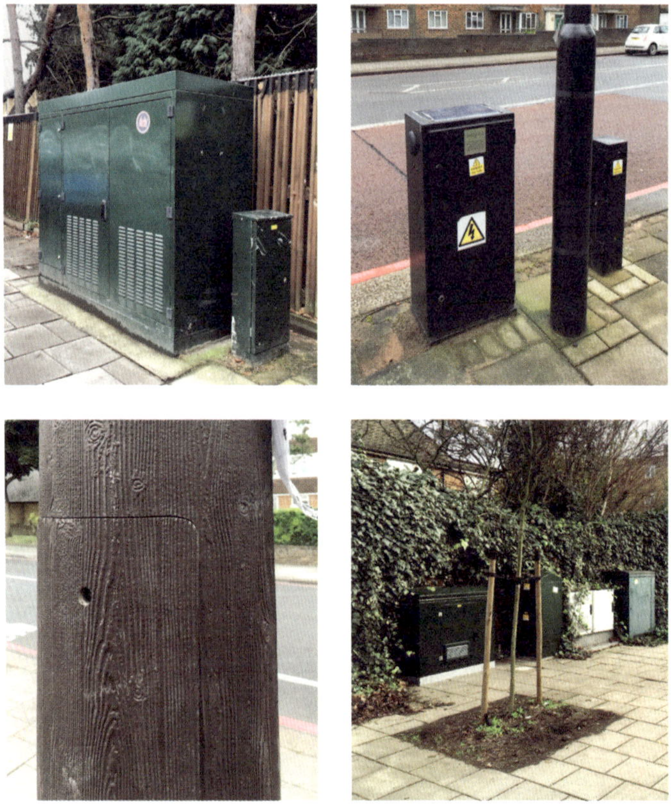

Communication boxes and poles, Putney, London

Street furniture now, however, is entering a new phase. Subsumed by big tech which has sensed an opportunity, the new generation of street furniture is less about utility and more about scraping data and hyperaccelerating the surveillance society. The picture that is likely to emerge might be compared to the way in which advertising companies colonised streetscapes with corporate imagery when they struck deals with underfunded councils and transport authorities to provide free bus shelters, seating, advertising columns and toilets in return for marketing space. It was a sell-out of a public utility to the sphere of capital, a privatisation of the most public of objects. The arrival of surveillance capitalism is profoundly accelerating and changing this privatisation.

There are streetlights which brighten and fade as we approach and pass, which monitor our movements, perhaps even filming us. There are Wi-Fi benches with charging points which also harvest data from your devices. There are smart bus stops which exude a halo of connectivity but in return pulse out targeted ads. Parking meters have long been smartened, necessitating online transactions and all the data flow that comes with them. That most seemingly stupid of items, the litter bin, has also been brought into the smart fold with sensors and data collection spewing information on its status. Will bins then turn against us if we throw the wrong kind of rubbish in? Will they film us and track us and report us? One project to install a new network of smart bins in the City of London was halted when it was found to be harvesting personal data of phones as their owners passed by, in order to tailor ads on their routes.

How can we possibly consent to the way our data is being used by all these inanimate objects and their networks of power and connectivity?

Street furniture at its best is a way of creating a node of utility, inserting a thing which will make our lives marginally better. A streetlight to guide us in the dark, a bench to relieve us, a toilet to relieve us in another way, a water fountain to slake our thirst. Yet the genesis of the Internet of Things, a new language of products which appeals to city leaders who see themselves as dynamic and tech-literate and all this as part of a thrusting new urban digital economy, is damaging the quality of that relationship. Rather than things to make us feel more human, these data-monetising objects are transforming us from humans into marks, not even customers but targets, flows of data, pure code. They are becoming dehumanising and depressing.

Every item of street furniture is metamorphosing into something else, deviating from its physical, visceral role (which becomes secondary) to concentrate on its primary role - the collection and monetisation of our data. What was once a tangible machine for making everyday life better has become a tool for more precise targeted advertising and gathering behavioural surplus. Our space is being scripted. As Marx wrote, 'All that is solid melts into air'. What could be more solid than a bench or a bollard? And what could be more ephemeral than data? Everything, ultimately, becomes advertising.

Spying

In the 1975 conspiracy thriller *Three Days of the Condor*, Robert Redford's bookish CIA agent kidnaps Faye Dunaway's boho-chic photographer to use her Brooklyn Heights apartment as a refuge, a place he can hole up and think while pursued by both the CIA and a gang of mysterious killers. In a strikingly cheesy scene in which Redford scans the walls and mansplains the meaning behind Dunaway's photos, the camera pans along a wall of black and white images. The first is an empty bench. So is the second. 'Lonely pictures', says Redford. Slowly we see more images: stark photos of railings, rows of street trees, deserted backlots. These are the spaces, of course, of espionage, the public benches and parks, the anonymous alleys, the spaces of the everyday that are intended to contrast with the world of spy networks, dead drops and conspiracies. The park bench, in its utter ordinariness and semi-invisibility, manages to embody both ends of this spectrum, the boring and the barely believable. We can't help, perhaps, but think of the telephoto lenses and recording devices, capturing encounters, snippets of conversation.

A movie of precisely that name, *The Conversation*, was released the previous year. Part of that same wave of conspiracy movies set against the background of the energy crisis, Watergate and the scandals of US political interference across the globe, it too centred around an encounter with street furniture and the way in which the public realm is used and surveilled, foreshadowing a very contemporary question. Gene Hackman's character, a sound surveillance expert, monitors a young couple's conversation in San Francisco's Union Square. Glitchy, incomplete and inconclusive, he nevertheless begins to fear for what his tapes and those fragments of sounds will mean for them. As the film opens, the camera follows Hackman's character through the square (then much more of a park than its current, harder landscaped incarnation). At a later point we see him sitting on a park bench with his directional recording equipment. In his grey plastic raincoat he appears to be Mr Average, a nobody. The square, with its throngs of people, looks very much like something from William H. Whyte's *Social Life of Small Urban Spaces*. Most scenes were filmed in secret, so real people are congregating, eating sandwiches, chatting. They perch on low walls and ledges and chat around the base of the monumental column, the Dewey Monument. It all seems to confirm Whyte's propositions about how to make a convivial public space and how people like to gather together and in the sun. It is all only spoilt by a busking mime in whiteface.

Both films feature scenes in phone booths (those curiously private/public spaces) as both protagonists retreat into paranoia. The phone booth becomes a space of revelation, akin to the confessional. The protagonists are speaking to unseen higher powers, mysterious, unknown and sinister. Through private conversations held in very public places, behind the most transparent of glass, the true extent of the conspiracies become clear. Now that we are followed and surveilled by our own phones, let alone the barrages of CCTV cameras, this impression of anonymity all seems rather quaint. Redford's character, a former army telecoms engineer, goes one step further by infiltrating the telephone exchange and tapping directly into the lines.

These films are all about unexpected connections, about conspiracies that run deep but which can be traced via the underground lines. It is a motif familiar to viewers of Carol Reed's *The Third Man* (1949), built around the paranoia following a yet deeper crisis, the Second World War. Here

Orson Welles's Harry Lime, the amoral presence at the heart of the film who nevertheless appears only a for a few memorable moments, uses the spaces under the city to move around unnoticed. Lime uses a Litfass column to escape into the underworld, the ephemerality of advertising covering up the disappearance of the real. But it is the light, or rather the lack of it, which makes the scenes of Vienna so memorable. The streetlights are barely visible and it is the shadows rather than the figures that provide the most striking presences. As in the earlier Expressionist films, the long, sinister shadows are cast on to the cobbles and the city's walls so that impressions of the figures are directly inscribed in darkness on to the architecture of the street. Lime is more present in the intangibility of the shadows he and his like cast on the city than in their actual reality, a true black economy. They are the sinister, cautionary tales that become part of the armature of urban life.

Back in the daytime, the park bench became one of the great (and much-parodied) clichés of the espionage movie. But it does throw some light on the curious and particular nature of the bench. A figure will usually arrive and join another already seated on the bench. As they both face ahead, they can avoid the impression of contact. Something enigmatic will be said, snippets of stilted conversation which might, initially, be code. Perhaps a newspaper will be involved, or a briefcase swap. And then they're gone, leaving at different times, with no goodbyes uttered. The nature of a random encounter and the specific qualities of side-by-side sitting paradoxically facilitates both physical proximity and a lack of intimacy and eye-contact - plausible deniability. From *The Spy Who Came in from the Cold* to *Red Joan*, the park bench is the liaison point par excellence. In *The Ipcress File*, the liaison occurs in a park by a bandstand, with the characters sitting on Parisian-type folding chairs. 'I think they're playing rather well', says Major Dalby about the band of the Irish Guards. 'Tell me who wins', replies Michael Caine's Harry Palmer, tartly, before striding off. But of course the military music of the brass band is the perfect cover for the conversation. There is the obligatory scene in a phonebox here too, the striking moment when Palmer realises he has been in London all along. It emphasises the familiarity and intimacy of the red phonebox, a familiar friend in the street with its glowing warmth. *The Ipcress File* is also a rare film in which a parking meter appears. At one point Palmer feeds a meter with a coin, one of Kenneth Grange's elegant, then very new designs. James Bond, of course, never had to pay for parking and that is the gag - Palmer exists in the far murkier and more complex everyday of uncertainty, a spy who is not above the law and who inhabits the same world as the rest of us.

If enigmatic encounters in parks combine the everyday with the extraordinary, there was another staple which highlighted a very particular condition. *The Spy Who Came in from the Cold* was filmed two years before *The Ipcress File* but its setting is closer to the fissure - Berlin. The Berlin Wall, indeed the whole of the once-metaphorical but ultimately increasingly physical Iron Curtain, became a kind of taxonomy of aggressive architecture: watchtowers, stripy barriers, sentry posts, tank traps, fences, spikes, bollards, arc lights, border guard booths. The street deteriorates into a landscape of control. Mythologised in the popular imagination, these concentrations of mechanisms of power become something different. Their components might be mundane, the ad hoc architecture of exclusion, but together they create a language of fear, containment, difference, dread. The intensity of otherwise banal items can radically alter their meaning, but so can the climate of fear and paranoia within which they are employed. And that is the key here, in the world of representation. The movies create a climate, chill, thrill or horror. Just as George Romero subverted that blandest of environments, the shopping mall, into a place of zombie apocalypse in *The Dawn of the Dead* (1978), the espionage thriller takes the most mundane items of street furniture and injects them with meaning. Some of that essence sticks to their reality so that it colours and taints our subsequent understanding of these objects, whether we realise it or not. A bench is rarely, if ever, just a bench.

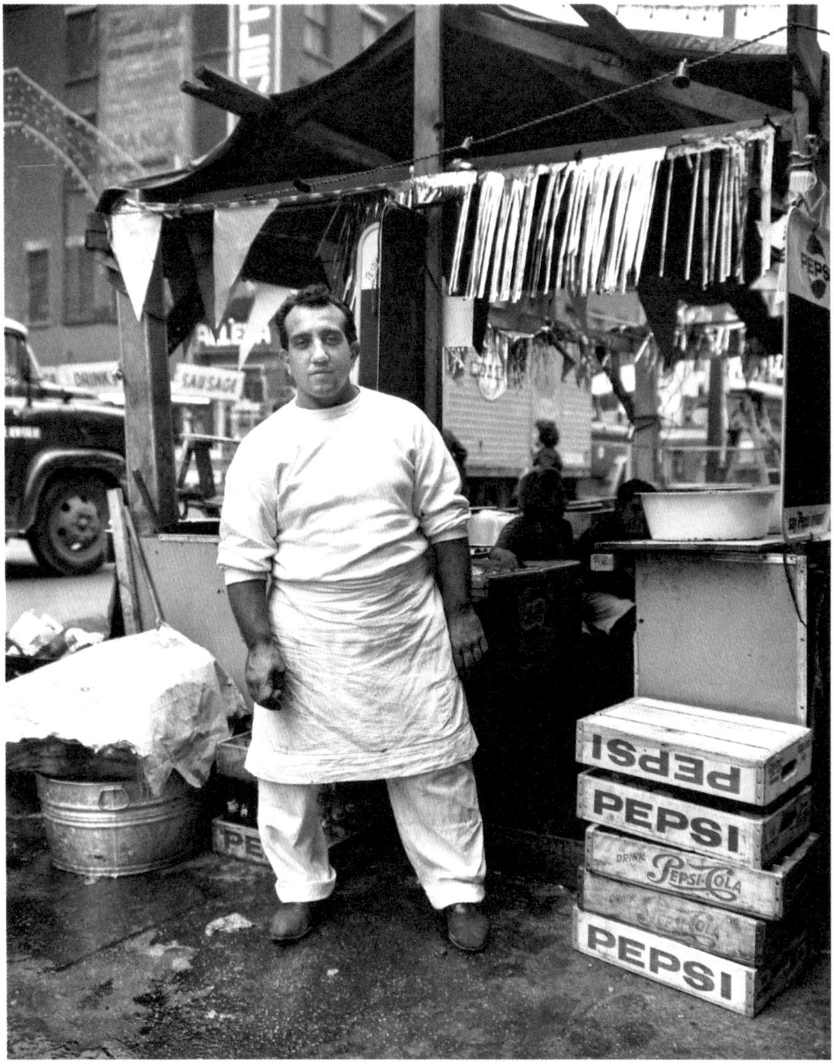

Hot Dog Stand, NY, 1965
Evelyn Hofer

Stalling

A costermonger's barrow can be an incredibly lovely thing. A little like Theseus's ship, they are old working things which have been repaired, rejigged, and have had pieces and wheels replaced over the years, and so there might only be very little of the original fabric remaining.

The few barrows left in my nearest market, North End Road in Fulham, look pretty ropey. But they maintain enough flamboyance and elegance to remain dignified artefacts in the streetscape, despite those years of rough treatment and abuse. They're pretty straightforward affairs: four cartwheels painted, like the whole undercarriage, in a pillar-box red and a surface cobbled together from sketchy lengths of a much-bodged and patched timber and steel section. At one end a fold-up bent bar acts as a handle to pull the barrow along by hand and stow it away in a lock-up around the corner overnight. The grips have been worn wonderfully smooth through decades of use.

The barrows have been relegated to the sides now. The colourful goods appear on simple stands of metal sections. On top a stripy plastic canopy gives a hint of seaside sauce, a fairground flavour painted red and green and enhanced by a row of bare bulbs twinkling in the drizzle as they drape low over the fruit which they echo in their ripe, rounded form. The barrow itself was only ever an armature, a cornucopia without its contents. But it is a transformative device. A row of stands, barrows, crates, trestles - with bellowing greengrocers behind, fake grass, and prodding, squeezing customers in front - makes a street into a market, a noisy, colourful, constantly changing riot of produce producing stacks of empty boxes and piles of rotten veg. They generate their own back-up of ancillary street furniture, mains ports disguised as bollards, sagging strung-up cables, massive bins and stacks of pallets. They create a world unto themselves.

This is London, but each city has its own vernacular of stalls. In Paris there are the Bouquinistes and their gorgeous fold-up boxes of books, in Istanbul the wheeled vitrines of the bread sellers, in Hong Kong the ramshackle green constructions of the Mid-Levels steps, and in Mainland China the box carts of hawkers on spindly bicycle wheels. Evelyn Hofer's famous 1963 Kodachrome of a New York hotdog seller perfectly captures this ad hoc adaptation. The beefy vendor, all in white, stands at the centre framed by plastic streamers hanging from the truss of his stand surrounded by the paraphernalia of selling. The streamers echo the colours of the cars, a little shabby tinsel above him perhaps a memory of Christmas. The structure itself is almost biblical, something you could imagine in a painting of the Nativity, a shoddily constructed barn with a draped tarp for a roof and an accidental crucifix emerging from its basic structure. This is New York, at this time the richest, most powerful city on earth. Yet this stall could be anywhere, from Manila to Mexico City. A stall or a stand levels the street out, creating a layer of universality amid the architecture of the city, whether that be skyscrapers or slums.

A market is also inevitably a theatrical moment in the city. It is an irony that the millions spent on huge buildings create less character, visual delight and intensity than these most fragile of structures. The piles of goods are displayed for impression, an abundance of colour and flavour, fruit and flowers; the smells and the sounds permeate the air. The aftermath of a market, too, is all spectacle with stacks of boxes and discarded goods, while the packing and unpacking has its own choreography developed over long, hard years of experience and practice.

In London at the moment many of the old market stalls, which catered for mostly poorer citizens and both long-established and immigrant communities, are being squeezed out and replaced by food trucks for office workers. This makes a different kind of market - lively at lunchtime, but less vital. These places are not about affordability any more but accessibility and, ironically, a self-proclaimed authenticity. They are wheeled but powered too and, like cars, they are not street furniture. The market creates a kind of magic from almost nothing, the food trucks isolate their vendors in a more private realm, insulating them from the street, above and apart from it, creating a barrier. Market traders become a part of the street, inseparable. Food trucks are more like ice-cream vans, come and then gone again with the sun.

New York's food carts and vendor stands are somehow more intimately tied in with the city, more akin in their regularity with the permanence of street furniture, from the hotdog stands and trailers with their quilted aluminium surfaces to the coffee and pastry carts providing a warm glow on bleak, still-dark winter mornings. There are the chicken and rice vendors, the falafel stands, the hand-carts which are the extortionately hired passports into the entrepreneurial city for new immigrants, so that they become a piece of the city even if only for part of the day. Vitrines full of bagels, Danish pastries, muffins and doughnuts, fruit for squeezing or candy bars cleave to the sidewalk, a radical contrast to the bleak corporate drugstores which are their all-night competition.

A newer appearance in the US is a recent arrival from Central America: the shopping cart repurposed as a street stall. Pushed by Latina women dispensing fresh potato crisps, mangoes or juice, or even with full frying kits inside as you might often see in Mexico City, they represent a fascinating reversal of use, from consumption to production, supermarket to street. Objects are always being reimagined and reappropriated for the street.

The world's cities are full of figures with their stalls who arrive and enliven the street, making it suddenly buzz. Theirs is an infrastructure of impermanence which is nevertheless a permanent feature of the pavement. A reassuring revenge of the little guy at street level serving his peers and somehow resisting the onslaught of big box retail and the chain coffee stores. It is furniture designed and evolved for the street, stripped down in its design, determined in its purpose and - at its best - a perfect embodiment of the resilience of life of the city.

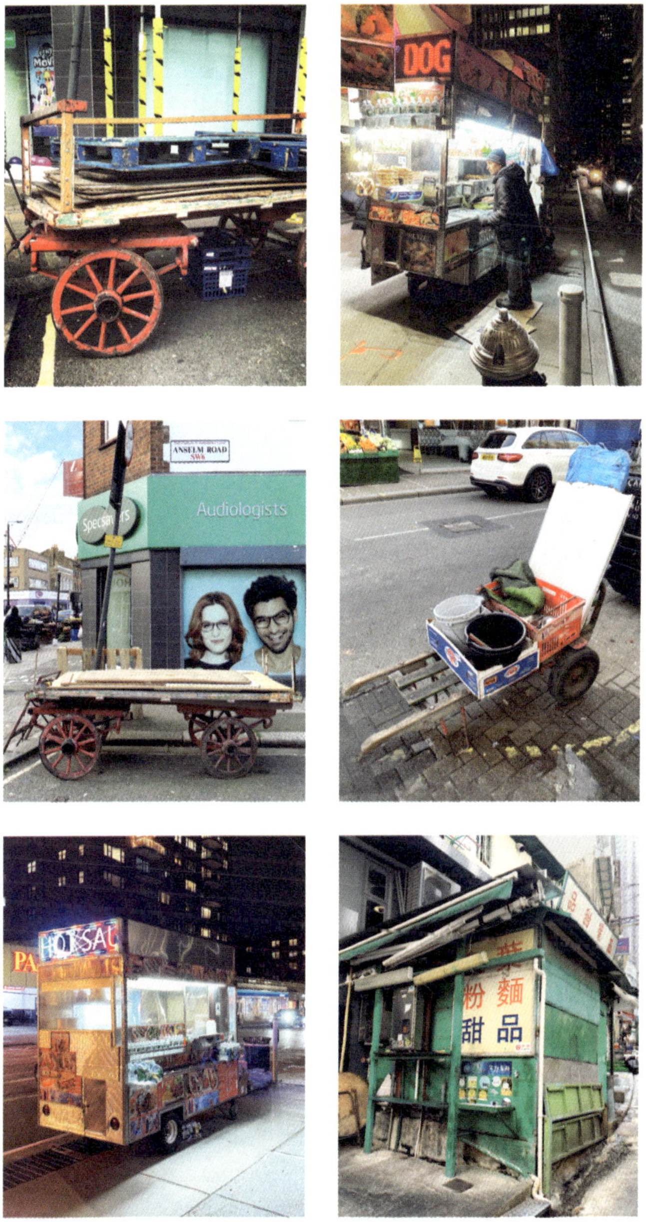

Top row, left: *London*; right: *New York*
Middle row: *London*
Bottom row, left: *New York*; right: *Hong Kong*

Stooping

The cover of my slightly ragged edition of Jane Jacobs's *The Death and Life of Great American Cities* features a photo of a busy city sidewalk and, at its heart, a stoop. The cover design is credited to Jan Pieńkowski (more famous for his later illustrations and pop-up books), though I couldn't find out who the photographer was, nor which city it depicts, though it'd be easy to guess it is Jacobs's then home city, New York.

The image perfectly chimes with her ideas about an active, mixed city in which generations and classes mingle, kids play in the street while gently being overseen by the community, and the line between inside and outside, public and private, is blurred. The city street becomes an additional social space to those living in often cramped conditions.

The book was seen, in part, as a reaction to the monolithic nature of modernism, its obsession with zoning and the attempts then underway (notably by Jacobs's nemesis, New York's powerful civil engineering and public works tsar, Robert Moses) to flatten huge swathes of historic New York to make way for new highways. Adopted by radical opponents of urban clearances and advocates of the historic preservation of buildings and complex communities, it was a powerfully influential work. In more recent years, though, there has been a turn against Jacobs, accusing her, in effect, of laying the ground for gentrification and the ultimate (if unintended) effect of a new kind of class homogeneity in the neighbourhoods she helped to valorise, popularise and save from the wrecking ball. Both angles have a little merit, but what interests us here is this image and, particularly, that stoop which was an architectural device at the heart of Jacobs's conception of the conviviality of the street.

A stoop is not street furniture. But then again, perhaps it is. The stoop is an in-between architecture, private but also in its way public, part of the house but projecting into the street. It acts as a small set of bleachers, a little strip of theatrical seating to watch what Jacobs famously called the 'ballet of the sidewalk'. It is useful to look at a British and an American urban house of the 19th century and to see how the stoop differs from the doorstep. In Britain the steps are very firmly on private property, beyond the line of iron railings, often bridging over a light well which acts as a ditch between private and public. With the stoop, the steps project into the street - the delineation is much less clear.

British flat-fronted brick houses might originally have been influenced by those in Amsterdam when the Dutch city was the wealthiest European centre of commerce in the 17th century, but the British did not adopt the stoop. The Dutch took it with them when they went to Manhattan and founded New Amsterdam. The words 'steep' and 'step' shares their roots with 'stoop', but so does the 'stoup' you find in a church, a vessel for holy water. That stoup acts as a threshold between sacred and profane but it is also very public, a tool for ritual welcome and blessing.

If we return to the photo on the cover of Jacobs's book we see, I think, a pair of priests wandering out of frame. The church and the other institutions which held the city together are here, in conversation with each other and the broader life of the street. The many generations of a family and their friends pose on the stoop, arranged almost professionally, while two boys look on from the foreground. If you turn the book to see the spine you see the picture rolls out, brilliantly positioned so that, on the shelf, it shows a small boy licking an ice cream standing next to a fire hydrant, the perfect picture of the happy streetscape. There are no cars.

The anonymous photo looks a little late to be by Helen Levitt, who may be the most obvious candidate. Levitt's photos of New York's Lower East Side and Spanish Harlem, which she surveyed so extensively in the 1930s and '40s, are almost an oeuvre of their own, documenting a city's life lived out on the stoops. Her shots capture what seems a remarkably vivid series of lives, African American, Latinx, recent European immigrant and white Americans. People, especially children, use the stoops like stages, conscious of the prominence a few steps gives them over the street, the elevation, the adulation. One particular photo of three children in Halloween masks shows them revelling in their outfits and their status, standing there, elevated. That some stoops extend into steps to the basement imparts a complex multi-tiering, a radical shift in the nature of the street from a single surface to an amphitheatre. Others of families consoling each other give a heartbreaking glimpse into lives which appeared so public and joyful yet which are clearly so full of hurt - scenes lived out in the public arena.

All of these images look very much like the idealised urban theatre that Jacobs extolled. In his excellent book *Looking at Photographs*, MoMA photography curator (and a fine photographer himself) John Szarkowski suggests that, sure, Levitt's catalogue might be a record of life in a city at its moment of optimal communality, but he also posits another possibility. 'Perhaps', he writes of the street of today, 'the children have forgotten how to pretend with style, and the women how to gossip and console, and the old how to oversee. Alternatively, perhaps the world that these pictures document never existed at all, except in the private vision of Helen Levitt, whose sense of the truth discovered those thin slices of fact that, laid together, create fantasy.'

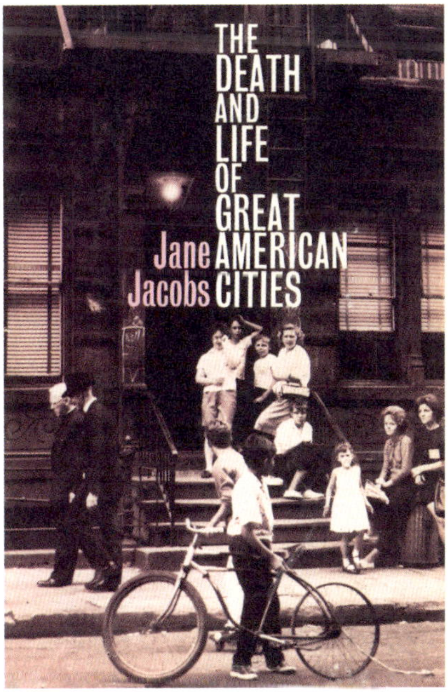

The Death and Life of Great American Cities, 1962
Cover by Jan Pieńkowski

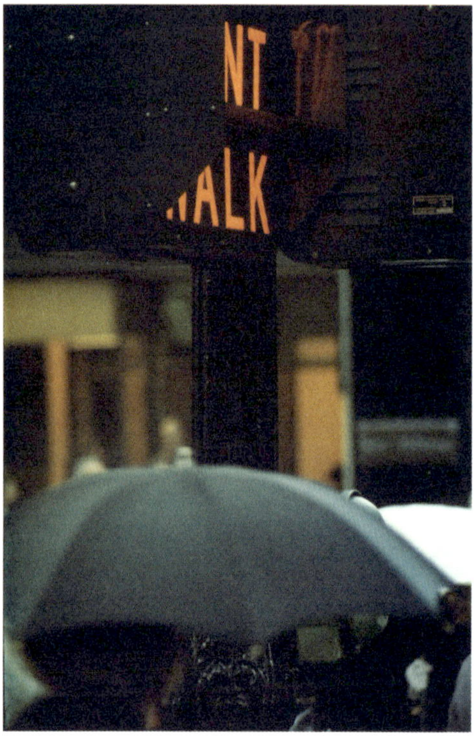

Don't Walk, 1952
Saul Leiter

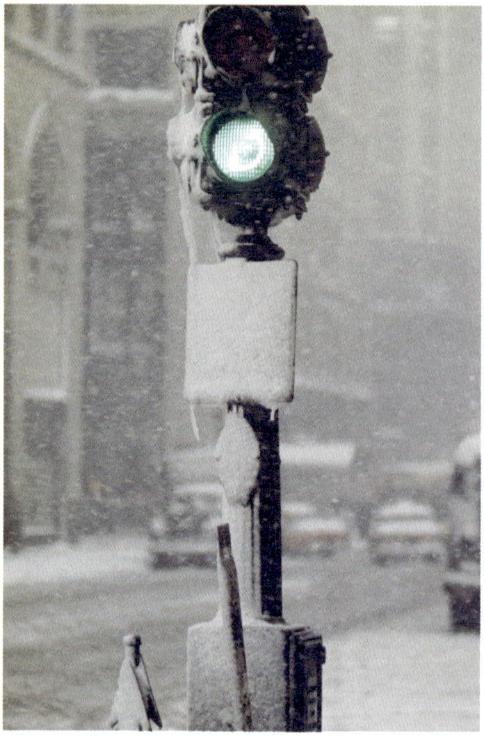

Green Light Against Grey, 1955
Saul Leiter

Stopping

In so many of Saul Leiter's photos you'll notice a vivid little splash of red or green, a half-obscured 'Don't Walk' sign, a suspended light or a partially visible traffic signal. Occasionally it'll be there as a red smudge, a Christmas tree light, at other times as part of a bigger system of signs, looming over a pedestrian. Just as the figures in Leiter's photos are only glimpsed, a fraction of a face or a body seen through the condensation of a café or taxi cab window, the traffic lights also appear as hints of something bigger. Which is what they are. We barely see traffic lights, even though we look at them all the time. They register only as signals but each light is a manifestation of a complex and connected network of traffic engineering, constantly calibrating itself to traffic flows and crowding conditions. It is the expression of the highly engineered rhythms of the city, a thing that looks as dumb as a lightbulb but which is actually the apex of an entire urban system.

The world's first traffic light was a bizarre-looking thing, not just to our eyes - it was parodied in *Punch* (depicted as the anthropomorphised 'Terrific Apparition', a haunted figure emerges, hands outstretched, its Cyclops-eye glowing though the London fog). Erected in 1868 in Bridge Street, New Palace Yard, Westminster, the first traffic light looked like a Gothic steampunk helicopter robot. Three blades protruded from a cast-iron column, tapering and with a barley-sugar twist and crowned by a lantern resembling a jewelled reliquary. The rotor-like blades mimicked railway signals in their language: up (horizontal) for 'Stop', down (flaccid) for 'Caution'. When they were down the light shone green; when they were up the light turned red. The gas lights did not exude much of a beam, notably in the city's perennial fogs, so the 'semaphore' blades acted as back-up. The contraption was controlled manually by a policeman standing on the traffic island. It was a disaster. At one point the gas power supply exploded, severely injuring the policeman. Cab drivers had no idea what the signals meant so either ignored them or paused, creating traffic chaos. Traffic lights wouldn't reappear on British roads until 1925.

Aimed mostly at drivers cocooned within their cars or cabs, traffic lights impinge only lightly on pedestrians. If you are not raging at the fast-changing lights they can have a kind of childishly cheerful presence, their colours a boiled sweet array of fruity flavours. For the walker the lights have a less abstract system: the standing/walking figures. Most famous among these outlines is the German Ampelmann with his urgent gait and hat (or standing, oddly, with a different hat, his arms spread wide). Designed by traffic psychologist Karl Peglau in 1961 in the Democratic Republic of Germany, they became deeply beloved for the figures' quirky attributes. After reunification in 1990, they began to be phased out, provoking widespread hostility until they were brought back and have now become synonymous, notably with Berlin where they vie with the city's more traditional bear logo as the city's de facto symbol. There have been attempts elsewhere to introduce female forms to the graphic language of crossings as well as families and LGBTQ+ versions (even, in Germany, Elvis silhouettes), though none have really taken hold beyond a few quirky and often very welcome examples.

There is something a little demeaning in the pressing of a button for a crossing which then tells you to wait. As if the walker needed permission. But, like the 'close door' buttons on lifts they impart a minimal sense of agency - having excluded us from most of the road they allow us again to feel a small, albeit largely fallacious, degree of control.

Streetlighting

Streetlighting expands the life of the metropolis through the hours of darkness, creating a negative version in which the sky is dark but the solid volumes are light. It throws light on the physical and yet, in struggling against the darkness of the night, creates a metaphysical world of artifice and shadow. It is perhaps the perfect example of how an apparently simple piece of street furniture can totally transform everyday life and the experience of the city. The streetlight might seem like a product of the modern age, but there is nothing new about it. The Romans illuminated their city streets at night, and Islamic cities from Baghdad to Córdoba were lit when most of Europe was living though what it is now unfashionable to call the Dark Ages but which was, from the point of view of streetlighting, exactly that.

The streets of London were illuminated, in a fashion, in the 15th century. Lord Mayor Henry Barton issued a decree in 1417 that inhabitants be required to hang lanterns outside their houses. But it isn't really until we get to Paris in the 18th century (during the reign, naturally, of Louis XIV - the Sun King) that we find more formalised statutes about the illumination of the streets. The inhabitants of Parisian dwellings were compelled to put a candle or a lamp in their street-facing windows so that the streets should be visible and navigable at night. It must have been quite a sight - a poetic inversion of the role of the window as a mechanism for allowing light in, instead using the private to illuminate the public realm. Parisians, however, failed to see the poetry and objected to the city dictating their habits. Candles (then either beeswax or tallow) were expensive, and it was seen as another unjust and unnecessary tax.

Cities across Europe made attempts to illuminate their streets using lanterns strung between houses on ropes or chains which could be lowered for lighting; in the narrow alleys of some Italian cities you can still see electrified examples of these. These lanterns however attracted new opprobrium - they became the targets of vandals and criminals who delighted in smashing them with stones. Some people, it turned out, didn't want to be seen at night.

A city can be divided into neighbourhoods, each with their own social mix and trades, but it is also divided by light and dark. In the dark, those uses and classes can shift, making the streets more permeable. Darkness facilitates transgression. The nighttime streets and back alleys of the city were once the domain of criminals, pickpockets, prostitutes, sexual adventurers and low-lifes, who liked it dark for their own reasons. Illuminating the corners of the nighttime city was seen as a colonisation of the dark by the bourgeoisie, a kind of gentrification through illumination, and it was deeply resented - quite often also by the middle classes, who themselves could now be recognised and identified as they went about their own shady transactions and assignations. Night allowed transgressions of class as well as activity.

By the 18th century, lighting had become intimately tied to commerce. Already in the 1760s there were reports of thousands of candles in the shopfronts of London making the commodities in the displays twinkle and shine. Artificial lighting extended business hours through the emerging metropolitan pastime of window shopping; the store might have been closed but desire could still be stimulated, perhaps even more effectively, in the dark. Shopping and lighting develop in tandem. Oxford Street in London became renowned as a place to wander in wonder at the illuminated shops in the late 18th century, despite its proximity to some of the worst slums in Europe.

When more concerted urban efforts began lighting streets in earnest, using lanterns hung on iron poles (the first 'lampposts'), it was the police who were usually responsible for their maintenance. In Paris, too, streetlighting would later be paid for from the police budget, and was suitably resented as another intrusion of authority. The mass imposition of public lighting on the city in the 1860s was seen as part of Baron Haussmann's reordering of the city as a place less amenable to revolution. During the 1848 uprisings, revolutionaries had smashed streetlights in order to be able to move around the city undetected. Streetlights were understood not as an act of municipal generosity but as an unwelcome tool of social control.

The spectacular leap forward in streetlighting arrived with the introduction of gas, which was pioneered in Britain with Pall-Mall being illuminated in a much-hyped spectacular in 1807. (Surprisingly, perhaps, gas lamps weren't new in the 19th century. The Chinese invented something similar as long ago as 500 BC, where they employed gas emanating from volcanoes to light flames in bamboo pipes and illuminate the streets of Beijing.) Within 15 years, 200 miles of London's streets were lit by gas, with lampposts bearing a huge array of designs. Most followed a standard format of base, decorated shaft and glass lantern. Cast iron's capacity for modelling lent itself to complex detail and ornament. The sculptural language of the streetlight is a story in itself, but tended to be an amalgam of lanterns and globes, curlicues and Baroque scrolls, with motifs including fish, monsters, lions (heads and feet), dragons, foliage, putti, crowns and classical columns. Paris beats London for lights, but there are some good examples, including some fine lights of globe design outside London's Royal Exchange and a single, elaborate three-globed version between Trafalgar Square and Admiralty Arch, complete with winged putti, garlands and overcooked monsters which blend fish-tails with lions' heads and gryphons. This rare piece of exuberant kit is marked 1878. More ornate examples were made for bridges or auspicious public places, highly decorated and made to resemble candelabras.

It is a little remarkable to learn that, up until 2021, there were still around 1,500 gas lamps in London. Those on the Embankment, some in Trafalgar Square and around Covent Garden and in Cecil Court were among those still powered by gas and retaining their characteristic soft glow. Although the lampposts are listed, and theoretically protected, Westminster Council has been (at the time of writing) replacing them, employing the usual excuses about maintenance. Other gas lamps survive in the Royal Parks, notably Green Park and Kensington Gardens, where their gentle glow is something wonderful to behold. They are remarkable survivals.

The gas lamp was a by-product of the industrial revolution, and went hand-in-hand with factory pollution. The halo around an illuminated streetlamp remains an evocative urban image, from representations of the London smog or the miasma of Sherlock Holmes's London to the *chiaroscuro* images of film noir. For a few decades after its introduction, the streetlight radically altered the city, not only prolonging the period in which work could be productively carried out in the street but also reversing expectations. The poor, unable to afford to light their rooms, began to occupy the streets at night in a manner disconcerting to the authorities. A device conceived in part as a mechanism for control inadvertently encouraged a not-always desirable nighttime economy, notably the huge and burgeoning sex industry. It has been estimated that one in five women in 18th-century London was a sex-worker. On the other hand, prints from the 18th and 19th century also show people reading beneath the bright lights of the big city, saving their eyes from dim domestic candle-light.

A morbid side of the streetlight is when it is transformed into public gallows. In the French Revolution one particular lamppost, at the corner of the Place de Grève and the Rue de la

Vannerie, became the most popular impromptu gallows. Until the invention of the guillotine, the lamppost was a de facto symbol of the revolution; the French still use the expression *à la Lanterne* in the way we might say 'kick the bucket'. German Expressionist artist Max Pechstein's shocking 1919 poster for the short-lived social democratic journal *An die Lantern* (*To the Lantern*) depicted a corpse hanging from a lamppost in a warning against the decline into mob rule. On the streets of Budapest during the 1956 revolution, members of the despised communist secret police, the AVO, were strung up from streetlights across the city.

For a brief time in the 19th century arc-lamps were trialled, blasting the streets with a powerful, steely cold light. Los Angeles was an early adopter in 1876, and Paris and London tried them out at a larger scale. It was a short-lived trend, replaced by the more efficient and less glaring incandescent bulbs. Among the earliest electric lights were those on the newly built Thames Embankment (1878) and they remain among the finest essays in sculptural street furniture, incorporating acanthus leaves, vines, lions' heads, classical capital and fluted shaft and coiled, Bernini-esque sea monsters (designated here, oddly, as dolphins).

All this makes it no surprise, then, that the streetlight embodies a curiously mixed iconography. There is the clichéd image of the behatted, rain-coated private detective, his face in shadow, or the femme fatale leaning dangerously against the post with a cigarette like Joan Bennett's character in the publicity stills and poster for Fritz Lang's 1945 *Scarlett Street*. Equally vivid is the famous poster for *The Exorcist*, in which the eponymous figure stands looking up towards the house while a streetlamp shines like the glow of a potential salvation.

Unlike other forms of street furniture, streetlighting captured the imagination of artists. In Giacomo Balla's *Street Light*, the humble lamppost is transformed into a sacred artefact, its light projected in hundreds of jewel-coloured shards. It is the final victory of engineering and electricity over nature as the streetlight outshines the crescent moon, artifice overcoming the cosmos. The light is modelled on one of the new electric versions then being installed in Rome's Piazza Termini. For Balla, the Futurist, the ancient landscape of Rome suffocated by its ruins and burdened by its history represented everything they wanted to destroy and the waning moon depicted here was similarly a symbol for everything mythical and tied to the past. The streetlight in Gustave Caillebotte's *Paris Street, Rainy Day*, however, acts not to illuminate but to regulate. Its verticality is echoed in the architecture, the umbrellas and the tall top hats, a stiff rectitude reflecting the regularity of the modern city. The lamppost splits the frame in two, perfectly down the centre, making a diptych in which the buildings appear as theatrical false perspective set-pieces and the citizens as cast members.

Eugène Atget managed to capture something of the paradox of the streetlight by day in his photo of a crowd gathering to watch an eclipse in Paris in 1912. Taken a year after Balla's exploding streetlight displaced the moon in the sky, here the crowd looks straight at the moon as it begins to hide the sun. Whatever streetlights do, the moon endures.

More, perhaps, than any other artist though, it was Martin Lewis who captured the city at night turned into artificial day. His densely hatched etchings foreshadow film noir as well as the work of Edward Hopper, on which Lewis had a huge and very visible influence. In *Relics (Speakeasy Corner)* (p.249), we have an upper-storey view of the city, looking down while the streetlight illuminates the field at the centre of the picture. This is the slightly sinister nighttime analogue to Jane Jacobs's ballet of the sidewalk - perhaps a darker cabaret. Figures become sinister shadows, amorphous, black-etched ghosts, attenuated and stretching across the street surface. The scene exists only because of the streetlight. Hopper turned a similar etching style into something more like foreboding. In *Night Shadows* (1921), the shadow cast

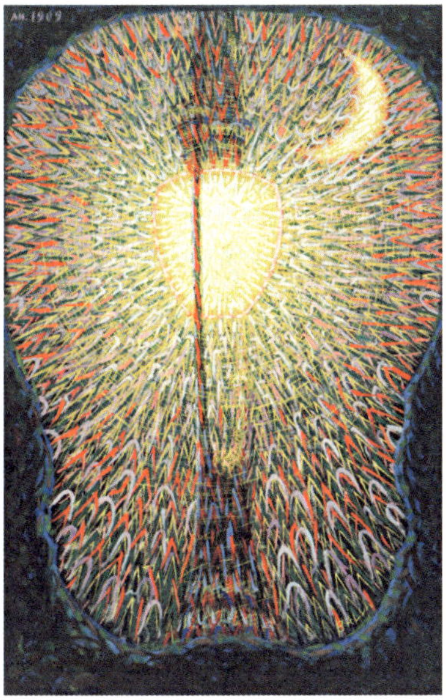

Street Light, 1909
Giacomo Balla

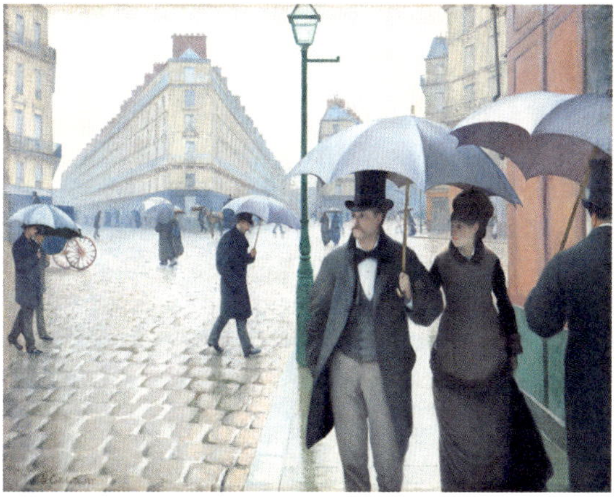

Paris Street, Rainy Day, 1877
Gustave Caillebotte

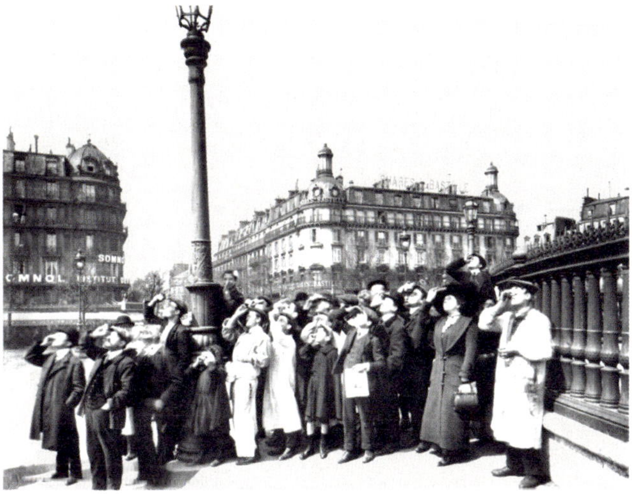

Eclipse, Paris, 1912
Eugène Atget

by the streetlight is like a slash through the picture frame, something, perhaps, like the black streak in the photographer's shots in *The Omen* which indicated that data is on the horizon and the method by which it would come. What, then is this? A barrier? Some kind of impaling?

The streetlight, and particularly the Victorian gas lamp, became central to horror, to a certain image of the 19th-century streets of Britain. Night was the time of transgression and crime, and the city, whether the London of Jack the Ripper or the Edinburgh of Burke and Hare, was defined in the popular imagination as a place of shadows cast by streetlight. The illustrator Sydney George Hulme Beaman captured this in his remarkable illustrations for the 1930 edition of Robert Louis Stevenson's *Strange Case of Dr Jekyll and Mr Hyde*. Hulme Beaman was mostly an illustrator and writer of children's stories, the creator of *Toytown* and *Larry the Lamb*, but in these dark illustrations he captured something of the hybrid horror cityscape. At the centre of almost every picture is a streetlight, a kind of artificial moon brought down to street level. The lamp itself becomes a character, a knowing witness to the terrible crimes.

Back in the real city, Fred Stein's nighttime photos of couples, one on a foggy night in Paris (1934) and another, more famous, image of a couple embracing in a streetscape covered by snow and scarred by tyre-tracks, reveal the transformations, the intersections between weather and light, and how both can transform the appearance and texture of the night. They see the streetlight as a kind of artificial sun, a miniaturised star with shadows cast to either side, creating a very distinctive kind of composition. In Paul Popper's much-reproduced scene of Soho at night, taken outside the Intrepid Fox pub, the object is unlit. Despite what appear to be scenes of darkness the light appears as a thing in its own right, appreciated for its form as a parallel to the verticality of the figures and not for the illumination it gives. When turned off, the streetlamp seems to turn into something else, a figure in the landscape. A gentler but equally unsettling transformation is embodied in Rene Magritte's haunting *L'empire des Lumieres*, in which a modest streetlight illuminates an uncanny nighttime streetscape under the canopy of a daytime sky above. The way in which night co-exists with day is the perfect cipher for a device which turns darkness into light, but is also an intimation of the unnatural state of the city, a place that comes alive and becomes completely public when it is darkest.

Modernism as a movement seemed to almost completely ignore the streetlamp. There is no Mies van der Rohe or Eileen Gray of streetlights. It was instead reduced to a utilitarian steel or concrete post. We barely noticed the steel tubes or faux-Victorian fittings. But with the reinforcement of CCTV cameras, phone tracking, police surveillance and even helicopters and now drones, lighting is itself now once again in the spotlight. At stake is the kind of lighting neighbourhoods are subject to. Upmarket districts with historic housing tend to be allowed to keep their heritage fittings, upgraded to the latest technology. Modern private housing estates might get something in between, perhaps a little throwback or something discretely contemporary. But areas deemed to be problem neighbourhoods get blasted with light. This is lighting as stigma, assuming that light must be washed over every corner to control crime and anti-social behaviour. In so doing, authorities further reinforce the status as a place to avoid rather than one in which to live. It is, undoubtedly, tricky territory. Lighting is a quick fix which enables local authorities to suggest they are doing something - about violence against women, about fear, about knife-crime or anti-social behaviour - without addressing the social and economic causes of the issues.

The contemporary urban nightscape is something else again. A complex ecosystem of light is created by a cocktail of streetlights, dazzling shopfronts, car-headlights, residential windows, bars draped with fairy-lights, Christmas-decorated houses and flickering smartphone screens. Streetlights are no longer alone in dictating the density and intensity of illumination.

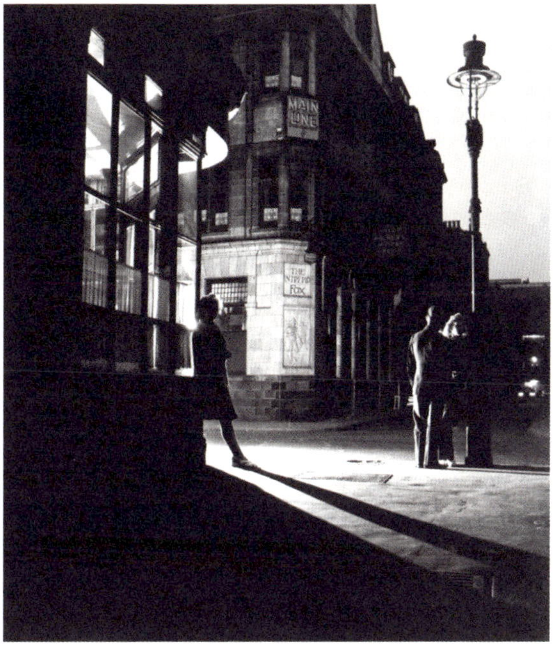

Intrepid Fox at Night, 1947
Paul Popper

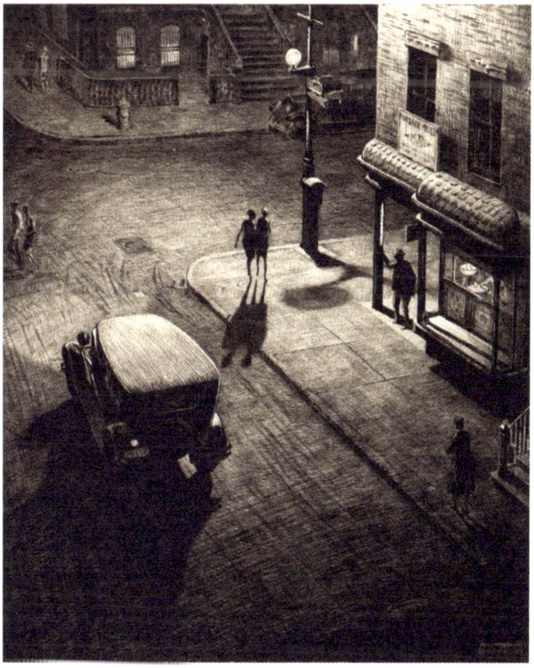

Relics (Speakeasy Corner), 1928
Martin Lewis

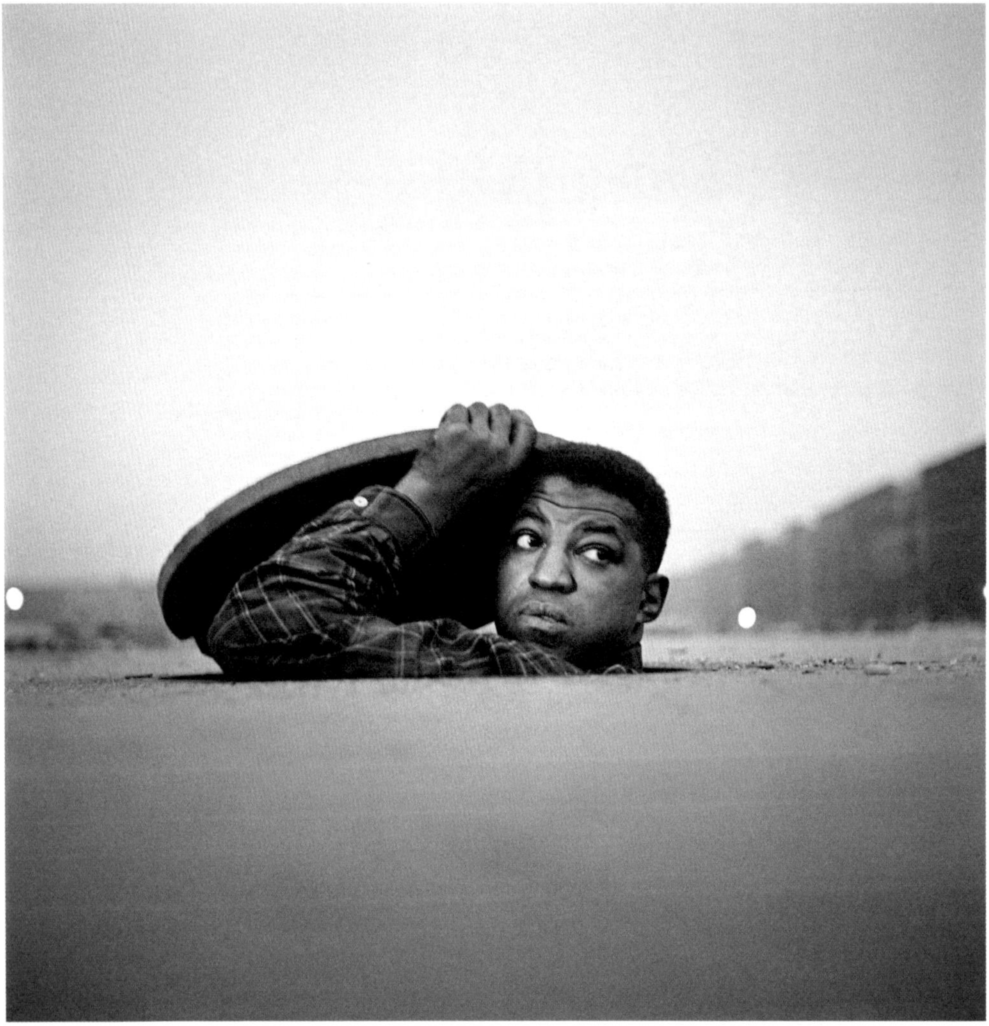

The Invisible Man, Harlem, New York, 1952
Gordon Parks

Submerging

As a child I used to suffer from a recurring bad dream. I would be walking down a familiar stretch of road (about half way from my house to the High Street), when I somehow fell through a hole in the pavement. Although it didn't seem to be particularly deep, it was dark down there and somehow my voice didn't seem to carry, no-one could hear me. I'm now not entirely sure if it was a manhole or one of those wooden trapdoors where beer was delivered to pub cellars but something of the memory has stayed with me and, although I'm no longer afraid of falling down a hole, there is a residual, eerie draw to the idea that there is an alternative, parallel city beneath the pavements. And the cast-iron, concrete, number and glass plates that cover them are the portals to that enigmatic underworld.

The Romans had manholes, of course (they were obsessed with sewers, the *cloaca*) and they were surprisingly similar to our own. There's one in the Vienna historical museum, chiselled from stone. It is rectangular and decorated with four almond-shaped openings (to allow a tool to gain purchase and lift it up, as well as to allow ventilation).

Our streets are even more full of holes - for pipes and cabling, for rainwater drainage, water hydrants for standpipes. The street can appear to be a quilt of covers stitched together in an often-frayed surface. It can lead to bizarre moments. A few yards from my house is a mad outbreak of water-hydrant covers, about a dozen packed into a couple of square feet, like an outbreak of iron shingles. Between them, the manholes reveal a huge amount about the changing technologies of the street, the rapid jumps in communications and transport and their seemingly equally rapid collapse. Many odd covers seem to survive the redundancy of their technologies, their utility being adopted ad hoc by other utilities.

The history of the city is there to see, inscribed in these covers. In London you might find iron plates embossed with the name of George Jennings, the sanitary engineer who introduced the flush toilet to London at the Great Exhibition of 1851 - an invention which quickly became so popular that the city's decrepit sewer system was unable to cope and the contents were flushed directly into the Thames, leading, famously to the Great Stink of the summer of 1858. You might find others featuring the name of the famously self-promoting Thomas Crapper, sanitary engineer, often with perforations to allow the escape of gas from sewers and avoid a build-up of pressure and the ultimate explosion which might propel a chunk of iron through the city at ferocious speeds. Which does, in fact, happen more frequently than you might expect (there was a spate of flying manholes in New York not long ago).

There are utilitarian rectangular covers with concrete panels and, around their edges, the names of telegraph or tramway companies, municipal gasworks or electric light companies. These date from the era of municipal munificence, when city councils in Britain owned the transport and the utilities and were busy fitting electrics for everything from telegraphs to trolleybuses. Part of the reason they became so wealthy, and were able to build such magnificent town halls, housing and libraries, was that they owned everything and were easily able to borrow against huge and stable public assets.

The evidence of changing material culture is also ingrained in these manhole covers. The cast iron of the Victorian era exemplifies the industrial might of the nation, just as the turn to concrete in the 20th century indicates the capture of urban planning by traffic engineering and a new vision of the streetscape as a highways system. The financial culture is equally inscribed, the slow transformation of all those municipal and nationalised utilities into shareholder value: General Post Office telephones give way to BT and so on. The quality takes a bit of a tumble too, these covers by now barely regarded as things which might potentially be elegant as well as useful. This is not the case everywhere.

In Tokyo, for instance, you might come across manhole covers in garish full colour, ornamented with the intricacy and vividness of *cloisonné*. They may portray samurai, swirling carp, Mount Fuji or wide-eyed Manga characters, and municipalities compete to install the most beautiful and most Instagrammed manhole covers. In New York the selection is a little more limited and literal, many just reading 'NYC Sewer', but I do like the ones embossed with 'DANGER' in caps, though not explaining quite what is so dangerous about them. In Seattle they have covers embossed with the city's own street plan, in Berlin with a rendering of its architectural highlights. In some cities you might find a manhole cover with the remains of a street-surface that has disappeared elsewhere. I've seen timber leftovers from the days when roads were lined with wood to dampen down the noise of iron carriage wheels trundling along the streets. Others may be concreted in, painted over, graffitied on or have fossils or stones inlaid in them.

Manhole covers are, in a way, a kind of street jewellery, little moments of making in the endless grey membrane of asphalt and granite. But perhaps more intriguingly, they are openings to an underworld which we only partly comprehend. They retain a touch of mystery, wormholes connecting the private and public realms, between pavement and property and between the worlds of light and dark. Gordon Parks's brilliant photo of a black man emerging from a manhole, lifting the iron cover above his head like a Greek soldier with his shield, plays on those perceptions and the imaginings of darkness and light, black and white (p.250). Taken as an illustration for his friend Ralph Ellison's book *Invisible Man*, the images were published in *Life* magazine in 1952 with the strapline 'A Man Becomes Invisible'. The implication is, of course, that people of colour led an existence in the city unseen. Like the parallel world of the underground systems, they were there, useful but invisible. Ellison's invisible man finds himself a basement: 'a hole in the ground, as you will'. The figure in the photo though is emerging, looking around. Suddenly seeing and seen.

Unexpectedly, a manhole cover became, quite possibly, the first spacecraft. Dr Robert Brownlee revealed that during the Operation Plumbbob nuclear tests in Nevada in 1957, a metal manhole cover over an underground explosion was expelled with such force that, according to the doctor's calculations, it would have quickly reached the earth's escape velocity and was blasted, in all probability, into outer space a few months before the Soviets launched the Sputnik. The manhole cover was never found.

One of the questions frequently asked of applicants for jobs in Silicon Valley used to revolve around manhole covers. Why are they round? Well, if they all were, perhaps I needn't ever have had that nightmare.

Telegraphing

The buzz of the city thrums through its wires: the overhead cables, the trolley and tram power, the phone lines (some submerged, others stretched high above the streets, kept taut between poles like musical strings to be strummed overhead). The decision to use buried or overhead cables can completely transform a cityscape. In Japanese streetscapes, for instance, now so familiar through pop culture images, public space is made super-distinctive by the tightly woven fabric of their electric power lines. These combine with the very particular houses and the alternatingly unsettling and thrilling aesthetic anarchy of the seemingly uncontrolled development of the backstreets and alleys. Radiating from corners and poles, an anarchic mesh contains the city streets below as a very visible manifestation of current communication.

There might be something slightly absurd in this approach in a country renowned for its high-tech industries and its fetishisation of the latest gadgets, but you might equally argue that the wires become a symbol of an electrified city which can change its configuration at a moment's notice. The ad hoc steampunk complexity is precisely what gives the city its electric buzz. There's even a sub-category of Japanese pixel art which creates gifs of subtly animated streetscapes in which the only real way you can tell the scenes are animated is though the gentle movement of overhead wires in the wind, and perhaps a few drops of drizzling rain or a gently flickering neon sign. The seeming insanity of the accumulated cables and junction boxes of endless variations, the weird and the wired, have become a kind of fetish in themselves. It is certainly easier to re-wire an overhead system after an earthquake than it is to excavate subterranean cables, but I wonder if it is also a kind of electrical analogue to the cherry blossoms and the paper lanterns. There is an awareness of the presence of things, a tangled web of strings and wires and twigs which perhaps allows people to see these as an extra layer of infrastructure - or perhaps not to notice them at all.

We have somehow forgotten how to see utility poles. In 1963 John Updike attempted to pour a little glory on them in his poem *Telegraph Poles*:

> Our eyes, washed clean of belief,
> Lift incredulous to their fearsome crowns of bolts, trusses,
> struts, nuts, insulators, and such
> Barnacles as compose
> These weathered encrustations of electrical debris
> Each a Gorgon's head, which, seized right,
> Could stun us to stone.

These stripped trees have a hint of torture about them. The steel spikes used as footholds for engineers bring them closer to totems, erections to worship at the feet of the gods of electricity. A visual metaphor for connection, the wires carry our voices and ideas. And they accumulate the detritus of other forms of communication: posters, lessons, jobs, lost pets, things nailed to their shafts. They amalgamate high and low tech, the metal of the wire and the timber of the trunk. They are a warning to street trees not to grow too straight, or this might be their fate.

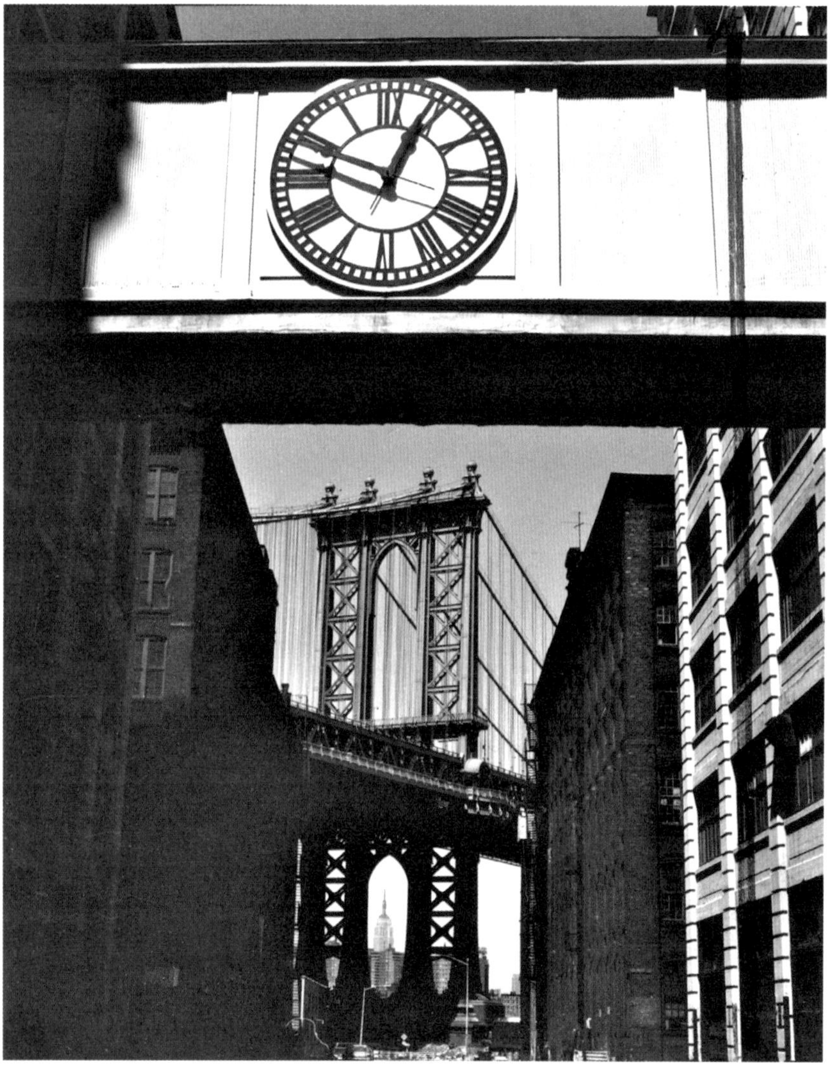

Overhead Cross Walk with Clock, Brooklyn, 1968
Arthur Tress

Timing

The time of the public clock is long gone. But the faces survive, still looking out over the city. Urban clocks embody an amalgam of apprehension, longing, regret, haste, rush, relief and stability. The standing timepiece is simultaneously the most mundane mechanism and the most theatrical of urban devices. That Christian Marclay could make one of the greatest artworks of modern times cobbled together from clock cameos in the movies illustrates the curious emotional range of their faces and the tension and expectation conveyed in their expressions. These machines are at the heart of so many human dramas. They frame and define the rhythm of our lives. They are also now virtually completely defunct as practical devices, long supplanted first by wristwatches and then phones, but their ritual role remains.

Listening for the bongs of Big Ben or waiting for the ball to drop in Times Square on New Year's Eve presents theatrical urban moments of gathering, communal anticipation and celebration. Then there are the clocks which are theatrical events in themselves - Prague's incredible Orloj astronomical clock for instance (1410) with a skeletal figure of Death striking the hour, or Bern's Zytglogge (1530) with its revolving cast of absurd bears and knights. These and others date from an era when the clock was a marvel in its own right, a thing of wonder and a miniaturisation of a clockwork cosmos. They are the exceptions. Most public clocks exist on a more mundane, less performative municipal level, in and outside stations, on town halls, hanging outside watchmakers' shops or on top of former newspaper offices. As our need to check the time has eroded so the clocks have stopped, unmaintained, or have become less visible. They now look as quaint as the sundials on church towers which preceded them, the relics of a lost religion of a mechanistic universe.

The story of the clock is a familiar one, a narrative of the industrial revolution and shift work in mills and factories - the necessity of clocking in and starting on time. The mechanisation of industry and labour spurred the mechanisation of time and of life itself. For urban historian Lewis Mumford it was the mechanical clock rather than the steam engine that powered the industrial revolution. He saw it as a machine which had passed from the monastery to the mill and was every bit as much about production as the engine or the loom, but its product was seconds and minutes, the sub-division of the day and the reconception of time as money.

The next phase was the arrival of the railways, necessitating a unification of time across nations so that timetables could be universalised. The railway clock became an icon of urban life, dictating not only times of travel but meetings and social patterns in the city. It was a manifestation of universal time, an idea that impossibly distant cities were nevertheless tied together, hence those ranks of clocks in offices and banks which showed the time in global cities across the world. To this day the hanging clock at Waterloo Station is a recognised point to wait for a date, slightly strange and fogeyish yet still an easily familiar, and suitably public, point.

Clocks gave a rationale to spires and towers on buildings once the simple urge to aspire to the heavens had been superseded, and town halls vied with cathedrals to define a civic identity. What else, for instance, is Big Ben (or, formally, the Elizabeth Tower) at the Palace of Westminster other than a clock to justify the construction of a Gothic skyscraper?

The 19th century saw clocks replacing sundials on churches, being erected on city streets and seaside promenades, on market halls and hanging outside shopfronts. The sudden explosion in the consciousness of time had a moral dimension to it, an imposition of urgency, an implicit condemnation of the wasting of time. But there was also the commercial angle, the opening times of pubs and shops, the starting times of shows, races and concerts, trains and hotel lunches; the clock came with its injunctions to consume before it was too late.

From the 1870s street clocks appeared as almost perfect pieces of street furniture: public amenities to help citizens adjust to the industrial, railway age. Mounted on posts, often quite elaborately cast and with double-sided clock faces, they looked like ornamental urban lollipops. The explosion in street clocks began in Vienna which, in 1877, established a network of timepieces powered by a citywide system of piped compressed air. The network, which sent a pulse of air each minute, pushing the minute hand one notch along, was described at the time not as a pneumatic power system but as a device for the distribution of time itself. Paris, which had already instigated a pneumatic postal system, was quick to adopt the Viennese innovation and from 1881 began installing an extensive network of 'Popp clocks' named after the system's inventor, Victor Popp. The clocks were often exquisite hybrid expressions of modern technics expressed in elaborate, Beaux Arts costume, a rich cocktail of classical columns, fine mouldings, straining caryatids, coats of arms, delicate crowns and often even moralising messages (one set in Paris exhorted people to be kind to their animals). They were often integrated into lampposts, occasionally with the clock cantilevered off to one side, more usually perched on top. Around the turn of the century there were around 7,800 clocks around the French capital, in an incredible array of designs and configurations, an entire layer of urban time. But time was short. By 1927 the system had become burdensome and apparently unprofitable and was abandoned.

Barely a handful of examples survive. There is one in Montmartre, below the steps of the Sacré Coeur and another not too far away integrated with a streetlight. The idea, however, has endured, even if the mechanics are long gone. Central Paris still features characteristic, vaguely Art Deco-inflected clocks with chamfered corners, usually stuck slightly incongruously on reproduction Belle Epoque streetlights. Simultaneous attempts at evoking different pasts.

The advent of pocket watches and then wristwatches undermined the status of the public clock, and the ubiquity of mobile phones has finally ended the hegemony of a dedicated device. But something about the anthropomorphisation of the clock, with its face and hands, has endeared it to us. Public clocks might have faded from our field of vision but they remain sentimentally valued, even when they have stopped.

The US adopted mechanical street clocks and they have survived better, not so much in the big cities perhaps, but in the provincial towns and smaller main streets. They remain popular civic markers, oddly visible in the city and now a firm part of the heritage industry - a gesture towards reviving a lost idea of Main Street - and they are still being manufactured. There was a time when street furniture, not only clocks, was almost entirely run on clockwork mechanisms. Parking meters and streetlighting operated on clockwork systems which governed when they were turned on or off or when time was up. Now that everything has been replaced by electronics and, increasingly, smart systems, all that remains is a few, mostly stopped, clocks which are, at least, accurate twice every day.

More visible still perhaps are the often monumental clocks suspended from buildings which exert a charismatic presence on the street in a similar manner to pub lanterns and signs. They act as a kind of branding, often representing businesses that had some kind of urgency built into their model; newspapers offer the best example perhaps. The former *Daily Telegraph* building in Fleet Street (Peterborough House, 1928) has a wonderful bronze Art Deco example, radiating colour and cheer in a manner which the newspaper could never have been accused of. Department stores also used time as an added branding mechanism, suggesting (as did newspapers) a level of public service and presence in the city beyond the product. Selfridges's incredible bronze clock with its blue-enamelled winged angel, or the rather fey footmen of the musical Georgian-revival version above Fortnum & Mason, illustrate the point. The ornate sculpting of Kaufmann's (now Macy's) store in Pittsburgh or the exotic protuberance at Marshall Field in Chicago (also Macy's) suggest a sense of self-importance too, as well as being a way to gain extra space in the city while suggesting the public good.

Now that newspapers and department stores are struggling to maintain custom or have long vacated their grand buildings, there is something apt in those defunct, often stopped clocks symbolising a presence in the cities with which they were once so synonymous. They hang, suspended and stopped over the street, still present beyond their use. Clocks convey the passing of time in myriad, often unpredictable ways.

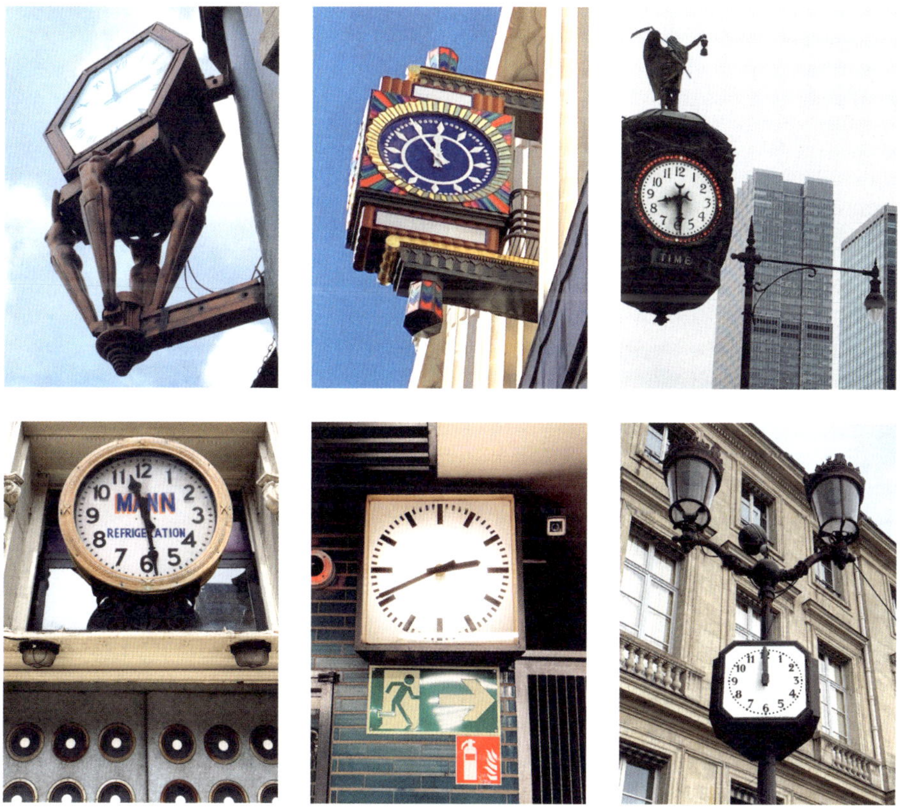

Top row, left: *London*; middle: *London*; right: *Chicago*
Bottom row, left: *New York*; middle: *Berlin*; right: *Paris*

Vending

Just off the North End Road in Fulham there is a faded orange pressed-metal box attached to a brick wall. It has two little slot windows. Scratched, sun-bleached and now almost milky white, you can still, just about, make out two small stacks of coloured balls behind them. On the front are two knobs to turn after a coin has been deposited after which you just might have received a small handful of hard, almost inedible bubblegum or, if you were lucky, a plastic ball containing a 'mystery gift'. It is an odd survival, a rarity, out of time, out of place, in what looks an altogether unlikely location at the street end of a shady, none-too-healthy smelling alley. Yet not so long ago the city was full of machines like this.

My childhood coincided with the tail-end of the vending machine boom. Streets, stations and shopfronts were studded with all kinds of machines, dispensing anything from cigarettes and milk to chocolate bars and stamps. There were bulky, fridge-sized units, there were boxes mounted on spindly legs and chained together, and there were dainty wall-mounted machines, painted in lurid colours or branded with logos. So seductive were vending machines seen to be that you could buy miniature versions for home consumption - miniature chocolate machines dispensing miniature bars for a penny a time. They were hugely successful as Christmas presents, I seem to remember. Something about street furniture seems to lend itself to savings: piggy banks shaped like postboxes or phone booths. Bubblegum and Jelly bean vending machines still seem to be a toyshop staple, a curious case of bad value but seductive imagery becoming fetishised as something deeply desirable.

Vending machines might once have looked like the future. Now they look very much like the past. But not quite everywhere. Japan, for instance, has somehow retained its culture for vending machines, covering your needs for everything from art-branded soda cans to umbrellas and underwear. At the time of writing, the Japanese vending machine industry appears to be worth an almost unbelievable $44 billion with over five million machines on the streets. Photographer Eiji Ohashi's haunting series *Time to Shine* reveals these ubiquitous and odd machines as something like street furniture shrines to consumption, glinting in the harshest conditions to keep people supplied with trashy snacks. Unlike my local bubblegum machine, the Japanese do not indulge sentimentality in their vending. Machines are ruthlessly replaced, much as are houses, when fashion, technology or demands change. So the curious impression from these photos - and indeed a whole raft of Japanese images of glowing vending machines in darkened streets - that these are permanent, almost sentient beings in the landscapes is very far from the truth. French photographer Edward Way's series on Japan's vending machines documents this curious kind of retail urbanism, the coloured machines contrasting with their banal settings. It takes a particular kind of low-crime society for these machines to survive in what are often out-of-the-way or desolate places. Following the Japanese example, South Korea and most of East Asia seems to have nurtured its culture of street vending machines, vivid blocks of kitsch and colour producing day-glo highlights in often bleak, generic cityscapes.

The Netherlands can seem like the one Western holdout, an outlier with its frites and croquette-dispensing machines and those 24-hour storefronts of the Automat type which was the craze in the US in the 1930s but now appears a bizarre cultural quirk. There are plenty of other vending machines as street furniture which we might barely notice. In the US it is newspaper boxes which punctuate the pavements. As print dies away they're becoming less common, their clunky technology (mechanical rather than electronic) unable to cope with anything more complex than quarters and balking at expensive papers like *The New York Times* Sunday edition (at current prices, 20 quarters).

The history of the street vending machine is surprisingly long, stretching back, apparently, to the Romans. Hero of Alexandria invented a coin-operated holy water dispensing machine sometime in the 1st century AD. There were tobacco dispensers in English inns already in the 17th century and newspaper vending machines in the 1820s, but the more familiar metal boxes arrived in the 1880s. The first models dispensed postcards, stationery and stamps. Drinks came soon after, and then just about everything including eggs, milk and chips. They seem to have reached a zenith in the mid-century and then stuck around in some places and fell away in others. Even in Italy you come across all-night shops with little glass-fronted cupboards of food. In other places they survive only as blocky fridges on station platforms or in unappealing subways.

As products they always promised a future of human obsolescence, in which transactions could be made between man and machine with no mediation. Except, of course, that the machine was the mediation. From chewing gum to cigarettes, the vending machines I encountered rarely seemed to work, perhaps victims of too much poking and prodding by teenagers attempting to squeeze a few coins out or, perhaps, just affected by the weather. If anything, they underlined why the future always seemed so far away. The sight of a frustrated patron banging or kicking a machine that had failed to deliver was once a slapstick staple of urban life and a pretty fine metaphor for life.

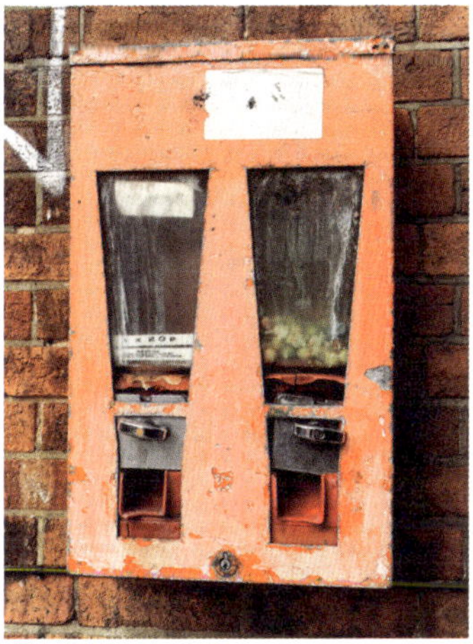

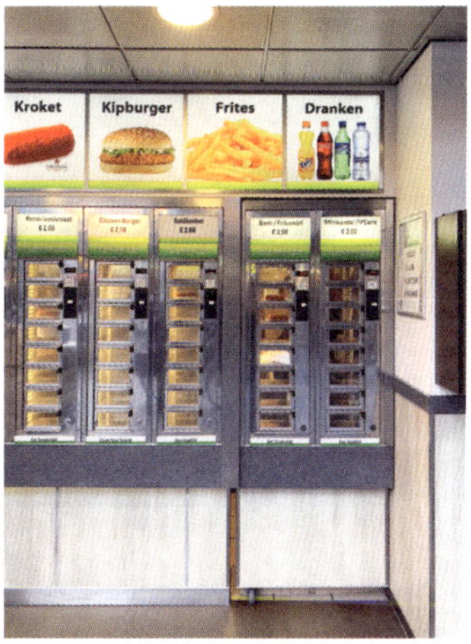

Vending in London, vending in Amsterdam

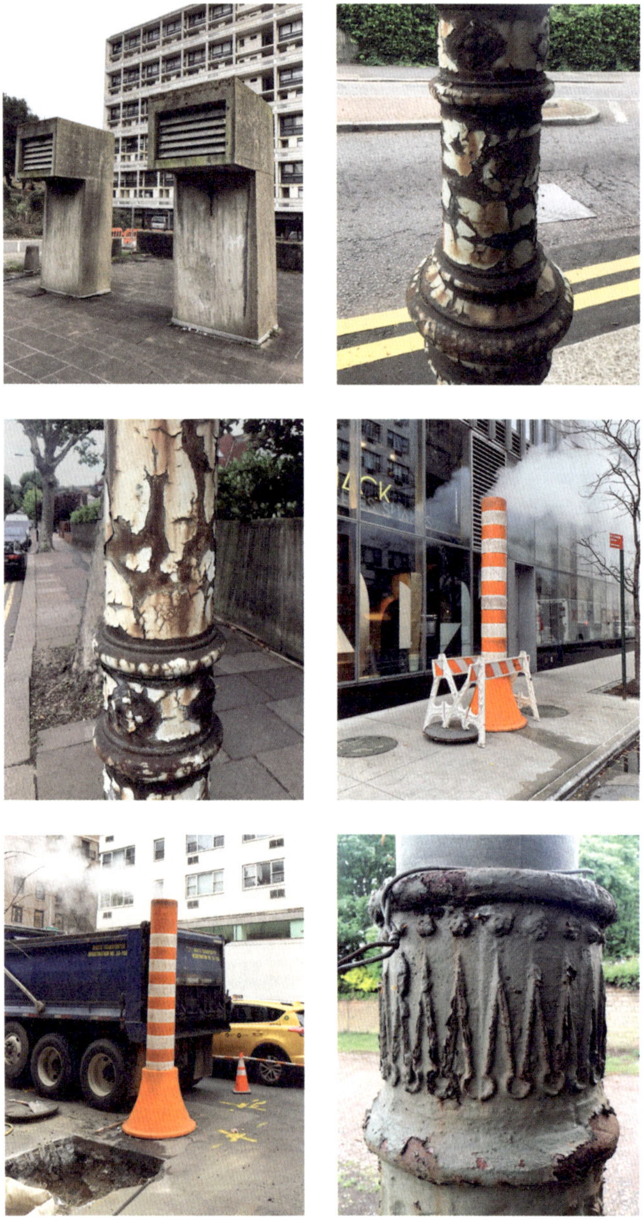

Stink stacks and vents in London and New York

Venting

The opening titles of Martin Scorsese's *Taxi Driver* show what appears to be a cloud or a fog until, to the percussive, urgent crescendo of Bernard Herrmann's hypnotic score, Travis Bickle's yellow taxi emerges and you realise you've been watching the steam billowing out from New York City's vents. As much as the yellow cab, the steam is a symbol of the city. It occupies a similar status to London's smogs and fogs, a condensing cloud, an amorphous vapour with no substance that somehow becomes synonymous with the city, a visual metaphor for the unknowability of the metropolis. More than that, however, the steam clouds suggest something else. They imply a condensed intensity, a vapour rising to suggest the presence of a steamy underworld - which is, of course, exactly the layer that Robert De Niro's disturbed, taxi-driving insomniac avenging dark angel Travis Bickle will seek to destroy. The clouds and the fog engulf the tops of skyscrapers, the immaterial overwhelming the material, while their bases are, on occasion, smothered in the hot steam of the vents. This is a city assailed by strange, intangible mists emanating from the depths and the heavens, aspiring to the extremes of both.

The modern metropolis has buried its bodily functions. The viscera of sewage, cabling, water, gas, steam heat and all the rest are submerged like the veins and arteries beneath the taut skin of tarmac and paving. But occasionally they return to remind us, when a road is dug up, when the membrane is operated upon, when a fire hydrant explodes into gushing metaphor, when a spindly stand-pipe emerges from the street, a single, tiny tap.

Many cities have steam systems, whether for district heating, exhaust, cooling or cleaning, but New York's is the only one where it totally defines a streetscape. There's something almost unbearably symbolic in those red-striped Cat-in-the-Hat vent chimneys fenced in by barriers letting off steam from underground, as if the city couldn't bear its own pressure.

Those steam clouds are supplemented on occasion by the warm draught of a passing subway train coming through a vent. Perfectly encapsulated in the image of Marilyn Monroe's white dress dancing up around her waist in the film *The Seven Year Itch*, the omnipresent roar and breeze suggests another set of spirits down below. That famous scene was a publicity stunt, filmed at 1am, on Lexington Avenue between 52nd and 53rd Street. Fans were forewarned and huge crowds as well as masses of media showed up. The footage proved unusable and the version that went into the movie was filmed on a sound stage in a Hollywood studio.

London has its own vents, but their product is a little less glamorous. I'm fond of the word 'stinkpipe' (though 'stenchpole' is just as good), which has a Surrealist quality to its hybrid formation. They were installed after the large-scale adoption of flushing lavatories in the city from the middle of the 19th century overwhelmed the city's sewers, and there were fears of methane build-up and noxious gas explosions. The stinkpoles vented the system. Part of the landscape of Victorian infrastructure, they are cast-iron columns with decorated bases like lampposts but curiously headless. If New York's steam vents allow the release of pressure from a system, London's are about bad smells. London was by then the seat of imperial power, and the greatest wealth ever accumulated. But it couldn't organise its own shit. What goes on underground is, sometimes, more purely representative of a place than what is visible above.

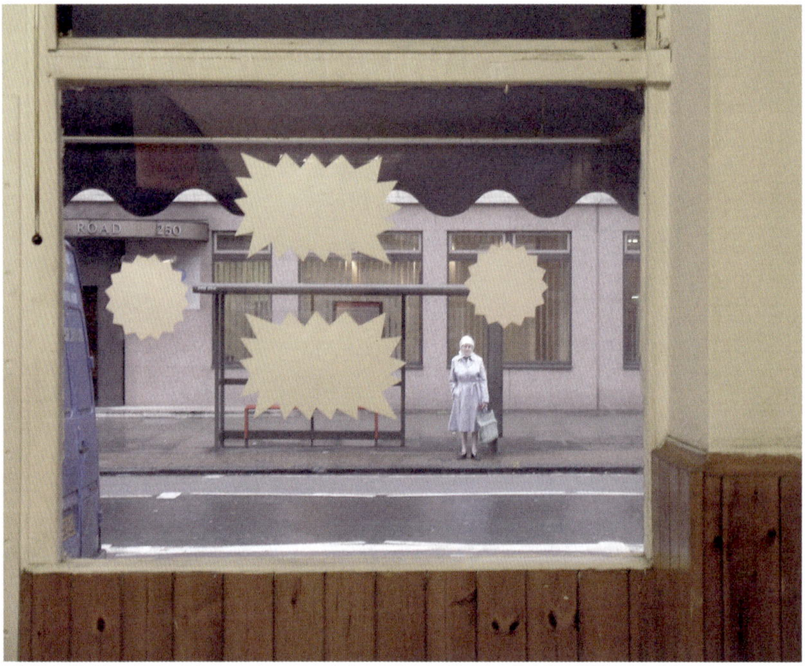

Mama's Snack Bar, SE1, 2003
Sue Barr

Waiting

Of all the dispiriting places in the city, a bus stop on a cold, damp night must surely rank among the worst: the municipal meanness and joylessness of a shelter which offers an uncomfortably angled plastic seat designed to give only the sparsest of relief, an object only allowed to exist because it supports the ads on its side so that the user is relegated to captive consumer. In my youth bus stops served, almost unbelievably, as social spaces. They were every bit as bad as they are today but, particularly for teens too young to drink, they were what there was. A swig, a cig and a snog, mostly without censure. They were the shelters for a critical rite of passage, an indispensable stop on the journey out as well as a reminder of home. They spoke both of longing to get away and needing to get back. They were public places of the most basic, but accessible, kind.

I don't drive, and use buses all the time. I like sitting on the top deck of a London bus, looking down at the streets; it feels dignified and slightly aloof. But waiting at a bus stop can exude a particular kind of impotence, a resignation to fate. The inhabitants of bus stops are destined to watch the stream of cars with their individuals wrapped in climate-controlled comfort pass them by without ever noticing them. That's why every photo of a bus stop ever taken is tinged with regret, ennui, even pain. Waiting are mostly women, often recent immigrants, and the elderly. They might be heavily laden with shopping trollies or buggies. They have bulky bags and awkward packages. Early in the morning the bus stops are inhabited by the cleaners and security guards, the transport workers and hospital porters.

During the day there are young and old men with too much time. Frustrated smokers who've just lit up and have to stub the expensive ciggy out because the bus came when they weren't expecting it. There are people looking at their phones, playing games, people speaking in every language to family back home. And then there are relentless waves of jostling schoolchildren, chaotic crowds of screaming, showing-off, unruly and joyful kids released from school and exploding with barely suppressed hormones and energy.

The advent of digital information boards has both improved and spoilt things (the TfL minute is an especially relative and elastic unit of time). There is now, at least, a sense of knowing when your bus might come but the anticipation that it might be just around the corner is now gone, that sheer, hopeful optimism we could once indulge. There is a sense that time spent waiting for a bus is wasted time. Car drivers, even those sitting in traffic, are being purposeful. The waiting are wasting time. Again, I can quite enjoy the waiting. It is a break. Perhaps I have fond memories of waiting with friends for night buses, or to get back from school myself. It is a rare moment to stop and watch the world. So in a way the shelter could be reconceived as a kiosk, a public viewing platform. Rather than submitting to the role of powerless potential passenger, you might assume the role of a privileged spectator, a stationery flâneur with a few moments of pure being in the city.

The real change in bus shelters in recent years has been the privatisation of this last public space. Bus stops were once refuges, cantilevered roofs against the rain. Now they are advertising kiosks. Bus stops have been outsourced to Adshel and J.C. Decaux - Texan and French megacorps respectively - and they supply and maintain the shelters in return for ad space. Not only are the passengers (consumers) secondary in this transaction, they are not even the target of the advertising. They are deemed too poor and downtrodden to be sold to and to qualify as bona fide consumers. The backlit ads are aimed at passing drivers. The shelters themselves have remained dumb steel structures, but the ads have got smarter. The corporates aim their innovation at advertising techniques and technologies, not at passengers or services.

J. Wesley Brown's series, *The Riders* – depicting figures waiting alone at Los Angeles bus stops around midnight – perfectly encapsulates this strange communication, the gap between the message and the users, or sometime the visual coincidence between then. The glow of marketing is both comforting and alienating. In one shot the illuminated poster reads 'Awake' while a homeless man wraps himself in a blanket for the night. The tableau is bookended by an illuminated ad and a shopping trolley, those symbols of contemporary consumption, here upended. The bus is, of course, antithetical to the self-image of Los Angeles, the car-centric city. Yet the poor travel by bus in huge numbers, just largely unseen by the middle classes.

Another thing about the ennui of the bus stop is that it is also often tinged with danger, even in what might seem the most public of places. For women travelling alone late at night, or for children and teenagers during the day, they can be lethal places. The racist murder of British black teenager Stephen Lawrence happened at a South London bus stop. Many terrible stories have their beginnings at lonely bus stops, including that of child-killer Levi Bellfield.

Most big cities continue to squander the opportunities presented by bus stops. In British villages, though, many take the form of thatched cottages, half-timbered pavilions or other pastiche miniature architectures. The Soviets meanwhile revelled in the construction of architecturally striking, often Constructivist-inflected concrete shelters. They weren't quite the 'palaces of the people' of the Moscow Metro, but they acknowledged a need for the investment of effort into the public realm. Ironically it is often their deterioration which has made these into cult structures, again with their own brand of ostlagic anomie. Photographer Christopher Herwig's irresistible surveys of this seemingly most mundane of building types reveals an incredible vocabulary of design. The finest of them have the eerie presence of deserted expo pavilions, exotic structures designed for a kinetic landscape of performative display and now abandoned and overacting to their humble surroundings. Others resemble art installations, as indeed do those in Western cities at night, their faint glow suggesting some deeper meaning, some charismatic presence not accorded their occupants.

Now relegated to advertising add-ons it can be difficult to remember that, even in Britain, bus stops were once the bridgehead of the avant-garde. Brighton's streamlined, Art Deco shelters with their curving, nautical prows were the height of seaside sophistication and still look sleek today. In the inter-war period, when most housing was still being built in Mock-Tudor or Neo-Georgian, London was building bus stops that appeared positively Miesian: elegant glass and steel structures with brightly coloured spandrels and overhanging eaves, like a modernist villa.

After the war, bus stops were part of a government initiative to gently persuade people of the benefits of modernist design, as if the aesthetic might sink into the queuing masses through osmosis. They became lessons in civics, carefully controlled by the Design Council and a list of approved industrial designers like Jack Howe, Sir Kenneth Grange, David Mellor or Arcon. Where there was no space for a shelter a single bus stop sign might be a perfectly integrated concrete column, with a timetable accommodated in its waist. It was sign, object, marker and information terminal in one – a simple stick made into a place.

Few of us, frankly, yearn to be in a bus shelter. They are places of necessity rather than venues of desire. But they are what we have. Perhaps only teens really understand them. But even they would probably rather not.

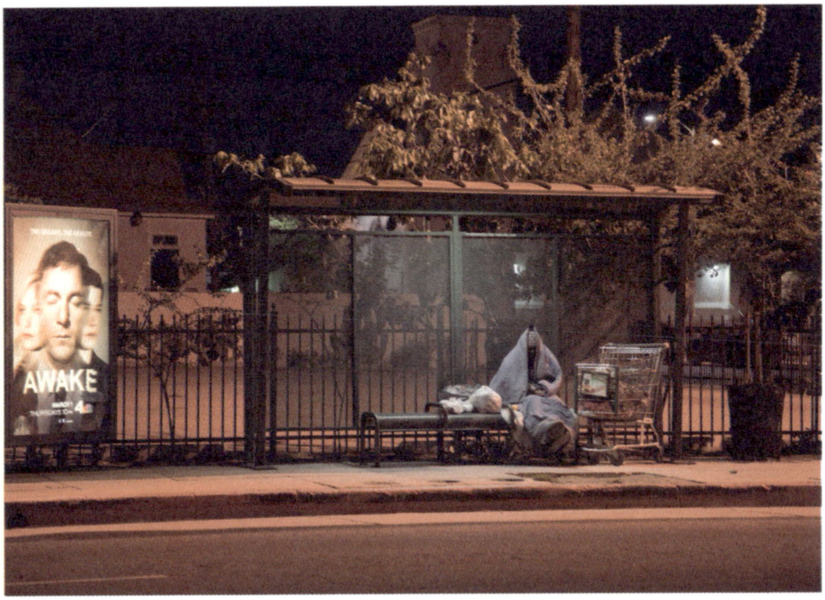

The Riders, Los Angeles, 2016
J. Wesley Brown

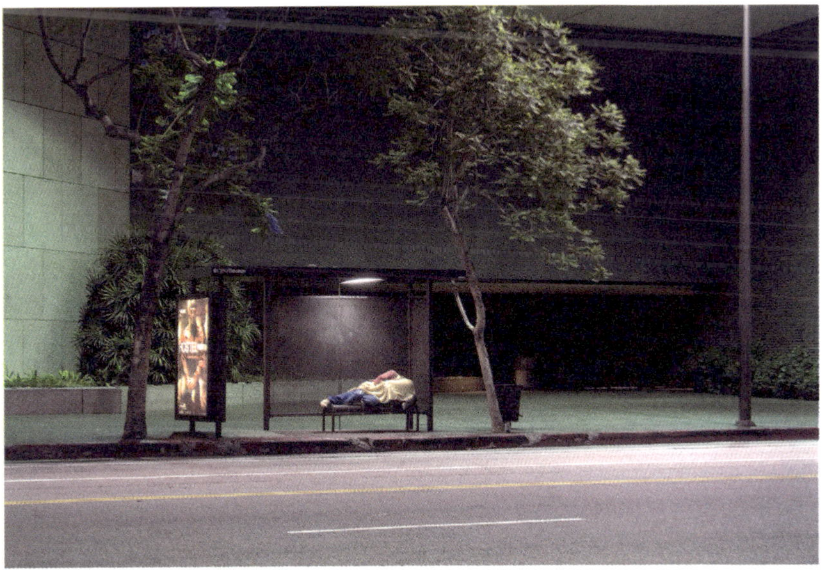

The Riders, Los Angeles, 2006
J. Wesley Brown

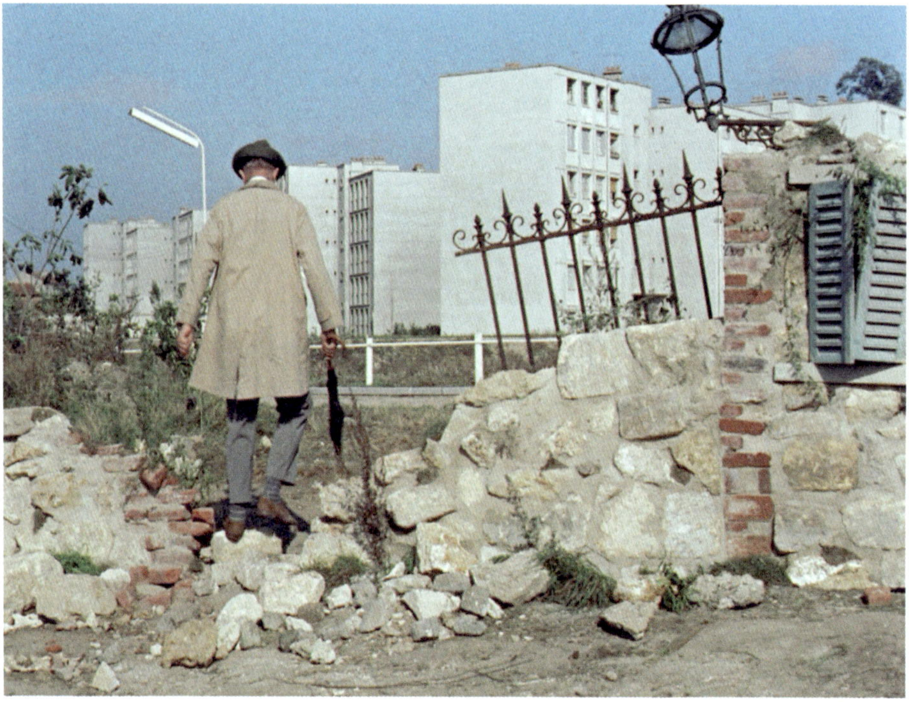

Still from Mon Oncle, 1958
Jacques Tati

Walling

There is a scene in Jacques Tati's film *Mon Oncle* (1958) where the protagonist, the raincoat-clad, pipe-smoking Monsieur Hulot, accidentally knocks a loose brick out of place as he steps through a gap in the remains of a wall. He turns, bends over, picks it up and carefully puts it back in its precarious original position. It looks like a pathetically futile gesture but it is, in a way, a synopsis of the spirit of the whole film. The wall and the plastered remains of a building beside it are what remains of the old neighbourhood. A delicate street lantern with an elaborate wrought-iron bracket juts out of the wall at an uncomfortable angle, while an ornate iron railing protrudes from the crumbling building. In the background a procession of identical white slab blocks is visible, modernity on the march. In this encroaching city of the future there is only a single stark streetlight, as blank in its aspect as the new housing, a piece of pure function.

A wall might not really belong in the taxonomy of street furniture, but it would certainly serve to define a public space and here it works with the other items - the lamp and the railing - to resist the creeping inevitability of development and modernisation, and the loss of the character of the old quartier. Monsieur Hulot is accompanied by jaunty accordion and guitar music, whereas the scenes in the new town are dominated by machine-made, percussive noises and the absurd choreography of cars, citizens enclosed in their privatised bubbles, their auto-consumables. Those in the old working-class neighbourhood, however, are clearly embedded in the eccentric, time-wasting but joyful world of the street, the public rather than the private life lived behind walls.

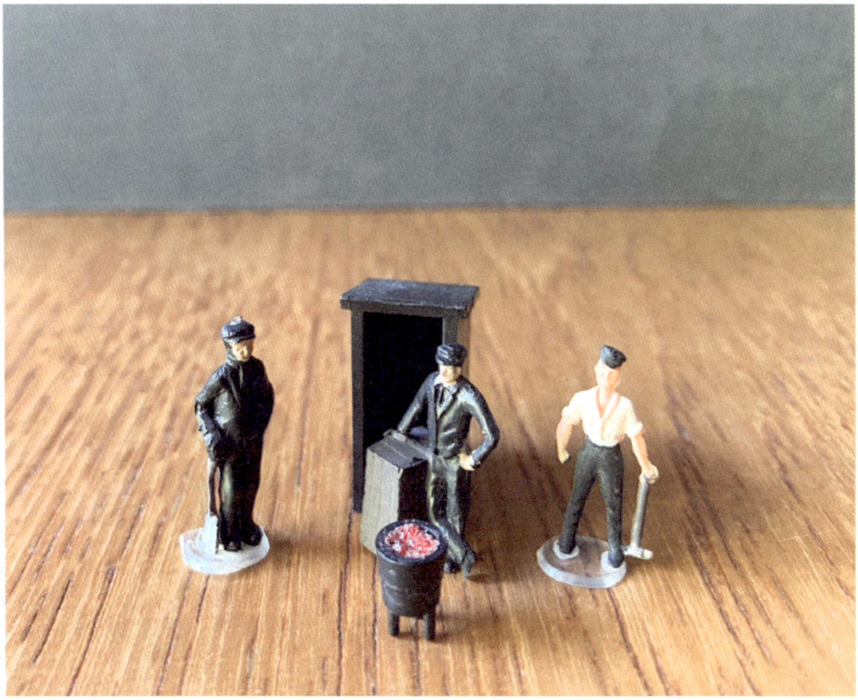

Plastic scale model of workers with brazier,
c. late 1970s

Working

When I was a child roadworks seemed to be a serious business. Workers would arrive in donkey jackets and flat caps with pickaxes and shovels. Then they'd set up a red-and-white stripy tent, sheet-metal 'Men at Work' signs, and a brazier for keeping warm and making tea. On occasion you might even catch the taste-bud tingling whiff of bacon frying inside. They looked well prepared for the long haul, and might stay there for weeks. Sometimes even working. The duration of the job allowed them to become almost part of the community. Passersby would greet them, they might pop into the local caff. My old train set included a small group of figures in flat caps, tools in hand, leaning on their pickaxes, sitting on boxes, not generally working. The little plastic brazier had a painted-on glow, like the end of a toy cigarette.

The stripy tent seemed an unmissable and inevitable element of street life and with it, the brazier. If you ever came across groups of homeless people, they too would have improvised a brazier from an old oil can or dustbin. The same was true at many markets where traders would go to warm their hands, and on the picket lines that seemed such a fixture of the 1970s. Battered, rusty, soot-stained but glowing and sending sparks into the wind, braziers were somehow simultaneously welcoming and sinister. They exuded an almost hypnotic warmth and attraction but also a kind of post-apocalyptic vibe, a post fossil-fuel future appropriate for the years of the oil crisis. The brazier became a staple of street photography, of the homeless clustering around burning cans, warming their hands in gloveless fingers or ranting uncontrollably.

And now they're gone. Not the homeless, they are there in ever greater numbers, but the braziers. Perhaps oil drums are in short supply now, or perhaps workers are just expected to be cold - outsourced, incentivised to do the work fast and get on to the next job. Work sites are now fenced off with plastic modular barriers. The engineers work alone. They are joyless, inhuman. Perhaps they have no time to relax or make cups of tea on the job any more and braziers have become redundant, or perhaps they contravene environmental regulations. You occasionally encounter workers in that marker of contemporary labour, the hi-vis jacket, down on their hands and knees in front of a green metal street cabinet, its insanely colourful viscera spilled out onto the pavement in a seemingly impossible tangle. Despite the apparent delicacy of their operations, they are afforded no shelter. They might be surrounded with some plastic folding fencing, isolated but not protected. The stripy tents and braziers belong to another, older, sootier, slower era.

In Italian, the word *umarell* is applied to the kind of elderly man (it is, almost always, a man) who stands, hands clasped behind his back, watching work being done. Occasionally he might give uncalled-for advice. These people properly inhabit the spirit of the street, understanding it as theatre, its activity a public spectacle and its spectating a public right. *Umarell* means 'little man' in Bolognese dialect. My set of little plastic men lacked an *umarell*. Too English perhaps. But it would have been a fine addition to those workers, their brazier and the stripy tent which exist, now, only in our memories. The streets are neater now, emptier and colder for their absence.

Street Walking

The more you look at things in the street – the objects rather than the field – the more your eye becomes drawn to them. After years of attempting to notice the details, the small events, the accidental convergences, the inadvertent humour and the clustering of things, I find that I now can't stop looking. This strata of street furniture becomes, at first, visible, and then unavoidable. It becomes endlessly fascinating in its small differences and its visual and material language.

I have taken thousands of pictures which now clog up my cloud, an endlessly renewing stream of streets and corners, of lights and kiosks, coal holes and drinking fountains. A small selection of these is reproduced on the following pages. They are the incidental pictures of travels and walks – the things in-between.

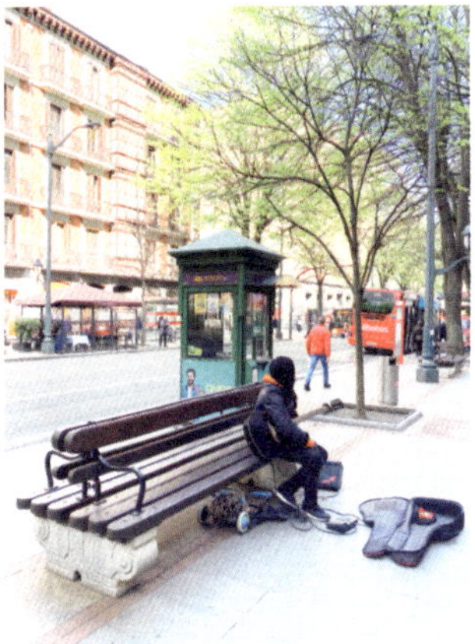

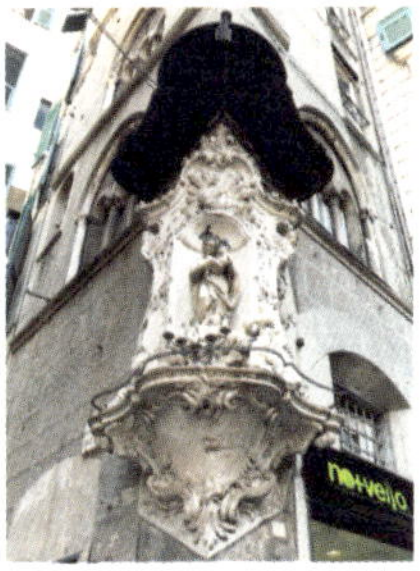

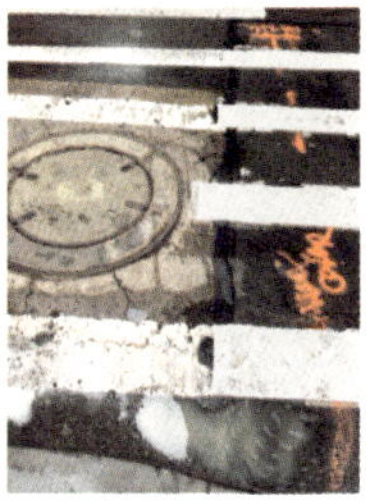

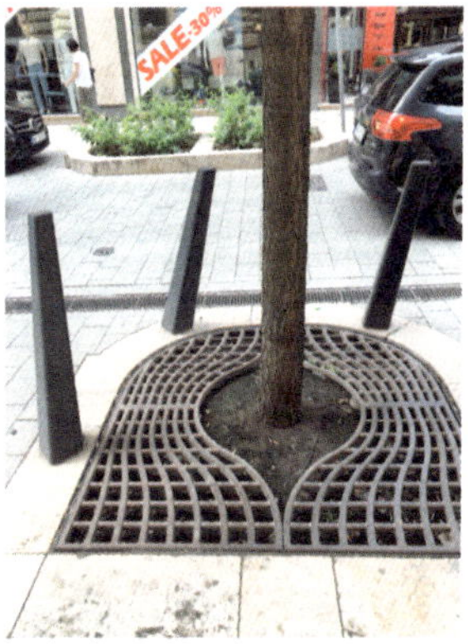
SALE -30%

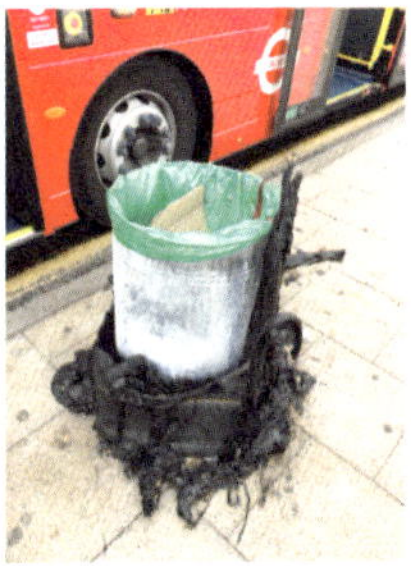

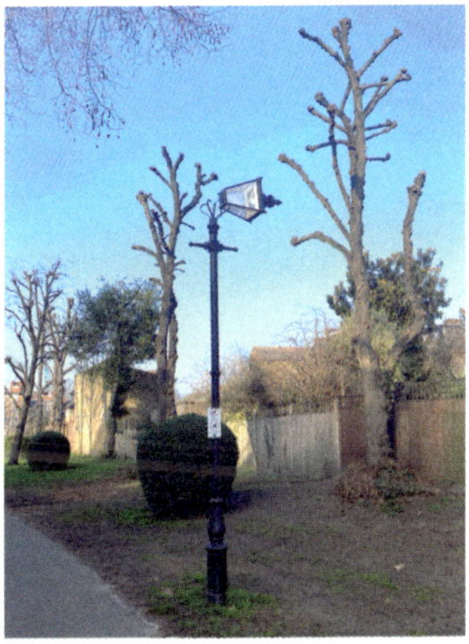

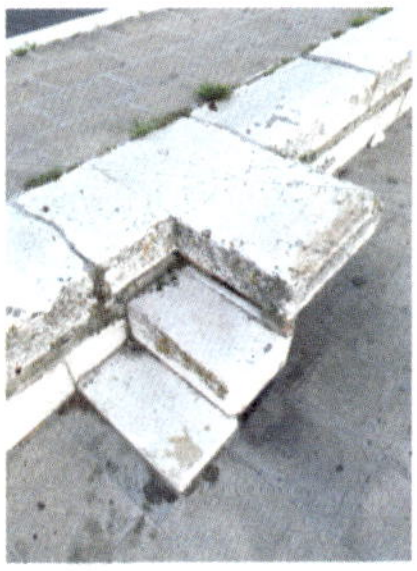

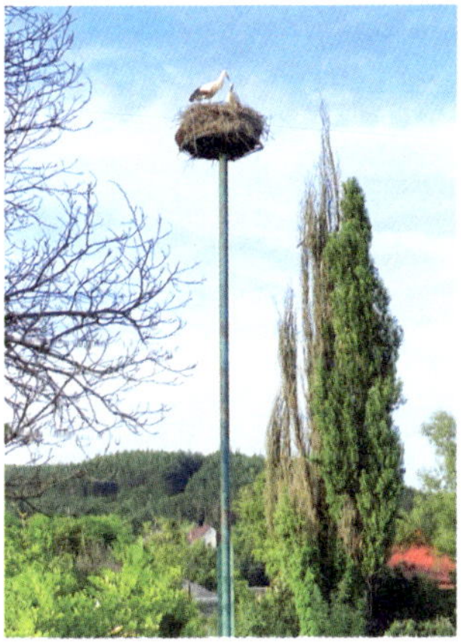

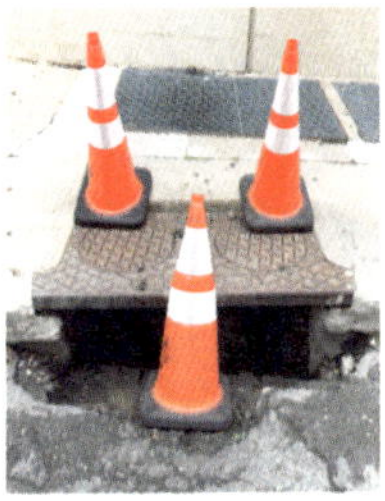

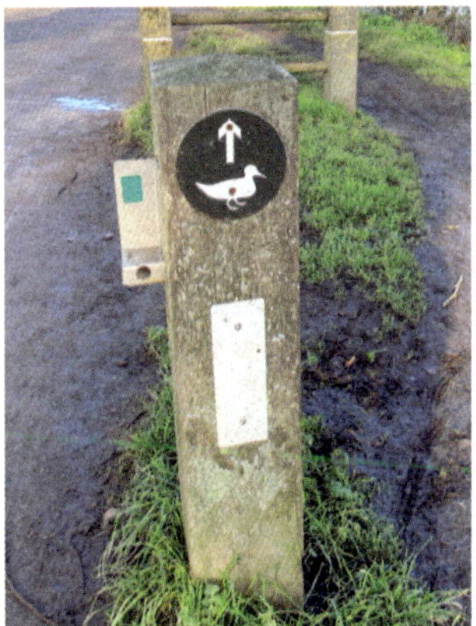

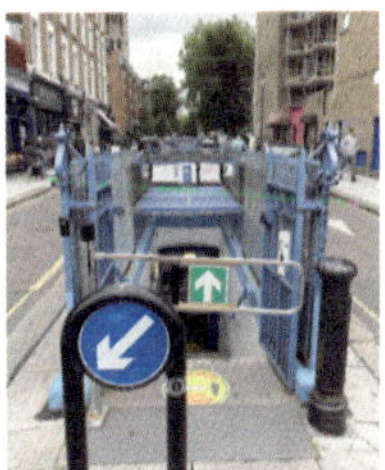

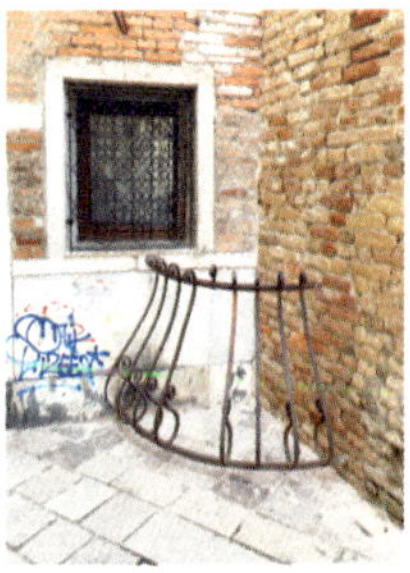

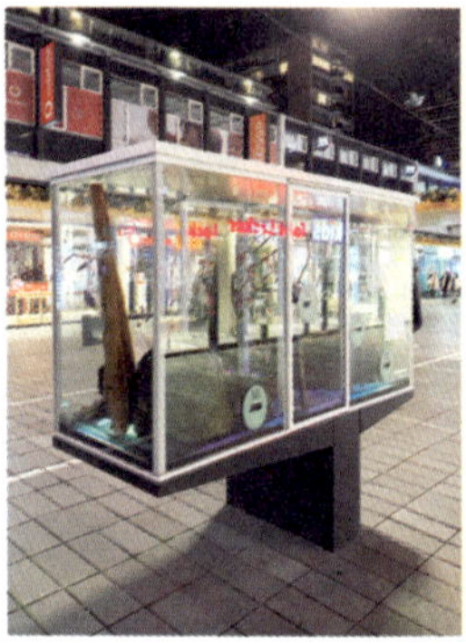

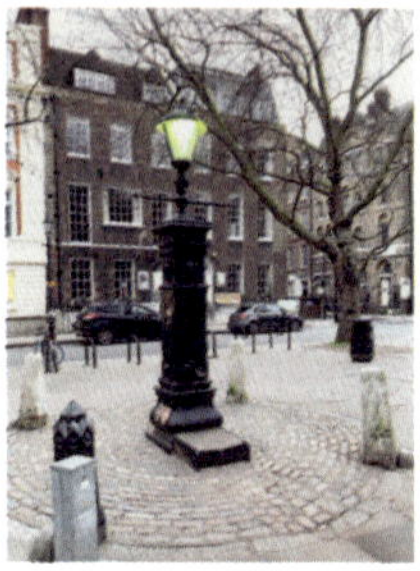

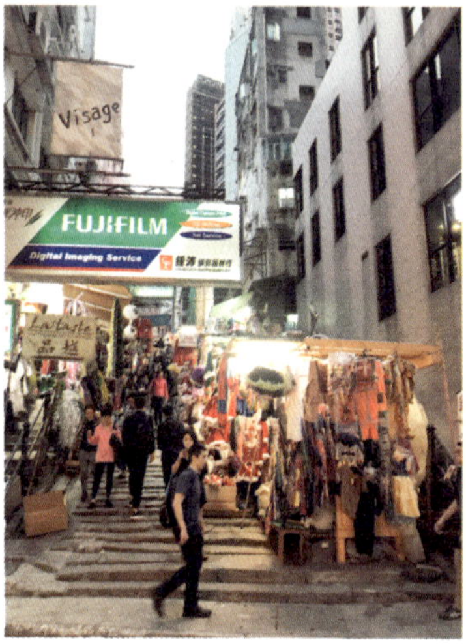
Visage
FUJIFILM
Digital Imaging Service

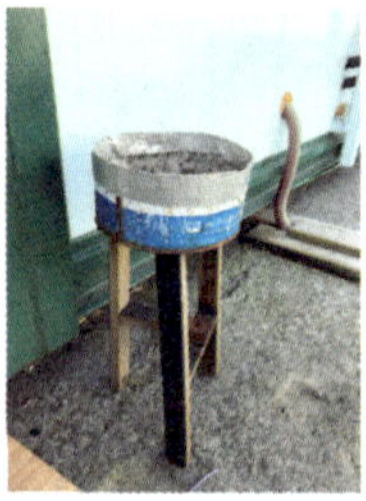

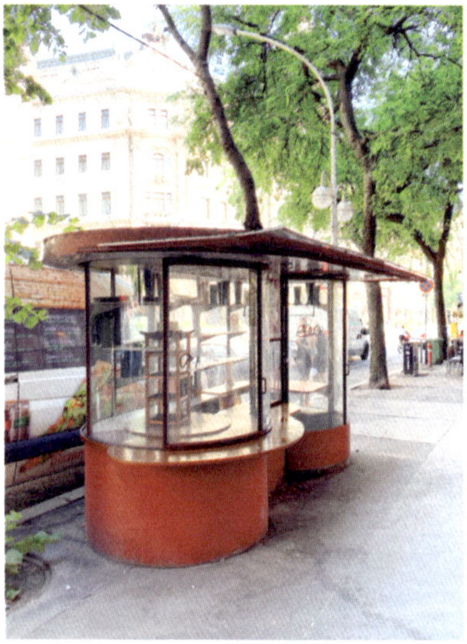

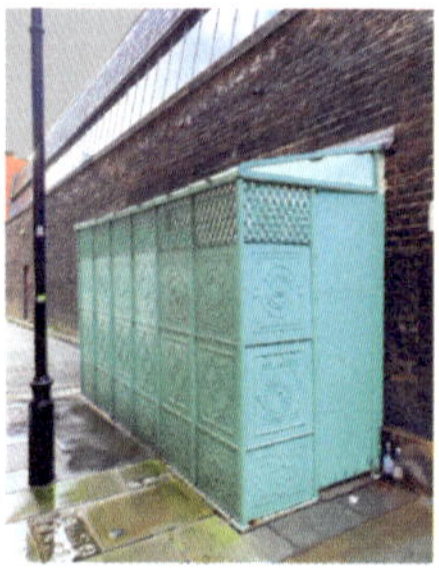

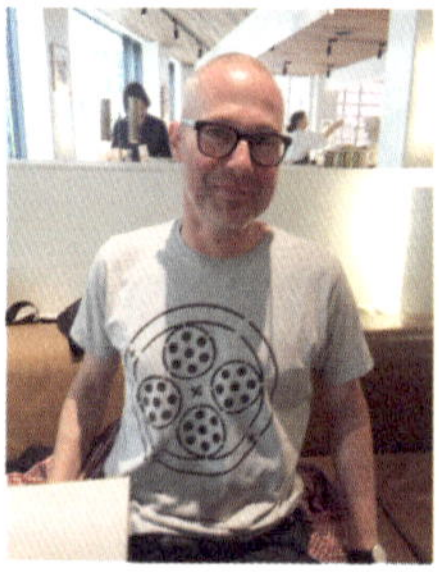

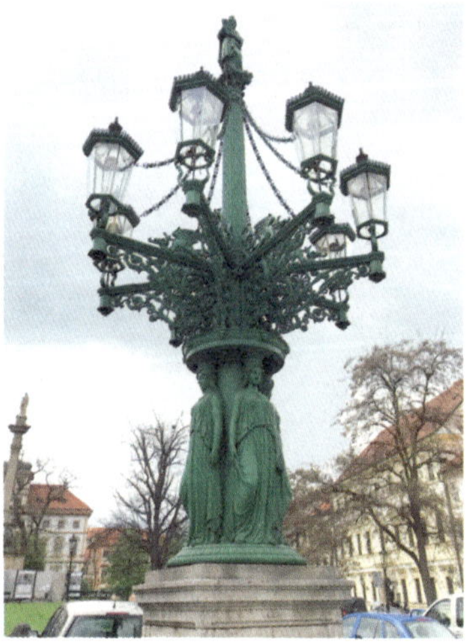

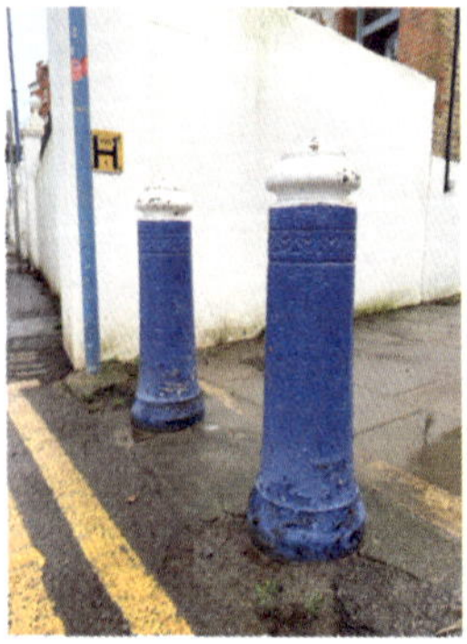
H

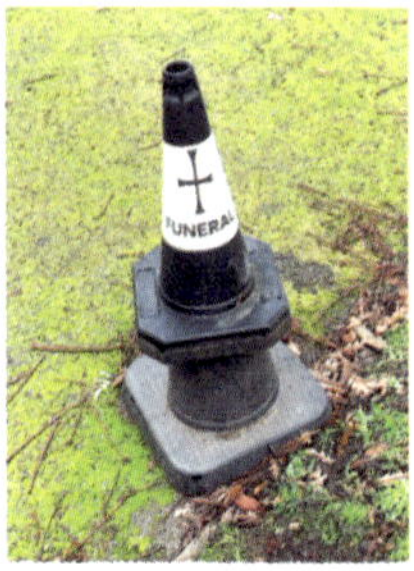
FUNERAL

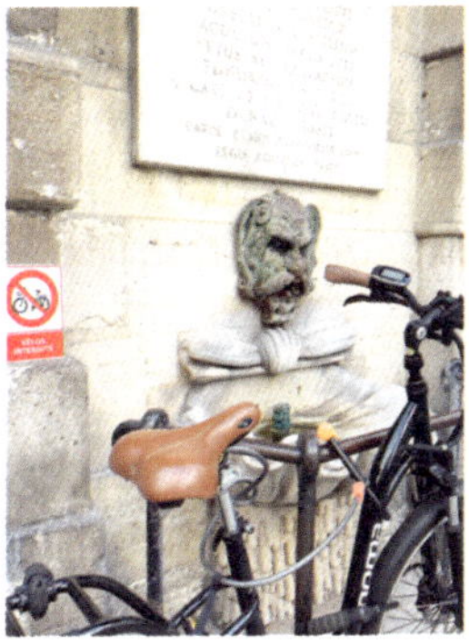

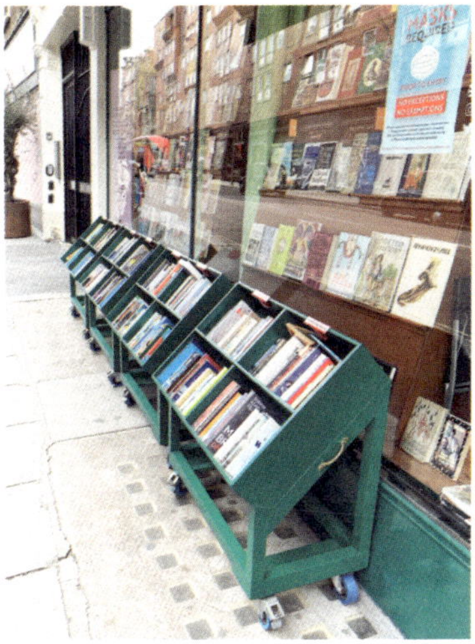

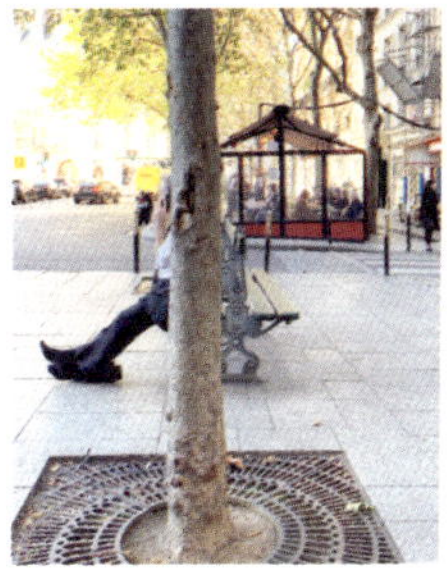

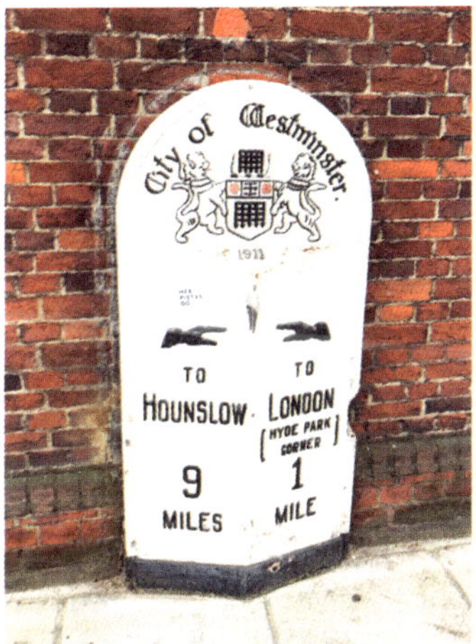
City of Westminster
1911
TO
HOUNSLOW
9
MILES
TO
LONDON
HYDE PARK
CORNER
1
MILE

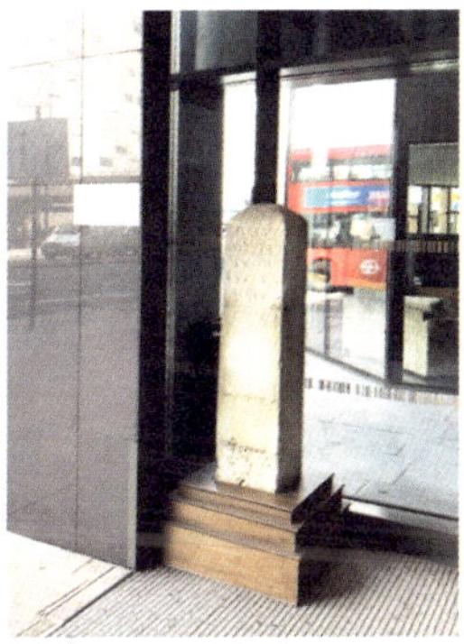

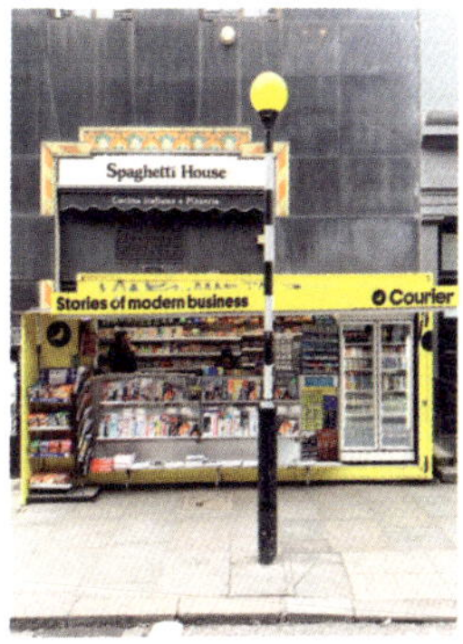
Spaghetti House
Stories of modern business
Courier

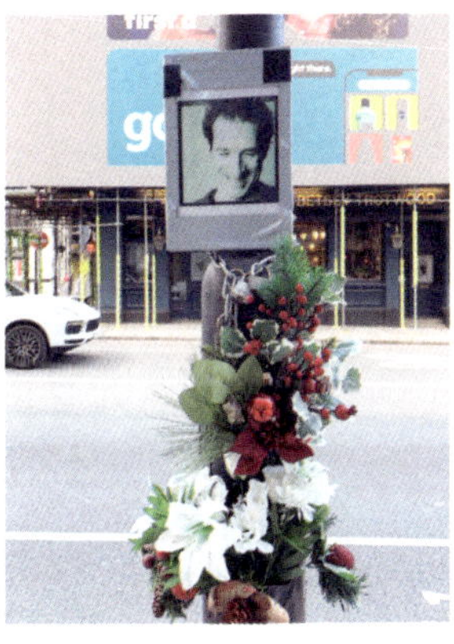

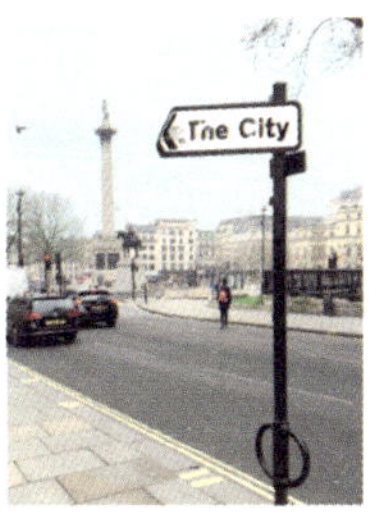
The City

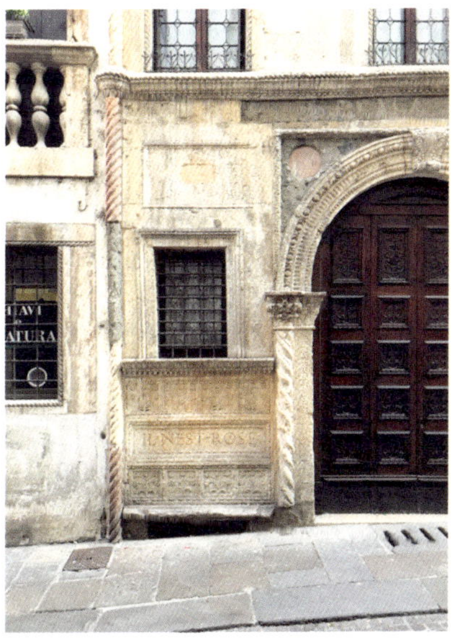

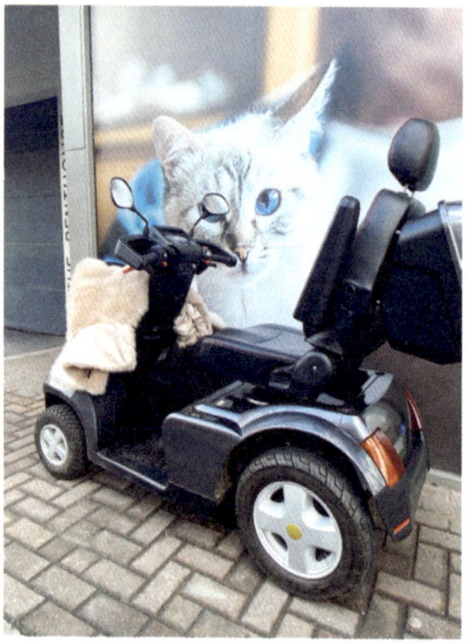

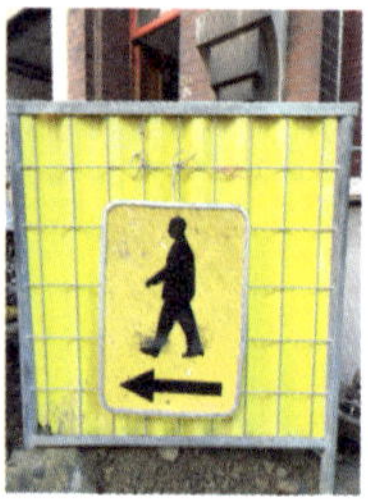

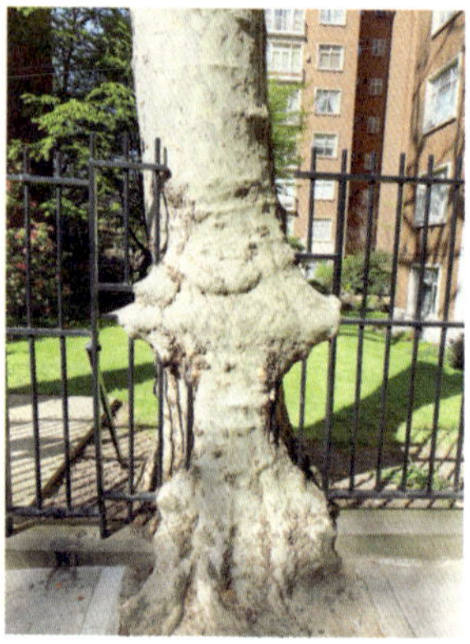

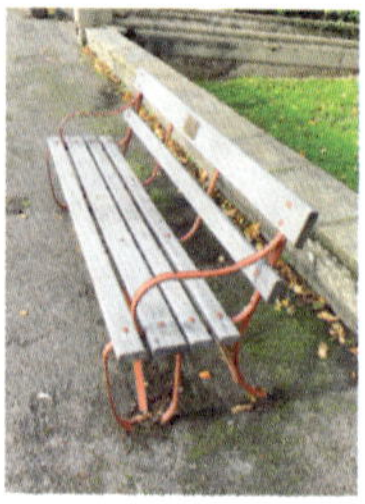

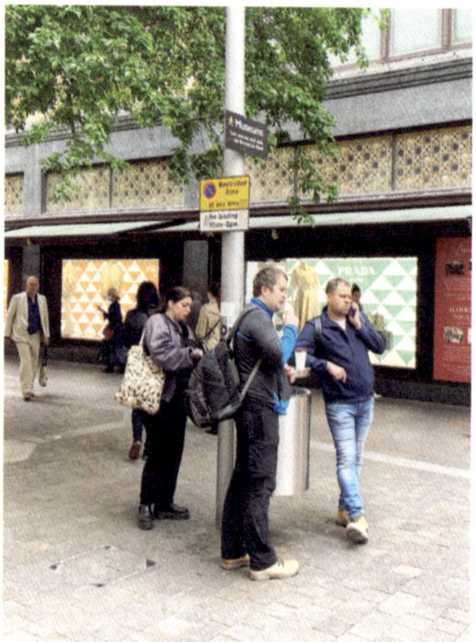

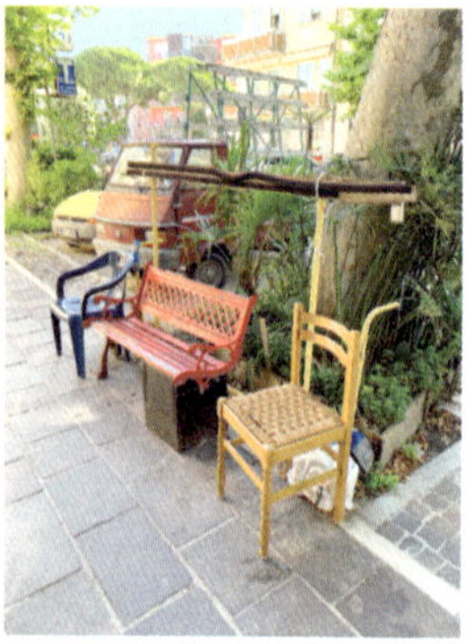

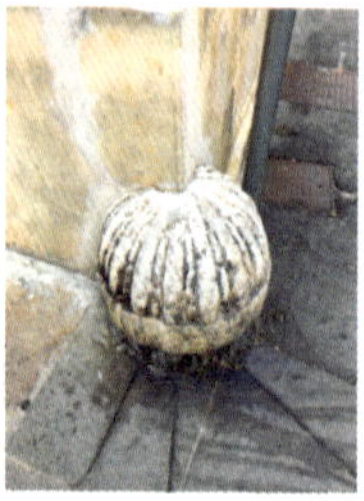

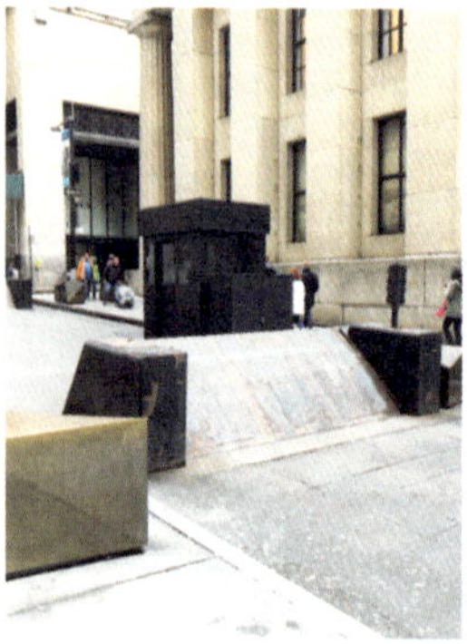

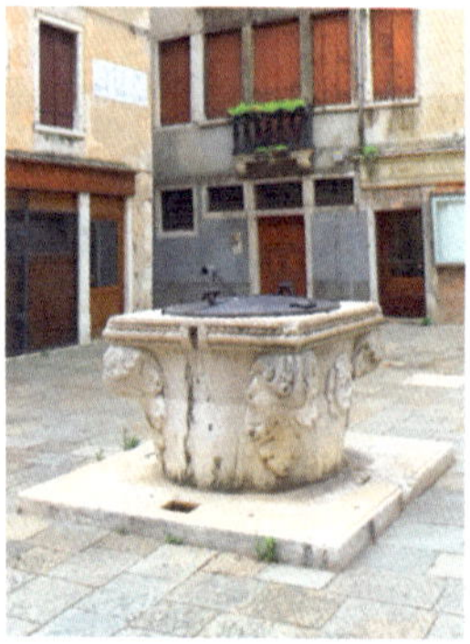

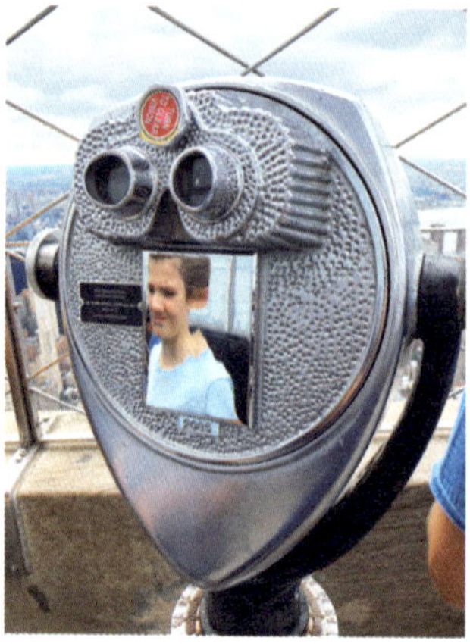

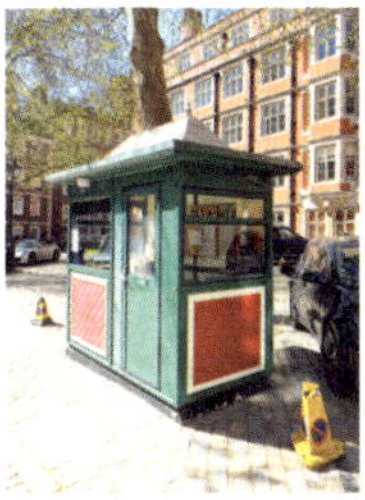

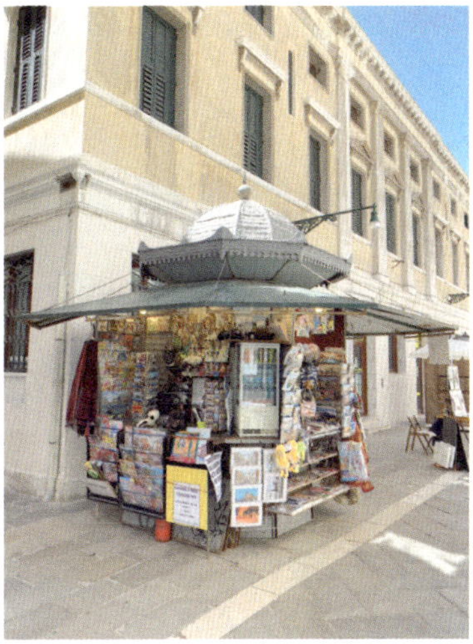

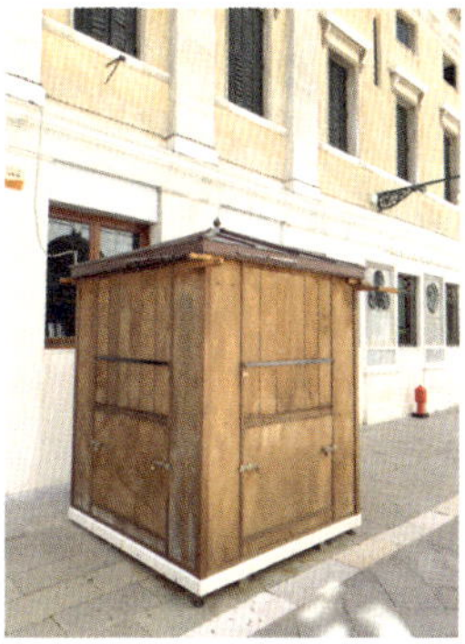

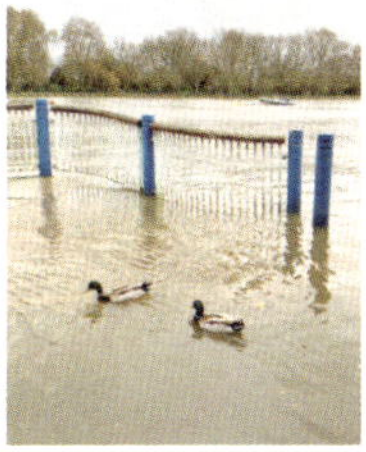

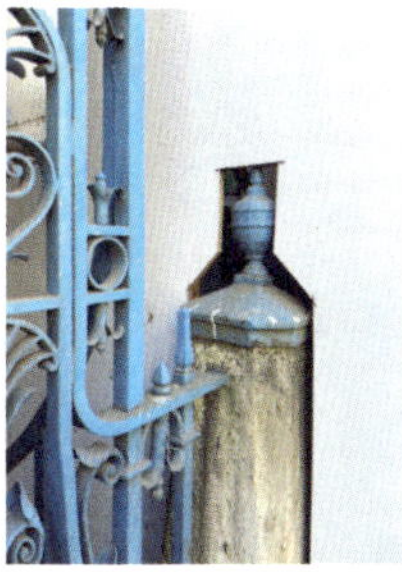

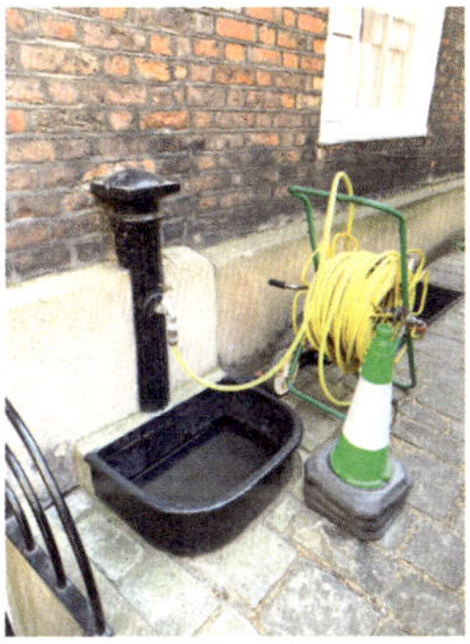

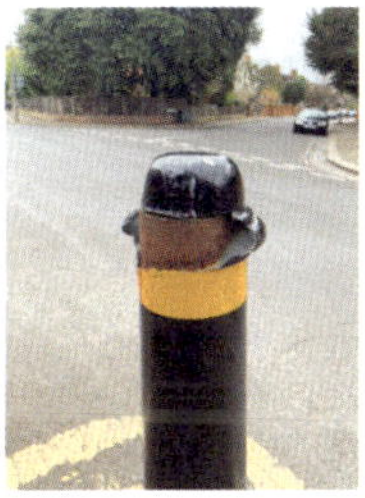

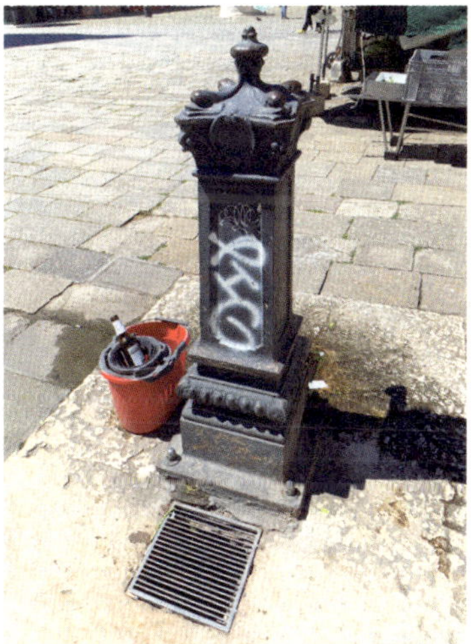

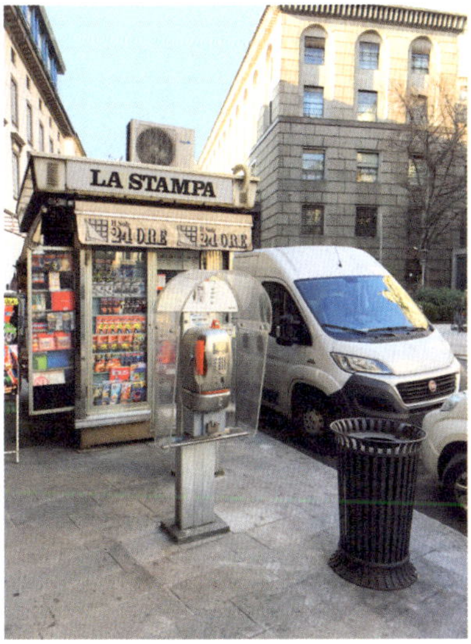
LA STAMPA

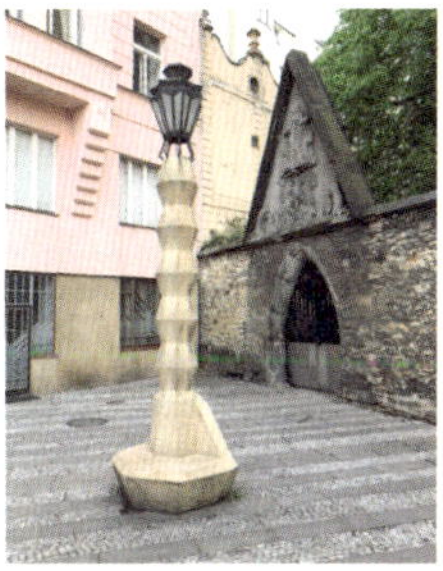

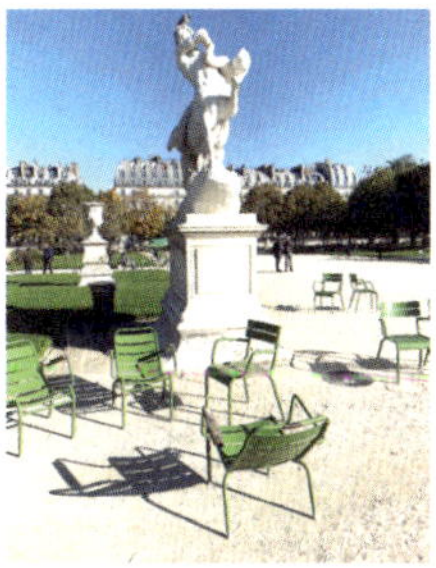

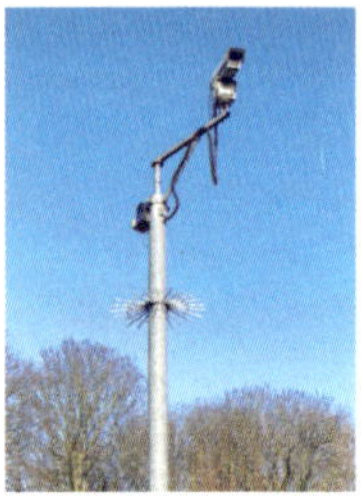

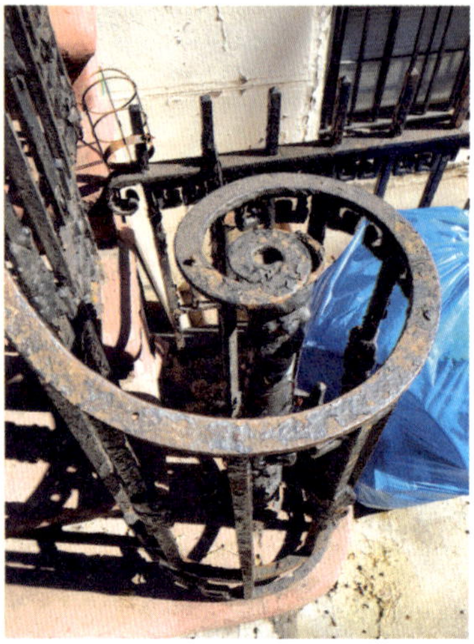

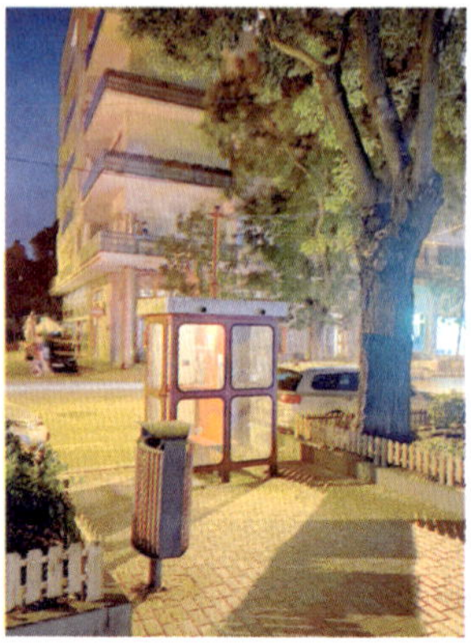

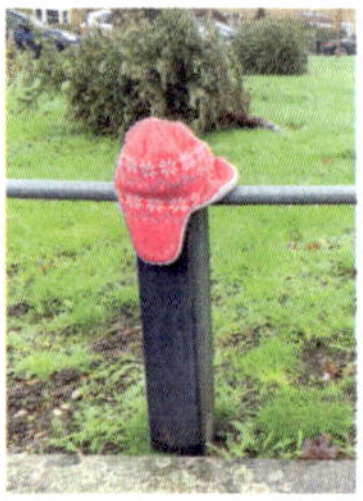

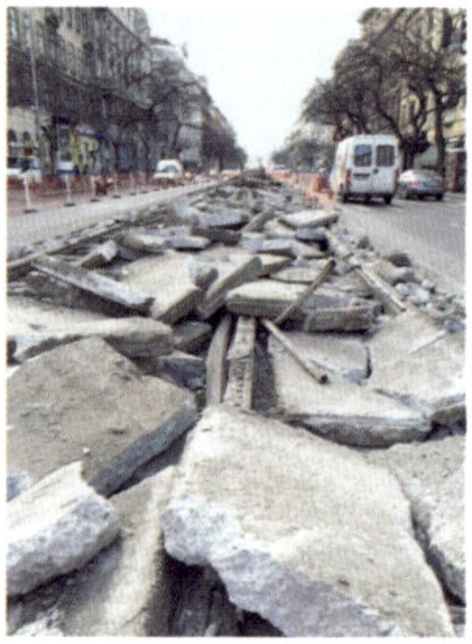

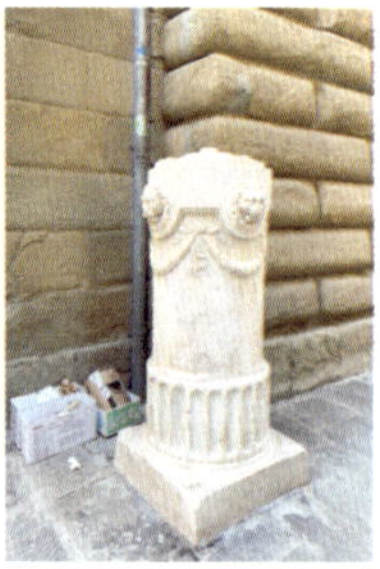

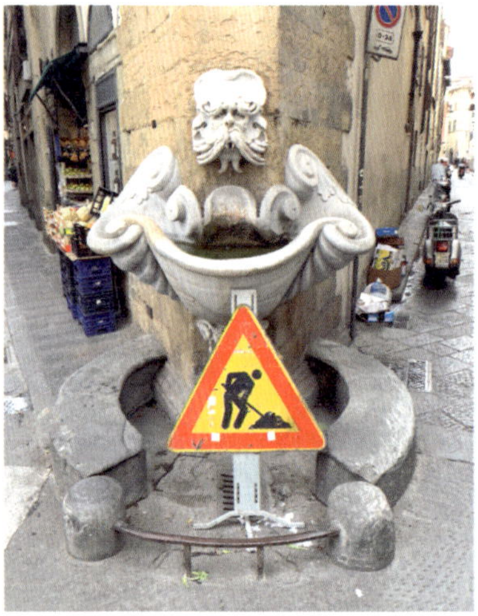

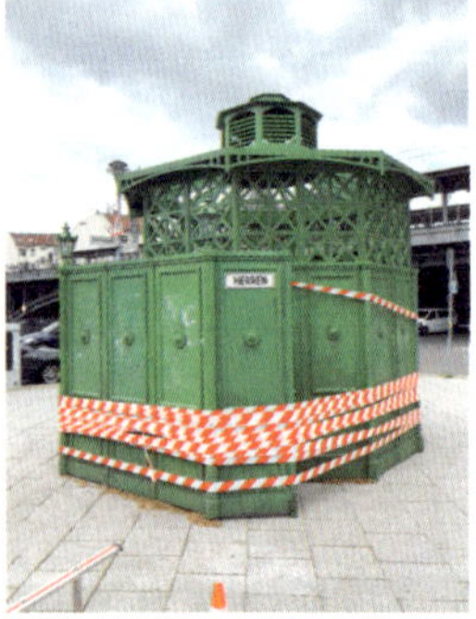

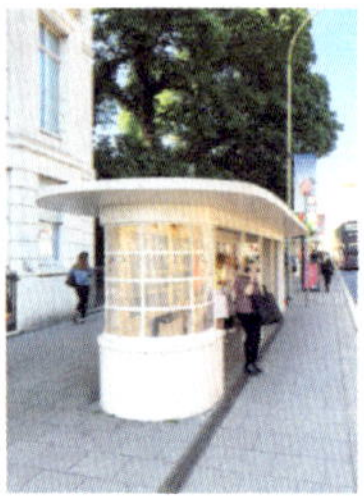

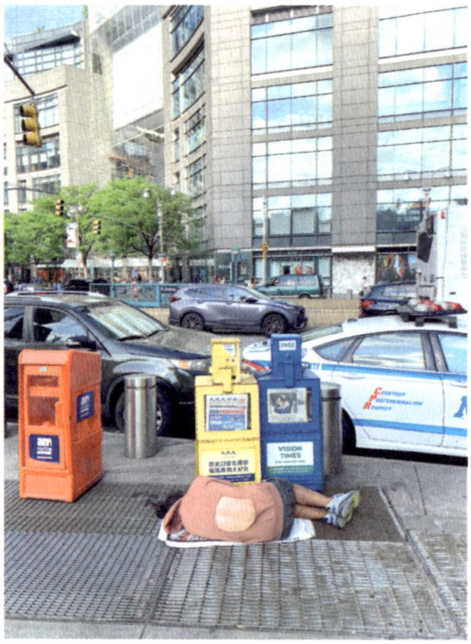
VISION TIMES

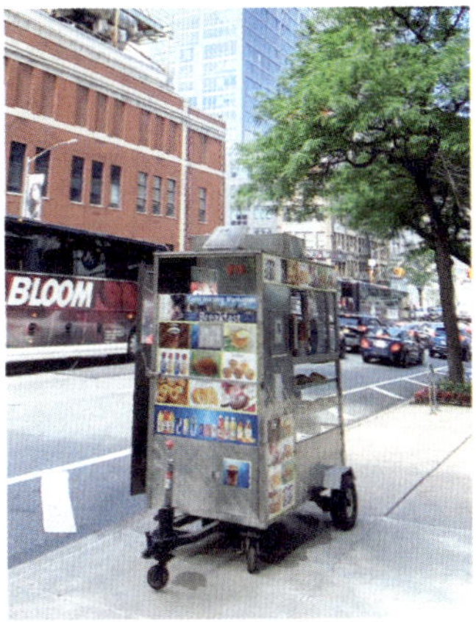
BLOOM
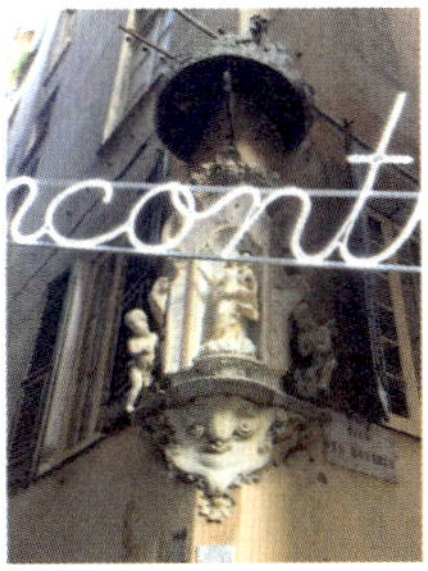
ncont
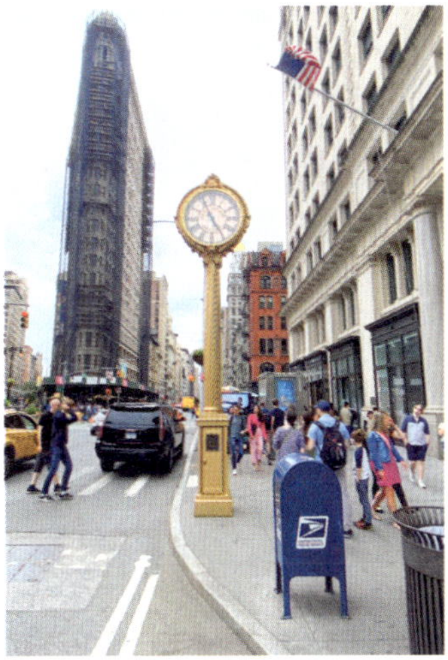
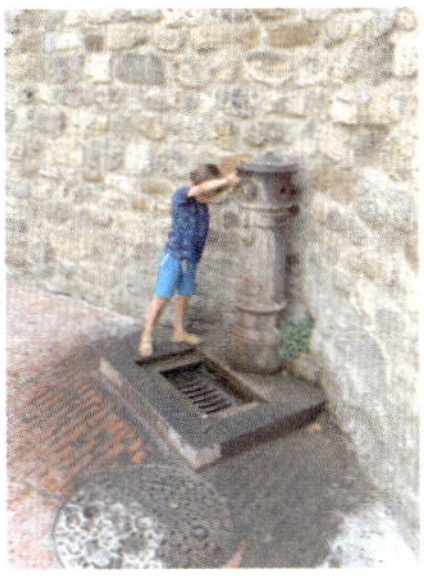
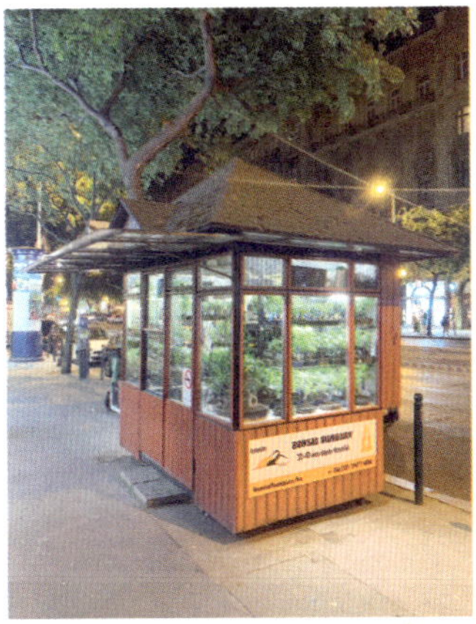
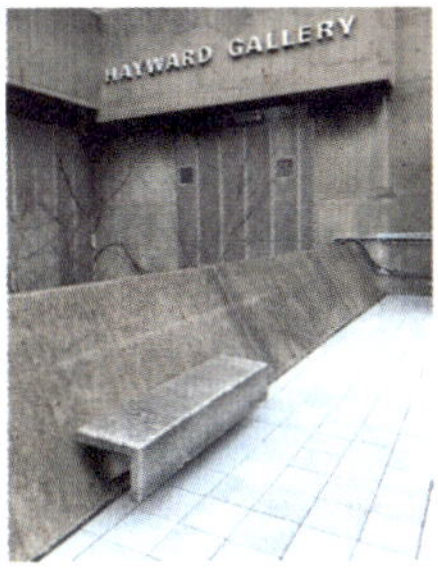
HAYWARD GALLERY
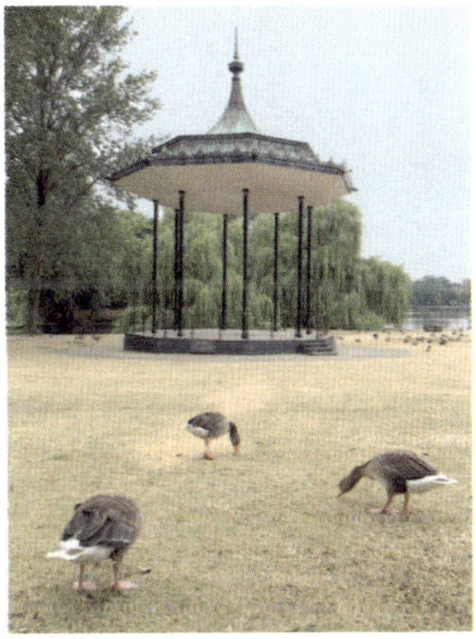
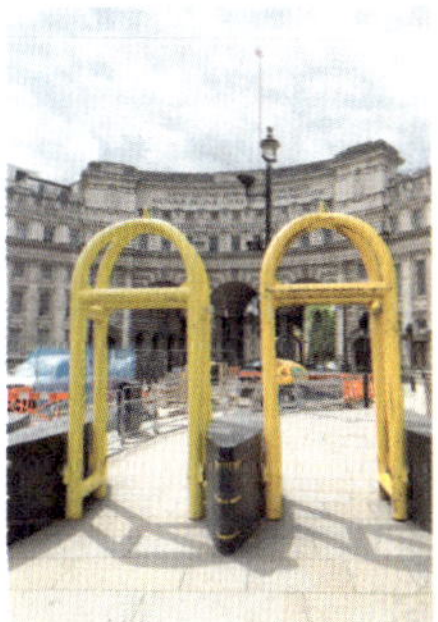
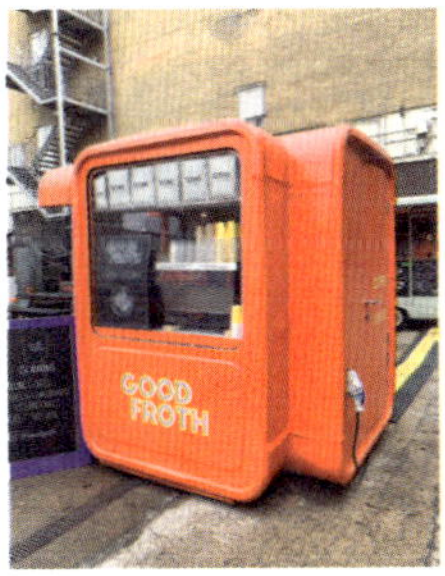
GOOD
FROTH
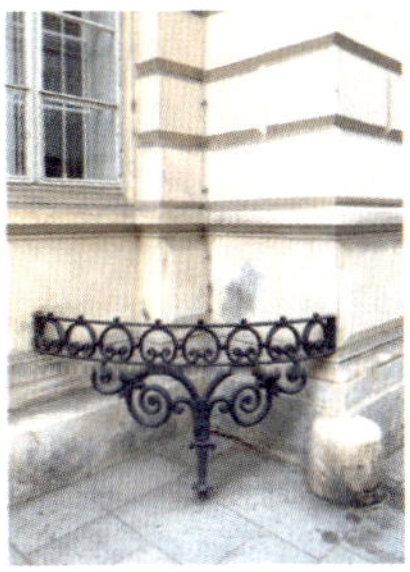
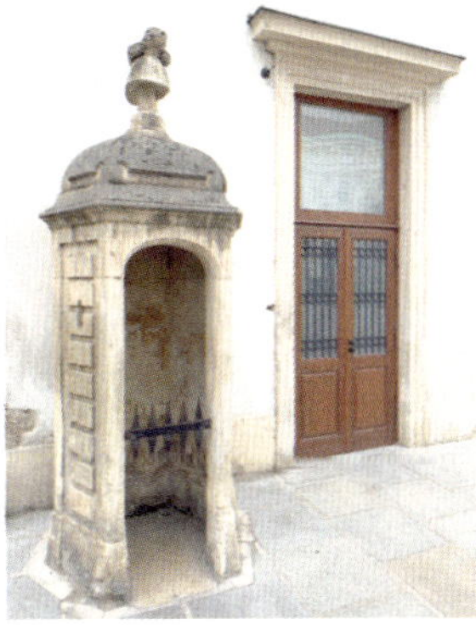
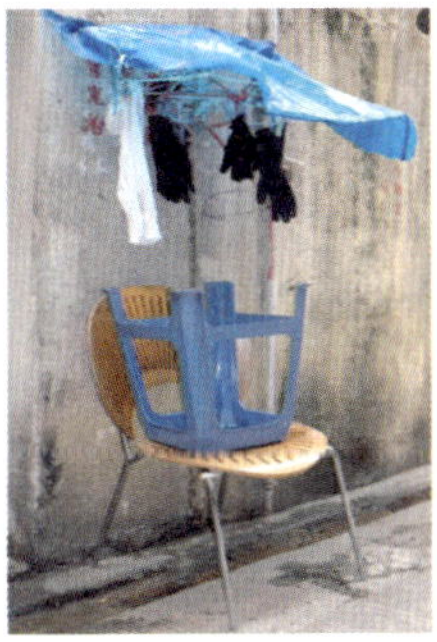

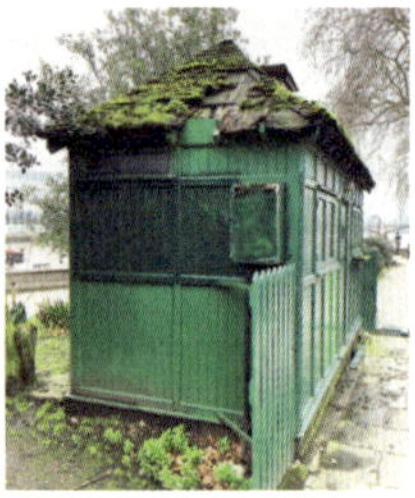

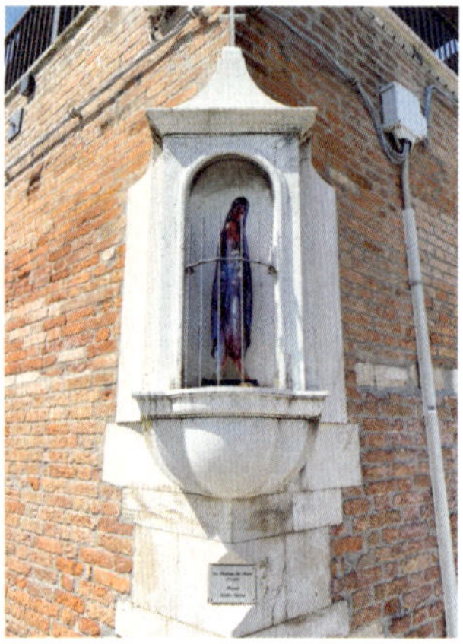

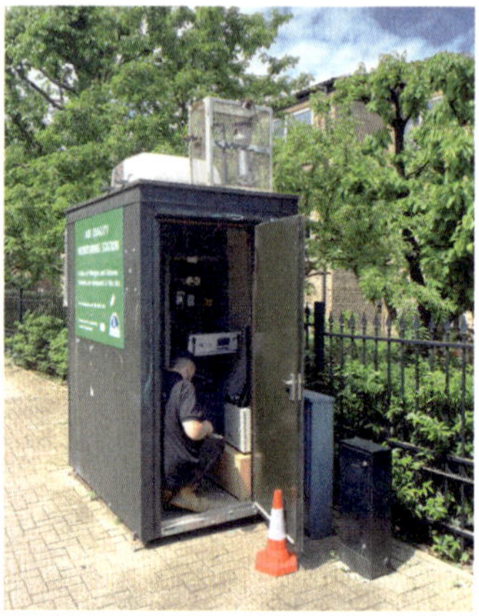

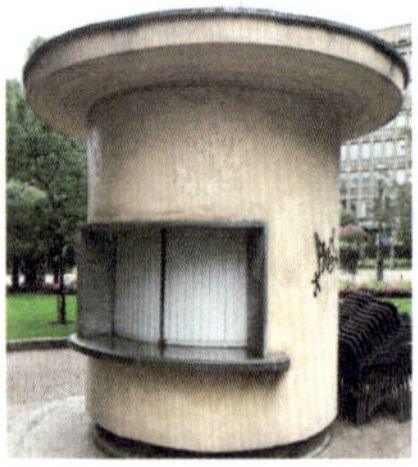

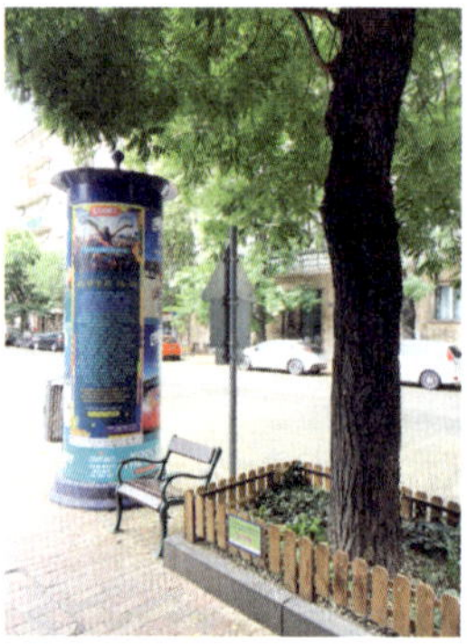

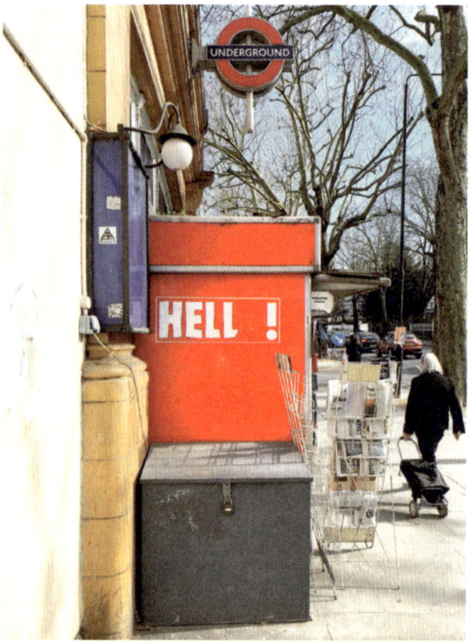
UNDERGROUND
HELL !

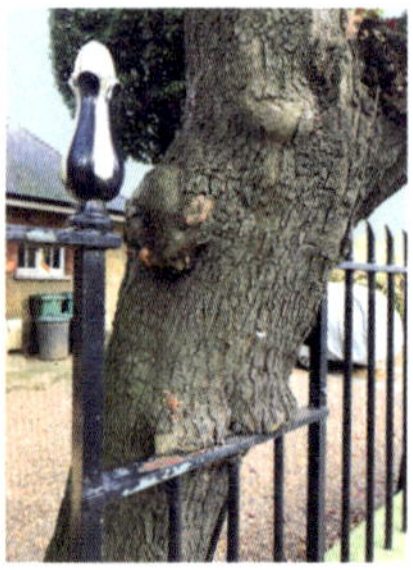

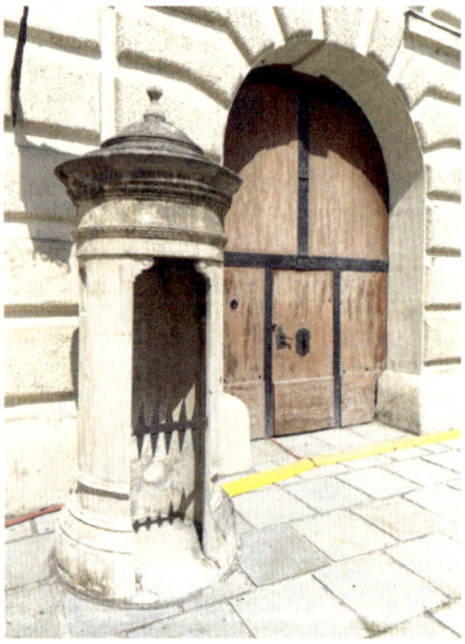

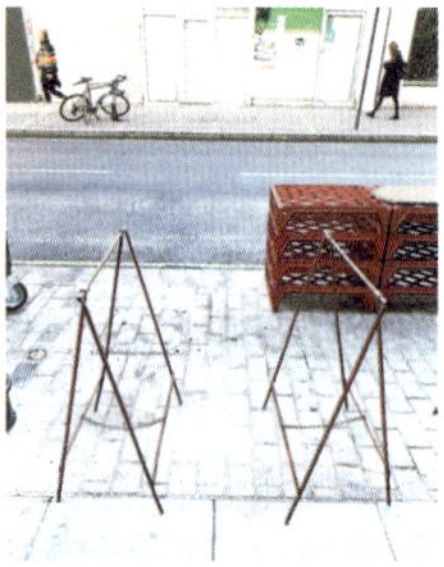

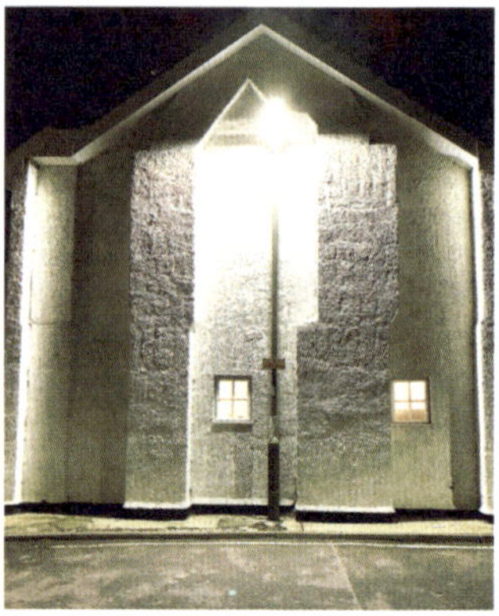

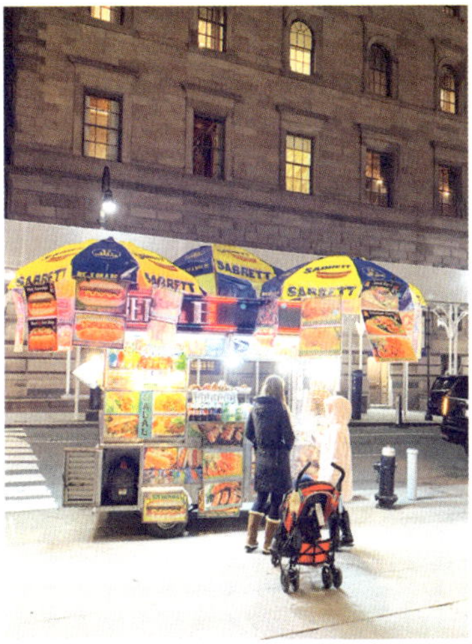
SABRETT

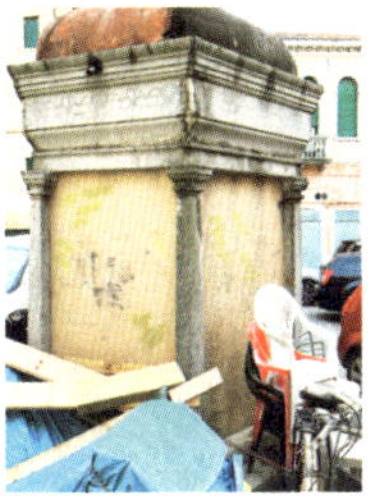

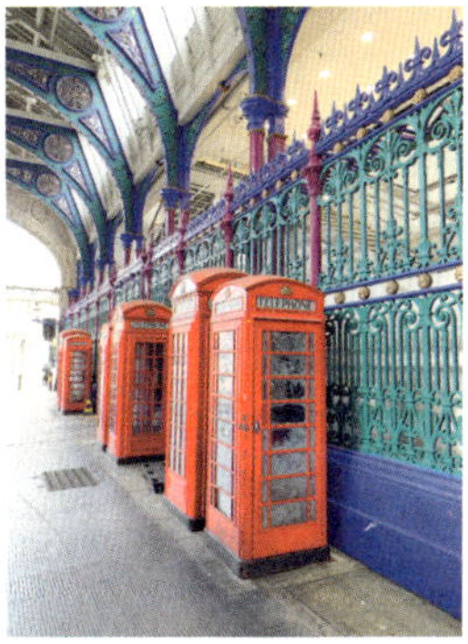

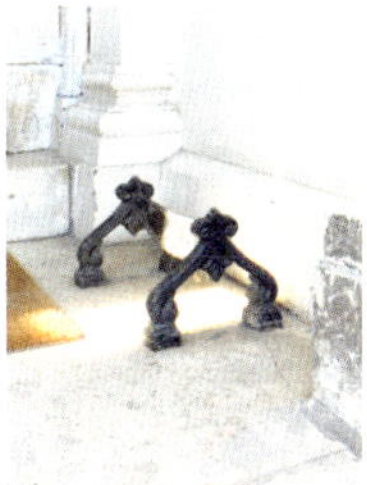

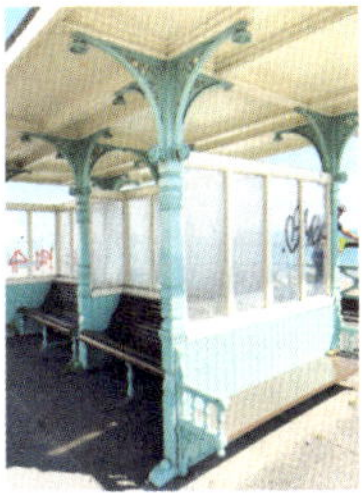

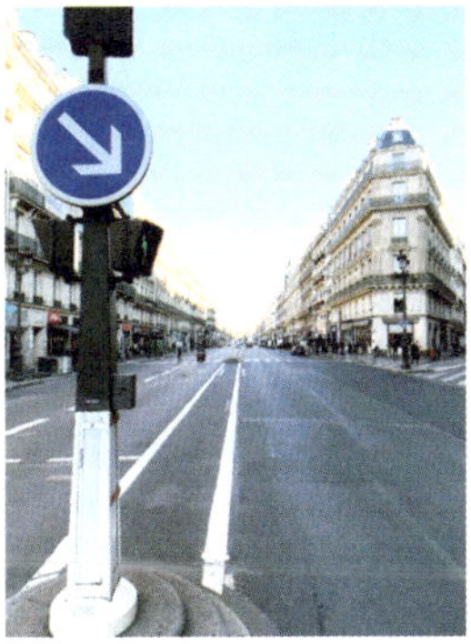

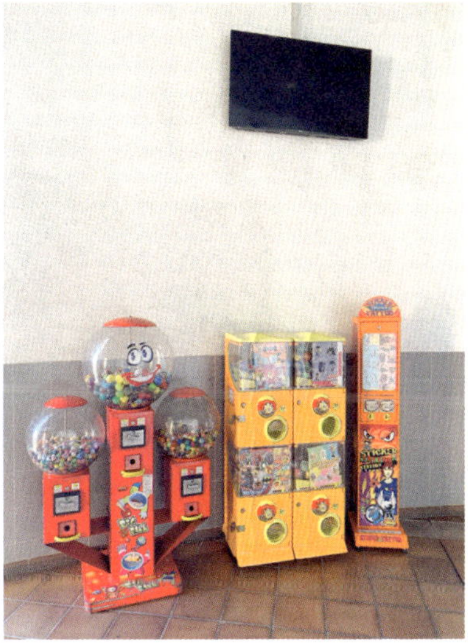

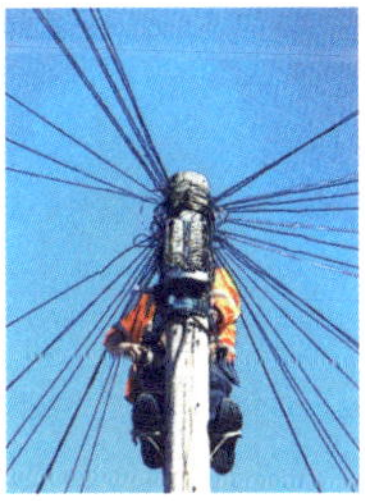

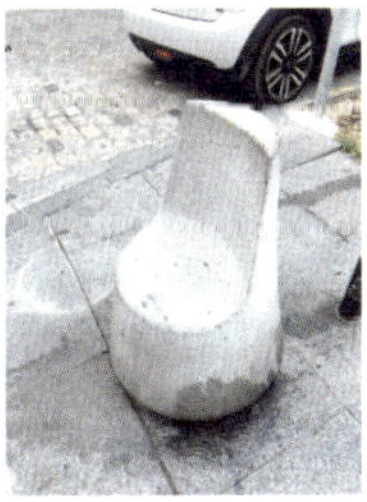

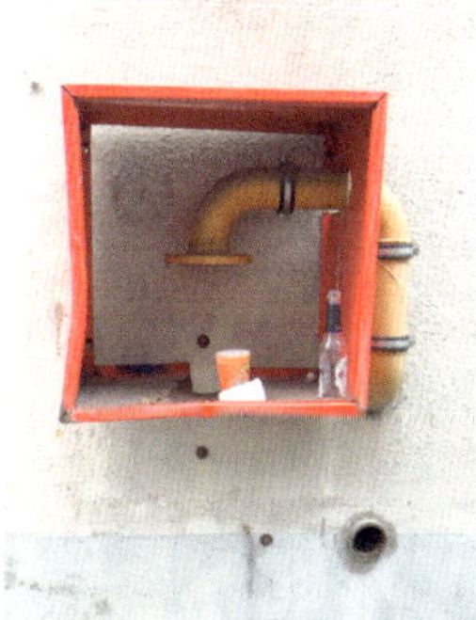

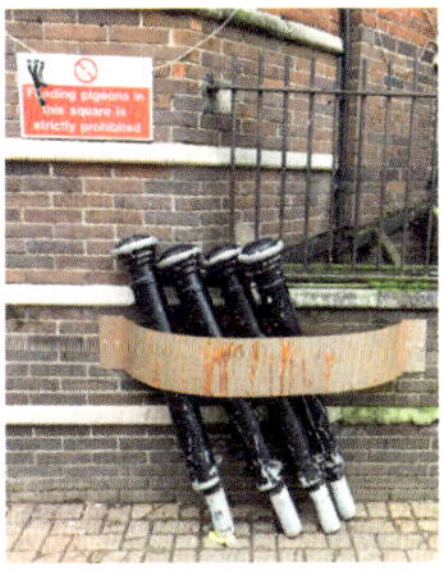

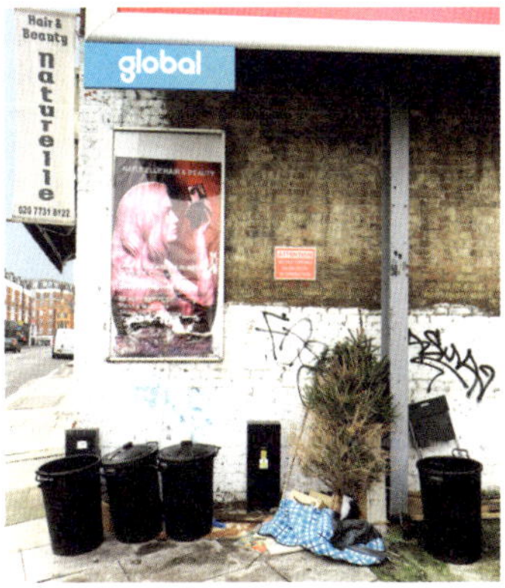
Hair &
Beauty
naturelle
global

Picture Credits

Every effort has been made to contact all copyright holders. The publishers will be pleased to amend in future printings any errors or omissions brought to their attention.

4: © Saul Leiter Foundation
6: © Mark Pimlott
9: © Andrea Frank Foundation. Photo SCALA, Florence
10: Courtesy Bibliothèque Nationale de France
16: © ESTATE BRASSAÏ - RMN-Grand Palais. Photo SCALA, Florence
19, top: © Arche Atrium AG; bottom: Courtesy Bibliothèque Nationale de France
24, top and bottom left: © Fondation Henri Cartier-Bresson/Magnum Photos; bottom right: © René Burri/Magnum Photos
30, top: © Inge Morath/Magnum Photos; bottom: © The Estate of W. Suschitzky
36: © Film Documents LLC, courtesy Galerie Thomas Zander, Cologne
45: Courtesy of Michael Wolf Estate
59: Courtesy Musée Carnavalet
60, 62, 63: © Design Council
70, 73: © Estate of Vivian Maier, Courtesy Maloof Collection and Howard Greenberg Gallery, New York
78, 79: Courtesy State Library Victoria www.slv.vic.gov.au
84: © Elliott Erwitt/Magnum Photos
87: © Estate of Vivian Maier, Courtesy Maloof Collection and Howard Greenberg Gallery, New York
93: © Sir Kenneth Grange
95: © Weegee (Arthur Fellig)/International Center of Photography via Getty Images
98: © Andrea Frank Foundation. Photo The Museum of Fine Arts, Houston
107: © Noah Sussman
120: © Arthur Tress
122, 125: Reproduced by permission of The Ironbridge Gorge Museum Trust
134: © Norman Parkinson/Iconic Images
137, top: © Lee Miller Archives, England 2022. All rights reserved. leemiller.co.uk; bottom: © Marilyn Stafford
144: © Metropolitan Museum of Art, New York. The Elisha Whittelsey Collection, The Elisha Whittelsey Fund, 1959
146: © ESTATE BRASSAÏ - RMN-Grand Palais. Photo SCALA, Florence
148: Scanned from book, *London Night* by John Morrison and Harold Burdekin (Collins, London, 1934). Courtesy of Bishopsgate Institute
149: Bill Brandt © Bill Brandt Archive Ltd
151, top: © heriheri; bottom: © Halowand
153: © Joji Hayashi
157: Reproduced by permission of The Ironbridge Gorge Museum Trust
158: © André Kertész Estate
160, top: © André Kertész Estate; bottom: © Martine Franck/Magnum Photos
163: © ESTATE BRASSAÏ - RMN-Grand Palais. Photo SCALA, Florence
171: © Marc Riboud/Fonds Marc Riboud au MNAAG/Magnum Photos
172: © Harry Gruyaert/Magnum Photos
176: © Condé Nast Ltd - Cecil Beaton/Trunk Archive
182, bottom: © Sheila Klein. Photo by Ian Byers-Gamber
185: © Jimmy Sime/Central Press/Hulton Archive via Getty Images
188: © John Pratt/Keystone Features via Getty Images
195: © Richard Wentworth/DACS 2022
206: Courtesy Library of Congress, Washington DC and Stanley Kubrick Film Archives LLC
209, top: © Metropolitan Museum of Art, New York. Gilman Collection, Purchase, Mr and Mrs Henry R. Kravis Gift, 2005; bottom: © Estate of Vivian Maier, Courtesy Maloof Collection and Howard Greenberg Gallery, New York
211, top: © Alexander Rodchenko, UPRAVIS, 2022. Photo Scala, Florence; bottom: © Trevor Traynor
220, 223: © Will Scott
227: © ESTATE BRASSAÏ - RMN-Grand Palais. Photo SCALA, Florence
229, top: © Estate of Garry Winogrand, courtesy Fraenkel Gallery, San Francisco; bottom: © André Kertész Estate
236: © Estate of Evelyn Hofer
241: First edition published by Jonathan Cape
242: © Saul Leiter Foundation
247, top: © Museum of Modern Art, New York/ DACS 2022. Photo SCALA, Florence; middle: Charles H. and Mary F.S. Worcester Collection; bottom: David Hunter McAlpin Fund, 1956
249, top: © Paul Popper/Popperfoto via Getty Images; bottom: © Metropolitan Museum of Art, New York. Photo SCALA, Florence
250: Courtesy of and © The Gordon Parks Foundation
254: © Arthur Tress
262: © Sue Barr
265: © J. Wesley Brown
266: © Les Films de *Mon Oncle* - Specta Films CEPEC
288: Courtesy State Library Victoria www.slv.vic.gov.au

Index

References to images are in **bold**.

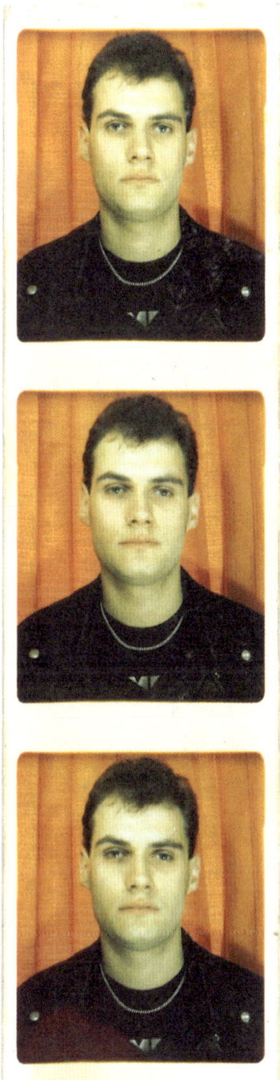

The Author

Edwin Heathcote is the architecture and design critic of The Financial Times. *He is author of about a dozen books including* The Meaning of Home *and is an architect and designer. Heathcote is also the Keeper of Meaning at The Cosmic House in London as well as the founder and editor of the online design writing archive readingdesign.org. He lives in London.*

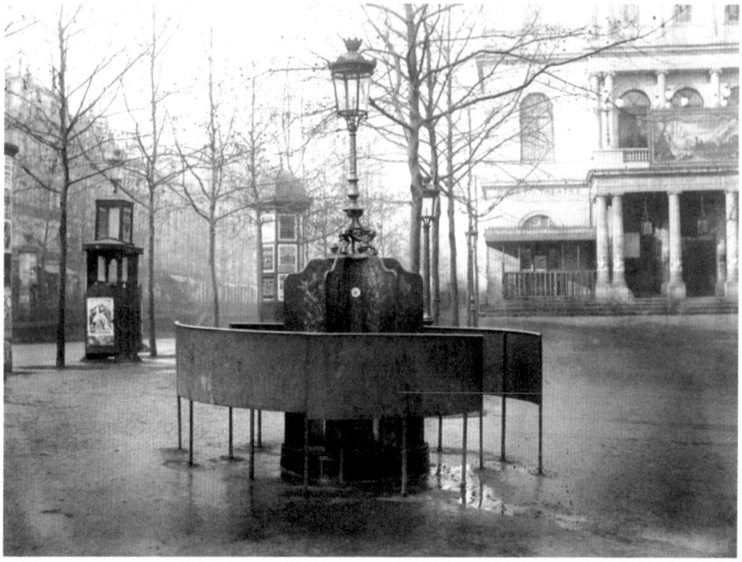

Urinal (Jennings System),
Plateau de l'Ambigu, c.1865
Charles Marville